Thank you very much for purchasing Haikyu!! volume 38! Mujinazaka High School, the team Fukurodani started playing last volume, is the representative of Oita Prefecture—an area known for a pretty thick accent. I was wondering what to do about that when I discovered that my new editor—who, conveniently enough, just joined me last volume—has lots of family connections in the Oita/Kyushu region. What a lucky break! Thank you very much to all of my editor's relatives who graciously looked over my storyboards every week!

WAKATTSAN

HARUICHI FURUDATE began his manga career when he was 25 years old with the one-shot Ousama Kid (King Kid), which won an honorable mention for the 14th Jump Treasure Newcomer Manga Prize. His first series, Kiben Gakuha, Yotsuya Sensei no Kaidan (Philosophy School, Yotsuya Sensei's Ghost Stories), was serialized in Weekly Shonen Jump in 2010. In 2012, he began serializing Haikyu!! in Weekly Shonen Jump, where it became his most popular work to date.

HAIKYU!!

VOLUME 38
SHONEN JUMP Manga Edition

Story and Art by
HARUICHI FURUDATE

Translation **1** ADRIENNE BECK
Touch-Up Art & Lettering **2** ERIKA TERRIQUEZ
Design **3** JULIAN [JR] ROBINSON
Editor **4** MARLENE FIRST

Published by VIZ Media, LLC
P.O. Box 77010
San Francisco, CA 94107

10 9 8 7 6 5 4 3 2 1
First printing, May 2020

VIZ MEDIA
viz.com

SHONEN JUMP
shonenjump.com

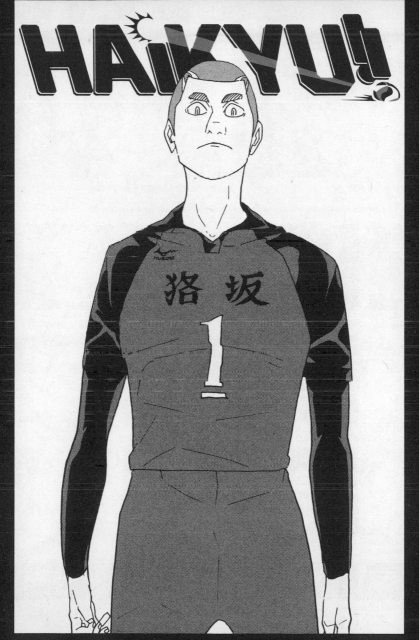

HARUICHI
FURUDATE

TASK FOCUS

38

Karasuno High School Volleyball Club

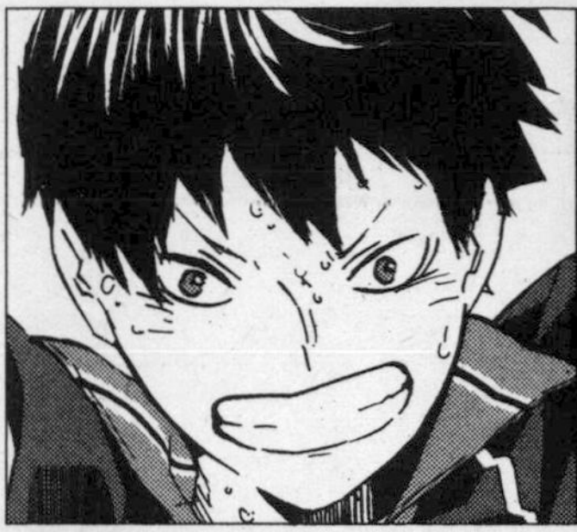

TOBIO KAGEYAMA

1ST YEAR / SETTER
His instincts and athletic talent are so good that he's like a "king" who rules the court. Demanding and egocentric.

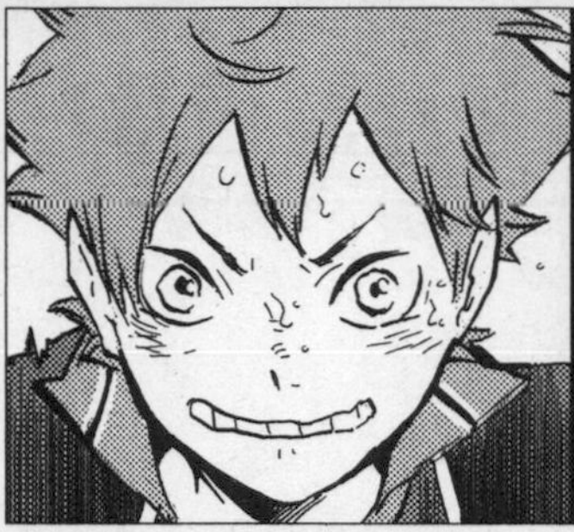

SHOYO HINATA

1ST YEAR / MIDDLE BLOCKER
Even though he doesn't have the best body type for volleyball, he is super athletic. Gets nervous easily.

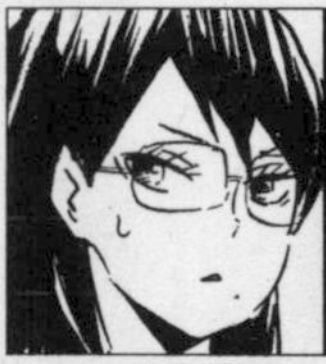

KIYOKO SHIMIZU
3RD YEAR
MANAGER

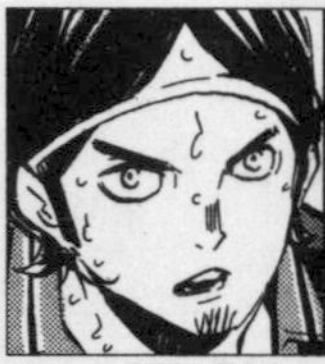

ASAHI AZUMANE
3RD YEAR
WING SPIKER

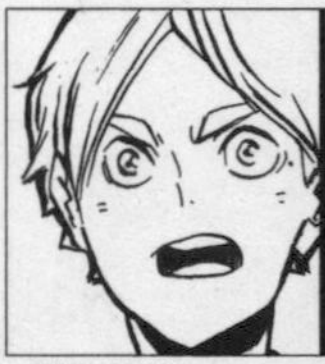

KOUSHI SUGAWARA
3RD YEAR (VICE CAPTAIN)
SETTER

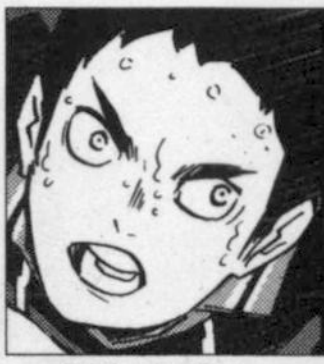

DAICHI SAWAMURA
3RD YEAR (CAPTAIN)
WING SPIKER

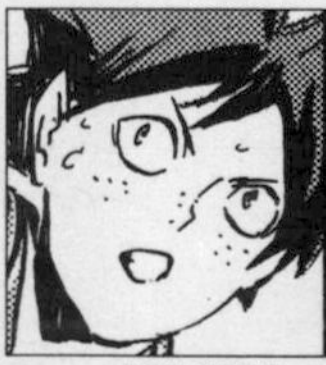

TADASHI YAMAGUCHI
1ST YEAR
MIDDLE BLOCKER

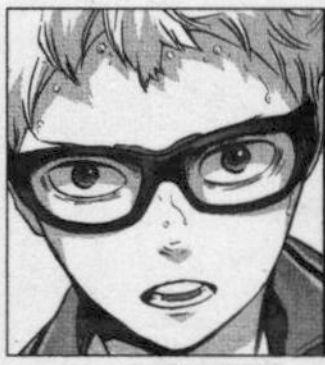

KEI TSUKISHIMA
1ST YEAR
MIDDLE BLOCKER

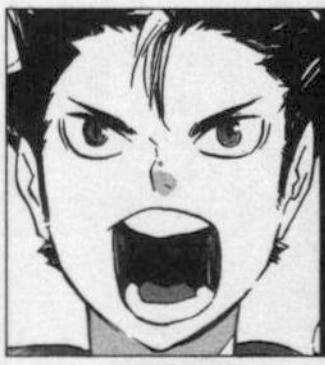

YU NISHINOYA
2ND YEAR
LIBERO

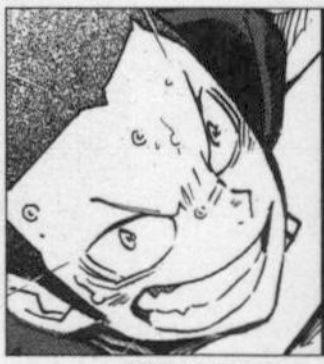

RYUNOSUKE TANAKA
2ND YEAR
WING SPIKER

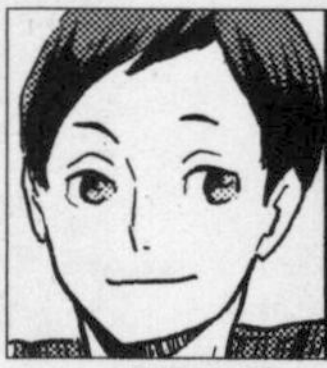

CHIKARA ENNOSHITA
2ND YEAR
WING SPIKER

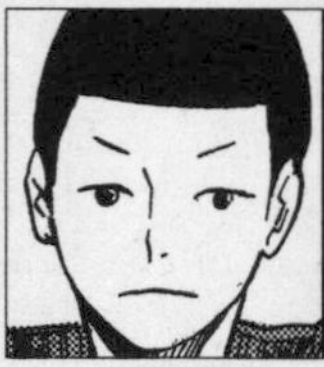

KAZUHITO NARITA
2ND YEAR
MIDDLE BLOCKER

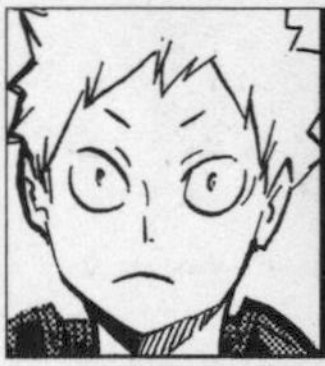

HISASHI KINOSHITA
2ND YEAR
WING SPIKER

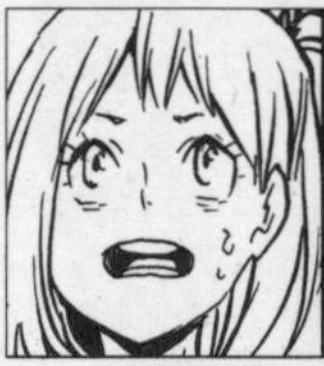

HITOKA YACHI
1ST YEAR
MANAGER

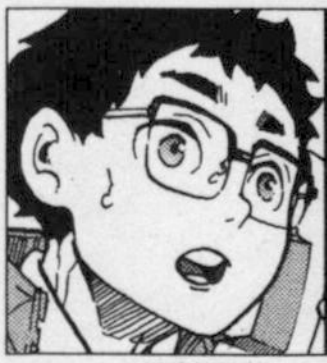

ITTETSU TAKEDA
ADVISER

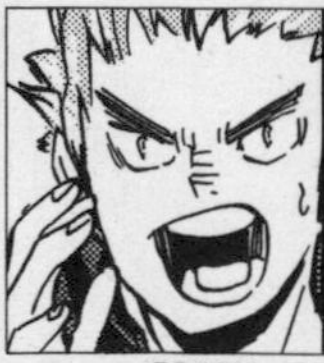

KEISHIN UKAI
COACH

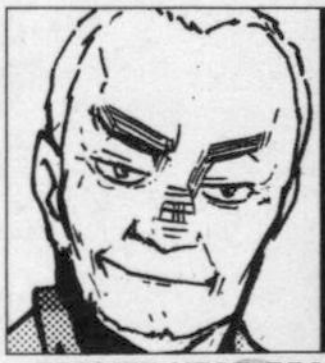

IKKEI UKAI
FORMER HEAD COACH

CHARACTERS

NATIONAL SPRING TOURNAMENT ARC

Fukurodani Academy Volleyball Club

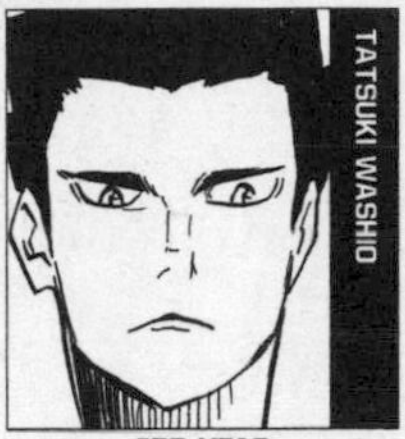
TATSUKI WASHIO
3RD YEAR
MIDDLE BLOCKER

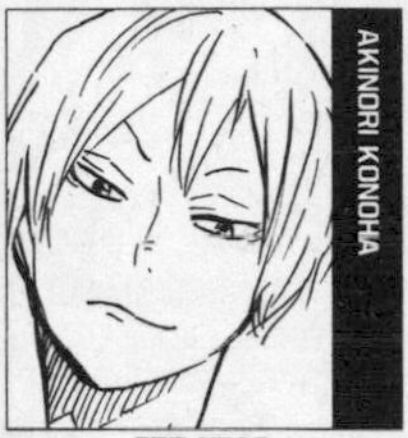
AKINORI KONOHA
3RD YEAR
WING SPIKER

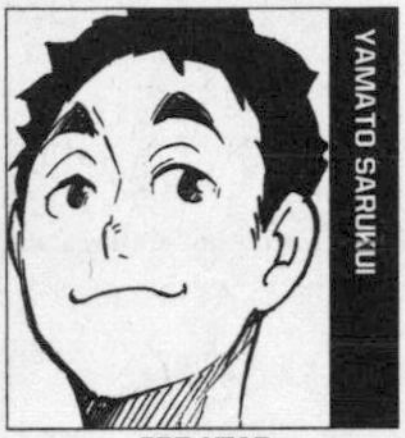
YAMATO SARUKUI
3RD YEAR
WING SPIKER

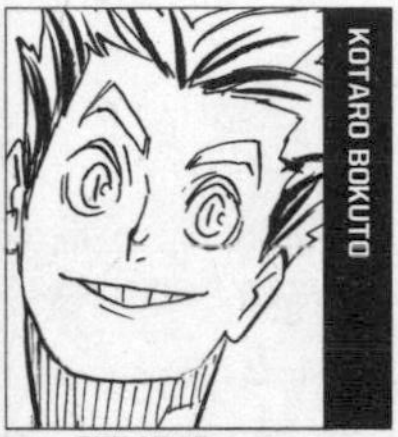
KOTARO BOKUTO
3RD YEAR (CAPTAIN)
WING SPIKER

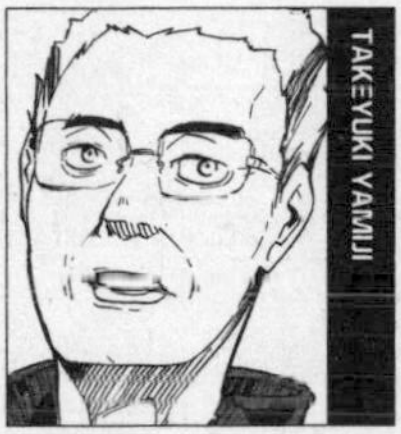
TAKEYUKI YAMIJI
HEAD COACH

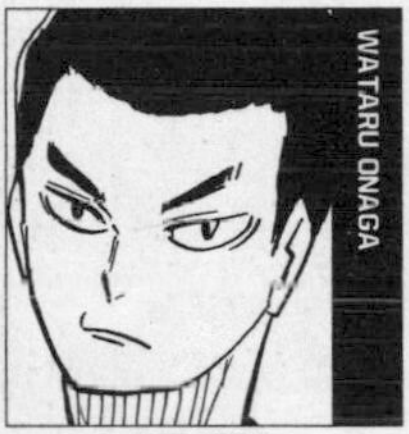
WATARU ONAGA
1ST YEAR
MIDDLE BLOCKER

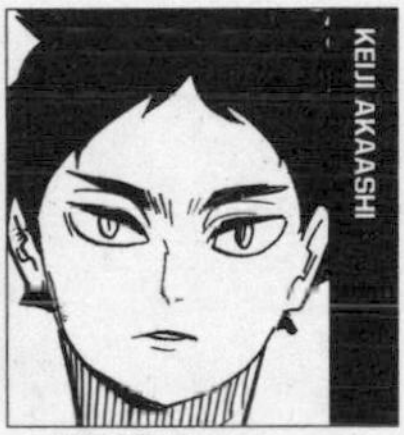
KEIJI AKAASHI
2ND YEAR (VICE CAPTAIN)
SETTER

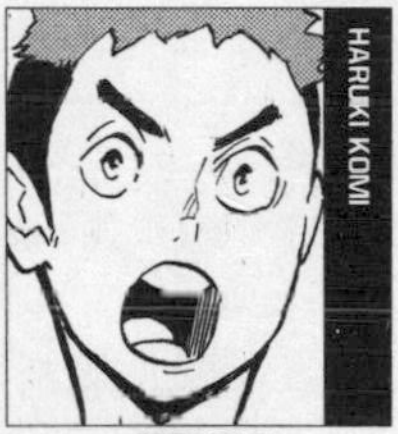
HARUKI KOMI
3RD YEAR
LIBERO

Kamomedai High School

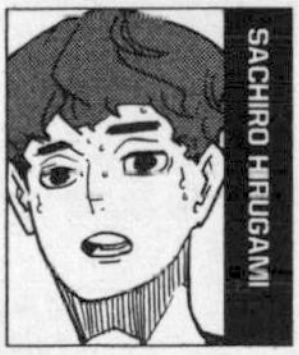
SACHIRO HIRUGAMI

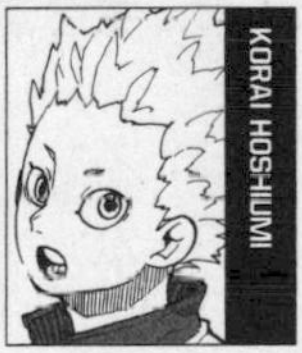
KORAI HOSHIUMI

Mujinazaka High School

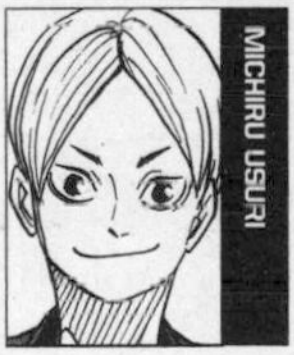
MICHIRU USURI

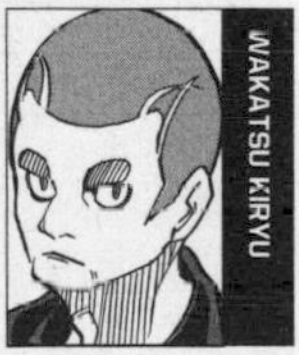
WAKATSU KIRYU

Ever since he saw the legendary player known as "the Little Giant" compete at the national volleyball finals, Shoyo Hinata has been aiming to be the best volleyball player ever! He decides to join the volleyball club at his middle school and gets to play in an official tournament during his third year. His team is crushed by a team led by volleyball prodigy Tobio Kageyama, also known as "the King of the Court." Swearing revenge on Kageyama, Hinata graduates middle school and enters Karasuno High School, the school where the Little Giant played. However, upon joining the club, he finds out that Kageyama is there too! The two of them bicker constantly, but they bring out the best in each other's talents and become a powerful combo. It's day 3 of the Spring Tournament. After a long and exhausting game, Karasuno finally beats Nekoma! Their next game, in the quarterfinals, starts later the same afternoon. Hinata will be duking it out with Korai Hoshiumi and Kamomedai in a match to decide who deserves the title of the New Little Giant! Meanwhile, Fukurodani plays their quarterfinal game against Mujinazaka and their star player, Kiryu, one of the top three aces in the nation. Thanks to Kiryu's ability to deftly turn poor sets into unbeatable hits, Mujinazaka takes the lead. Akaashi begins to panic, leading to more lost points for Fukurodani. But then Bokuto steps up and declares he's going to start being the team's ace...period.

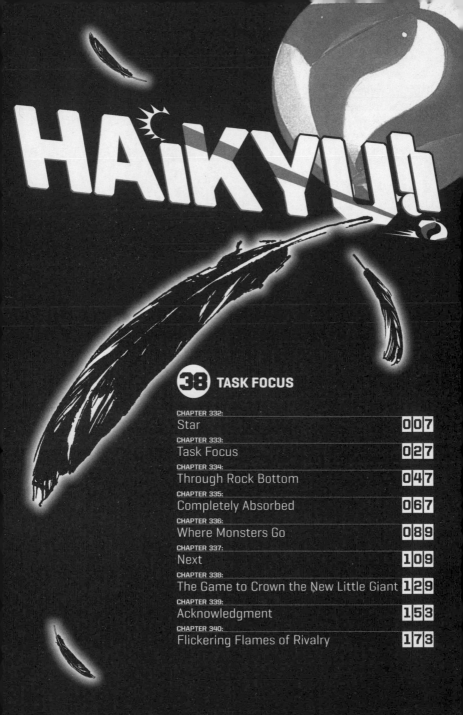

HAIKYU!!

38 TASK FOCUS

CHAPTER 332:
Star — 007

CHAPTER 333:
Task Focus — 027

CHAPTER 334:
Through Rock Bottom — 047

CHAPTER 335:
Completely Absorbed — 067

CHAPTER 336:
Where Monsters Go — 089

CHAPTER 337:
Next — 109

CHAPTER 338:
The Game to Crown the New Little Giant — 129

CHAPTER 339:
Acknowledgment — 153

CHAPTER 340:
Flickering Flames of Rivalry — 173

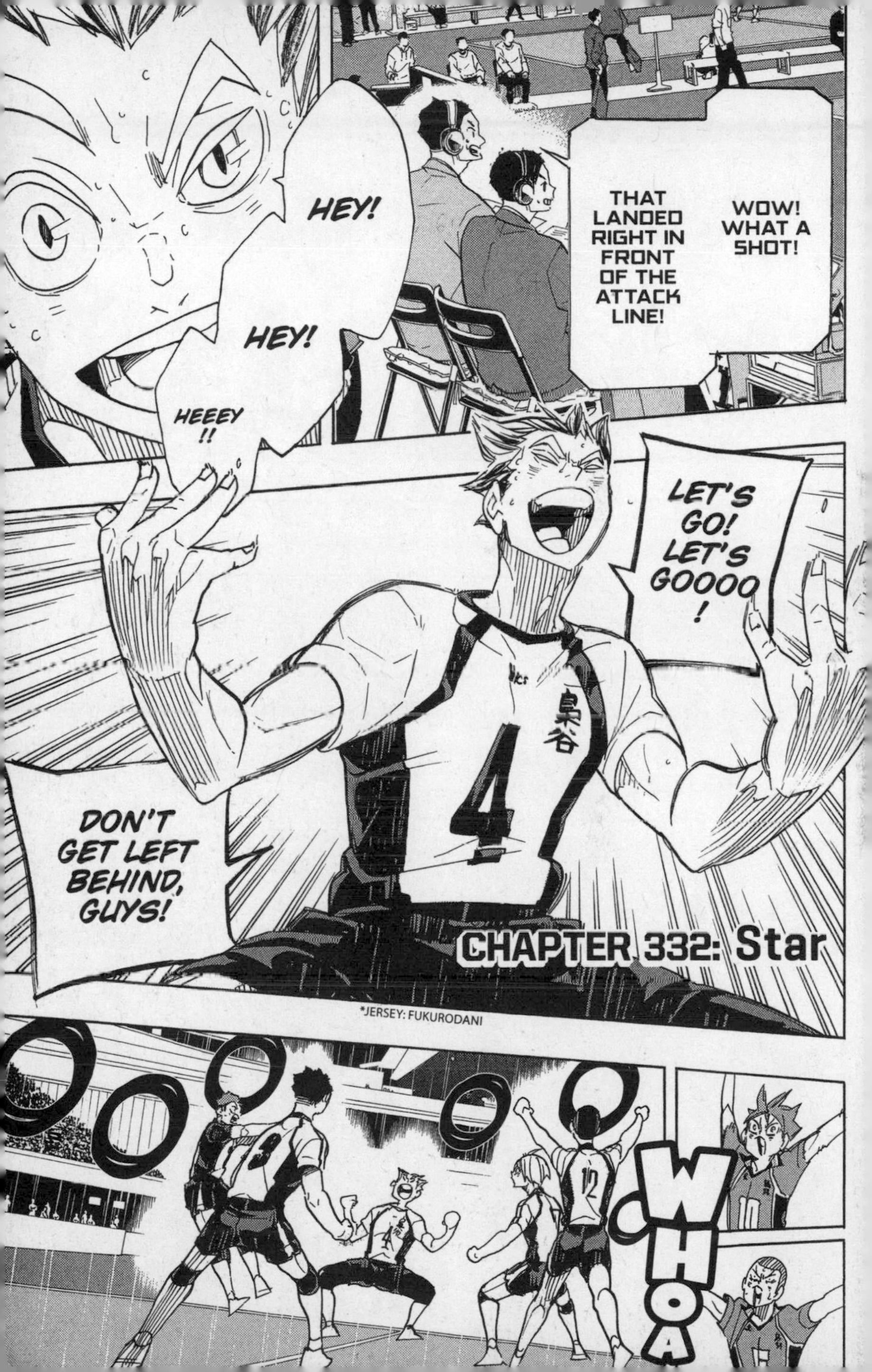
WOW! WHAT A SHOT!
THAT LANDED RIGHT IN FRONT OF THE ATTACK LINE!
HEY!
HEY!
HEEEY!!
LET'S GO! LET'S GOOOO!
DON'T GET LEFT BEHIND, GUYS!
CHAPTER 332: Star
*JERSEY: FUKURODANI
WHOA

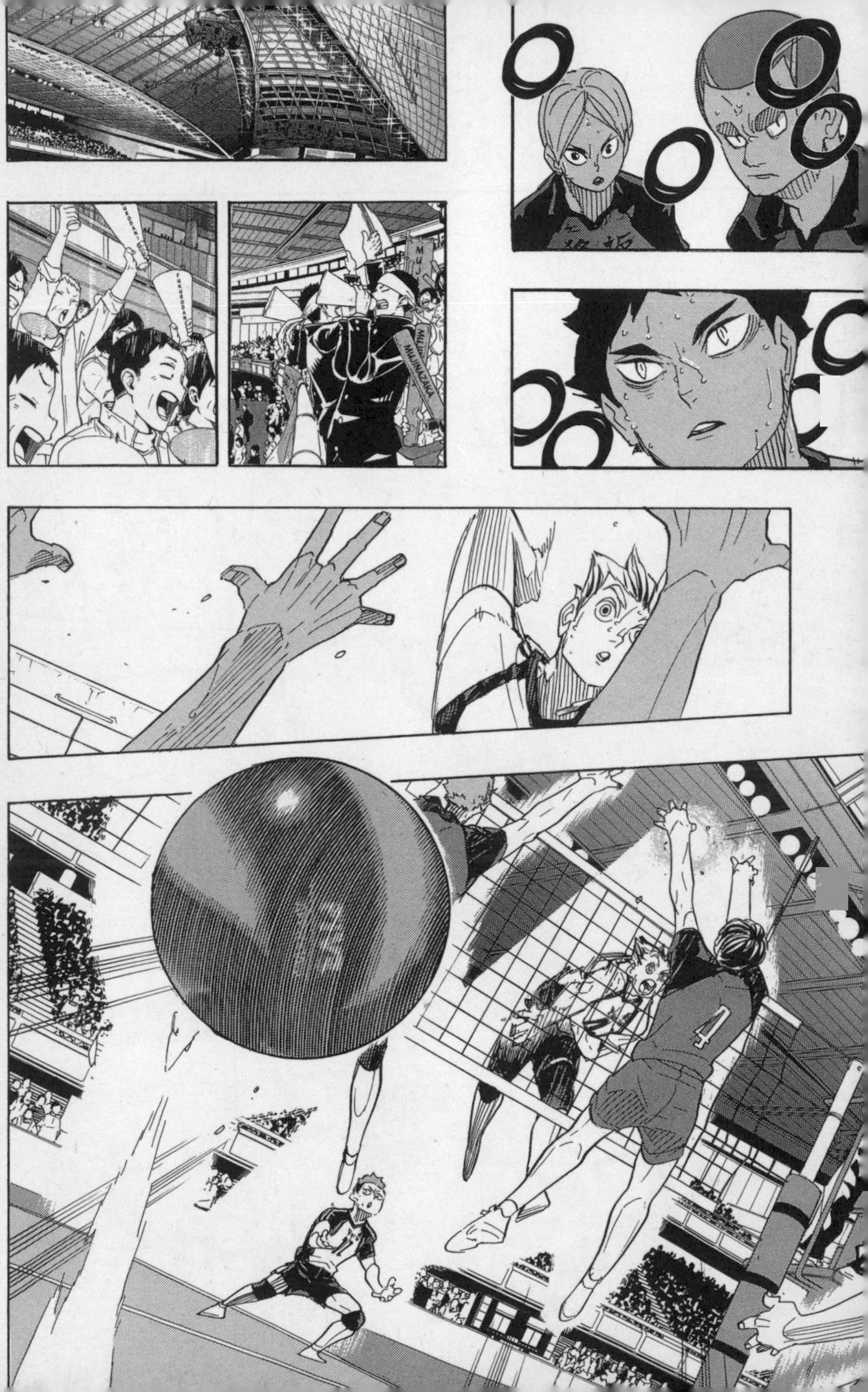
MUJINAZAKA

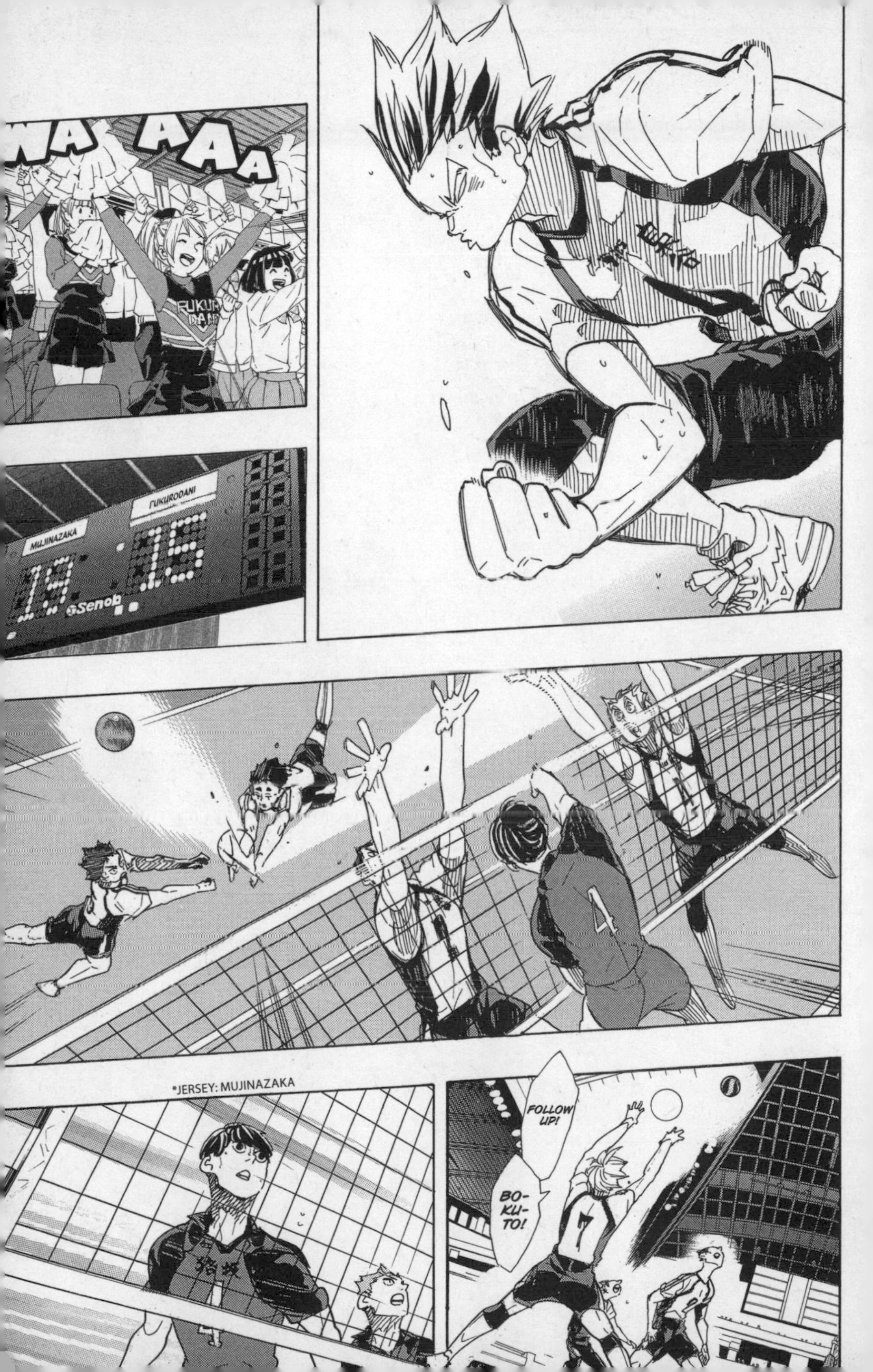
WA AAAA
FUKURODANI
MUJINAZAKA
19
15
Senob
*JERSEY: MUJINAZAKA
FOLLOW UP!
BO-KU-TO!

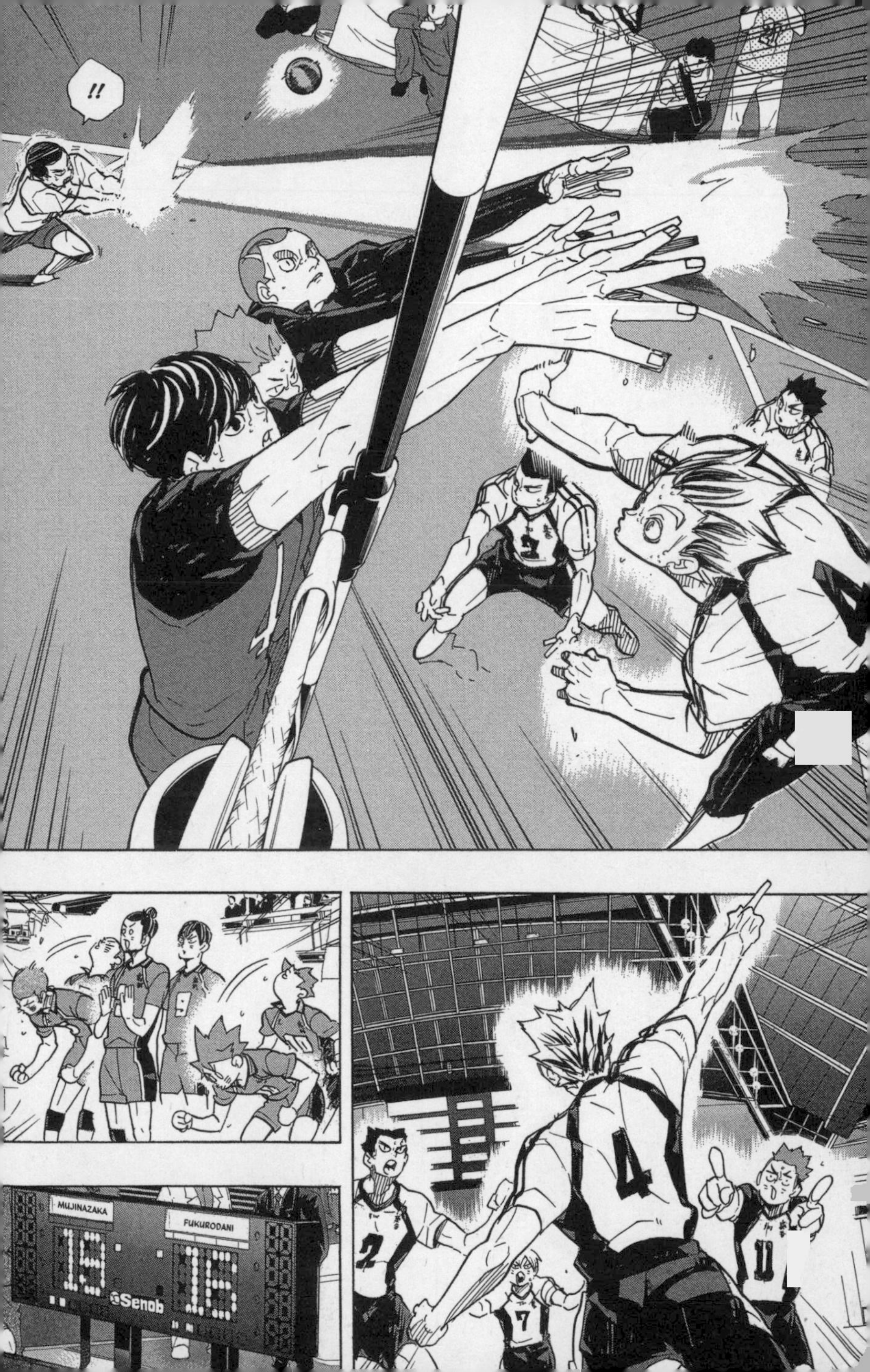
!!
MUJINAZAKA
FUKURODANI
19
16
Senob

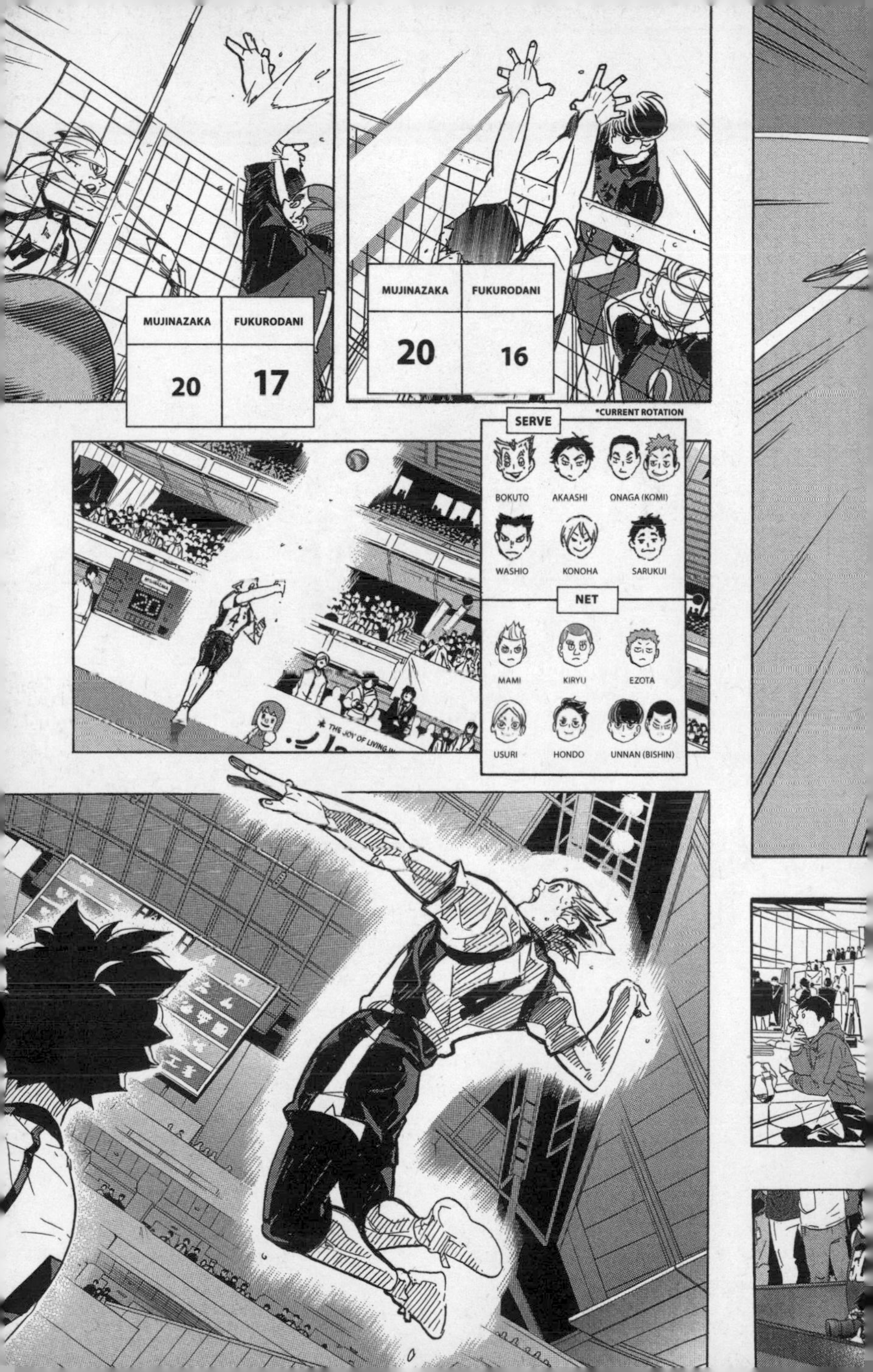
MUJINAZAKA
20
FUKURODANI
16
MUJINAZAKA
20
FUKURODANI
17
*CURRENT ROTATION
SERVE
BOKUTO
AKAASHI
ONAGA (KOMI)
WASHIO
KONOHA
SARUKUI
NET
MAMI
KIRYU
EZOTA
USURI
HONDO
UNNAN (BISHIN)
THE JOY OF LIVING

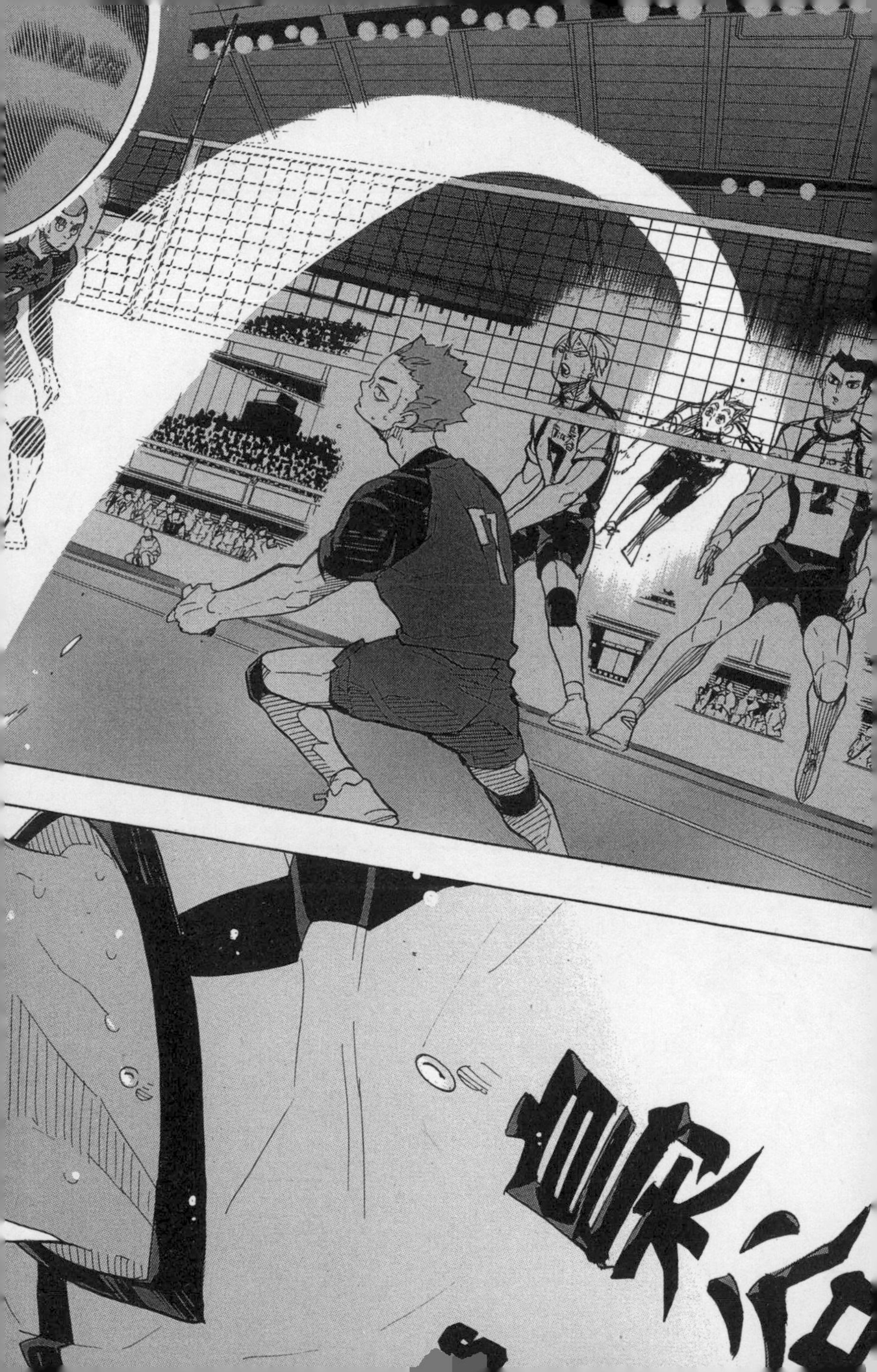

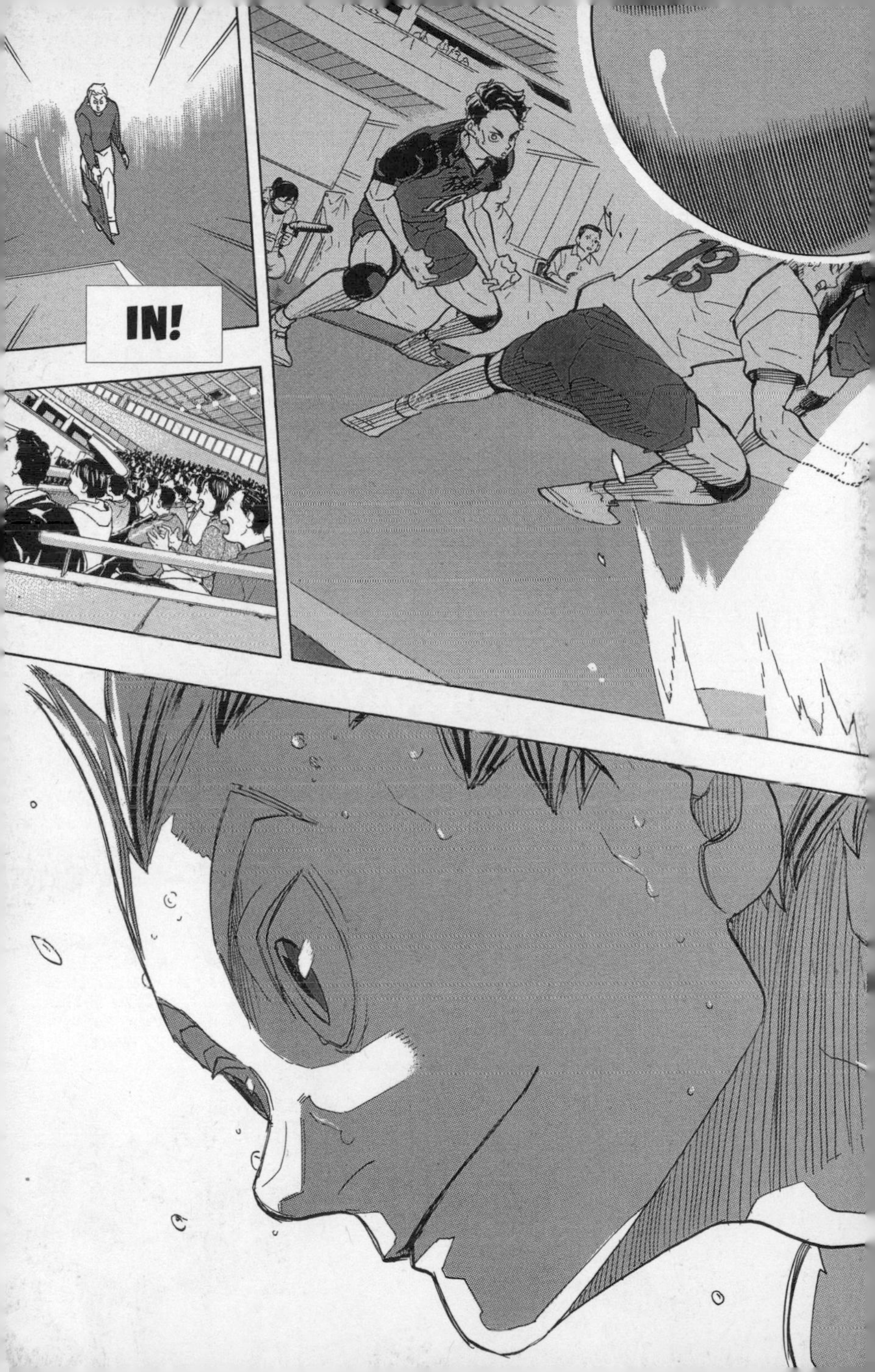
IN!

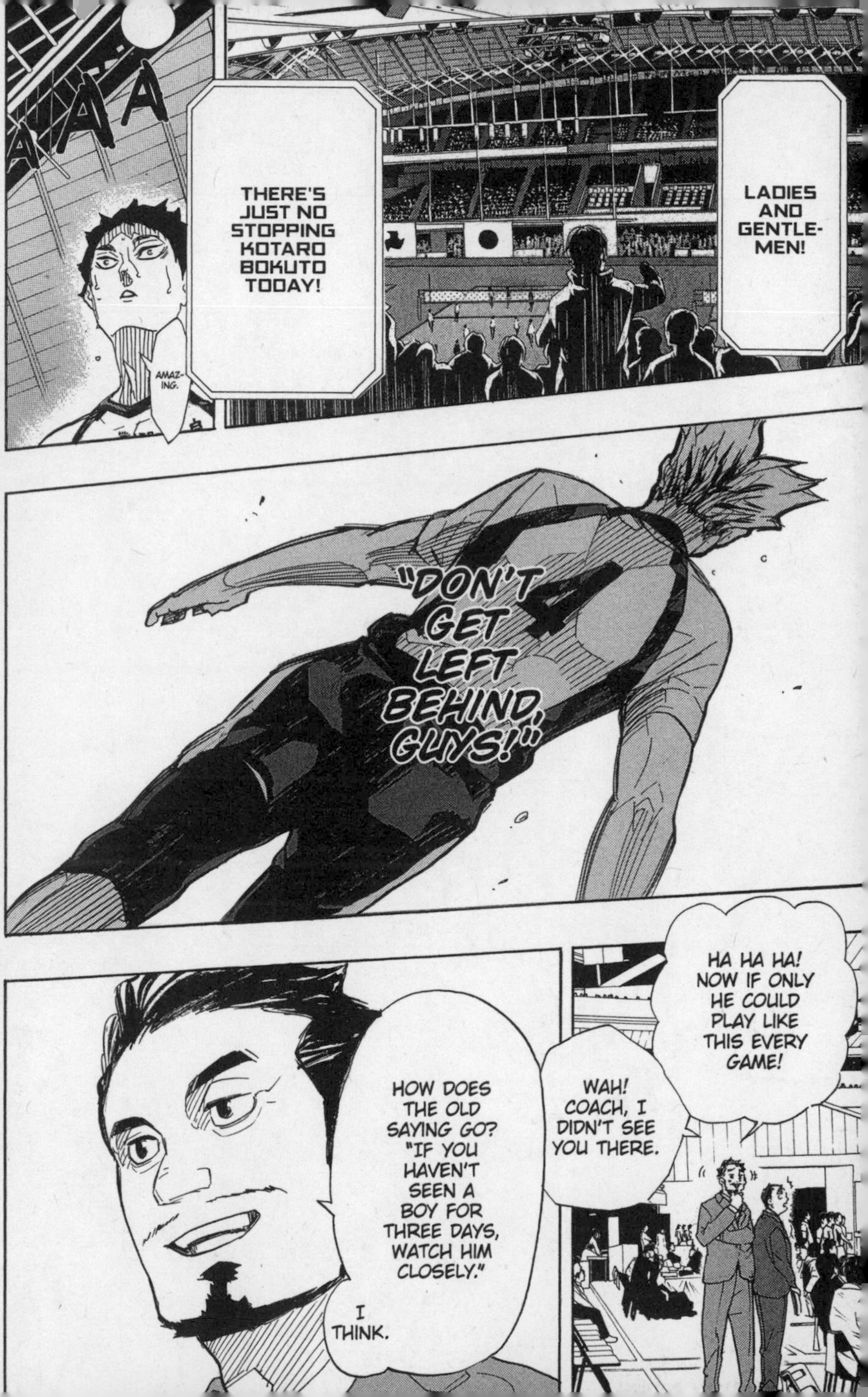
LADIES AND GENTLE-MEN!
THERE'S JUST NO STOPPING KOTARO BOKUTO TODAY!
AAA
AMAZ-ING.
"DON'T GET LEFT BEHIND, GUYS!"
HA HA HA! NOW IF ONLY HE COULD PLAY LIKE THIS EVERY GAME!
WAH! COACH, I DIDN'T SEE YOU THERE.
HOW DOES THE OLD SAYING GO? "IF YOU HAVEN'T SEEN A BOY FOR THREE DAYS, WATCH HIM CLOSELY."
I THINK.

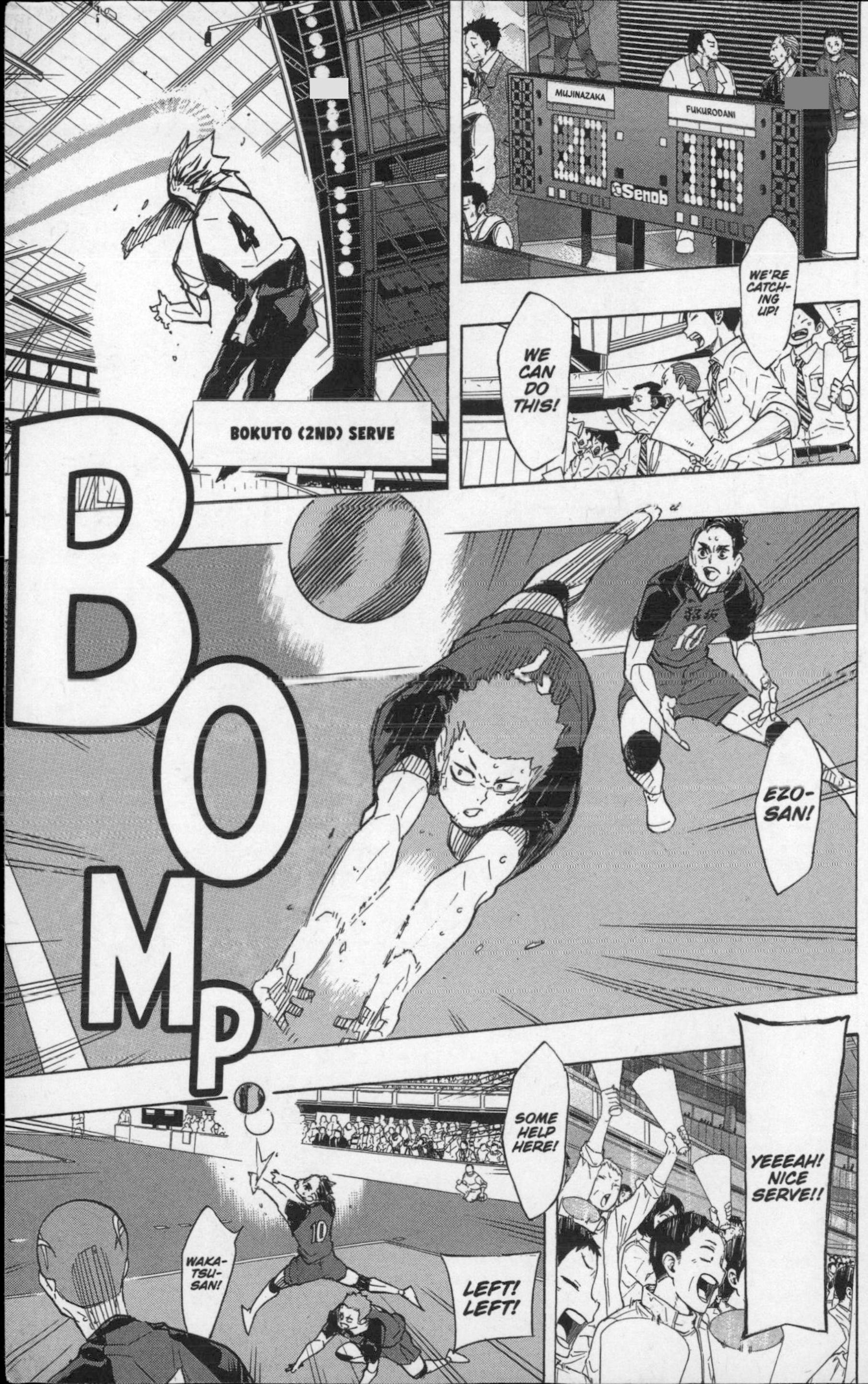
MUJINAZAKA
FUKURODANI
Senob
WE'RE CATCHING-UP!
WE CAN DO THIS!
BOKUTO (2ND) SERVE
BOMP
EZO-SAN!
YEEEAH! NICE SERVE!!
SOME HELP HERE!
LEFT! LEFT!
WAKATSU-SAN!

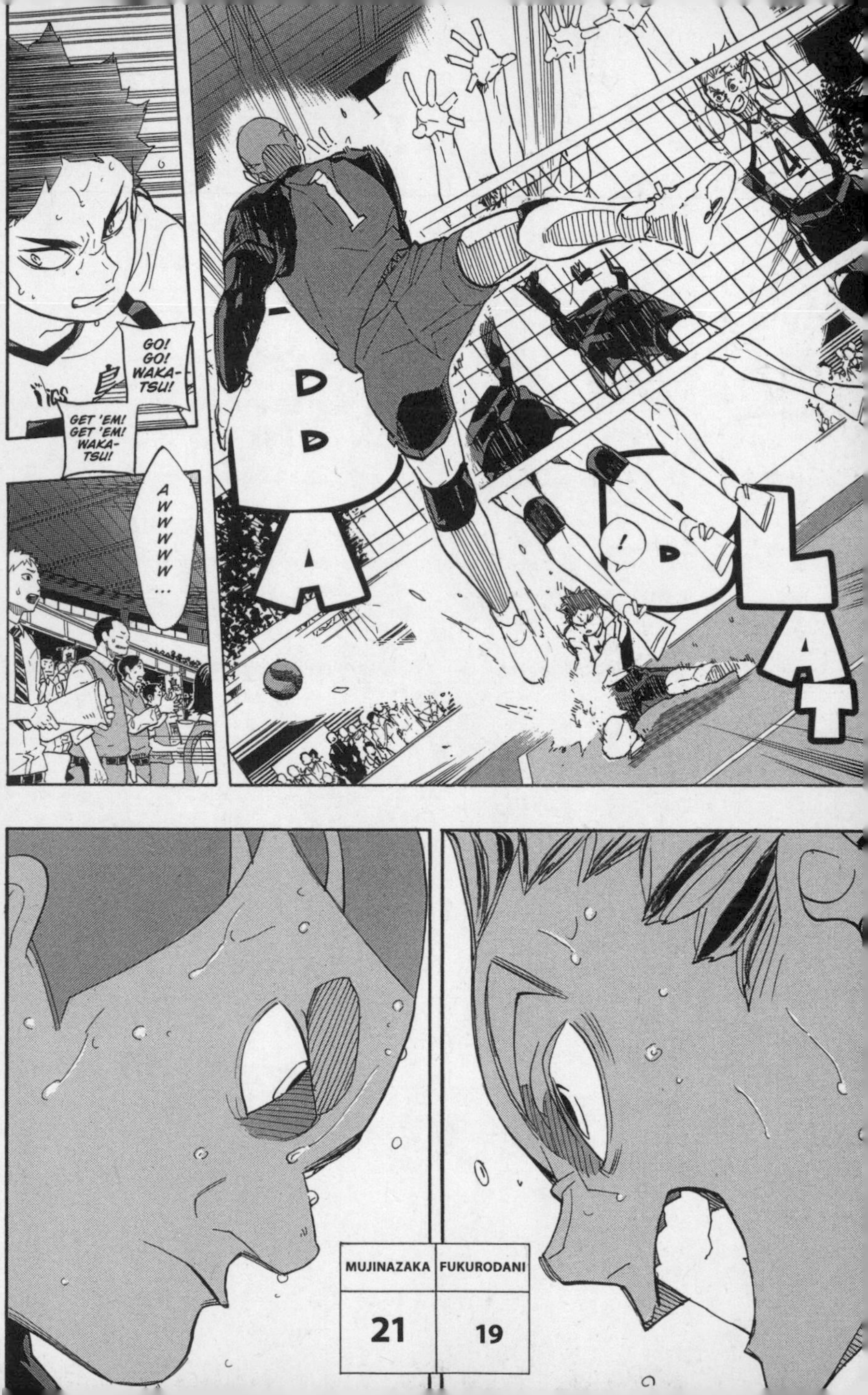
DA
!
DLAT
GO! GO! WAKA-TSU!
GET 'EM! GET 'EM! WAKA-TSU!
AWWWWW...
MUJINAZAKA
FUKURODANI
21
19

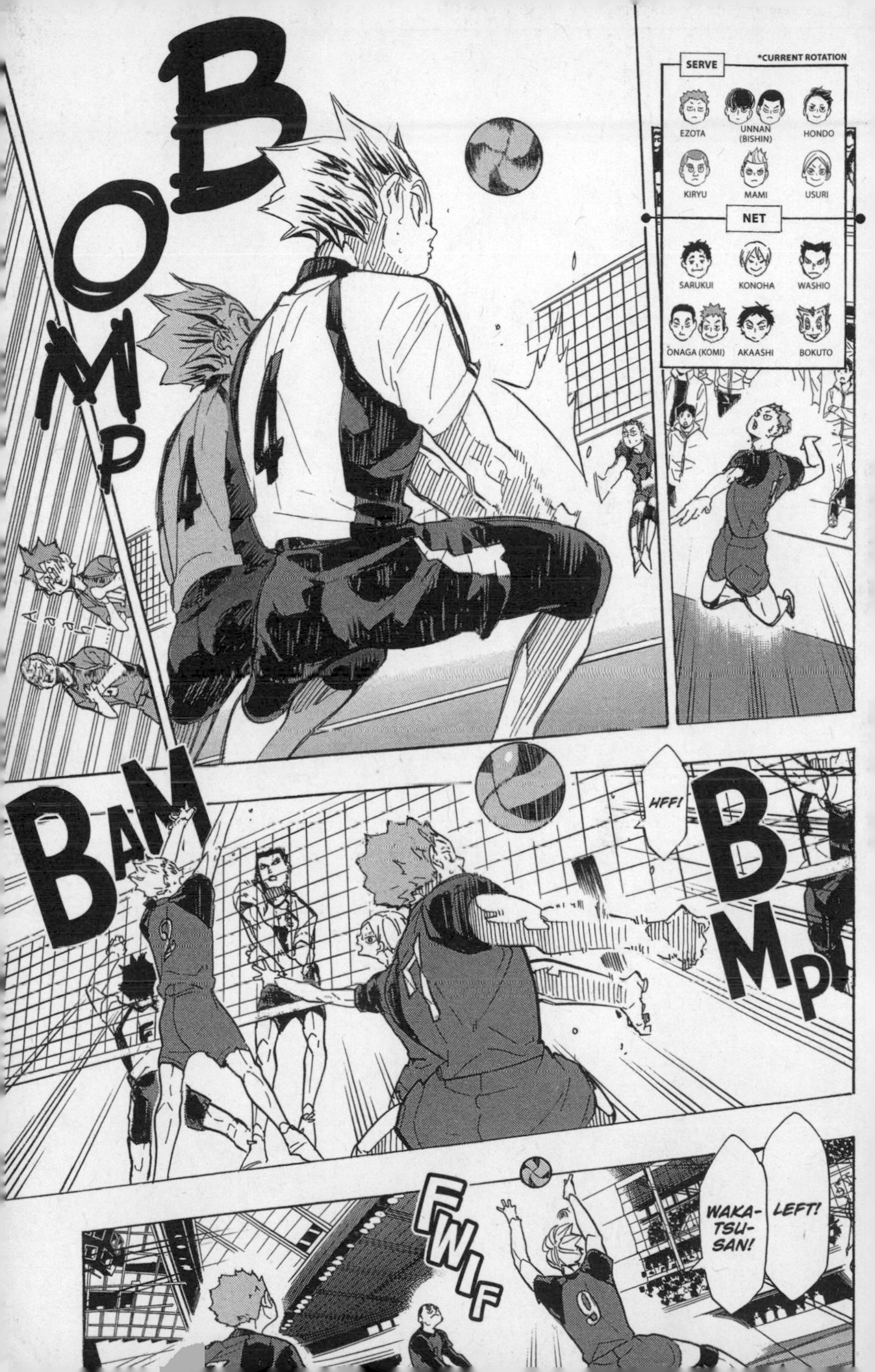
*CURRENT ROTATION
SERVE
EZOTA
UNNAN (BISHIN)
HONDO
KIRYU
MAMI
USURI
NET
SARUKUI
KONOHA
WASHIO
ONAGA (KOMI)
AKAASHI
BOKUTO
BOMP
HFF!
BMP
BAM
LEFT!
WAKA-TSU-SAN!
FWIF

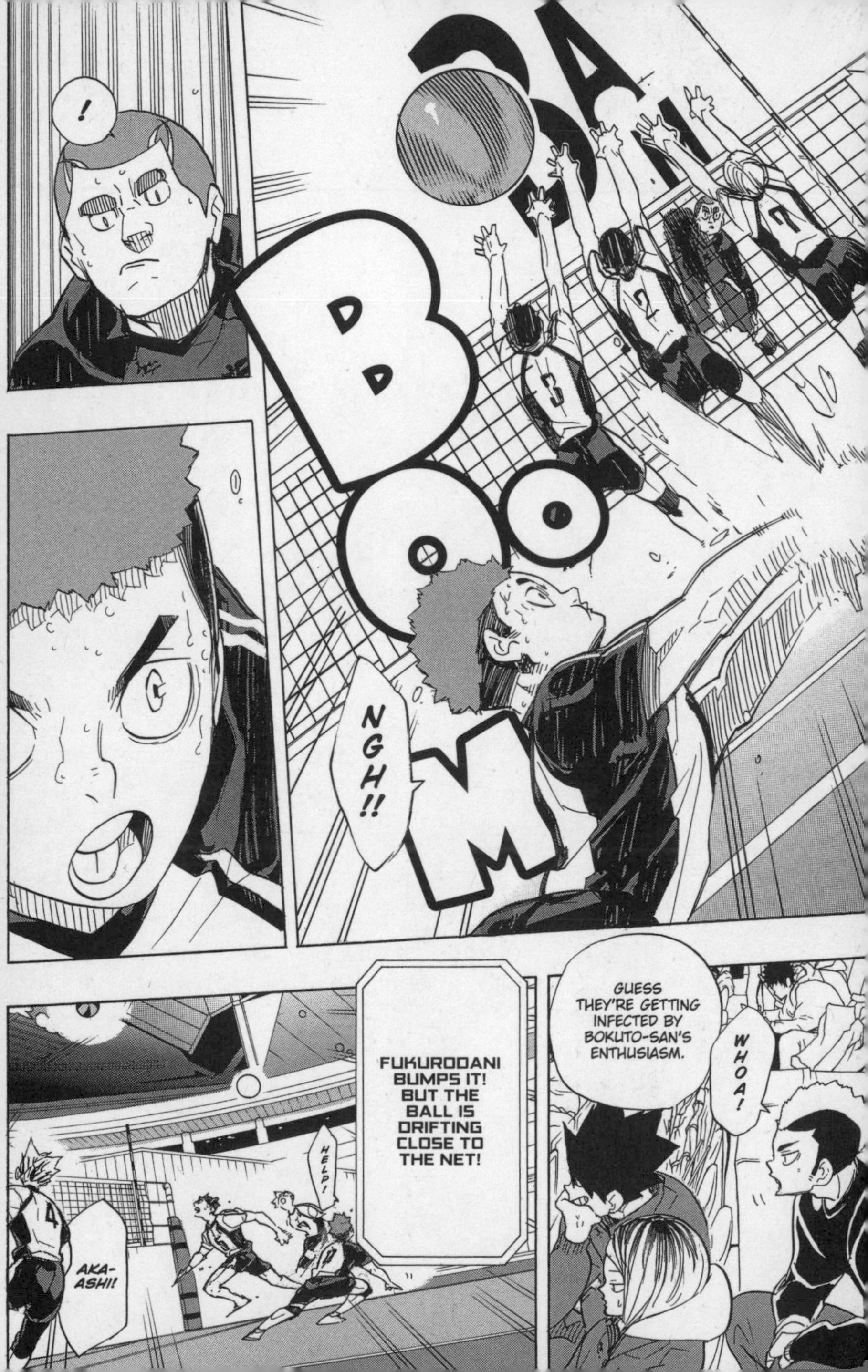
DASH
BOOM
NGH!!
!
GUESS THEY'RE GETTING INFECTED BY BOKUTO-SAN'S ENTHUSIASM.
WHOA!
FUKURODANI BUMPS IT! BUT THE BALL IS DRIFTING CLOSE TO THE NET!
HELP!
AKA-ASHI!

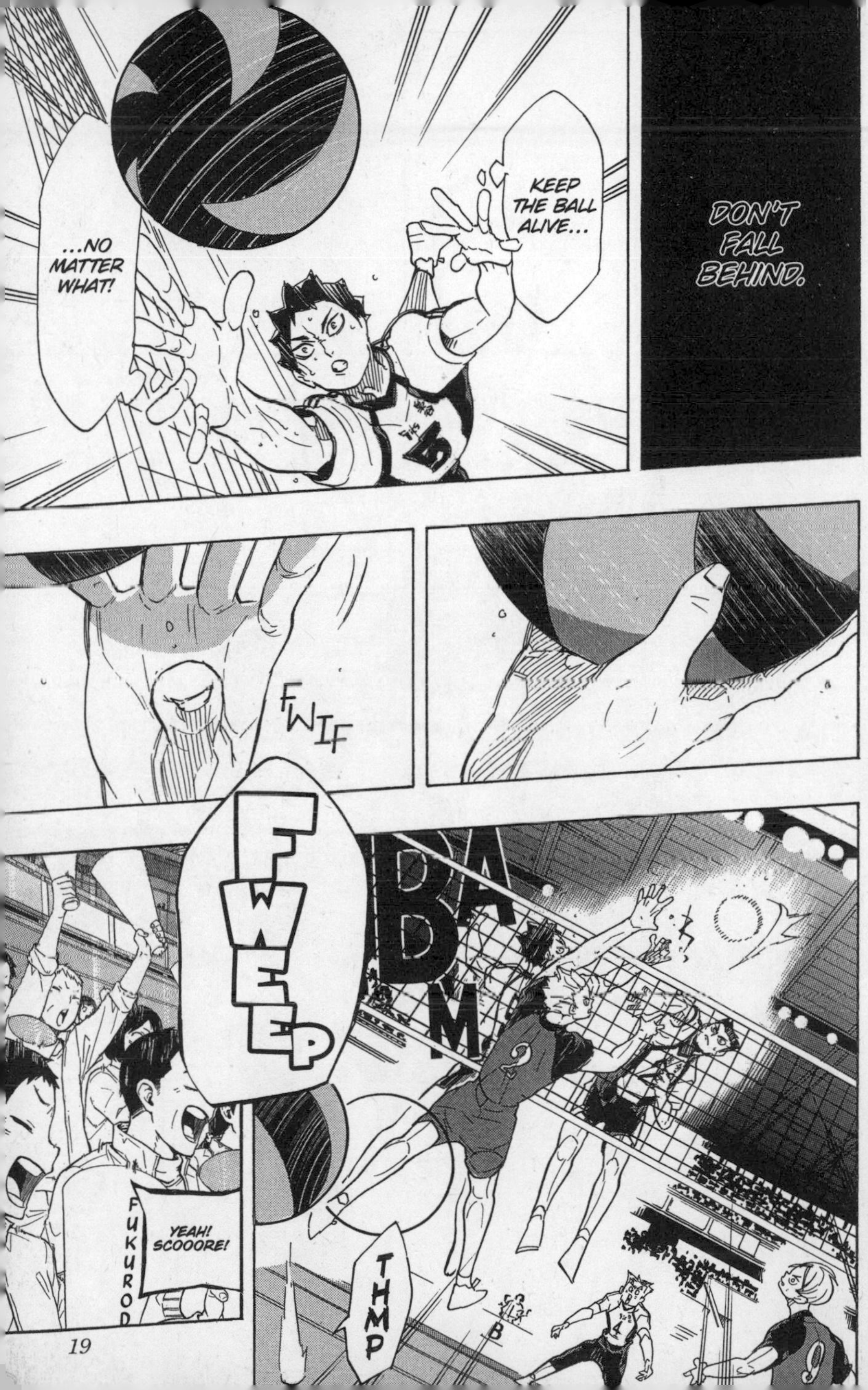
DON'T FALL BEHIND.
KEEP THE BALL ALIVE...
...NO MATTER WHAT!
FWIF
FWEEP
BADAM
THMP
YEAH! SCOOORE!
FUKUROD

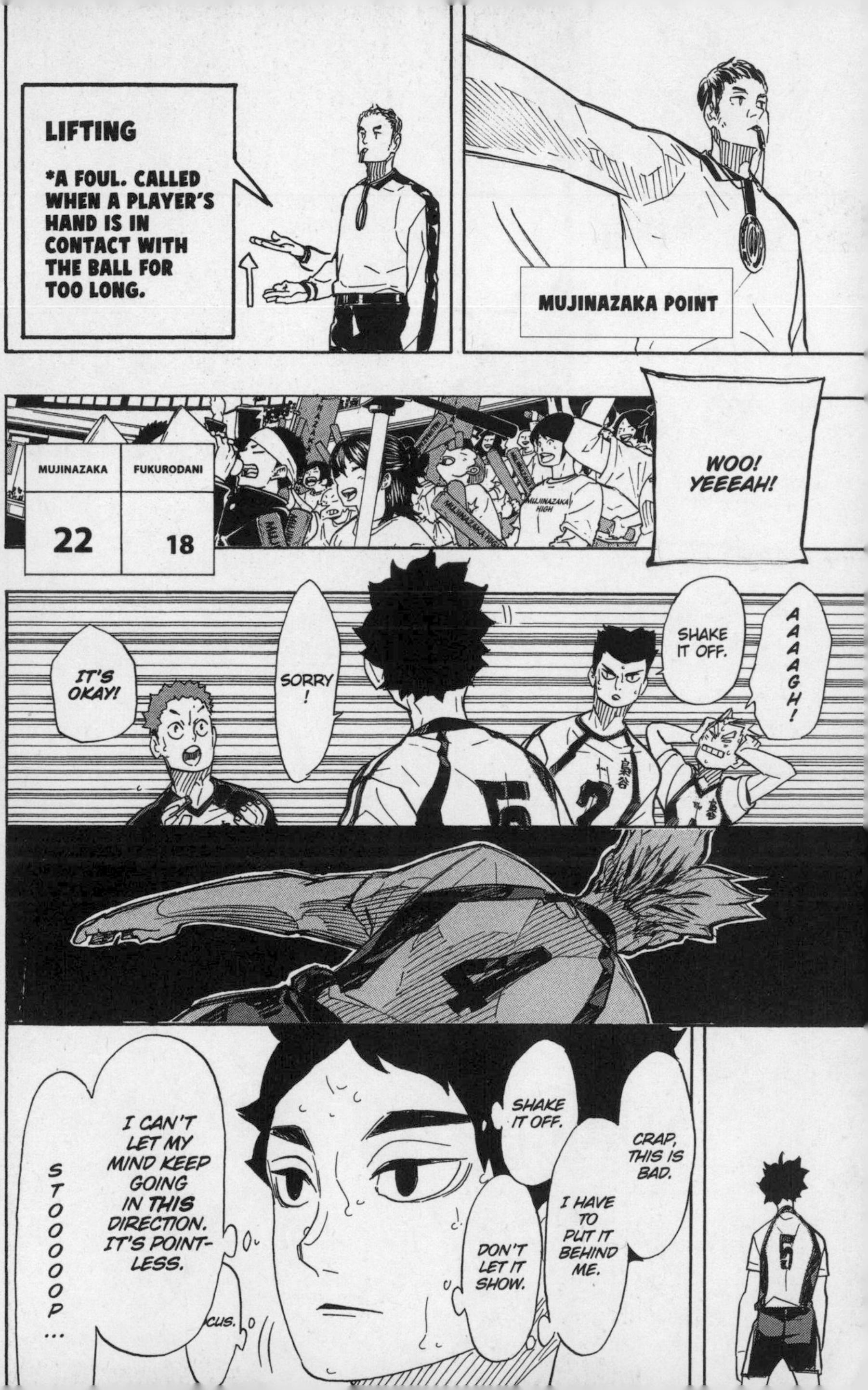
MUJINAZAKA POINT
LIFTING
*A FOUL. CALLED WHEN A PLAYER'S HAND IS IN CONTACT WITH THE BALL FOR TOO LONG.
WOO! YEEEAH!
MUJINAZAKA HIGH
MUJINAZAKA 22
FUKURODANI 18
AAAAGH!
SHAKE IT OFF.
SORRY!
IT'S OKAY!
CRAP, THIS IS BAD.
SHAKE IT OFF.
I HAVE TO PUT IT BEHIND ME.
DON'T LET IT SHOW.
CUS.
I CAN'T LET MY MIND KEEP GOING IN THIS DIRECTION. IT'S POINTLESS.
STOOOOOOP...

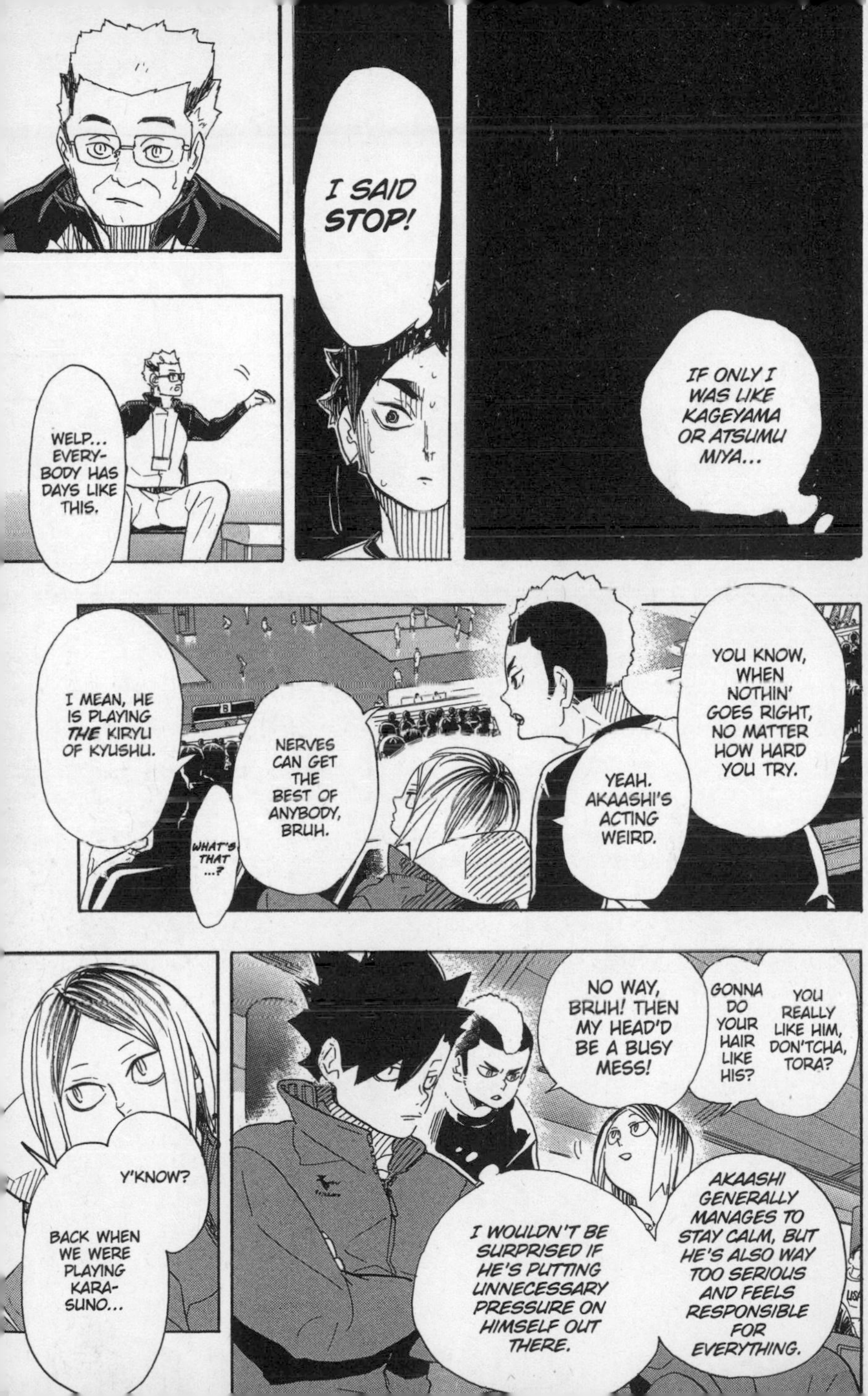
IF ONLY I WAS LIKE KAGEYAMA OR ATSUMU MIYA...
I SAID STOP!
WELP... EVERYBODY HAS DAYS LIKE THIS.
YOU KNOW, WHEN NOTHIN' GOES RIGHT, NO MATTER HOW HARD YOU TRY.
YEAH. AKAASHI'S ACTING WEIRD.
NERVES CAN GET THE BEST OF ANYBODY, BRUH.
I MEAN, HE IS PLAYING *THE* KIRYU OF KYUSHU.
WHAT'S THAT ...?
YOU REALLY LIKE HIM, DON'TCHA, TORA?
GONNA DO YOUR HAIR LIKE HIS?
NO WAY, BRUH! THEN MY HEAD'D BE A BUSY MESS!
AKAASHI GENERALLY MANAGES TO STAY CALM, BUT HE'S ALSO WAY TOO SERIOUS AND FEELS RESPONSIBLE FOR EVERYTHING.
I WOULDN'T BE SURPRISED IF HE'S PUTTING UNNECESSARY PRESSURE ON HIMSELF OUT THERE.
Y'KNOW?
BACK WHEN WE WERE PLAYING KARA-SUNO...

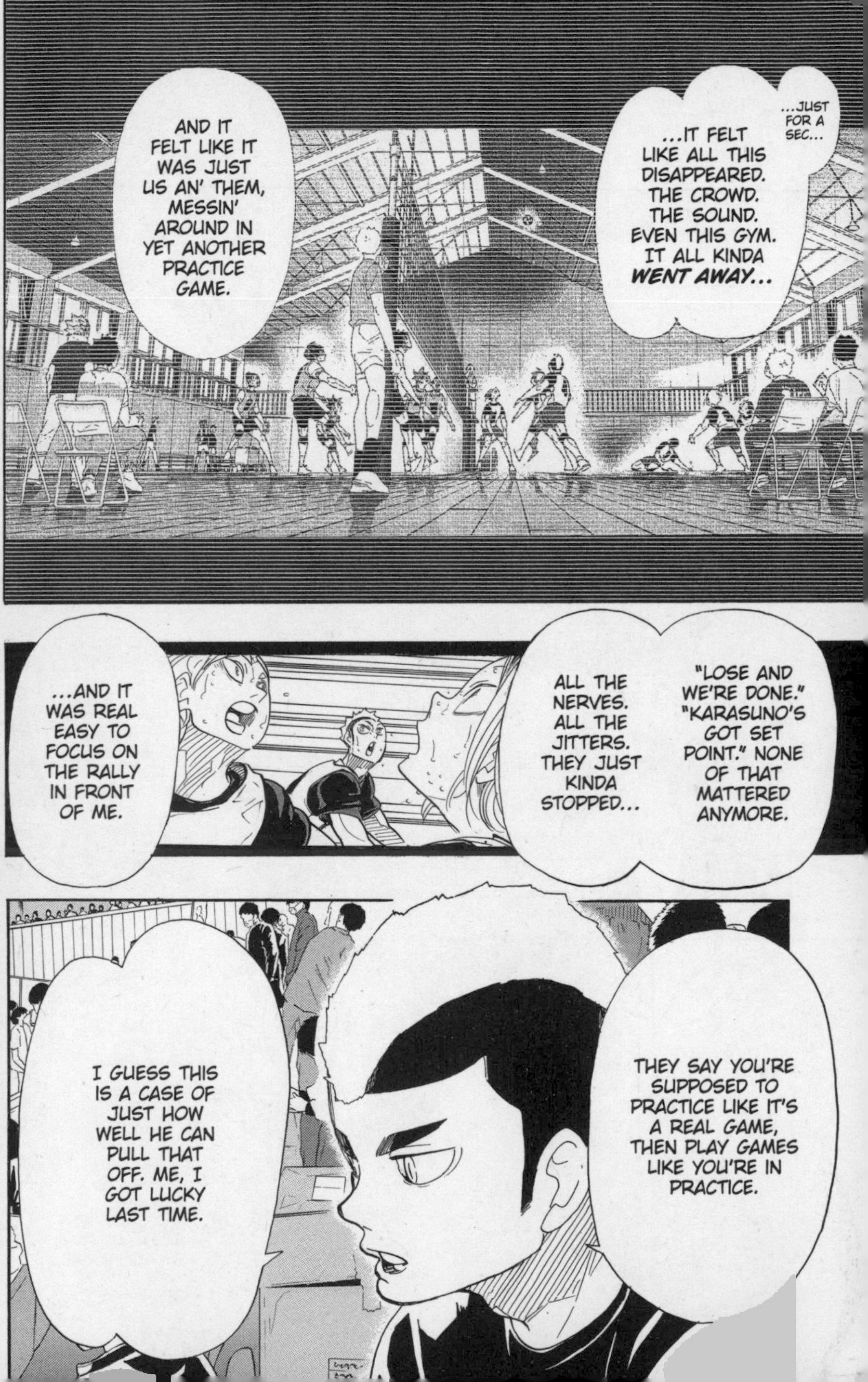

...IT FELT LIKE ALL THIS DISAPPEARED. THE CROWD. THE SOUND. EVEN THIS GYM. IT ALL KINDA **WENT AWAY...**
...JUST FOR A SEC...
AND IT FELT LIKE IT WAS JUST US AN' THEM, MESSIN' AROUND IN YET ANOTHER PRACTICE GAME.
"LOSE AND WE'RE DONE." "KARASUNO'S GOT SET POINT." NONE OF THAT MATTERED ANYMORE.
ALL THE NERVES. ALL THE JITTERS. THEY JUST KINDA STOPPED...
...AND IT WAS REAL EASY TO FOCUS ON THE RALLY IN FRONT OF ME.
THEY SAY YOU'RE SUPPOSED TO PRACTICE LIKE IT'S A REAL GAME, THEN PLAY GAMES LIKE YOU'RE IN PRACTICE.
I GUESS THIS IS A CASE OF JUST HOW WELL HE CAN PULL THAT OFF. ME, I GOT LUCKY LAST TIME.

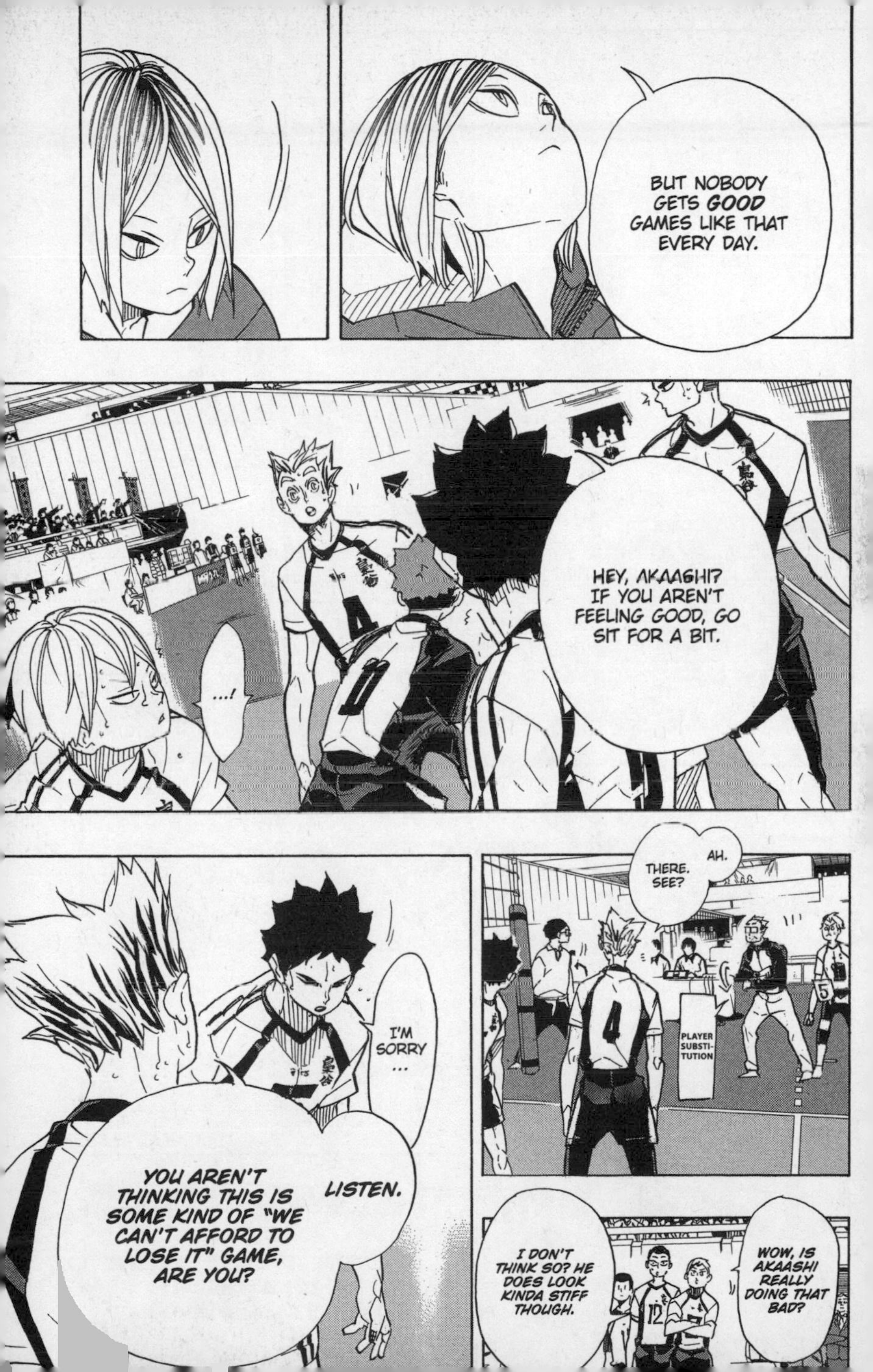
BUT NOBODY GETS **GOOD** GAMES LIKE THAT EVERY DAY.
HEY, AKAASHI? IF YOU AREN'T FEELING GOOD, GO SIT FOR A BIT.
...!
AH.
THERE. SEE?
PLAYER SUBSTITUTION
WOW, IS AKAASHI REALLY DOING THAT BAD?
I DON'T THINK SO? HE DOES LOOK KINDA STIFF THOUGH.
I'M SORRY ...
LISTEN.
YOU AREN'T THINKING THIS IS SOME KIND OF "WE CAN'T AFFORD TO LOSE IT" GAME, ARE YOU?

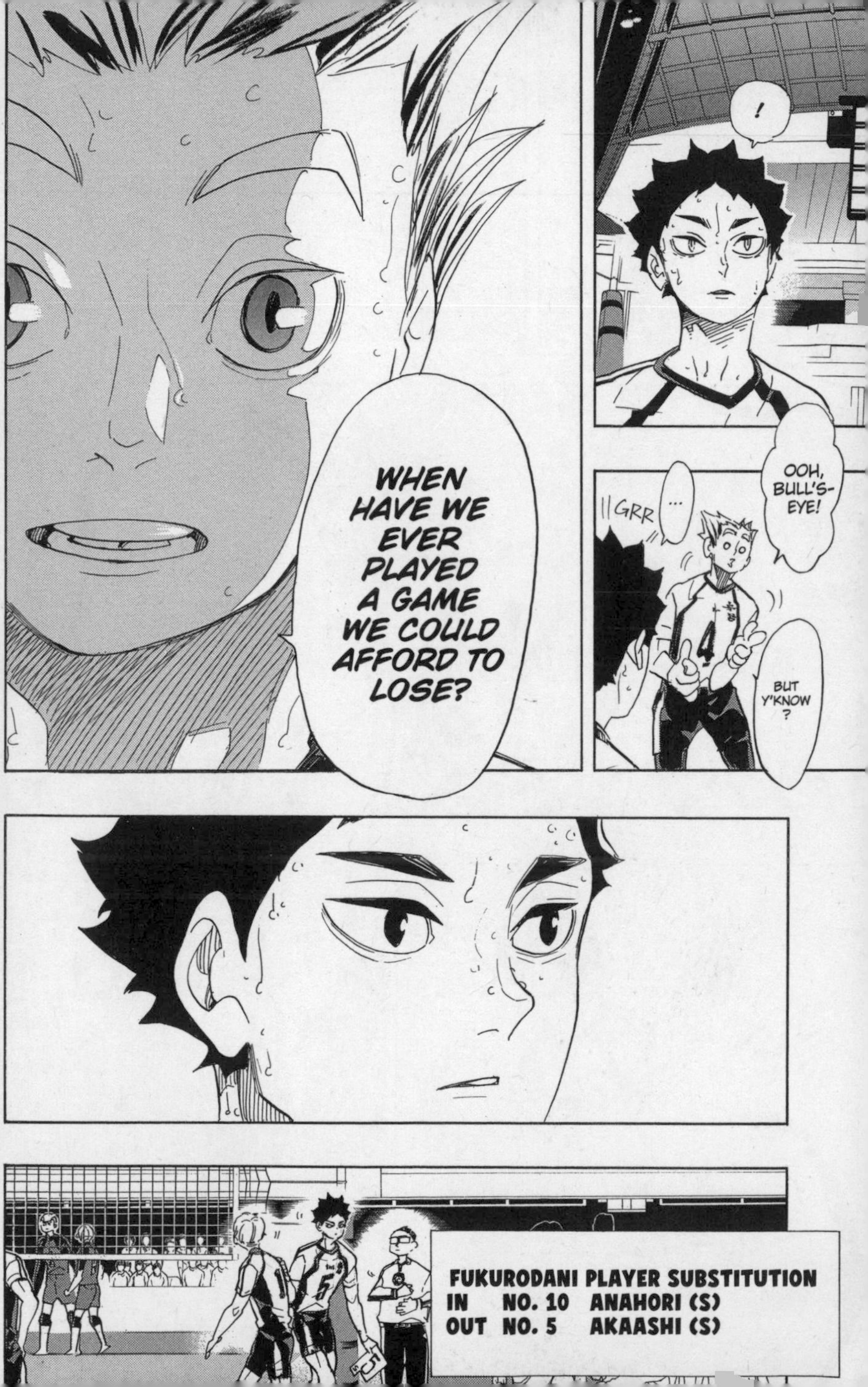
!
OOH, BULL'S-EYE!
...
GRR
BUT Y'KNOW?
WHEN HAVE WE EVER PLAYED A GAME WE COULD AFFORD TO LOSE?
FUKURODANI PLAYER SUBSTITUTION
IN NO. 10 ANAHORI (S)
OUT NO. 5 AKAASHI (S)

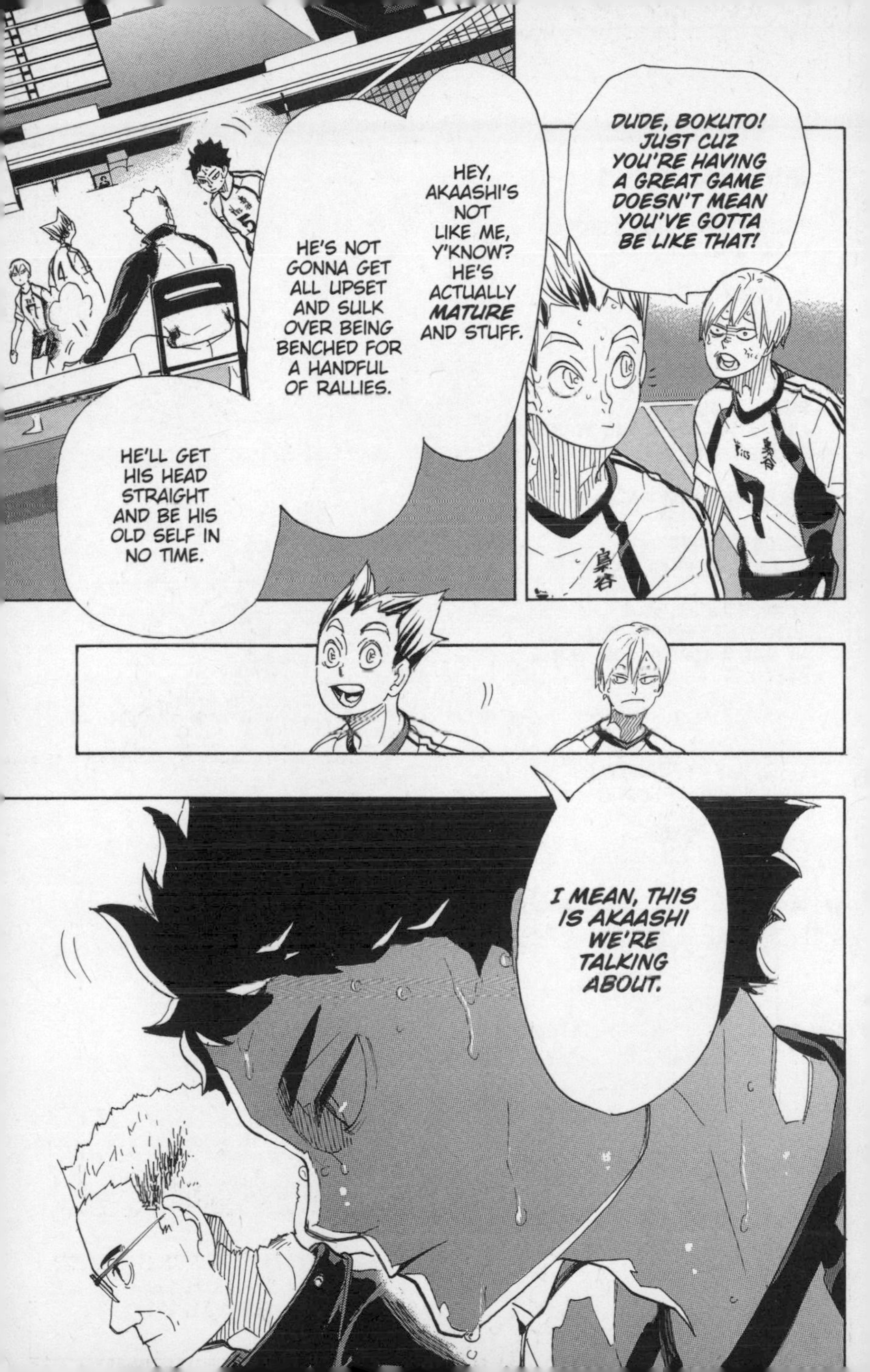
DUDE, BOKUTO! JUST CUZ YOU'RE HAVING A GREAT GAME DOESN'T MEAN YOU'VE GOTTA BE LIKE THAT!
HEY, AKAASHI'S NOT LIKE ME, Y'KNOW? HE'S ACTUALLY MATURE AND STUFF.
HE'S NOT GONNA GET ALL UPSET AND SULK OVER BEING BENCHED FOR A HANDFUL OF RALLIES.
HE'LL GET HIS HEAD STRAIGHT AND BE HIS OLD SELF IN NO TIME.
I MEAN, THIS IS AKAASHI WE'RE TALKING ABOUT.

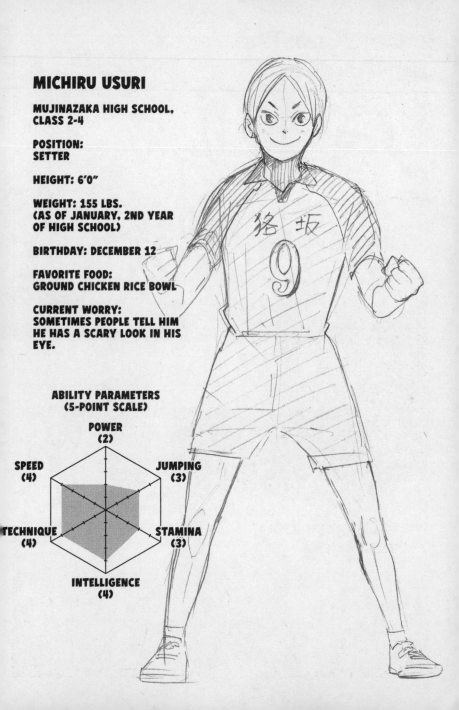

MICHIRU USURI

MUJINAZAKA HIGH SCHOOL, CLASS 2-4

POSITION:
SETTER

HEIGHT: 6'0"

WEIGHT: 155 LBS.
(AS OF JANUARY, 2ND YEAR OF HIGH SCHOOL)

BIRTHDAY: DECEMBER 12

FAVORITE FOOD:
GROUND CHICKEN RICE BOWL

CURRENT WORRY:
SOMETIMES PEOPLE TELL HIM HE HAS A SCARY LOOK IN HIS EYE.

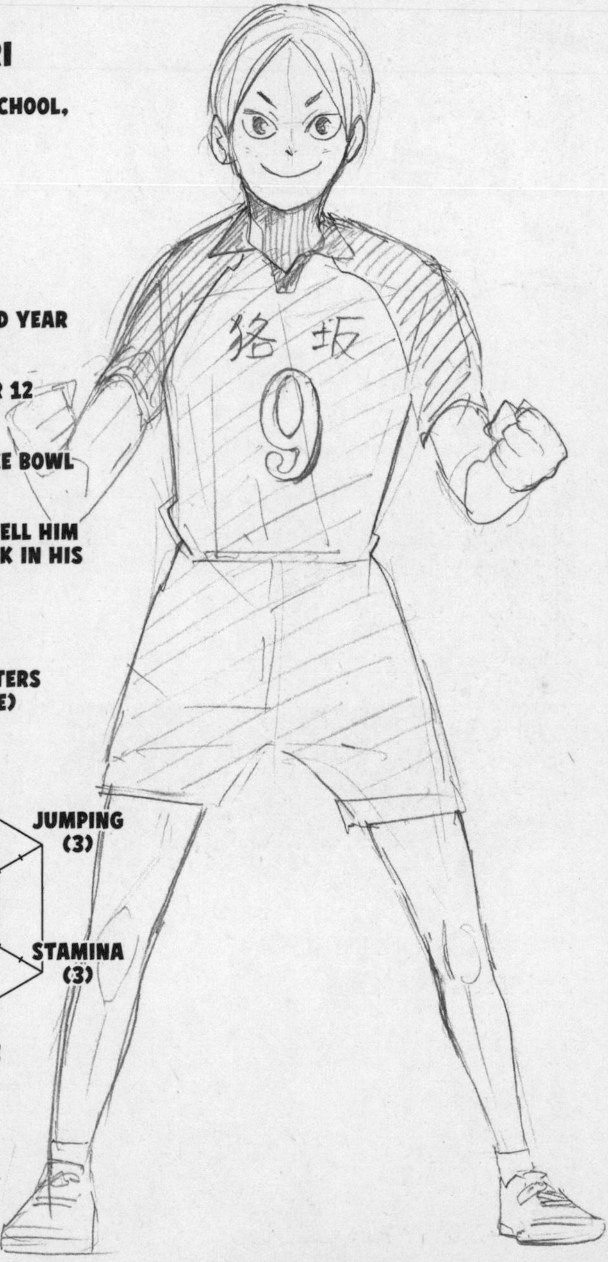
狢坂
9

ABILITY PARAMETERS
(5-POINT SCALE)

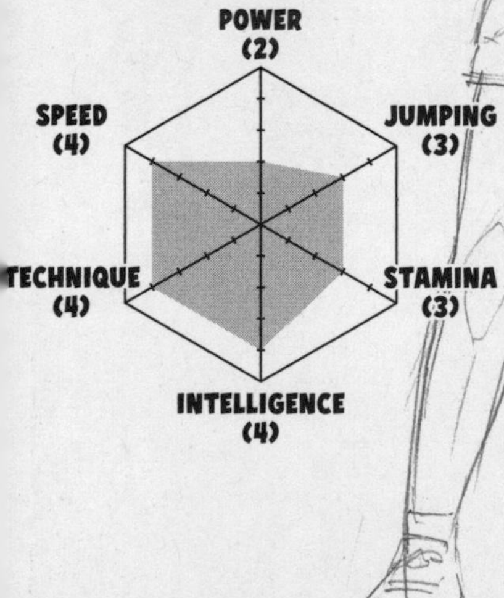
POWER
(2)
JUMPING
(3)
STAMINA
(3)
INTELLIGENCE
(4)
TECHNIQUE
(4)
SPEED
(4)

CHAPTER 333: Task Focus

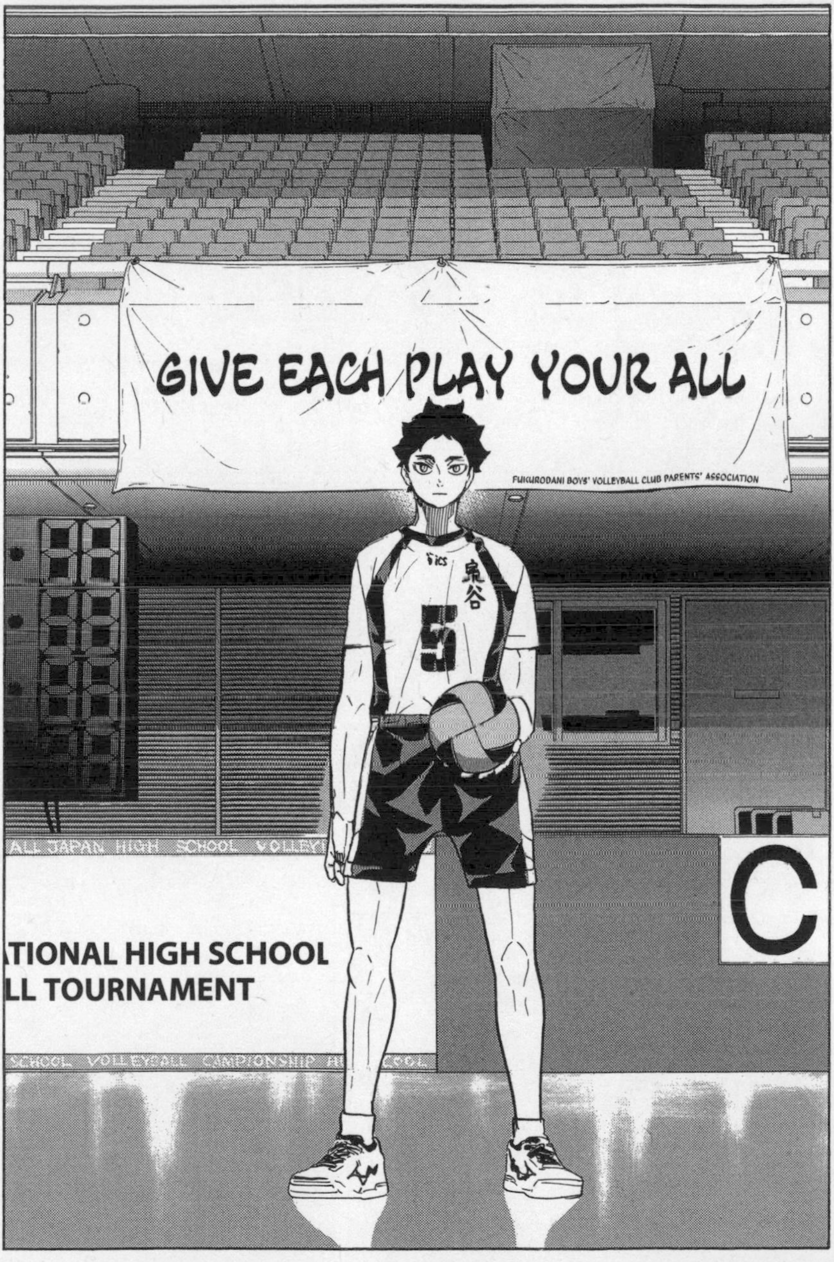
GIVE EACH PLAY YOUR ALL
FUKURODANI BOYS' VOLLEYBALL CLUB PARENTS' ASSOCIATION
ATIONAL HIGH SCHOOL
LL TOURNAMENT
C

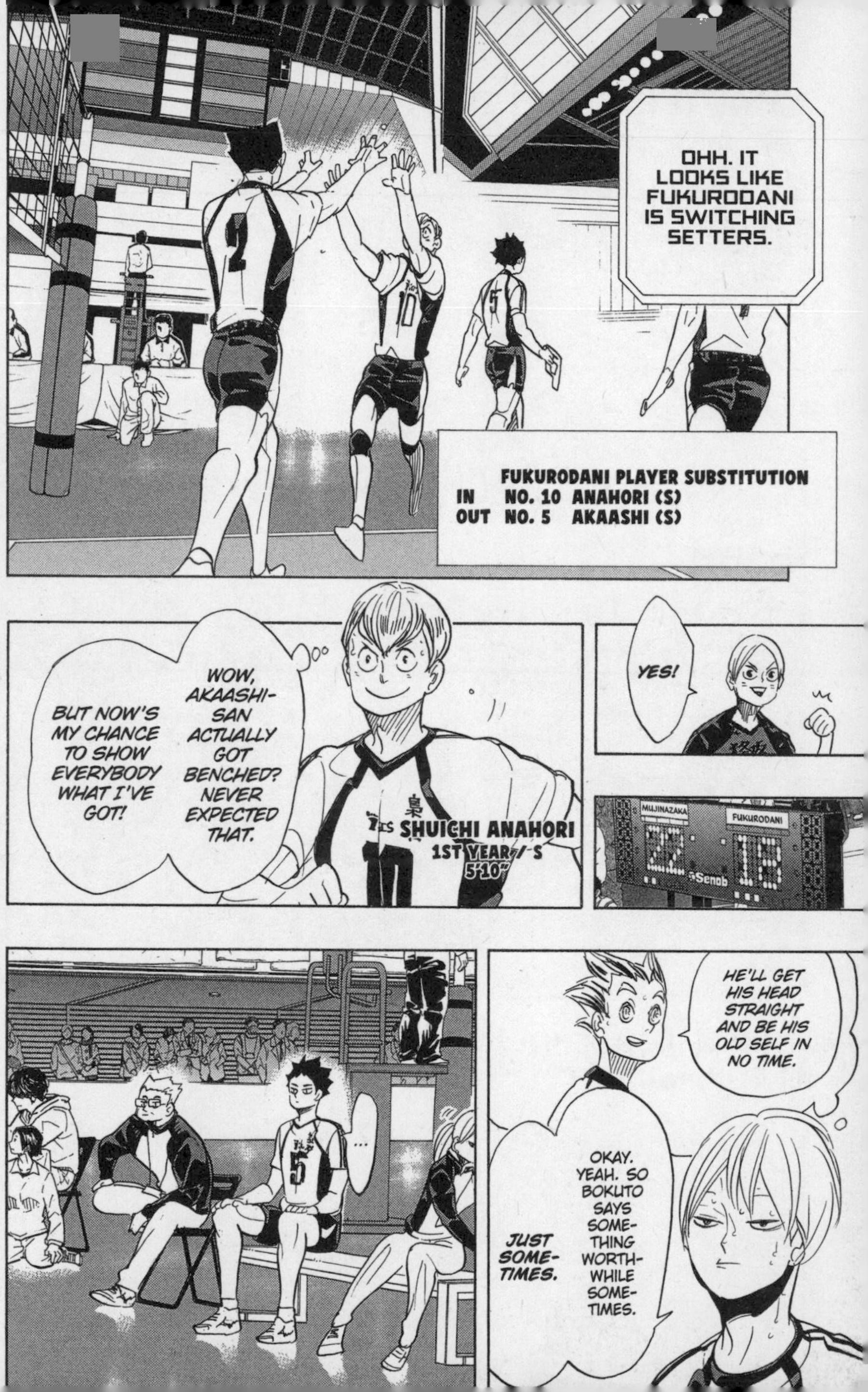
OHH. IT LOOKS LIKE FUKURODANI IS SWITCHING SETTERS.
FUKURODANI PLAYER SUBSTITUTION
IN NO. 10 ANAHORI (S)
OUT NO. 5 AKAASHI (S)
YES!
MUJINAZAKA
FUKURODANI
Senob
WOW, AKAASHI-SAN ACTUALLY GOT BENCHED? NEVER EXPECTED THAT.
BUT NOW'S MY CHANCE TO SHOW EVERYBODY WHAT I'VE GOT!
SHUICHI ANAHORI
1ST YEAR / S
5'10"
HE'LL GET HIS HEAD STRAIGHT AND BE HIS OLD SELF IN NO TIME.
OKAY. YEAH. SO BOKUTO SAYS SOMETHING WORTHWHILE SOMETIMES.
JUST SOMETIMES.
...

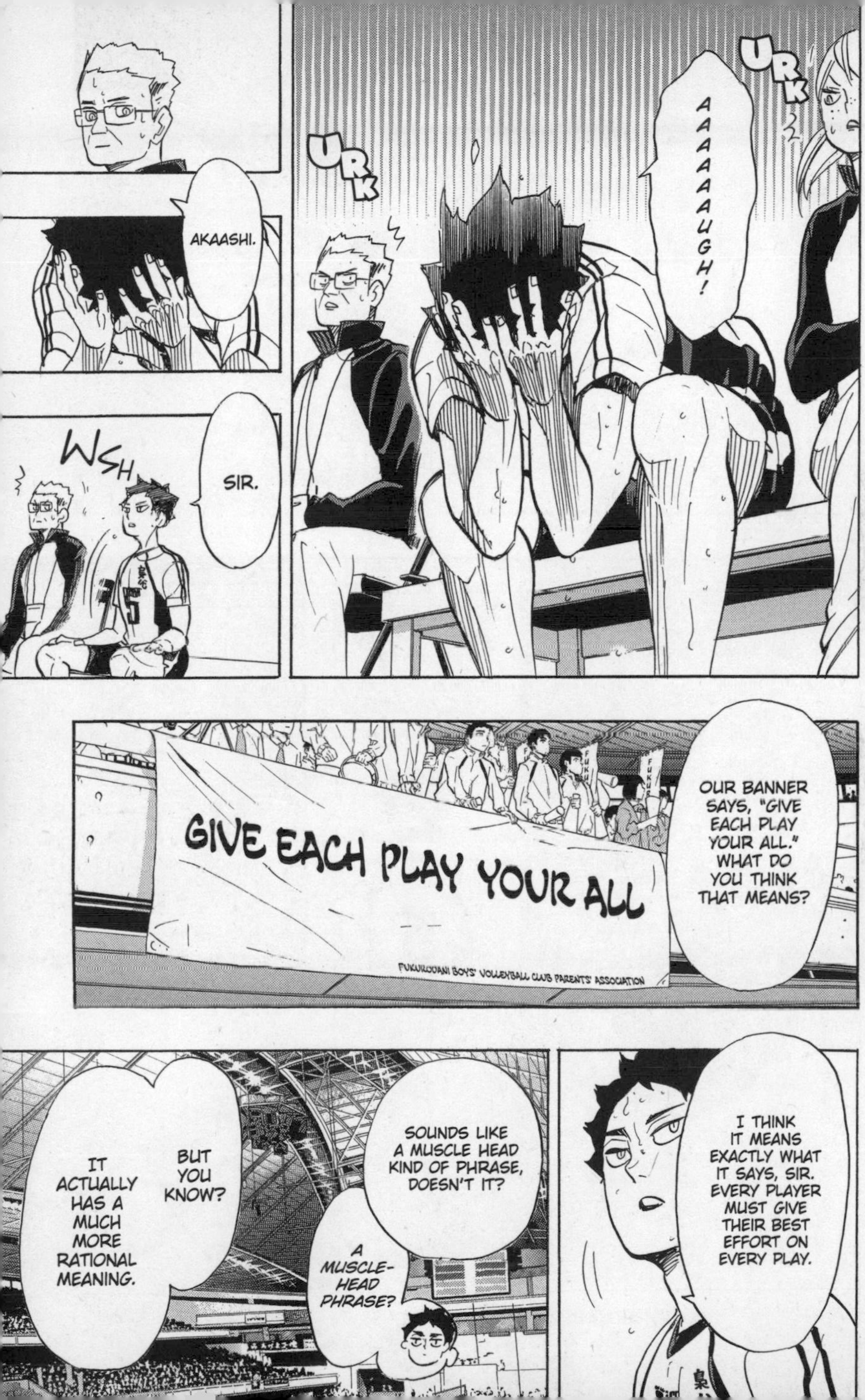
URK
AAAAAAUGH!
URK
AKAASHI.
SIR.
WSH
OUR BANNER SAYS, "GIVE EACH PLAY YOUR ALL." WHAT DO YOU THINK THAT MEANS?
GIVE EACH PLAY YOUR ALL
FUKURODANI BOYS' VOLLEYBALL CLUB PARENTS' ASSOCIATION
I THINK IT MEANS EXACTLY WHAT IT SAYS, SIR. EVERY PLAYER MUST GIVE THEIR BEST EFFORT ON EVERY PLAY.
SOUNDS LIKE A MUSCLE HEAD KIND OF PHRASE, DOESN'T IT?
A MUSCLE-HEAD PHRASE?
BUT YOU KNOW?
IT ACTUALLY HAS A MUCH MORE RATIONAL MEANING.

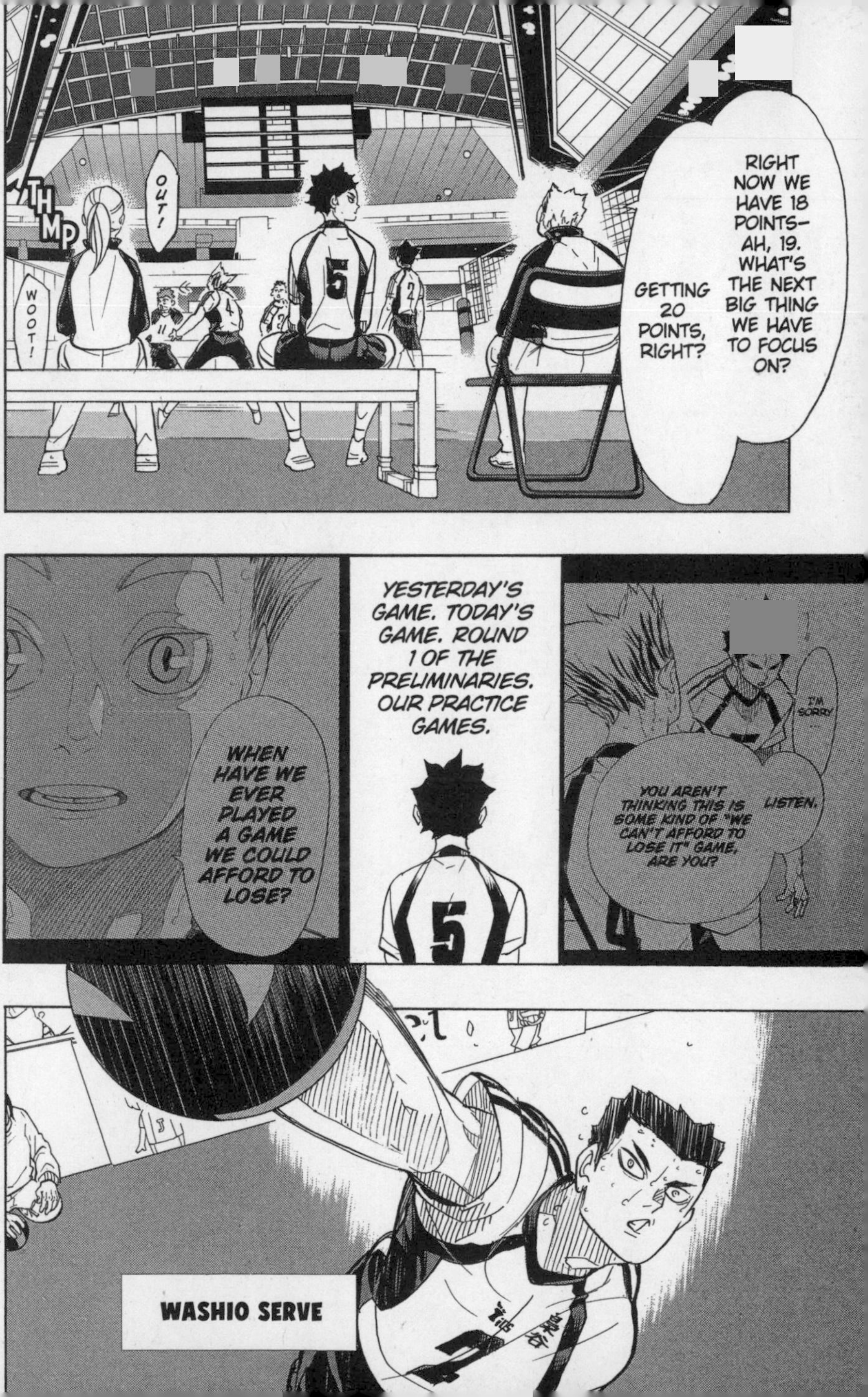
RIGHT NOW WE HAVE 18 POINTS— AH, 19. WHAT'S THE NEXT BIG THING WE HAVE TO FOCUS ON?
GETTING 20 POINTS, RIGHT?
OUT!
THMP
WOOT!
I'M SORRY
LISTEN.
YOU AREN'T THINKING THIS IS SOME KIND OF "WE CAN'T AFFORD TO LOSE IT" GAME, ARE YOU?
YESTERDAY'S GAME. TODAY'S GAME. ROUND 1 OF THE PRELIMINARIES. OUR PRACTICE GAMES.
WHEN HAVE WE EVER PLAYED A GAME WE COULD AFFORD TO LOSE?
WASHIO SERVE

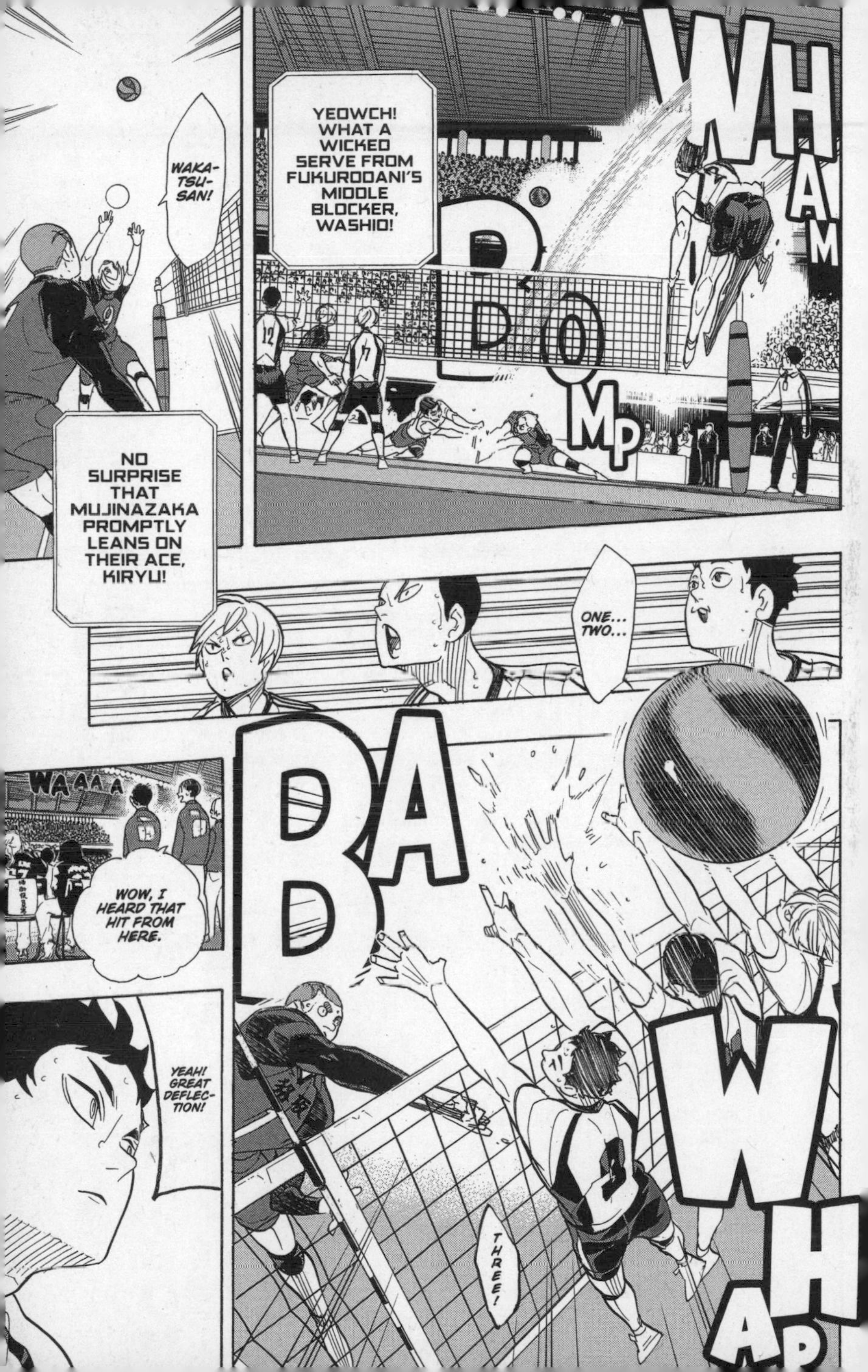
WHAM
YEOWCH! WHAT A WICKED SERVE FROM FUKURODANI'S MIDDLE BLOCKER, WASHIO!
DOMP
WAKA-TSU-SAN!
NO SURPRISE THAT MUJINAZAKA PROMPTLY LEANS ON THEIR ACE, KIRYU!
ONE... TWO...
WHAP
BADA
THREE!
WAAAA
WOW, I HEARD THAT HIT FROM HERE.
YEAH! GREAT DEFLEC-TION!

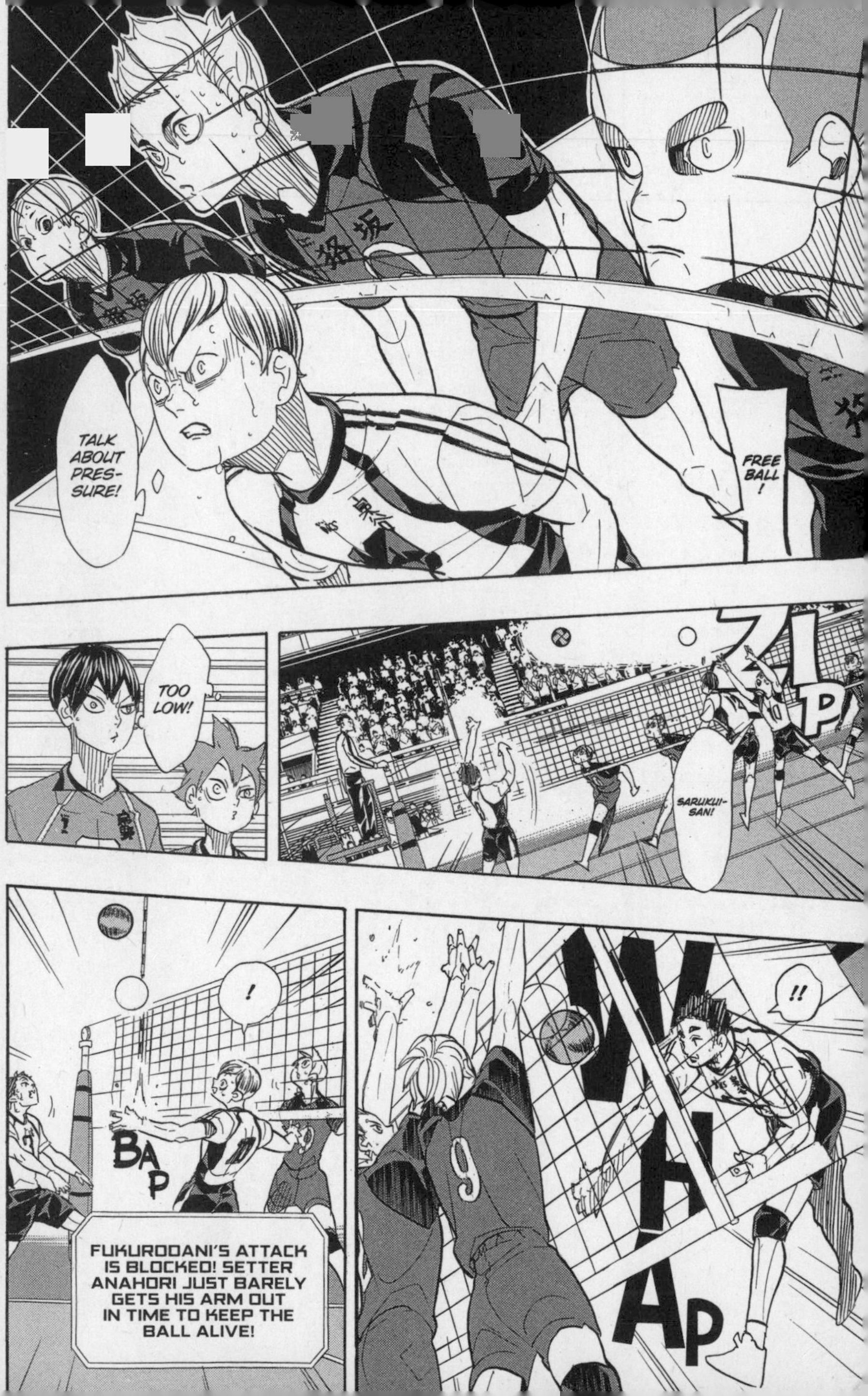
FREE BALL!
TALK ABOUT PRES-SURE!
ZIP
SARUKUI-SAN!
TOO LOW!
WHAP
!!
!
BAP
FUKURODANI'S ATTACK IS BLOCKED! SETTER ANAHORI JUST BARELY GETS HIS ARM OUT IN TIME TO KEEP THE BALL ALIVE!

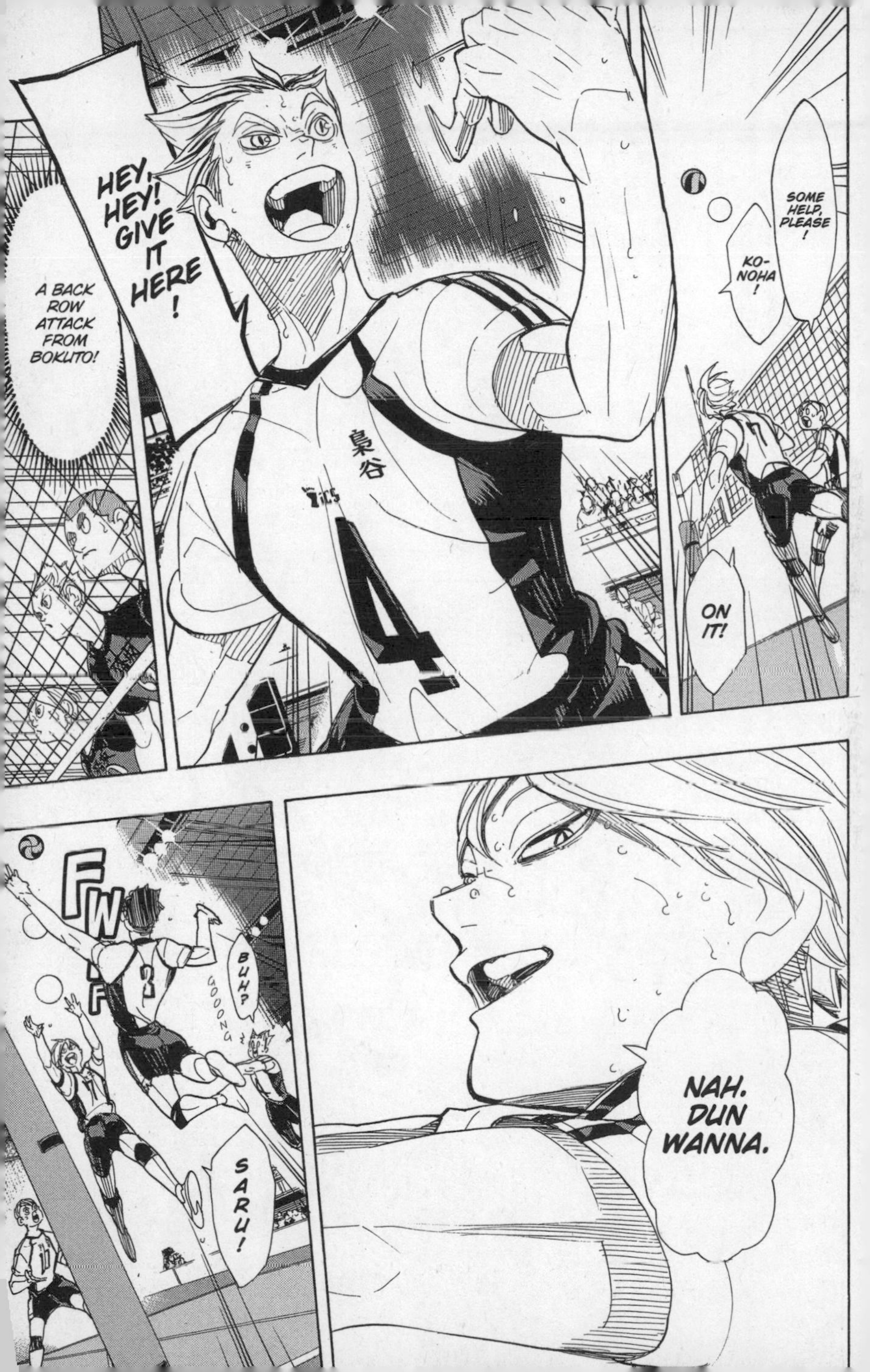
SOME HELP, PLEASE!
KO-NOHA!
ON IT!
HEY, HEY! GIVE IT HERE!
A BACK ROW ATTACK FROM BOKUTO!
NAH. DUN WANNA.
FWF
BUH?
GOOONG
SARU!

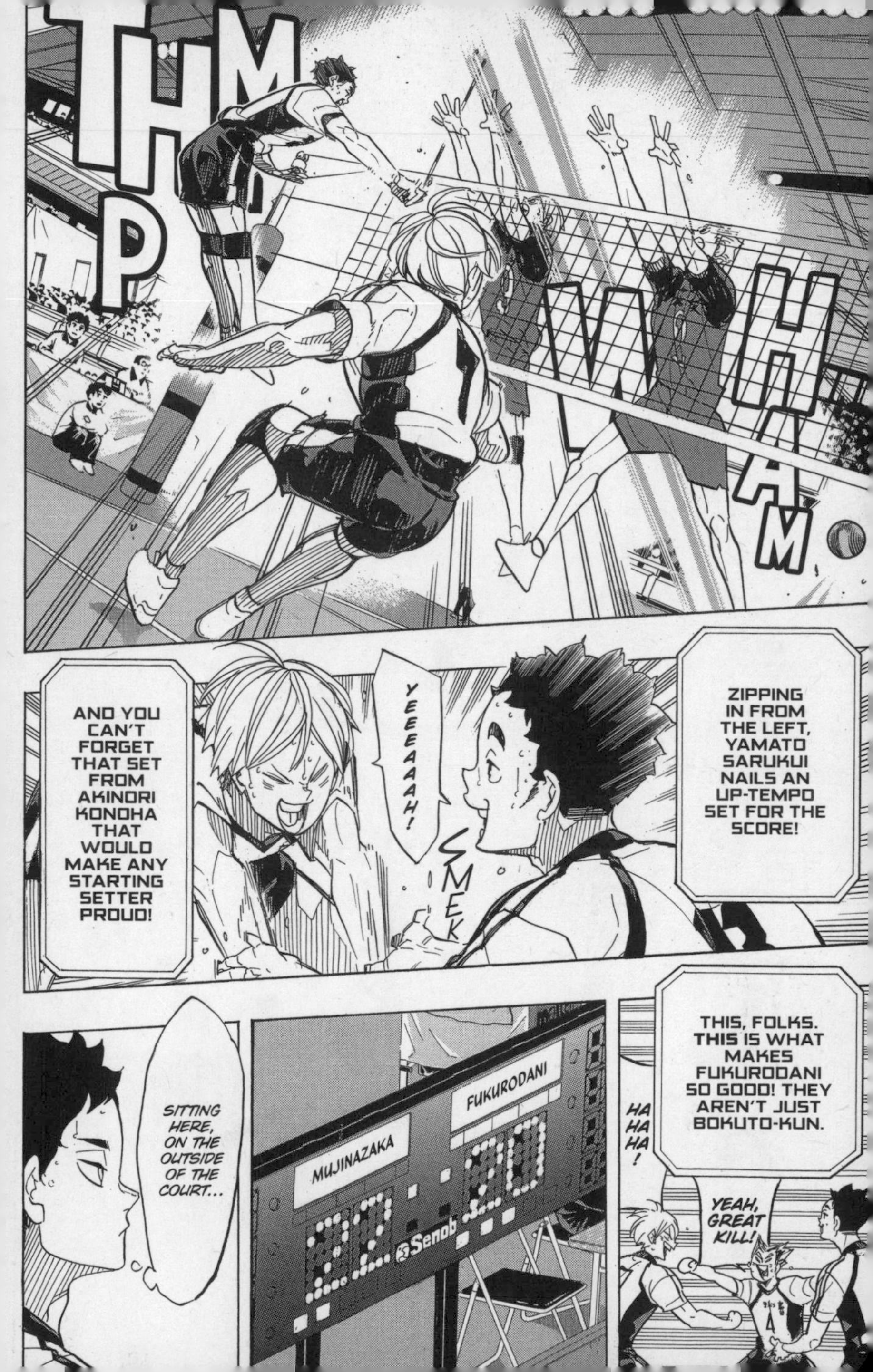
THMP
WHAM
ZIPPING IN FROM THE LEFT, YAMATO SARUKUI NAILS AN UP-TEMPO SET FOR THE SCORE!
YEEEAAAH!
SMEK
AND YOU CAN'T FORGET THAT SET FROM AKINORI KONOHA THAT WOULD MAKE ANY STARTING SETTER PROUD!
THIS, FOLKS. THIS IS WHAT MAKES FUKURODANI SO GOOD! THEY AREN'T JUST BOKUTO-KUN.
HA HA HA!
YEAH, GREAT KILL!
FUKURODANI
MUJINAZAKA
Senob
SITTING HERE, ON THE OUTSIDE OF THE COURT...

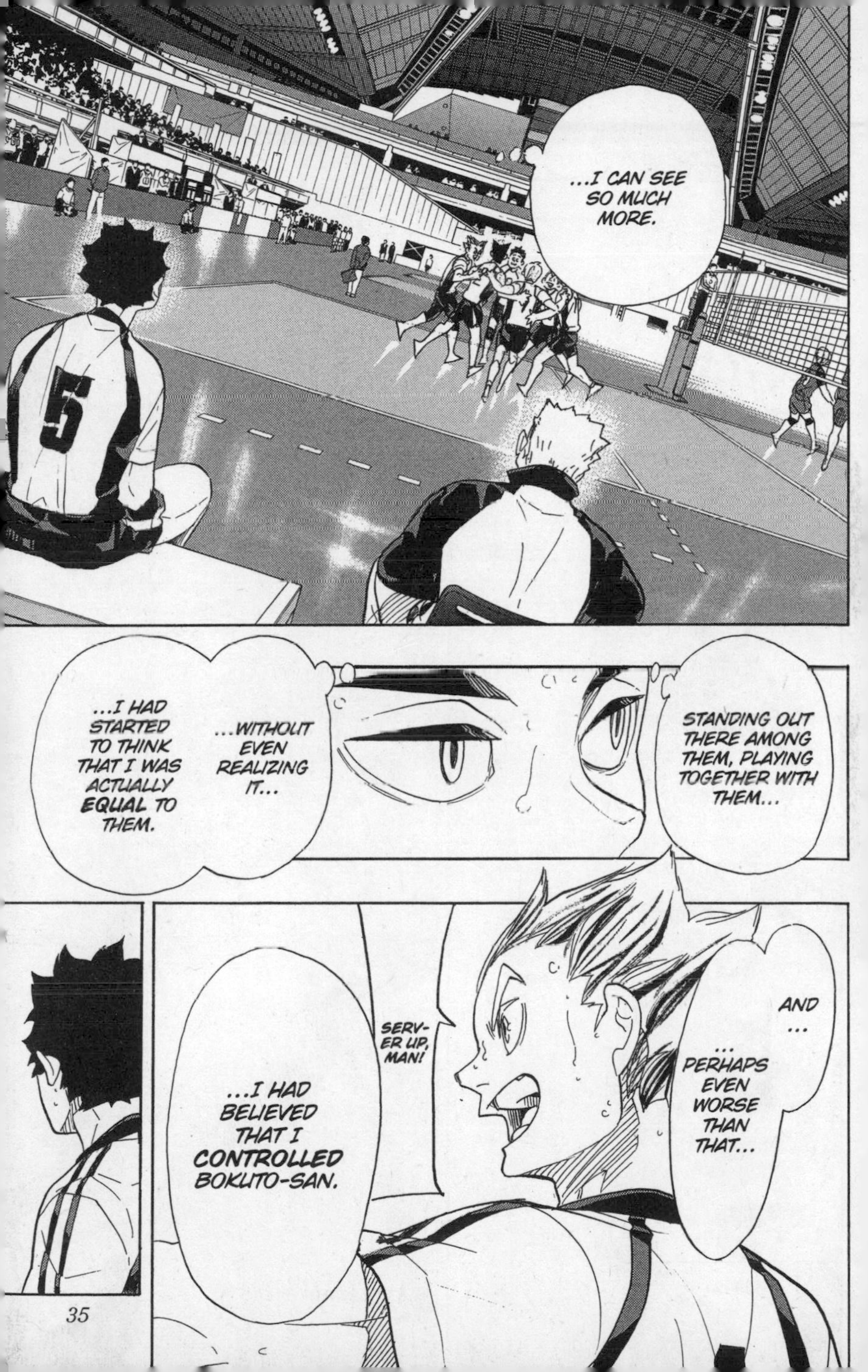
...I CAN SEE SO MUCH MORE.
STANDING OUT THERE AMONG THEM, PLAYING TOGETHER WITH THEM...
...WITHOUT EVEN REALIZING IT...
...I HAD STARTED TO THINK THAT I WAS ACTUALLY EQUAL TO THEM.
AND ... ... PERHAPS EVEN WORSE THAN THAT...
SERV-ER UP, MAN!
...I HAD BELIEVED THAT I CONTROLLED BOKUTO-SAN.

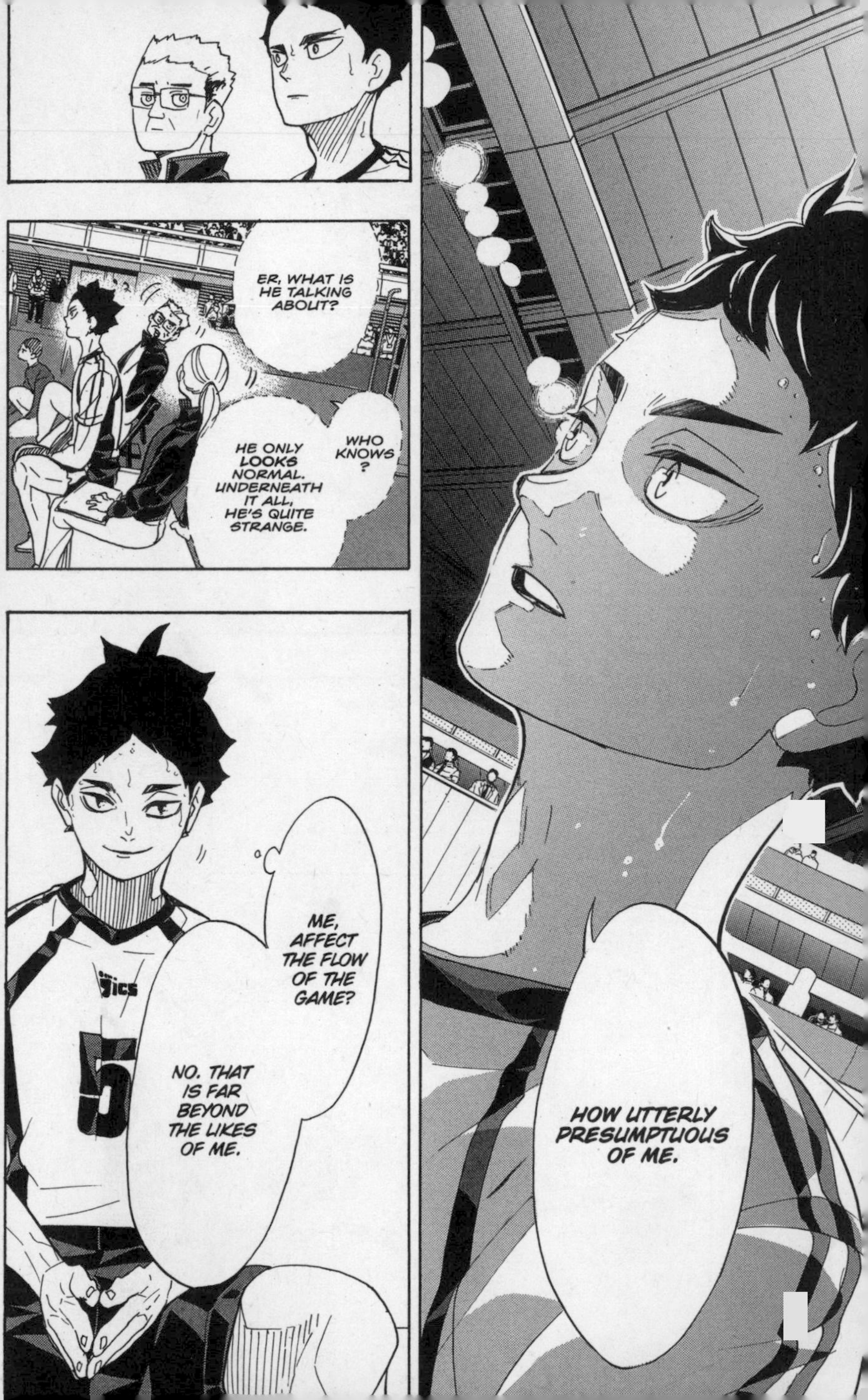
ER, WHAT IS HE TALKING ABOUT?
WHO KNOWS?
HE ONLY LOOKS NORMAL. UNDERNEATH IT ALL, HE'S QUITE STRANGE.
ME, AFFECT THE FLOW OF THE GAME?
NO. THAT IS FAR BEYOND THE LIKES OF ME.
HOW UTTERLY PRESUMPTUOUS OF ME.

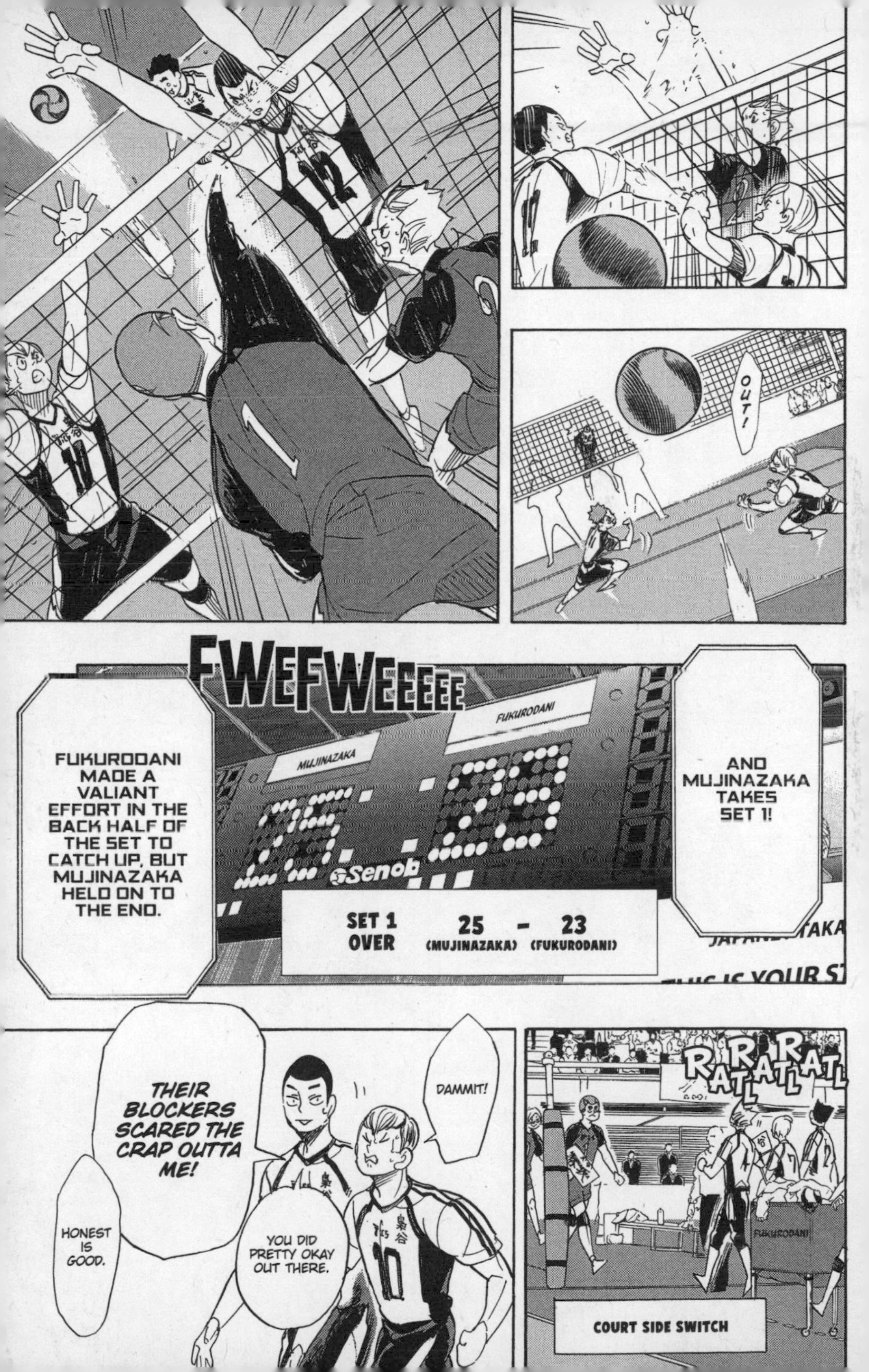
OUT!
FWEFWEEEEE
AND MUJINAZAKA TAKES SET 1!
FUKURODANI
MUJINAZAKA
FUKURODANI MADE A VALIANT EFFORT IN THE BACK HALF OF THE SET TO CATCH UP, BUT MUJINAZAKA HELD ON TO THE END.
SET 1 OVER 25 - 23 (MUJINAZAKA) (FUKURODANI)
RATLRATLRATL
FUKURODANI
COURT SIDE SWITCH
DAMMIT!
THEIR BLOCKERS SCARED THE CRAP OUTTA ME!
YOU DID PRETTY OKAY OUT THERE.
HONEST IS GOOD.

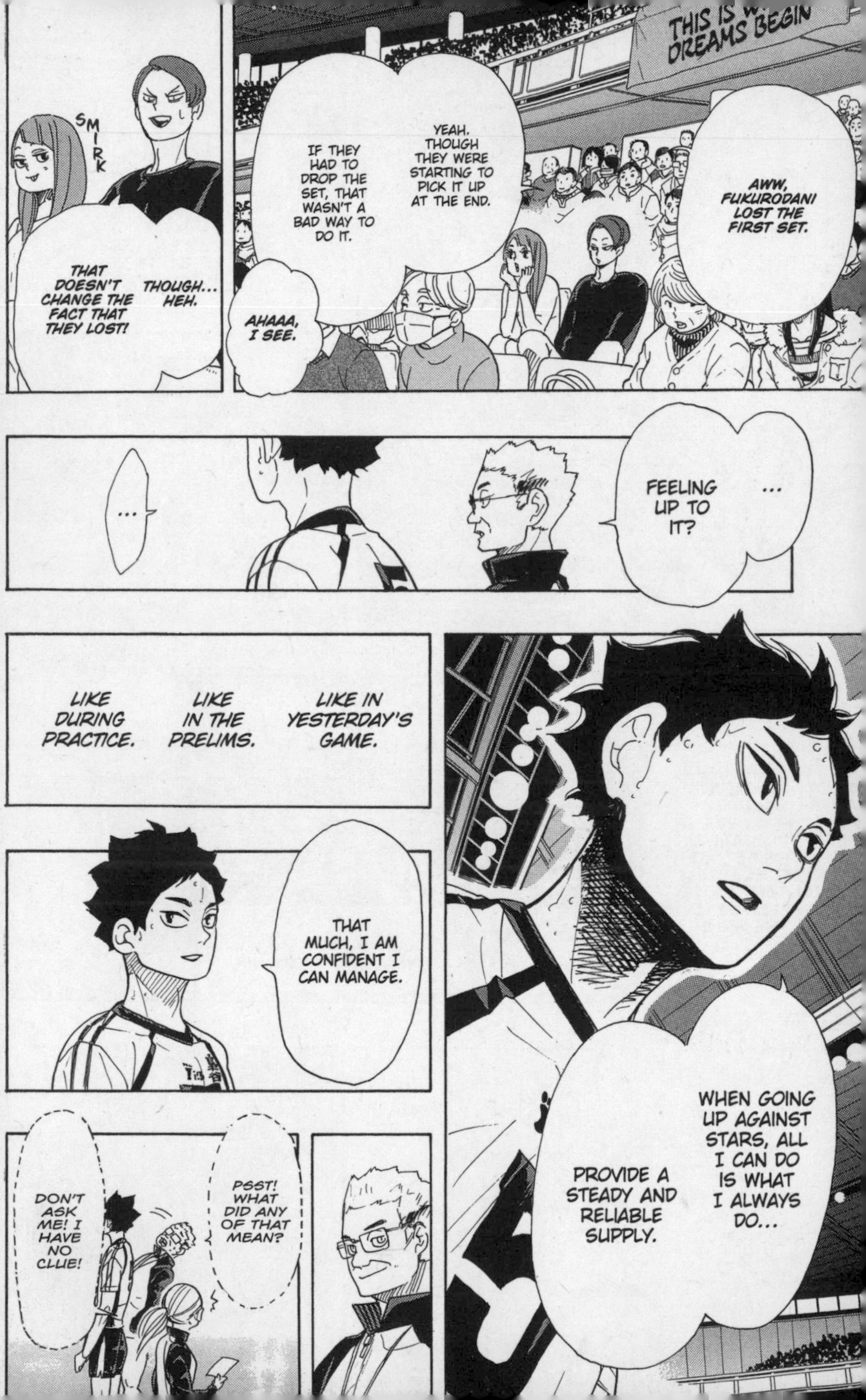

THIS IS
DREAMS BEGIN
AWW, FUKURODANI LOST THE FIRST SET.
YEAH. THOUGH THEY WERE STARTING TO PICK IT UP AT THE END.
IF THEY HAD TO DROP THE SET, THAT WASN'T A BAD WAY TO DO IT.
AHAAA, I SEE.
SMIRK
THOUGH... HEH.
THAT DOESN'T CHANGE THE FACT THAT THEY LOST!
FEELING UP TO IT? ...
...
WHEN GOING UP AGAINST STARS, ALL I CAN DO IS WHAT I ALWAYS DO...
PROVIDE A STEADY AND RELIABLE SUPPLY.
LIKE IN YESTERDAY'S GAME.
LIKE IN THE PRELIMS.
LIKE DURING PRACTICE.
THAT MUCH, I AM CONFIDENT I CAN MANAGE.
PSST! WHAT DID ANY OF THAT MEAN?
DON'T ASK ME! I HAVE NO CLUE!

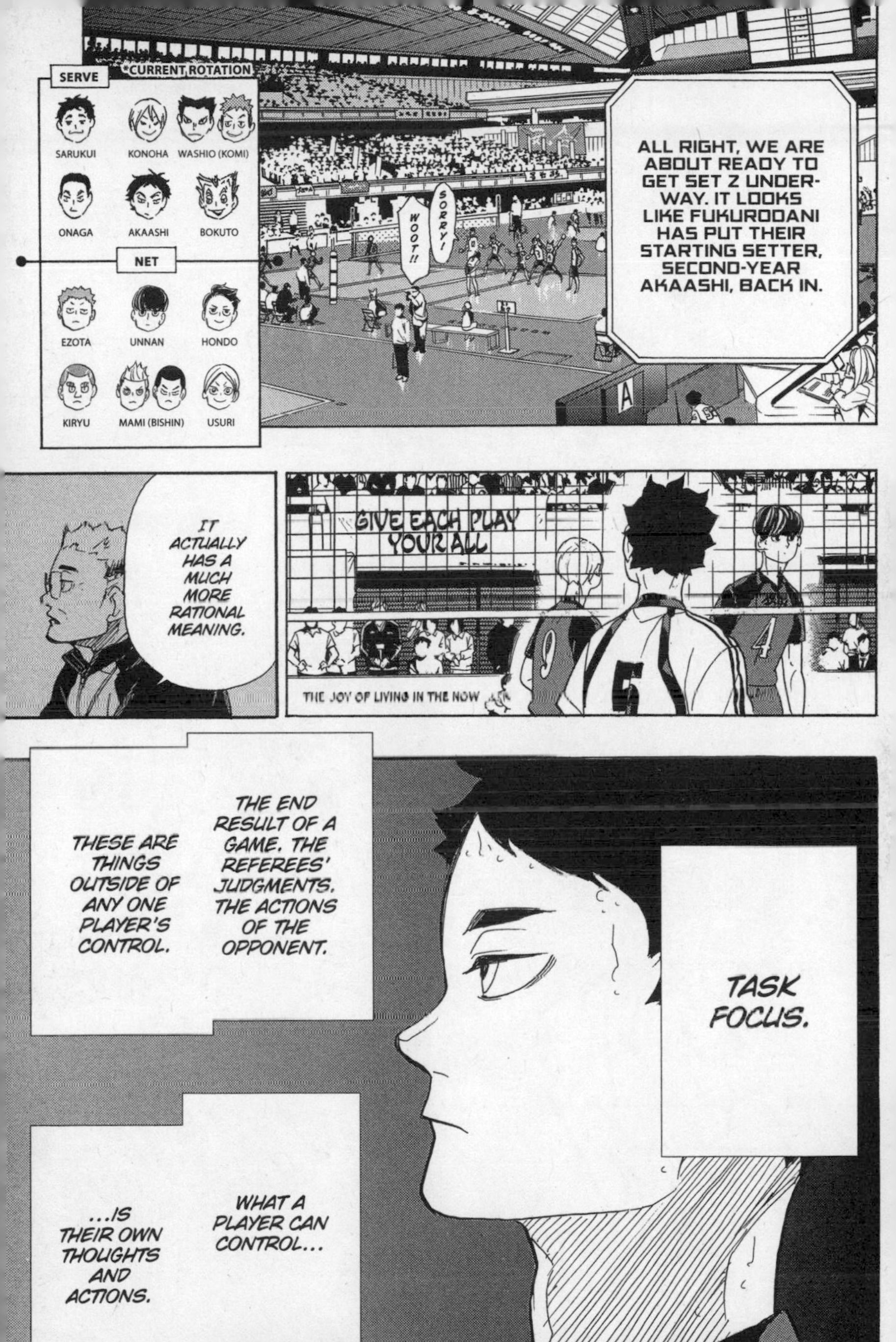
ALL RIGHT, WE ARE ABOUT READY TO GET SET 2 UNDERWAY. IT LOOKS LIKE FUKURODANI HAS PUT THEIR STARTING SETTER, SECOND-YEAR AKAASHI, BACK IN.
SORRY!
WOOT!!
*CURRENT ROTATION
SERVE
SARUKUI
KONOHA
WASHIO (KOMI)
ONAGA
AKAASHI
BOKUTO
NET
EZOTA
UNNAN
HONDO
KIRYU
MAMI (BISHIN)
USURI
GIVE EACH PLAY YOUR ALL
THE JOY OF LIVING IN THE NOW
IT ACTUALLY HAS A MUCH MORE RATIONAL MEANING.
TASK FOCUS.
THE END RESULT OF A GAME. THE REFEREES' JUDGMENTS. THE ACTIONS OF THE OPPONENT.
THESE ARE THINGS OUTSIDE OF ANY ONE PLAYER'S CONTROL.
WHAT A PLAYER CAN CONTROL...
...IS THEIR OWN THOUGHTS AND ACTIONS.

*REFERENCE: *VOLLEYBALL MENTAL KYOKA METHOD* BY EIJI WATANABE (JIKKYO NO NIHONSHA)

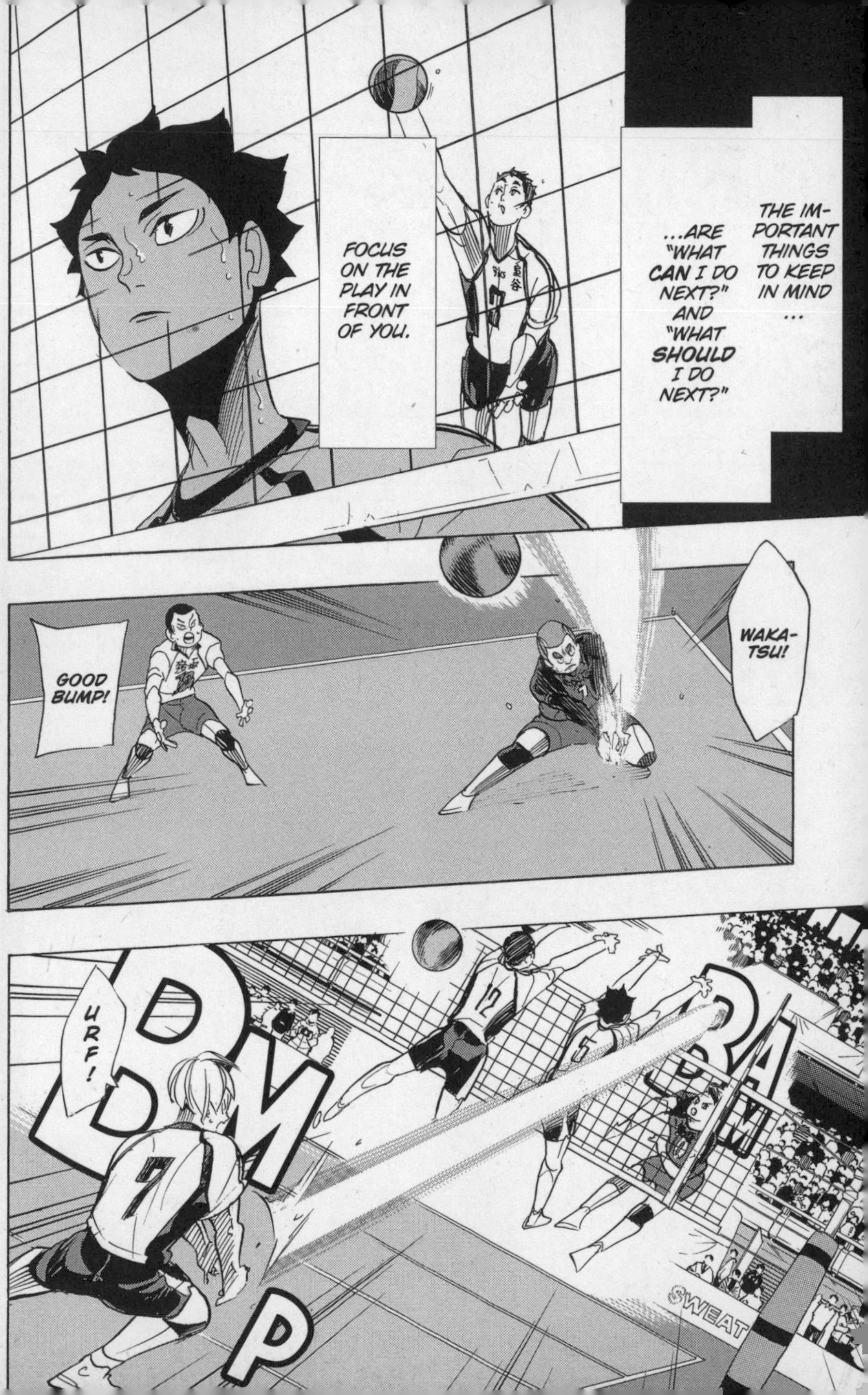
THE IMPORTANT THINGS TO KEEP IN MIND...
..."ARE "WHAT CAN I DO NEXT?" AND "WHAT SHOULD I DO NEXT?"
FOCUS ON THE PLAY IN FRONT OF YOU.
WAKATSU!
GOOD BUMP!
URF!
SWEAT

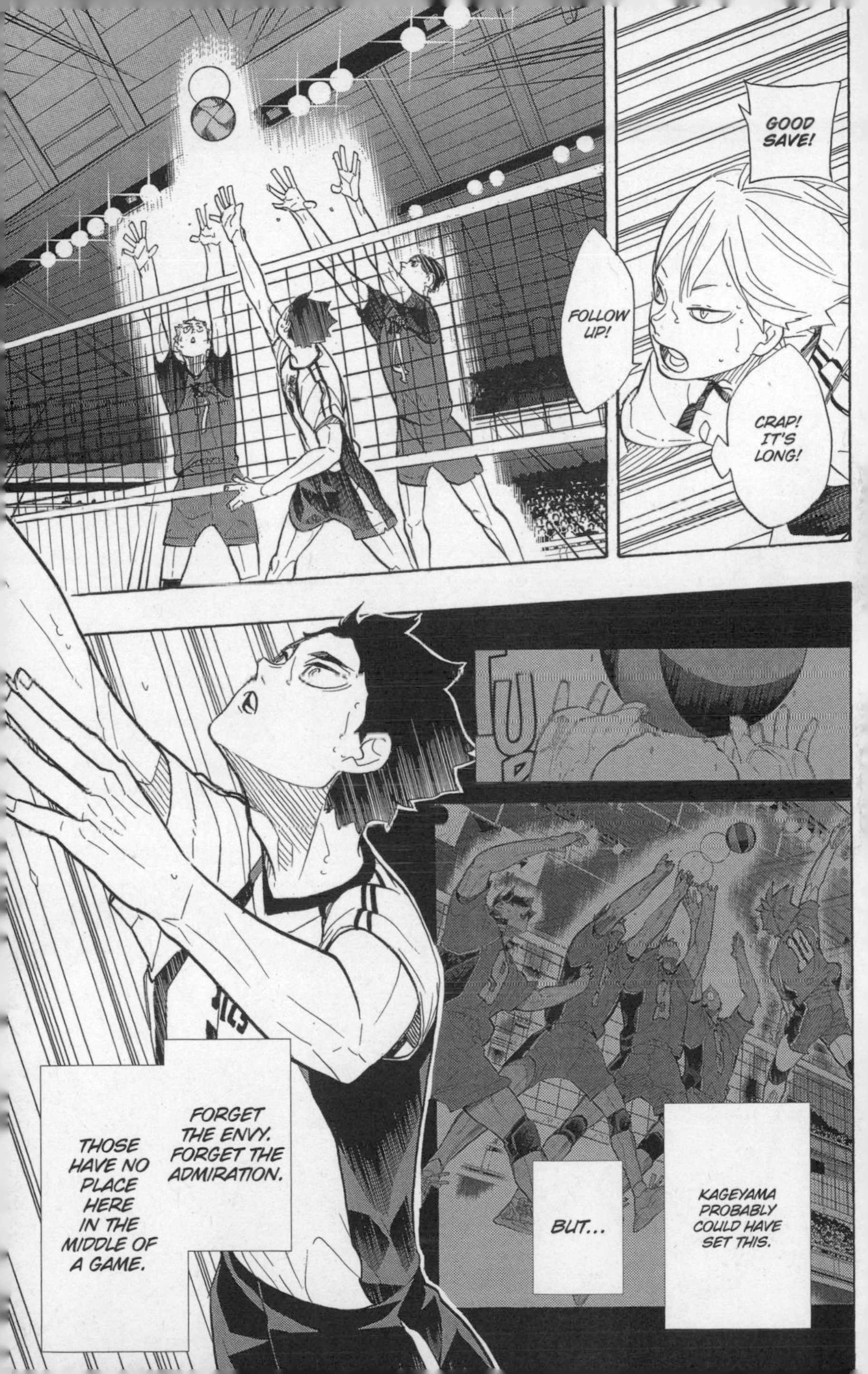
GOOD SAVE!
FOLLOW UP!
CRAP! IT'S LONG!
KAGEYAMA PROBABLY COULD HAVE SET THIS.
BUT...
FORGET THE ENVY. FORGET THE ADMIRATION.
THOSE HAVE NO PLACE HERE IN THE MIDDLE OF A GAME.

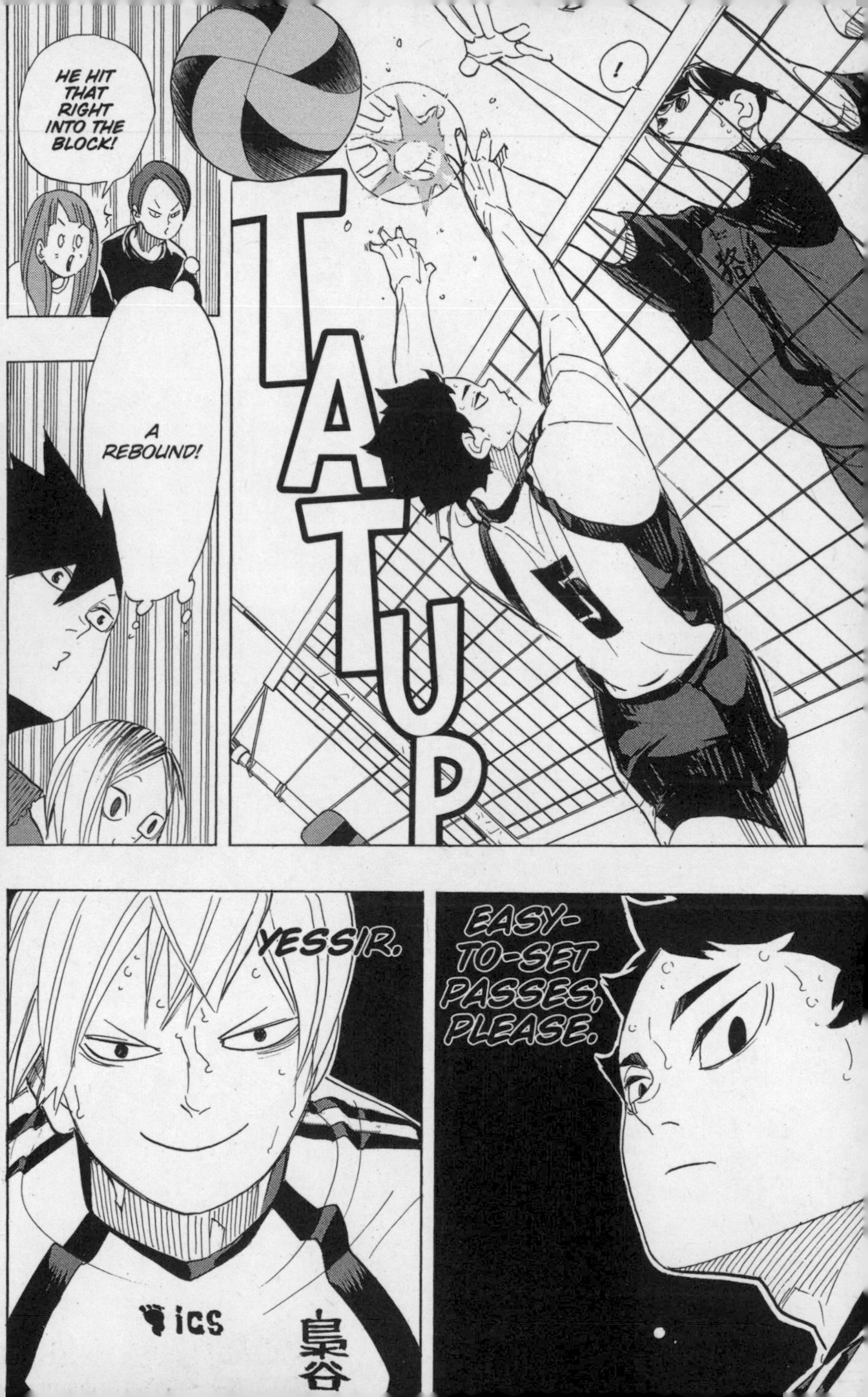
!
TATUP
HE HIT THAT RIGHT INTO THE BLOCK!
A REBOUND!
EASY-TO-SET PASSES, PLEASE.
YESSIR.

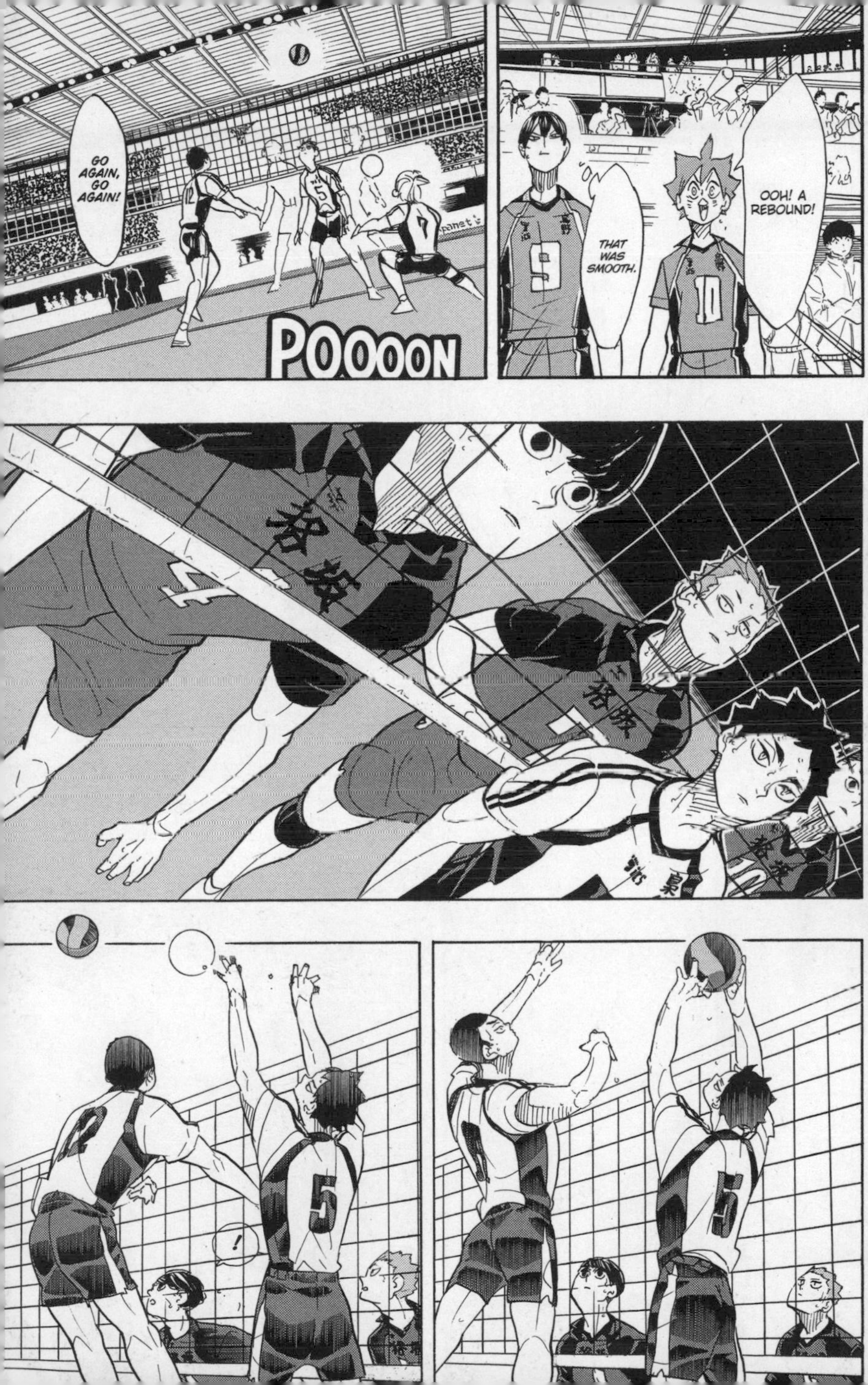
OOH! A REBOUND!
THAT WAS SMOOTH.
GO AGAIN, GO AGAIN!
POOOON
!

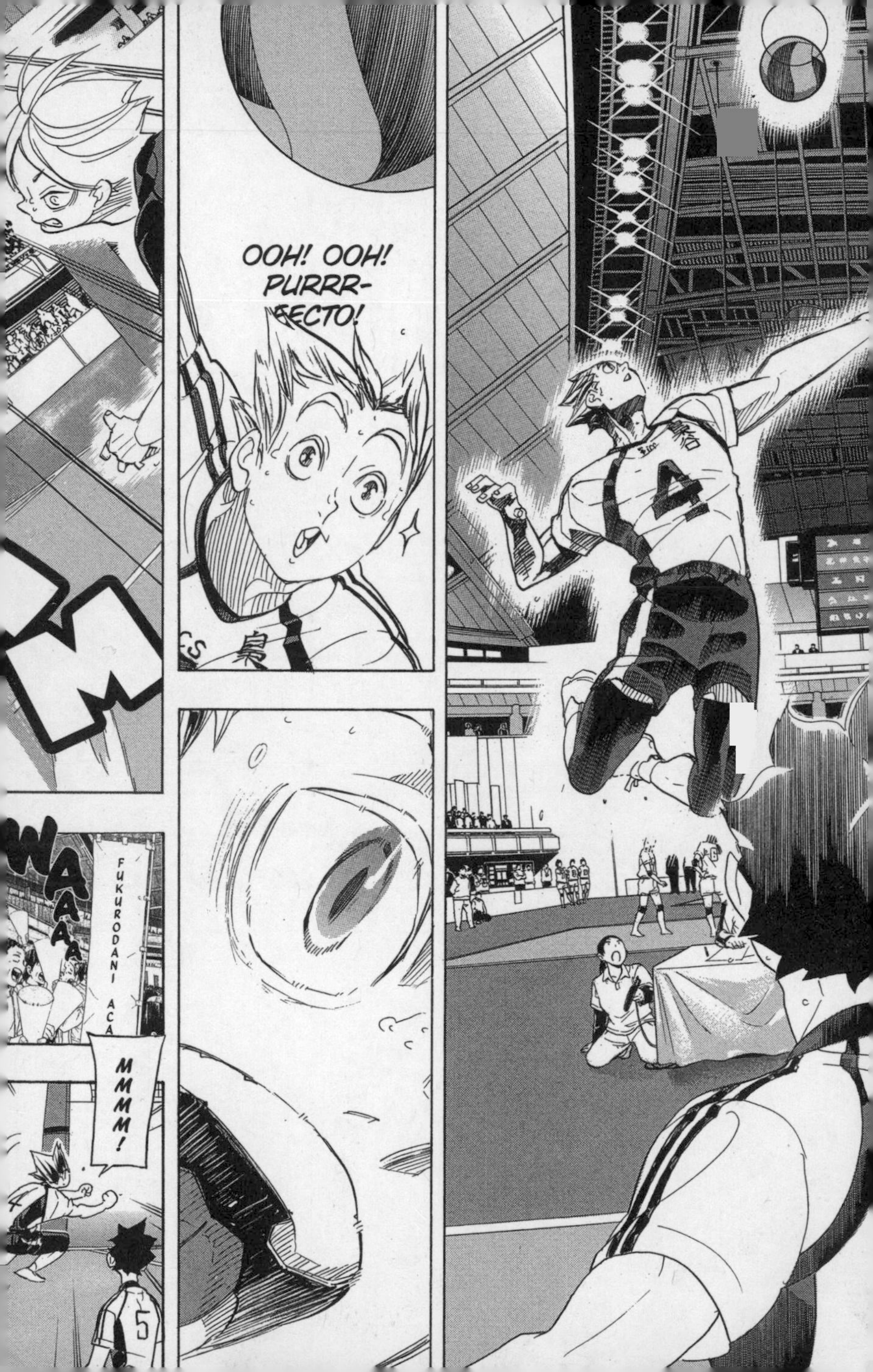
OOH! OOH! PURRR-FECTO!
WAAAA
FUKURODANI ACA
MMMM!

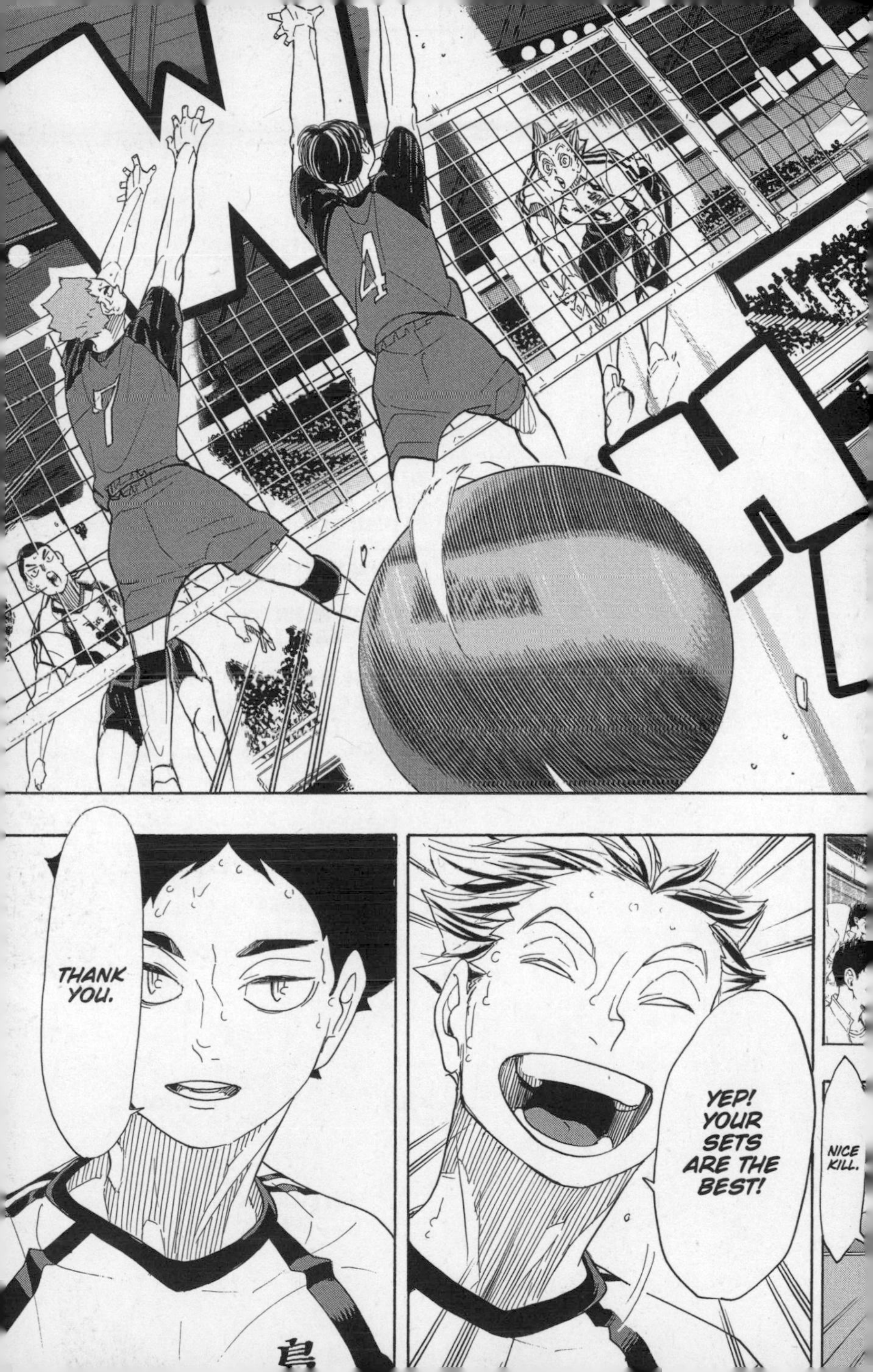
NICE KILL.
YEP! YOUR SETS ARE THE BEST!
THANK YOU.

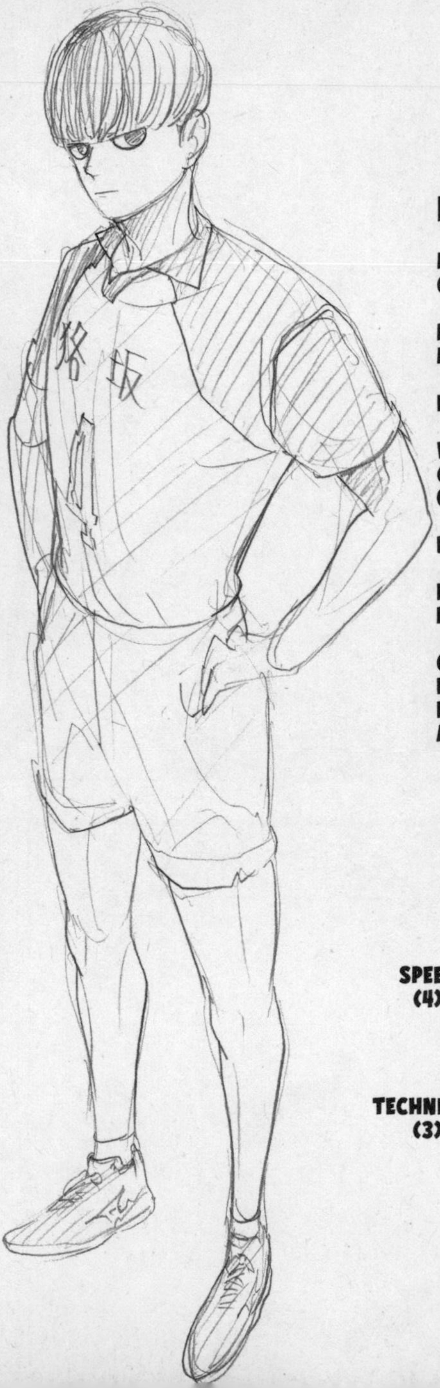

KEISUKE UNNAN

MUJINAZAKA HIGH SCHOOL, CLASS 3-3

POSITION:
MIDDLE BLOCKER

HEIGHT: 6'3"

WEIGHT: 176 LBS.
(AS OF JANUARY, 3RD YEAR OF HIGH SCHOOL)

BIRTHDAY: JANUARY 29

FAVORITE FOOD:
RED CAVIAR

CURRENT WORRY:
HE WANTS TO BE TALLER, EVEN IF IT'S ONLY HALF AN INCH.

ABILITY PARAMETERS
(5-POINT SCALE)

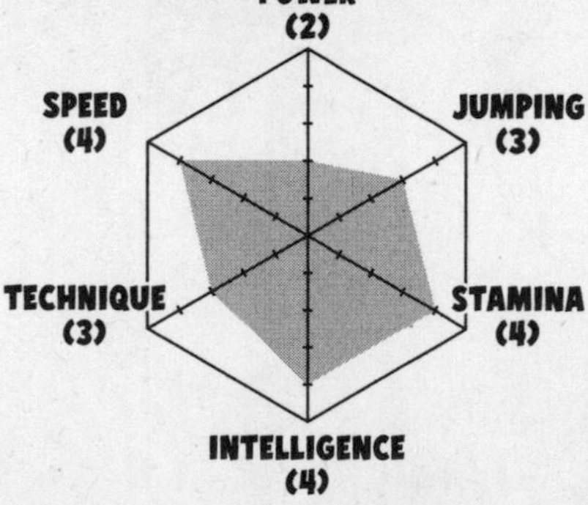
POWER (2)
JUMPING (3)
STAMINA (4)
INTELLIGENCE (4)
TECHNIQUE (3)
SPEED (4)

LESS THAN TEN SECONDS PASS BETWEEN A POINT AND THE NEXT SERVE.

THERE'S NO TIME TO WASTE REGRETTING EARLIER MISTAKES OR LAMENTING THE CURRENT SCORE.

ANALYZE THE OPPONENT'S PRESENT ROTATION AND PREPARE FOR HOW THEY MIGHT ATTACK US.

ONLY THINK ABOUT WHAT I CAN AND SHOULD BE DOING.

SERVE *CURRENT ROTATION

EZOTA | UNNAN (BISHIN) | HONDO

KIRYU | MAMI | USURI

NET

KONOHA | WASHIO | BOKUTO

SARUKUI | ONAGA (KOMI) | AKAASHI

CHAPTER 334: Through Rock Bottom

KONOHA!

ZIP

FOLLOW UP!

LEFT!

BOMP

GLANCE

SARU!

B-BVMP

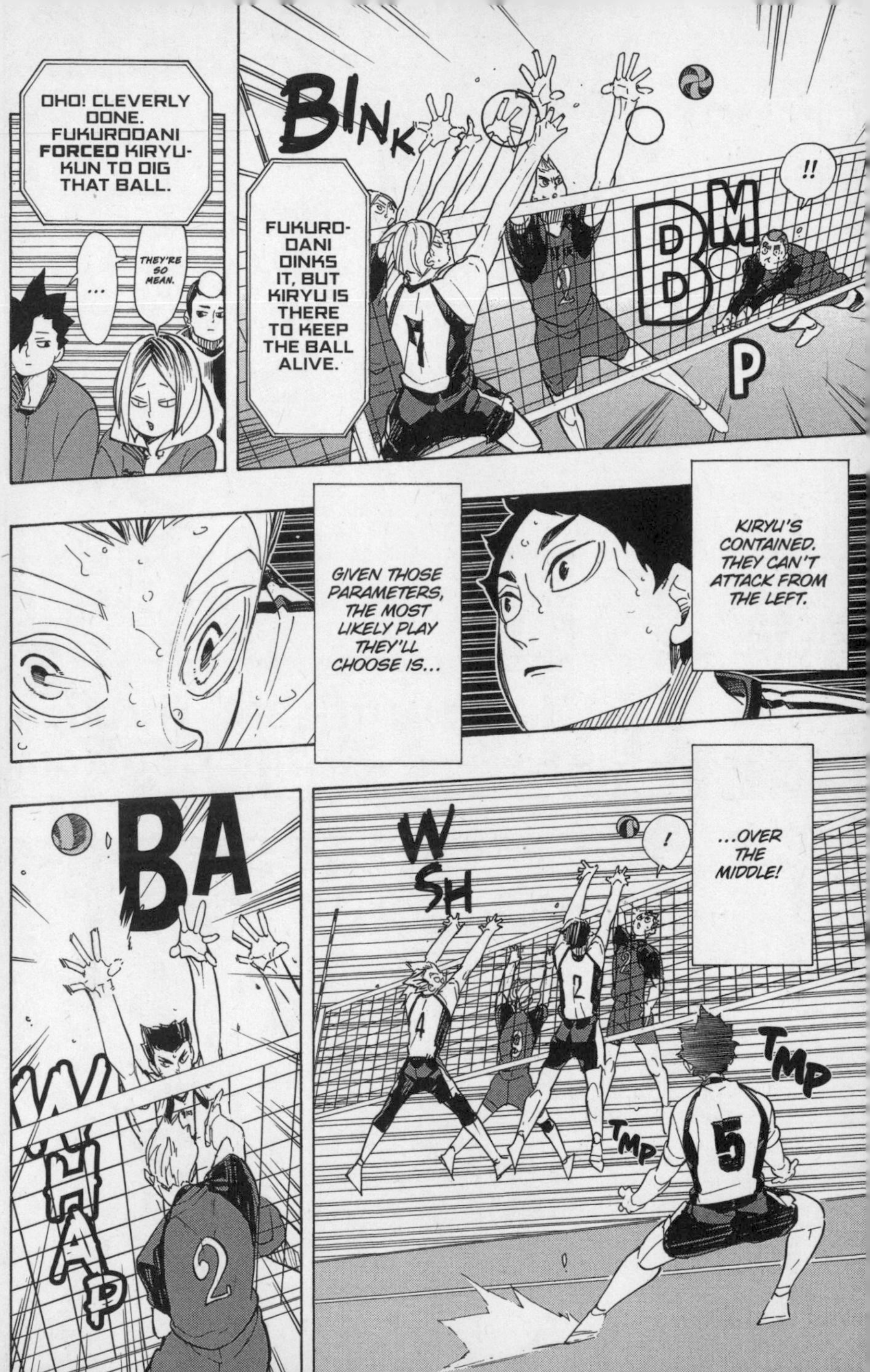
!!
BINK
FUKURODANI DINKS IT, BUT KIRYU IS THERE TO KEEP THE BALL ALIVE.
BMP
OHO! CLEVERLY DONE. FUKURODANI FORCED KIRYU-KUN TO DIG THAT BALL.
THEY'RE SO MEAN.
...
KIRYU'S CONTAINED. THEY CAN'T ATTACK FROM THE LEFT.
GIVEN THOSE PARAMETERS, THE MOST LIKELY PLAY THEY'LL CHOOSE IS...
...OVER THE MIDDLE!
!
WSH
TMP
TMP
BA
WHAP

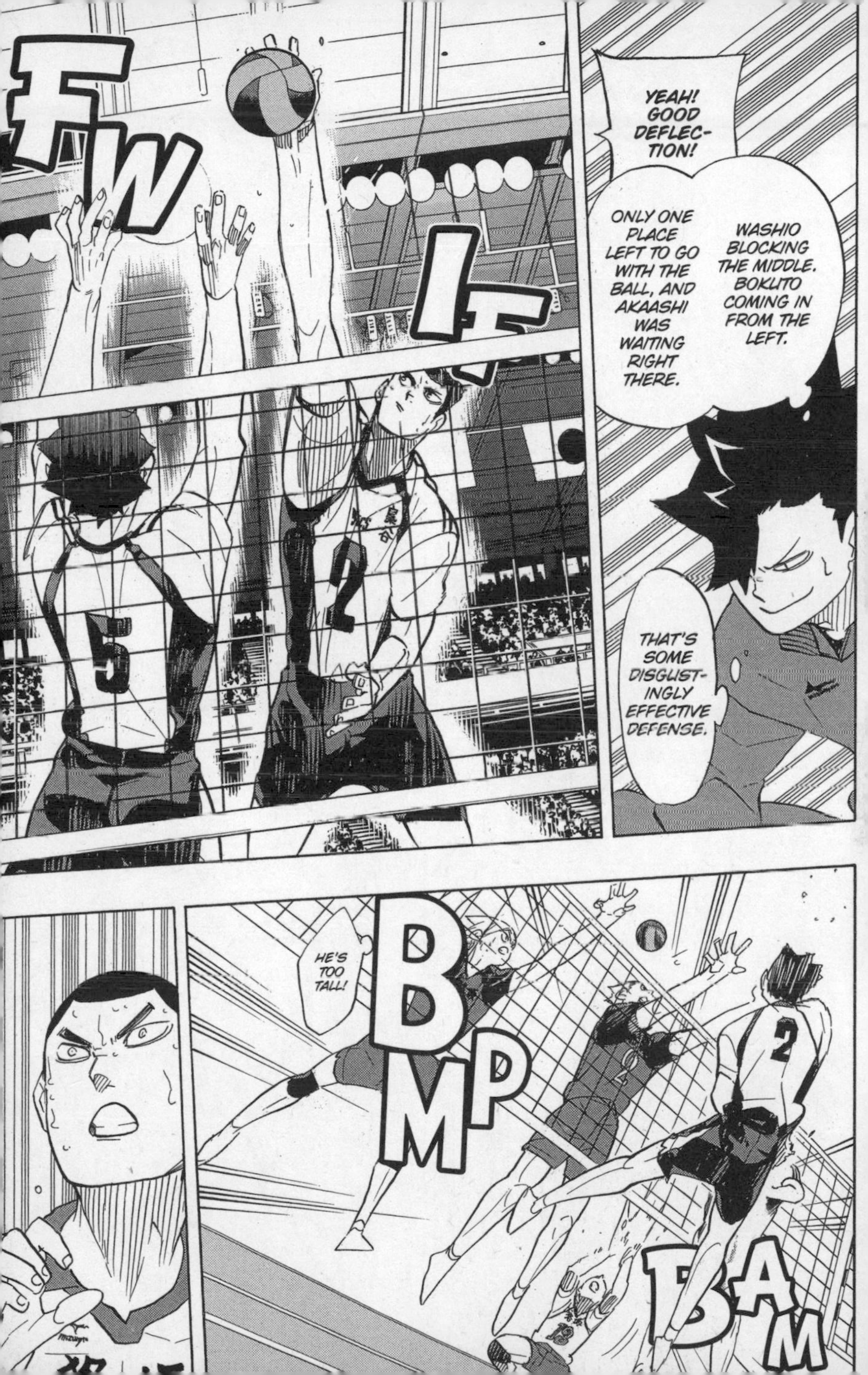
YEAH! GOOD DEFLEC-TION!
WASHIO BLOCKING THE MIDDLE. BOKUTO COMING IN FROM THE LEFT.
ONLY ONE PLACE LEFT TO GO WITH THE BALL, AND AKAASHI WAS WAITING RIGHT THERE.
THAT'S SOME DISGUST-INGLY EFFECTIVE DEFENSE.
FWIP
HE'S TOO TALL!
BMP
BAM

WHAM

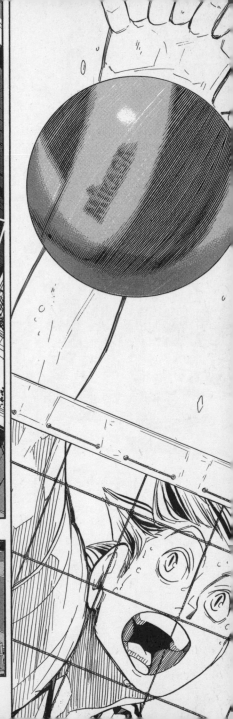

BOKUTO IS THERE TO SMASH IT BACK OVER ON ONE!

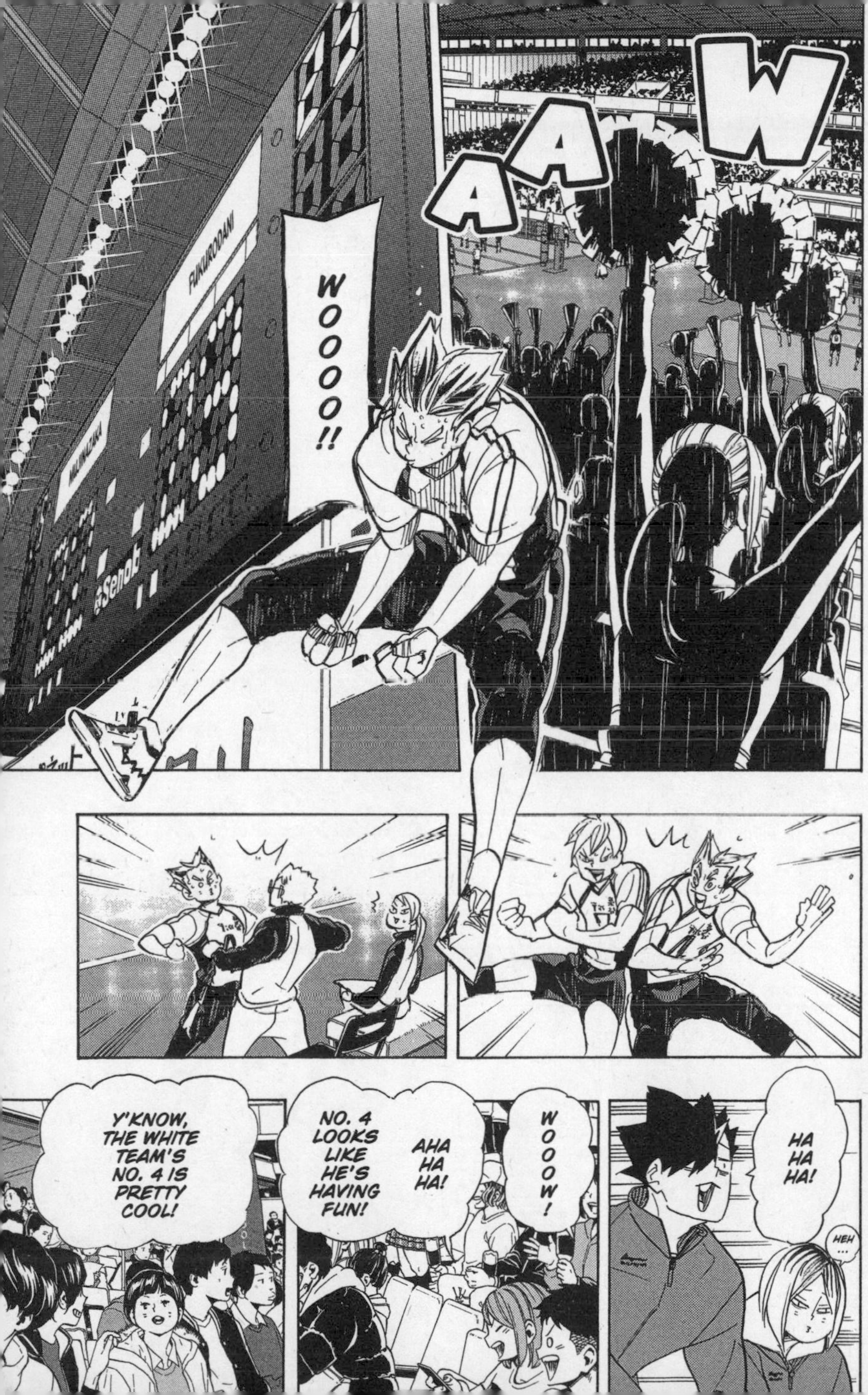
AAAW
WOOOOO!!
FUKURODANI
HA HA HA!
HEH...
WOOOOW!
AHA HA HA!
NO. 4 LOOKS LIKE HE'S HAVING FUN!
Y'KNOW, THE WHITE TEAM'S NO. 4 IS PRETTY COOL!

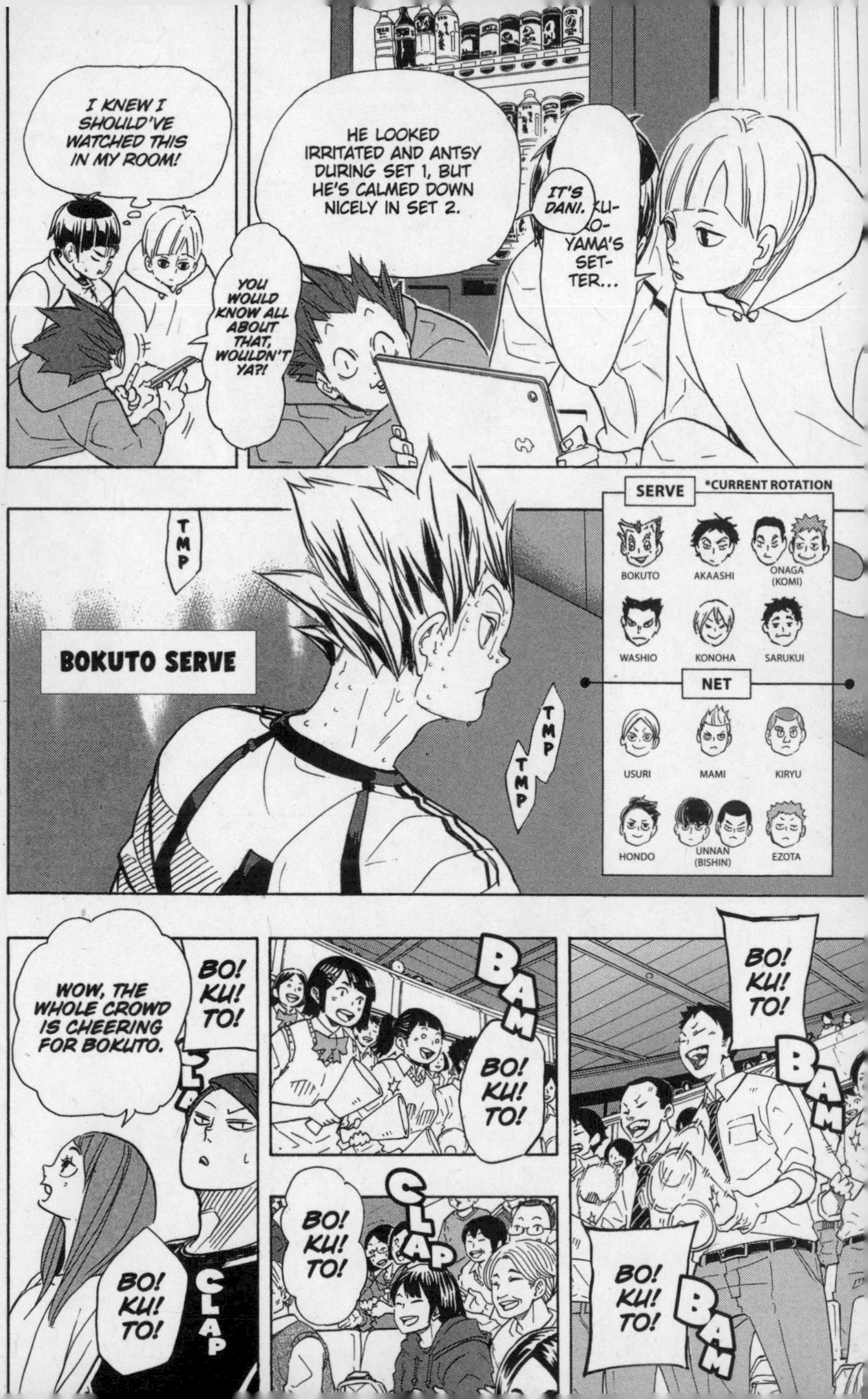
HE LOOKED IRRITATED AND ANTSY DURING SET 1, BUT HE'S CALMED DOWN NICELY IN SET 2.
IT'S DANI.
KU- O- YAMA'S SET- TER...
YOU WOULD KNOW ALL ABOUT THAT, WOULDN'T YA?!
I KNEW I SHOULD'VE WATCHED THIS IN MY ROOM!
SERVE
*CURRENT ROTATION
BOKUTO
AKAASHI
ONAGA (KOMI)
WASHIO
KONOHA
SARUKUI
NET
USURI
MAMI
KIRYU
HONDO
UNNAN (BISHIN)
EZOTA
TMP TMP
BOKUTO SERVE
TMP
BO! KU! TO!
BAM
BAM
BO! KU! TO!
BAM
BO! KU! TO!
BAM
CLAP CLAP
BO! KU! TO!
BO! KU! TO!
WOW, THE WHOLE CROWD IS CHEERING FOR BOKUTO.
CLAP
BO! KU! TO!
CLAP

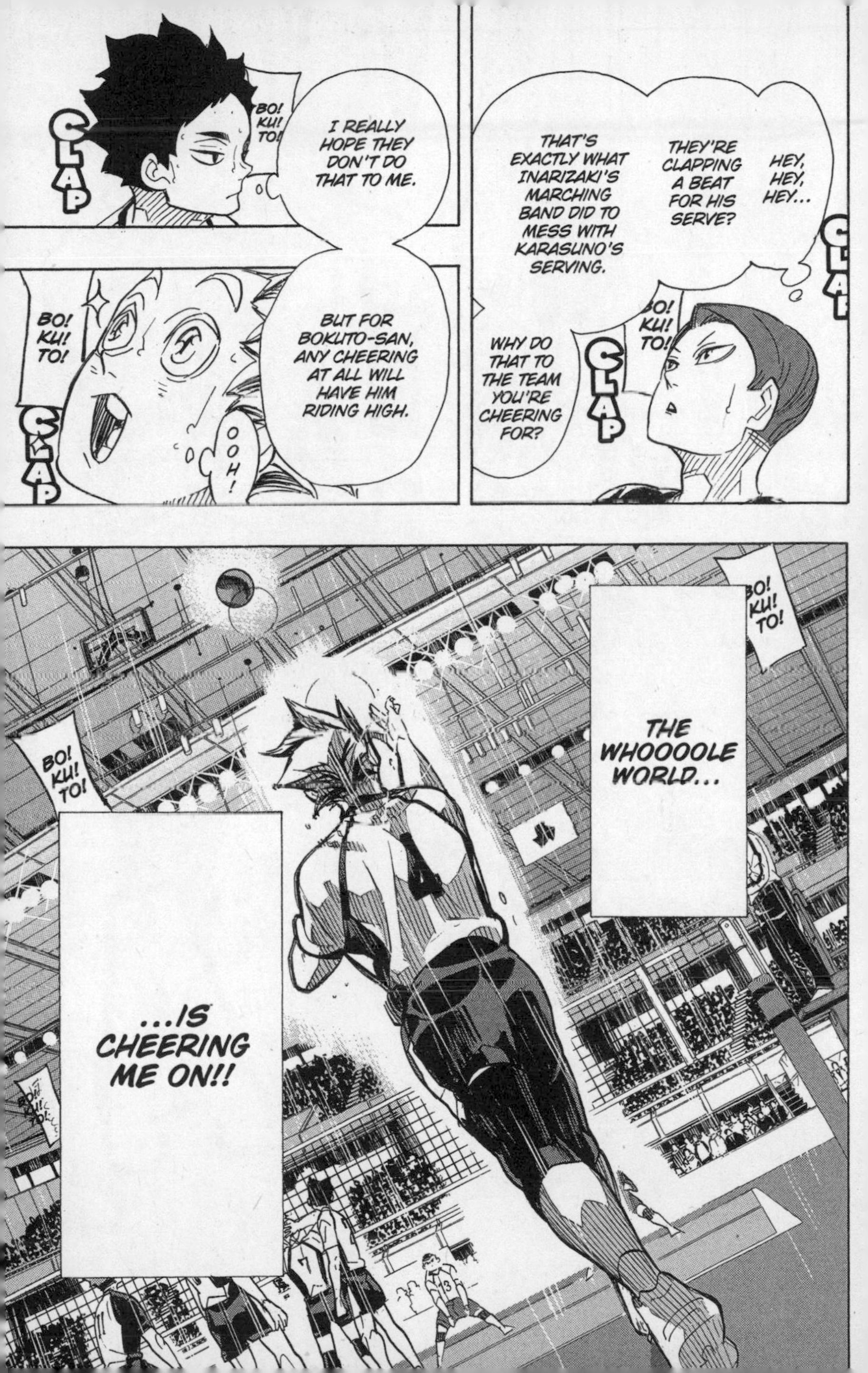
CLAP
HEY, HEY, HEY...
THEY'RE CLAPPING A BEAT FOR HIS SERVE?
THAT'S EXACTLY WHAT INARIZAKI'S MARCHING BAND DID TO MESS WITH KARASUNO'S SERVING.
BO! KU! TO!
CLAP
WHY DO THAT TO THE TEAM YOU'RE CHEERING FOR?
BO! KU! TO!
CLAP
I REALLY HOPE THEY DON'T DO THAT TO ME.
BUT FOR BOKUTO-SAN, ANY CHEERING AT ALL WILL HAVE HIM RIDING HIGH.
OOH!
BO! KU! TO!
CLAP
BO! KU! TO!
THE WHOOOOLE WORLD...
BO! KU! TO!
...IS CHEERING ME ON!!
BO! KU! TO!

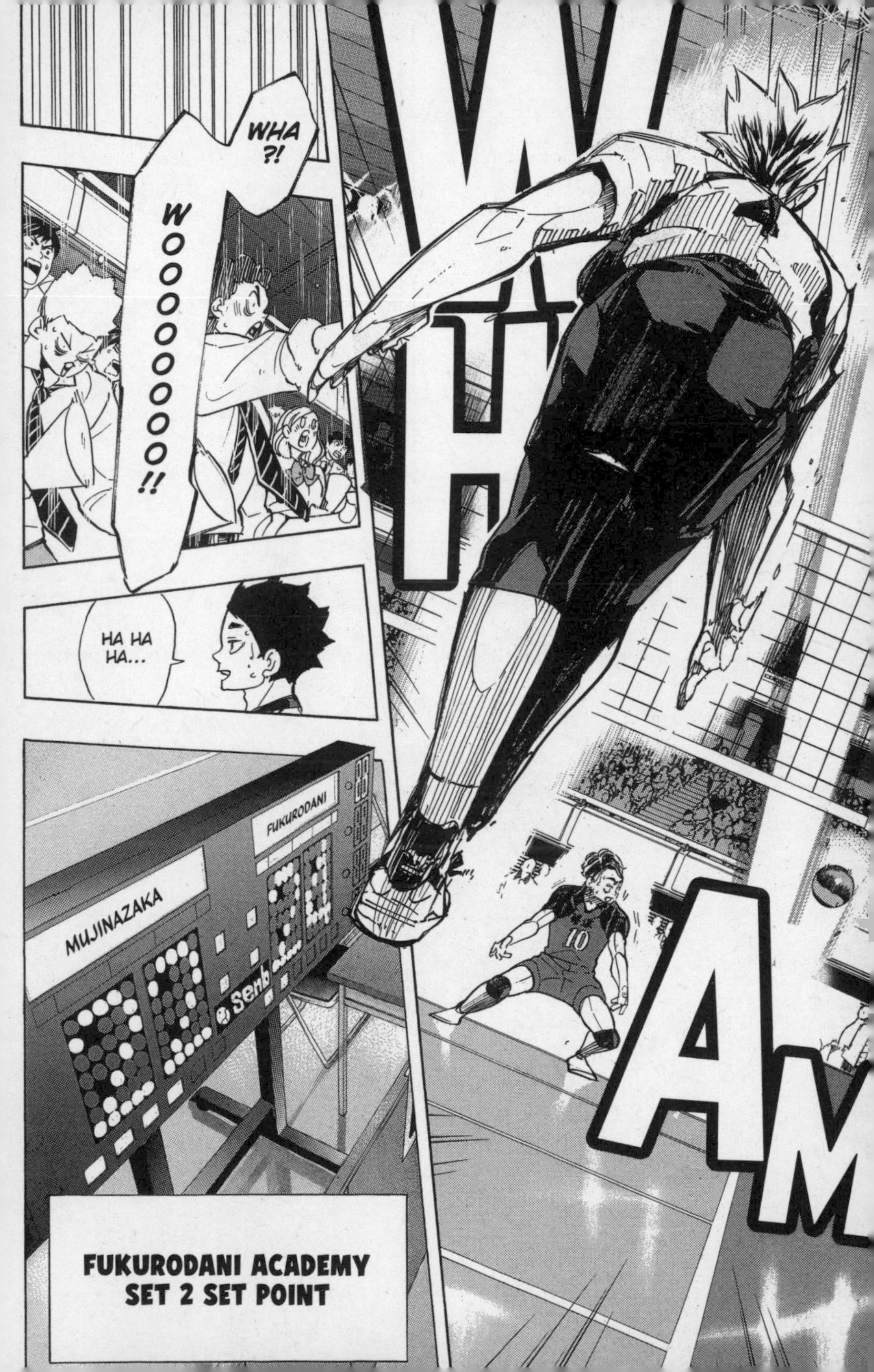
WHAM
WHA?!
WOOOOOOOOOO!!
HA HA HA...
FUKURODANI
MUJINAZAKA
FUKURODANI ACADEMY SET 2 SET POINT

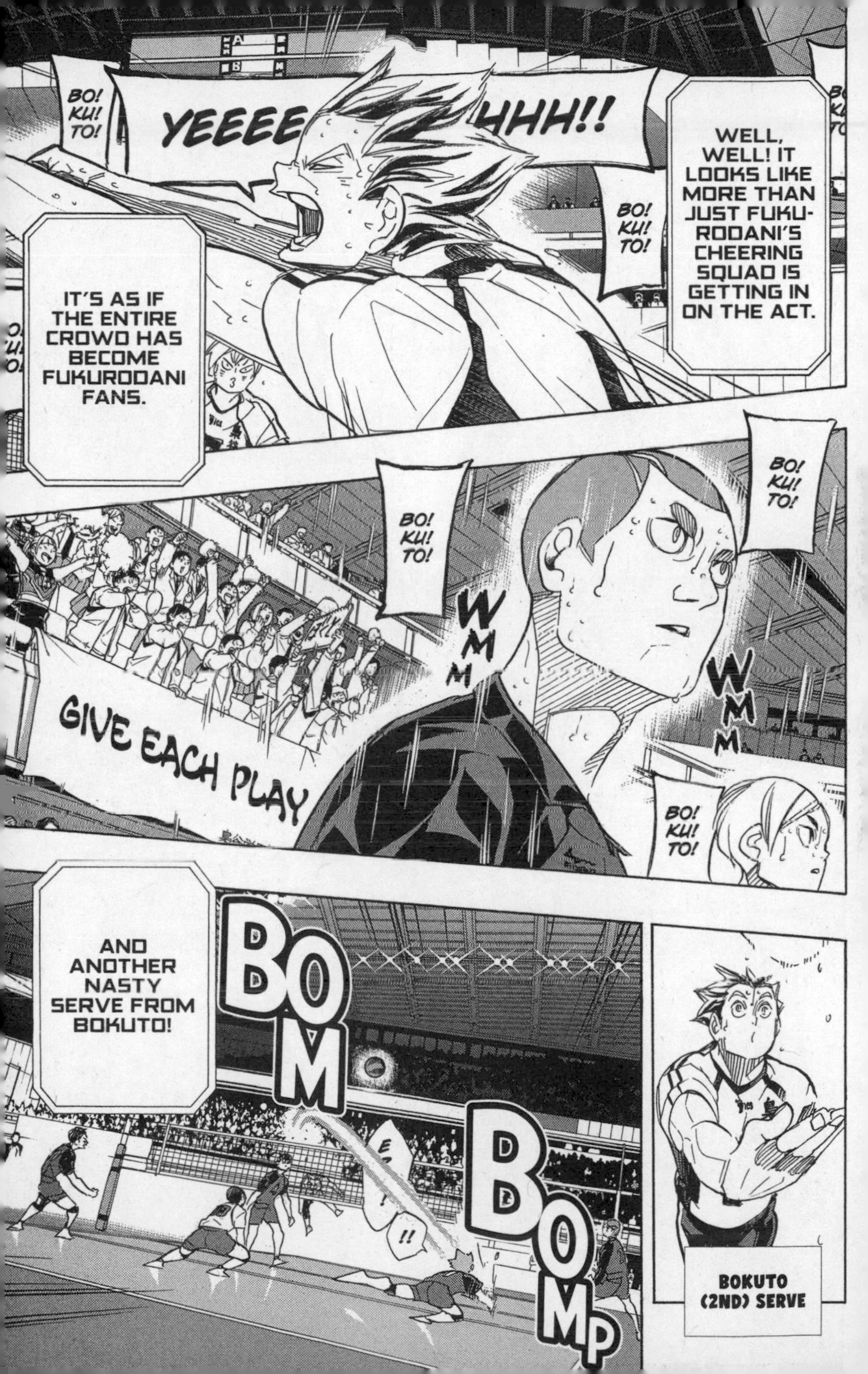
WELL, WELL! IT LOOKS LIKE MORE THAN JUST FUKURODANI'S CHEERING SQUAD IS GETTING IN ON THE ACT.
BO! KU! TO!
YEEEE
HHH!!
BO! KU! TO!
IT'S AS IF THE ENTIRE CROWD HAS BECOME FUKURODANI FANS.
BO! KU! TO!
BO! KU! TO!
WMM
WMM
BO! KU! TO!
GIVE EACH PLAY
BOKUTO (2ND) SERVE
AND ANOTHER NASTY SERVE FROM BOKUTO!
BOM
BOMP
!!

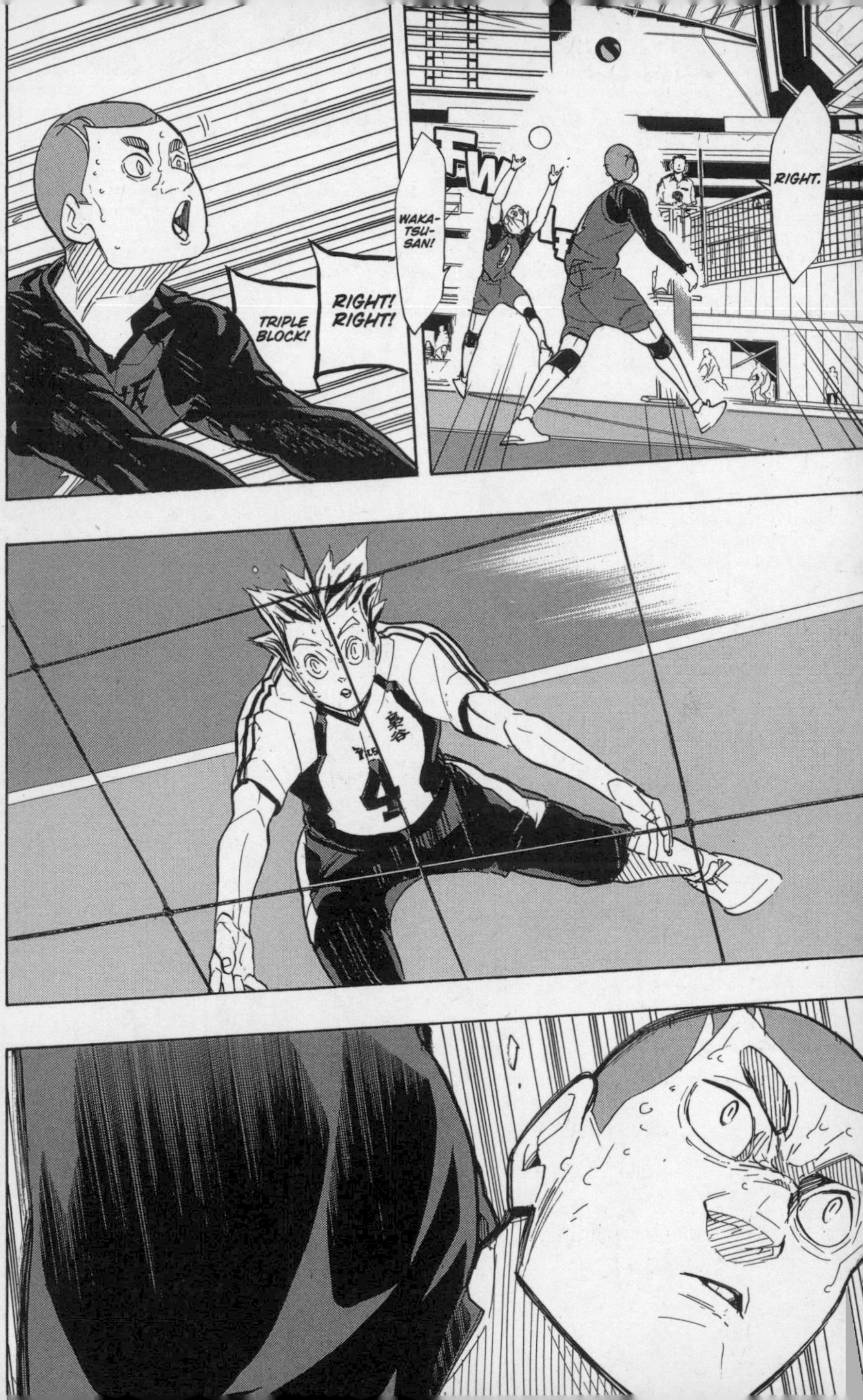
RIGHT.
WAKA-TSU-SAN!
RIGHT! RIGHT!
TRIPLE BLOCK!

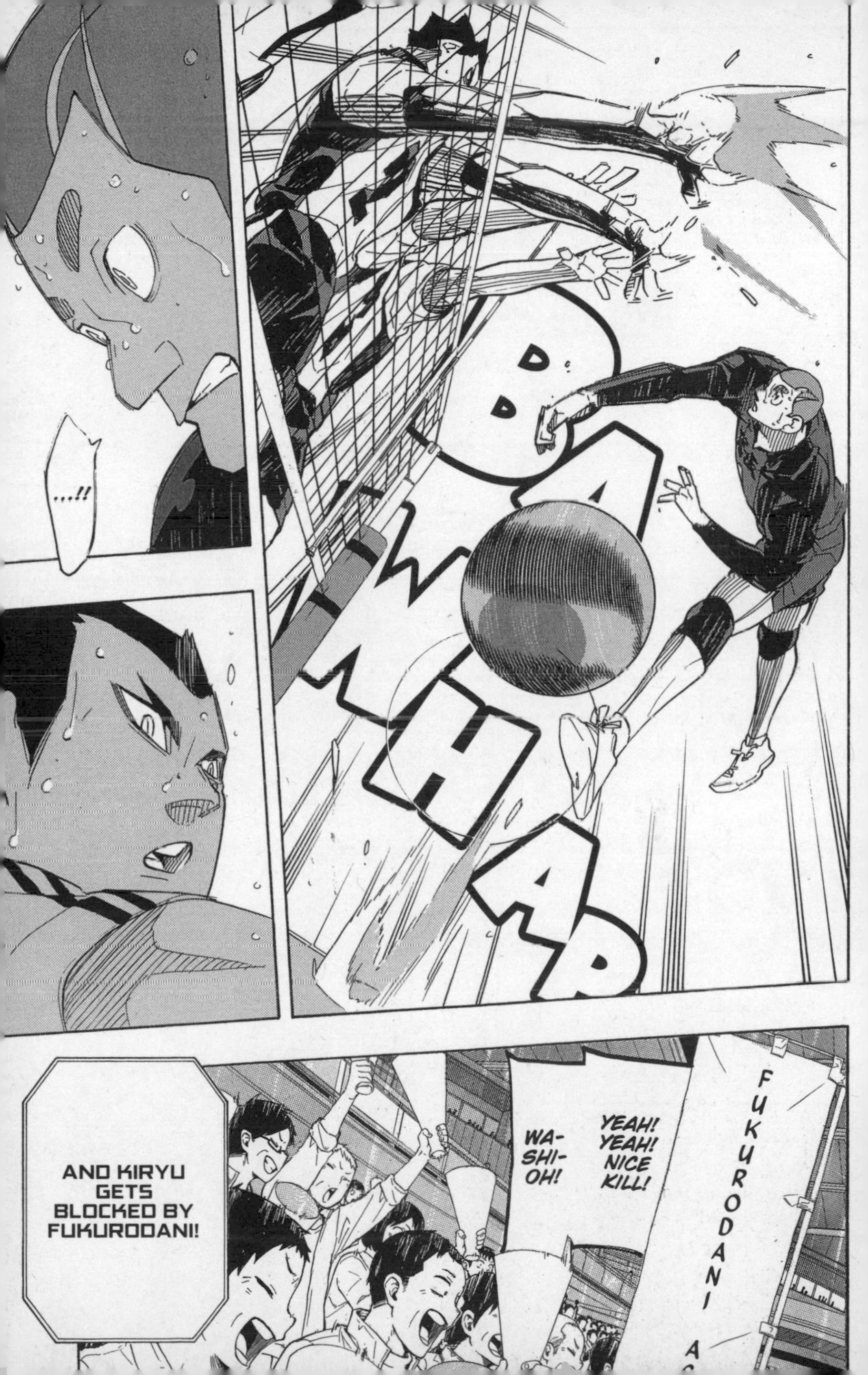
WHAP
...!!
FUKURODANI
YEAH! YEAH! NICE KILL!
WA-SHI-OH!
AND KIRYU GETS BLOCKED BY FUKURODANI!

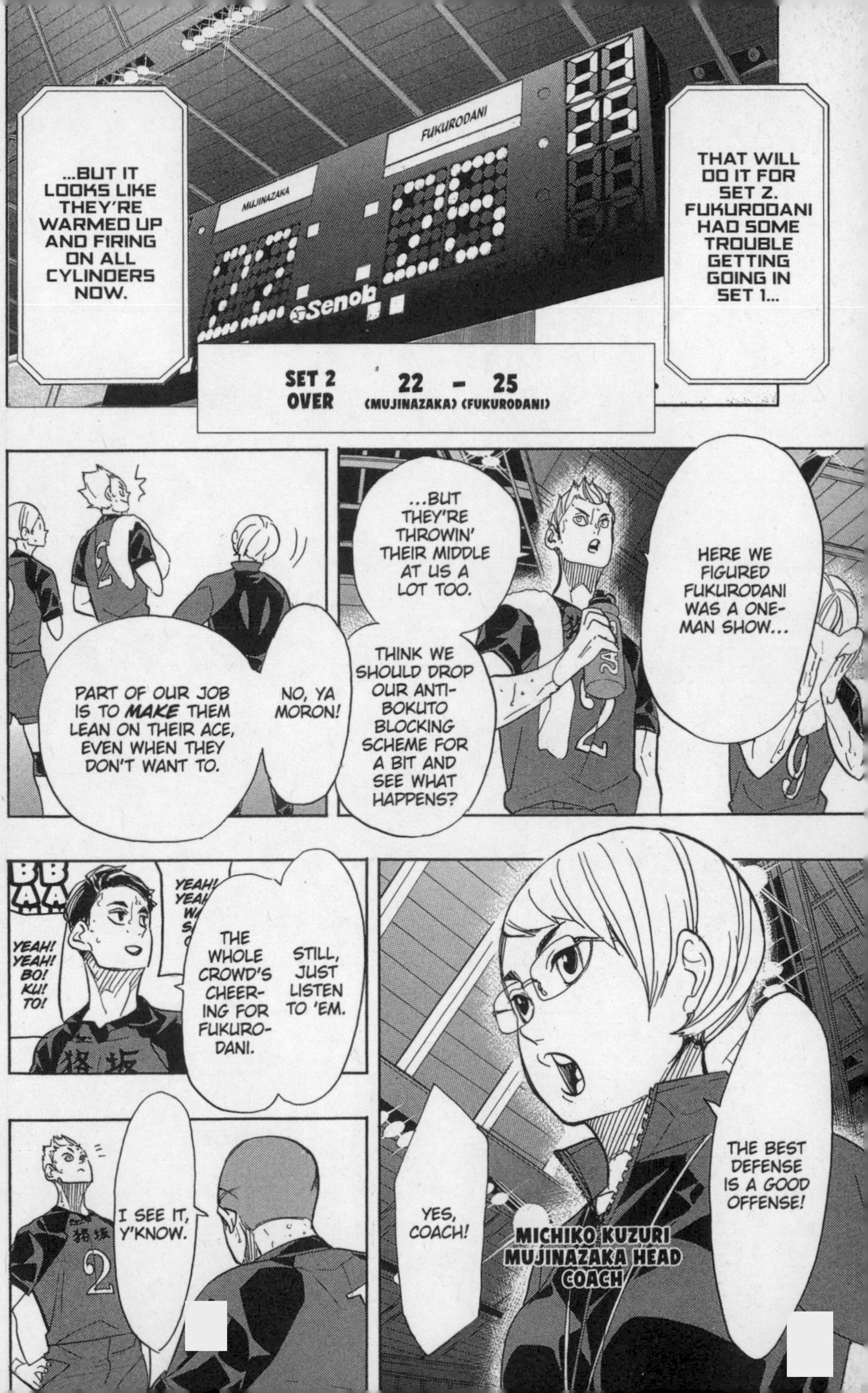
THAT WILL DO IT FOR SET 2. FUKURODANI HAD SOME TROUBLE GETTING GOING IN SET 1...
FUKURODANI
MUJINAZAKA
...BUT IT LOOKS LIKE THEY'RE WARMED UP AND FIRING ON ALL CYLINDERS NOW.
SET 2 OVER 22 - 25 (MUJINAZAKA) (FUKURODANI)
HERE WE FIGURED FUKURODANI WAS A ONE-MAN SHOW...
...BUT THEY'RE THROWIN' THEIR MIDDLE AT US A LOT TOO.
THINK WE SHOULD DROP OUR ANTI-BOKUTO BLOCKING SCHEME FOR A BIT AND SEE WHAT HAPPENS?
NO, YA MORON!
PART OF OUR JOB IS TO MAKE THEM LEAN ON THEIR ACE, EVEN WHEN THEY DON'T WANT TO.
THE BEST DEFENSE IS A GOOD OFFENSE!
YES, COACH!
MICHIKO KUZURI MUJINAZAKA HEAD COACH
STILL, JUST LISTEN TO 'EM.
THE WHOLE CROWD'S CHEERING FOR FUKURODANI.
YEAH! YEAH! BO! KU! TO!
I SEE IT, Y'KNOW.

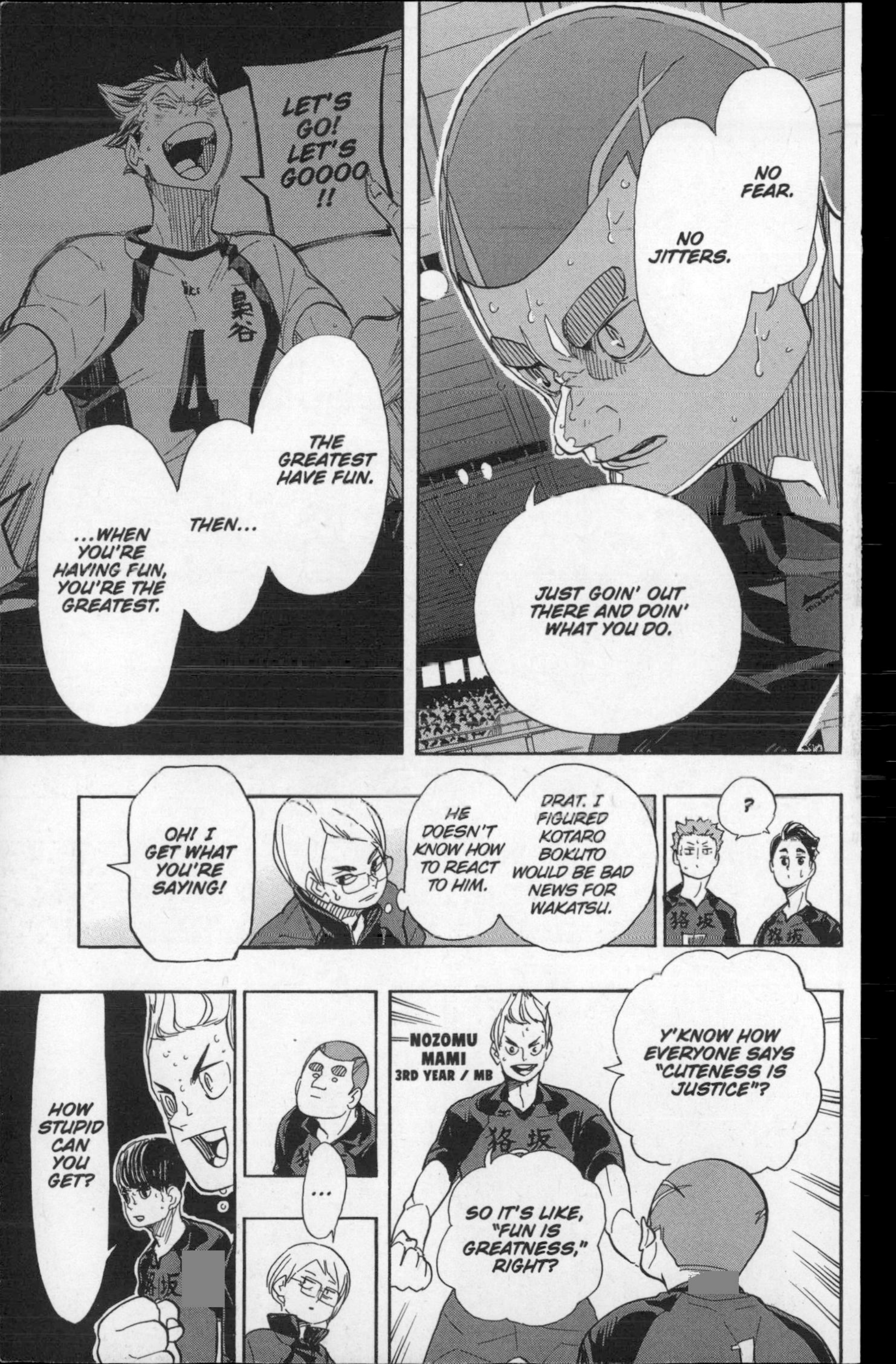
NO FEAR.
NO JITTERS.
JUST GOIN' OUT THERE AND DOIN' WHAT YOU DO.
LET'S GO! LET'S GOOOO !!
THE GREATEST HAVE FUN.
THEN...
...WHEN YOU'RE HAVING FUN, YOU'RE THE GREATEST.
?
DRAT. I FIGURED KOTARO BOKUTO WOULD BE BAD NEWS FOR WAKATSU.
HE DOESN'T KNOW HOW TO REACT TO HIM.
OH! I GET WHAT YOU'RE SAYING!
Y'KNOW HOW EVERYONE SAYS "CUTENESS IS JUSTICE"?
NOZOMU MAMI 3RD YEAR / MB
SO IT'S LIKE, "FUN IS GREATNESS," RIGHT?
...
HOW STUPID CAN YOU GET?

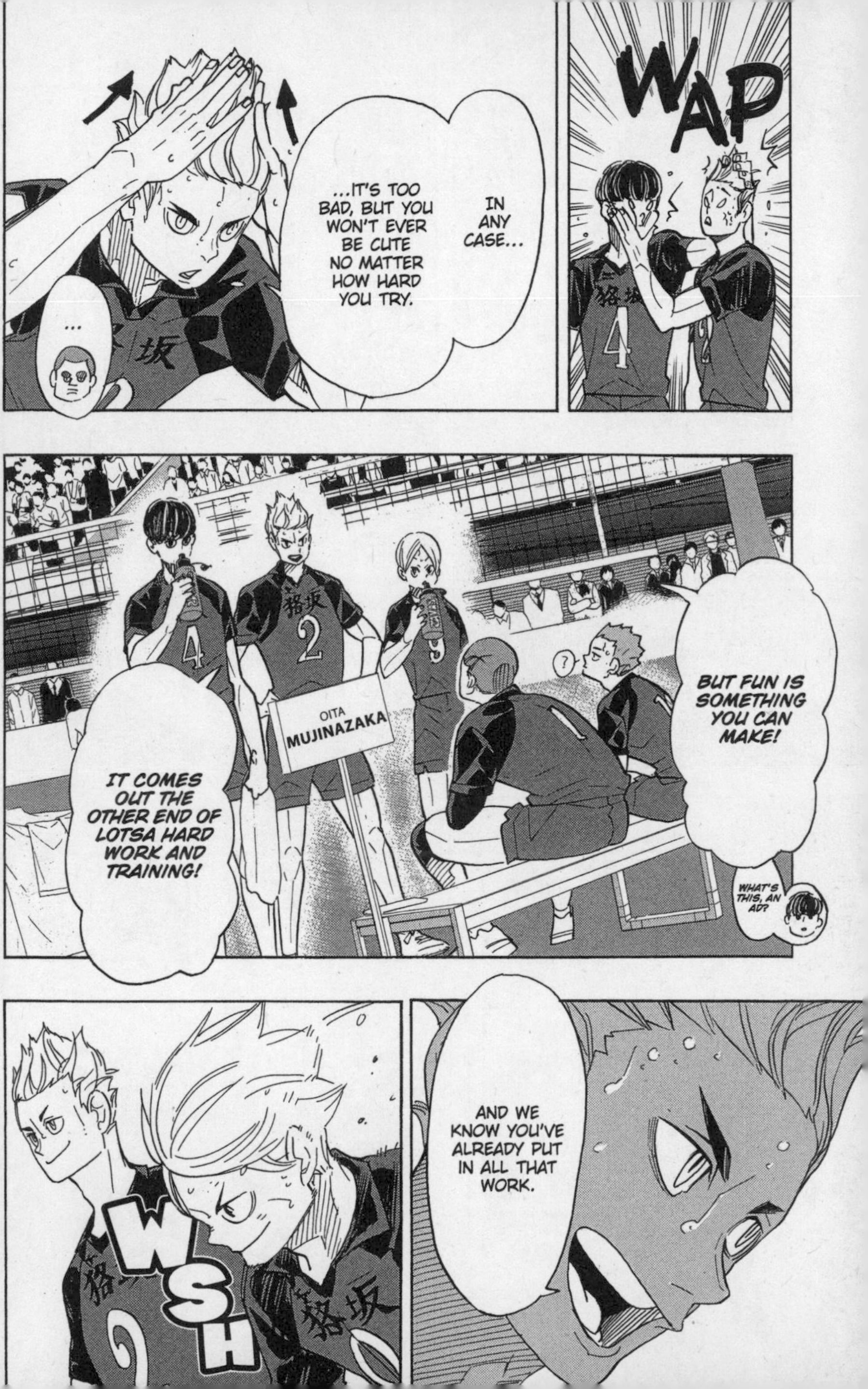
WAP
IN ANY CASE...
...IT'S TOO BAD, BUT YOU WON'T EVER BE CUTE NO MATTER HOW HARD YOU TRY.
...
BUT FUN IS SOMETHING YOU CAN MAKE!
?
OITA MUJINAZAKA
IT COMES OUT THE OTHER END OF LOTSA HARD WORK AND TRAINING!
WHAT'S THIS, AN AD?
AND WE KNOW YOU'VE ALREADY PUT IN ALL THAT WORK.
WSH

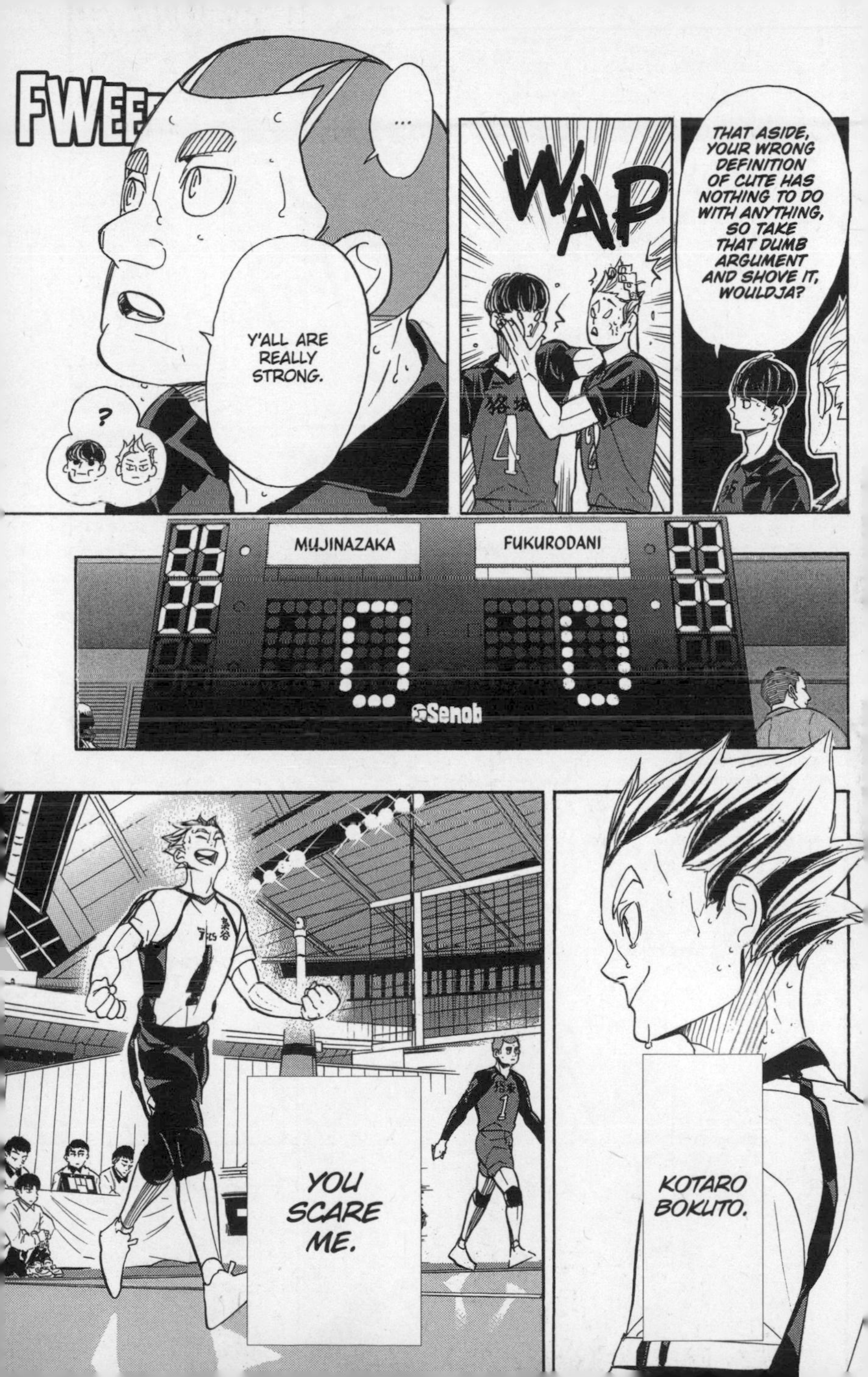
THAT ASIDE, YOUR WRONG DEFINITION OF CUTE HAS NOTHING TO DO WITH ANYTHING, SO TAKE THAT DUMB ARGUMENT AND SHOVE IT, WOULDJA?
WAP
FWEEE
...
Y'ALL ARE REALLY STRONG.
?
MUJINAZAKA
FUKURODANI
Senob
KOTARO BOKUTO.
YOU SCARE ME.

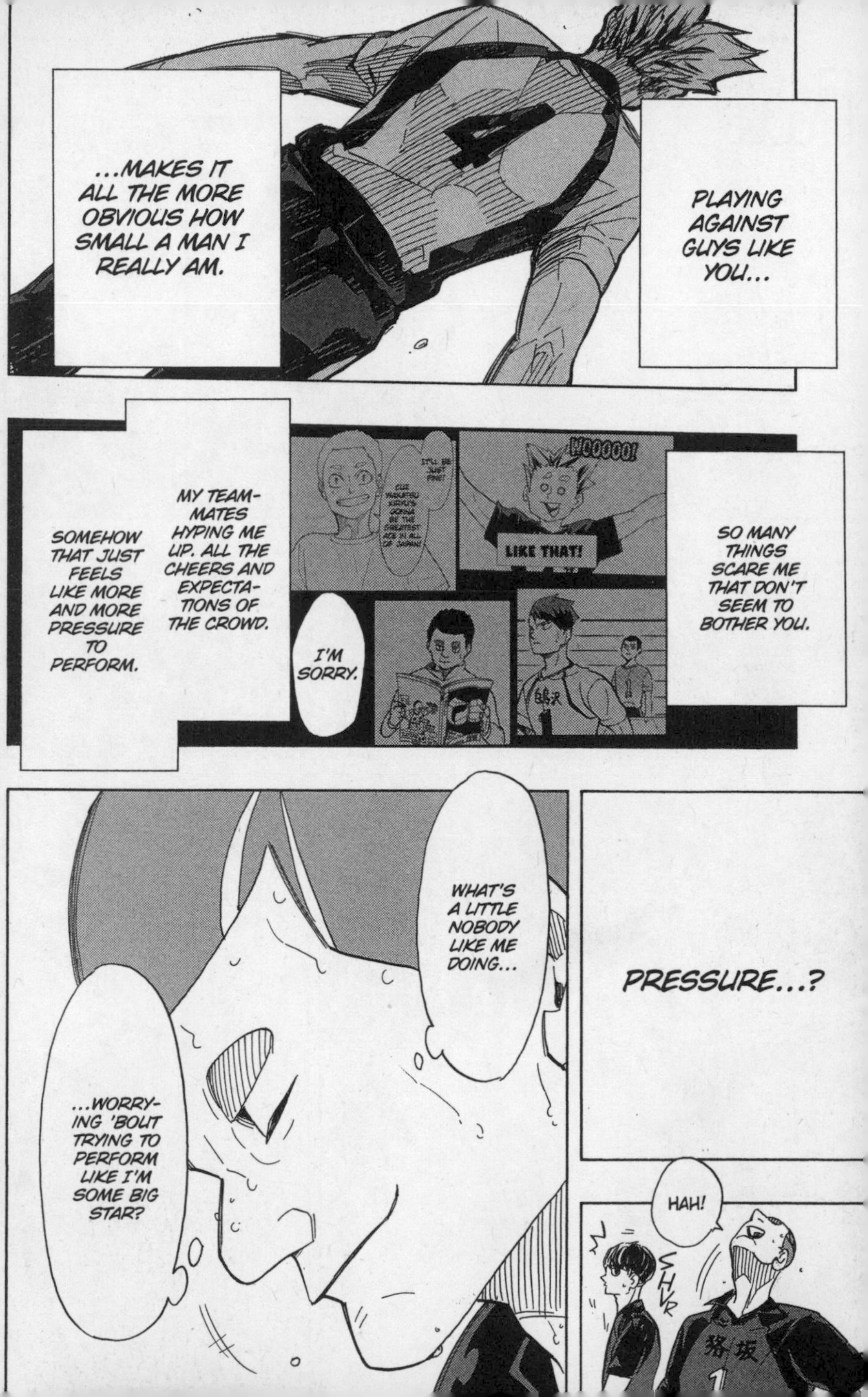
PLAYING AGAINST GUYS LIKE YOU...
...MAKES IT ALL THE MORE OBVIOUS HOW SMALL A MAN I REALLY AM.
SO MANY THINGS SCARE ME THAT DON'T SEEM TO BOTHER YOU.
WOOOOO!
LIKE THAT!
I'M SORRY.
MY TEAM-MATES HYPING ME UP. ALL THE CHEERS AND EXPECTA-TIONS OF THE CROWD.
SOMEHOW THAT JUST FEELS LIKE MORE AND MORE PRESSURE TO PERFORM.
PRESSURE...?
HAH!
SHVR
WHAT'S A LITTLE NOBODY LIKE ME DOING...
...WORRY-ING 'BOUT TRYING TO PERFORM LIKE I'M SOME BIG STAR?

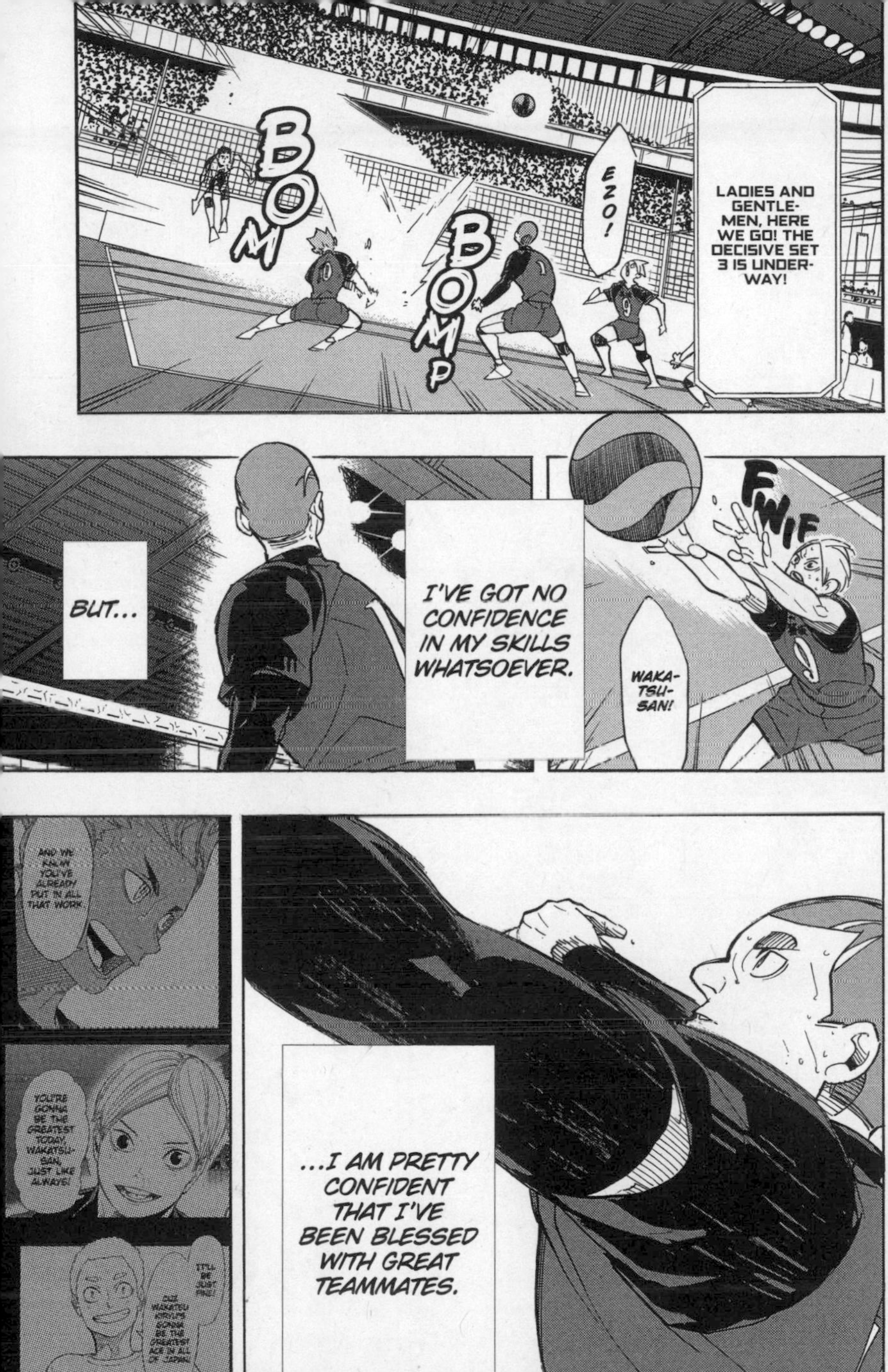
LADIES AND GENTLE-MEN, HERE WE GO! THE DECISIVE SET 3 IS UNDER-WAY!
EZO!
BOMP
BOM
FWIF
WAKA-TSU-SAN!
I'VE GOT NO CONFIDENCE IN MY SKILLS WHATSOEVER.
BUT...
...I AM PRETTY CONFIDENT THAT I'VE BEEN BLESSED WITH GREAT TEAMMATES.
AND WE KNOW YOU'VE ALREADY PUT IN ALL THAT WORK.
YOU'RE GONNA BE THE GREATEST TODAY, WAKATSU-SAN, JUST LIKE ALWAYS!
IT'LL BE JUST FINE!
OUR WAKATSU KIRYU'S GONNA BE THE GREATEST ACE IN ALL OF JAPAN.

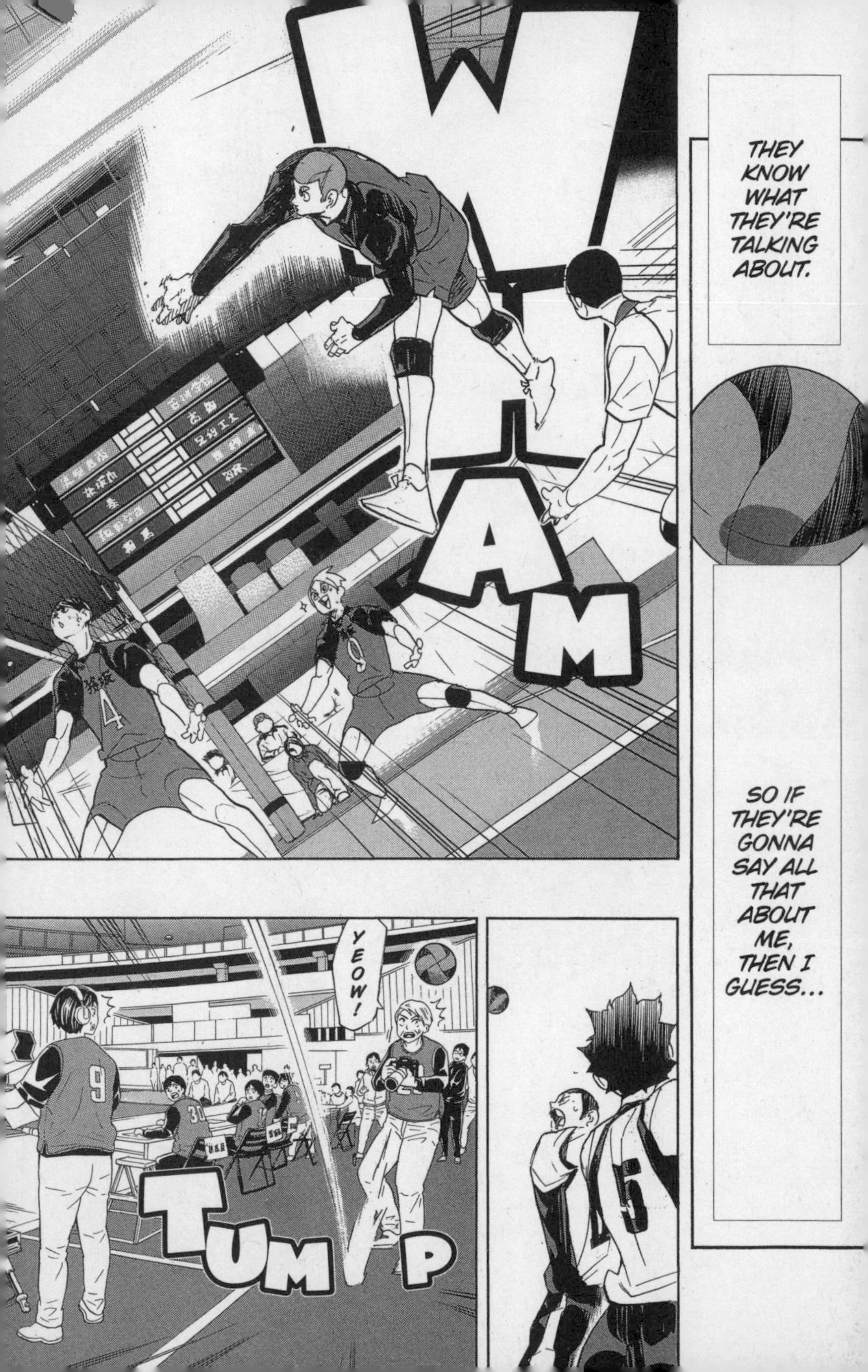
THEY KNOW WHAT THEY'RE TALKING ABOUT.
WHAM
SO IF THEY'RE GONNA SAY ALL THAT ABOUT ME, THEN I GUESS...
YEOW!
TUM P

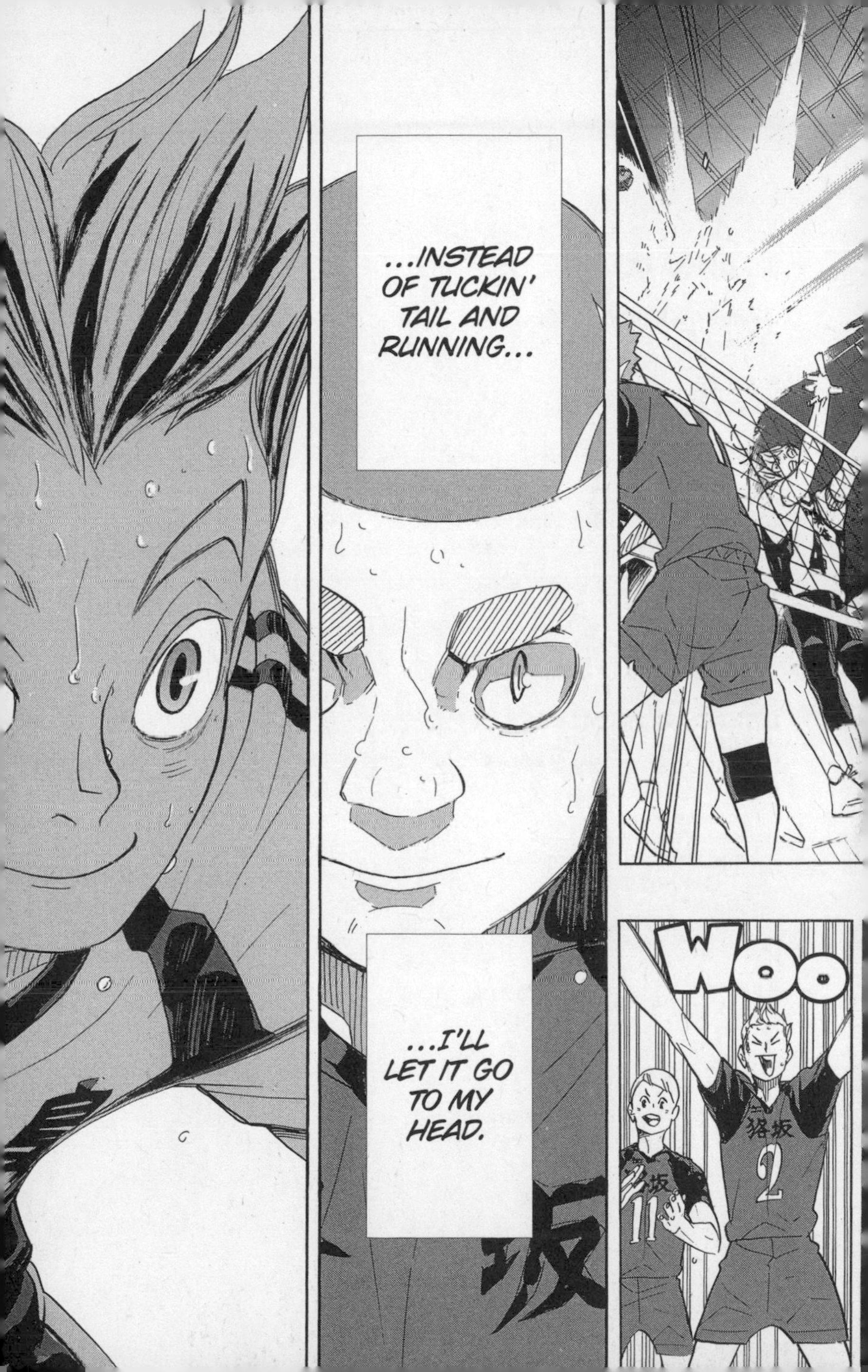
WOO
...INSTEAD OF TUCKIN' TAIL AND RUNNING...
...I'LL LET IT GO TO MY HEAD.

NOZOMU MAMI

MUJINAZAKA HIGH SCHOOL,
CLASS 3-6

POSITION:
MIDDLE BLOCKER

HEIGHT: 6'3"

WEIGHT: 186 LBS.
(AS OF JANUARY, 3RD YEAR OF HIGH SCHOOL)

BIRTHDAY: AUGUST 1

FAVORITE FOOD:
SEA BREAM *CHAZUKE*

CURRENT WORRY:
IS THERE ANY POSSIBLE WAY HE COULD MEET SATOMI ISHIHARA AND MAYBE MARRY HER?

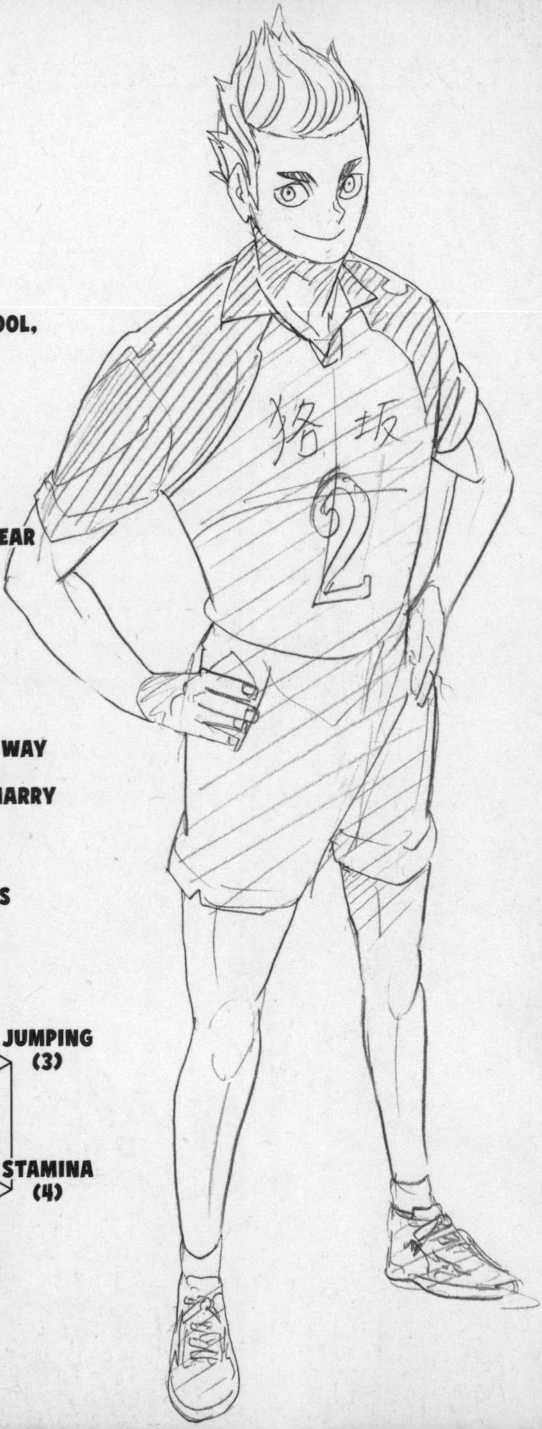

狢坂
2

ABILITY PARAMETERS
(5-POINT SCALE)

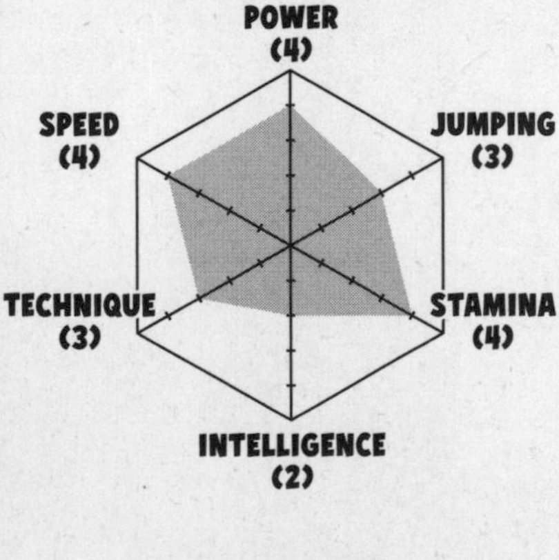

POWER (4)
JUMPING (3)
STAMINA (4)
INTELLIGENCE (2)
TECHNIQUE (3)
SPEED (4)

CHAPTER 335: Completely Absorbed

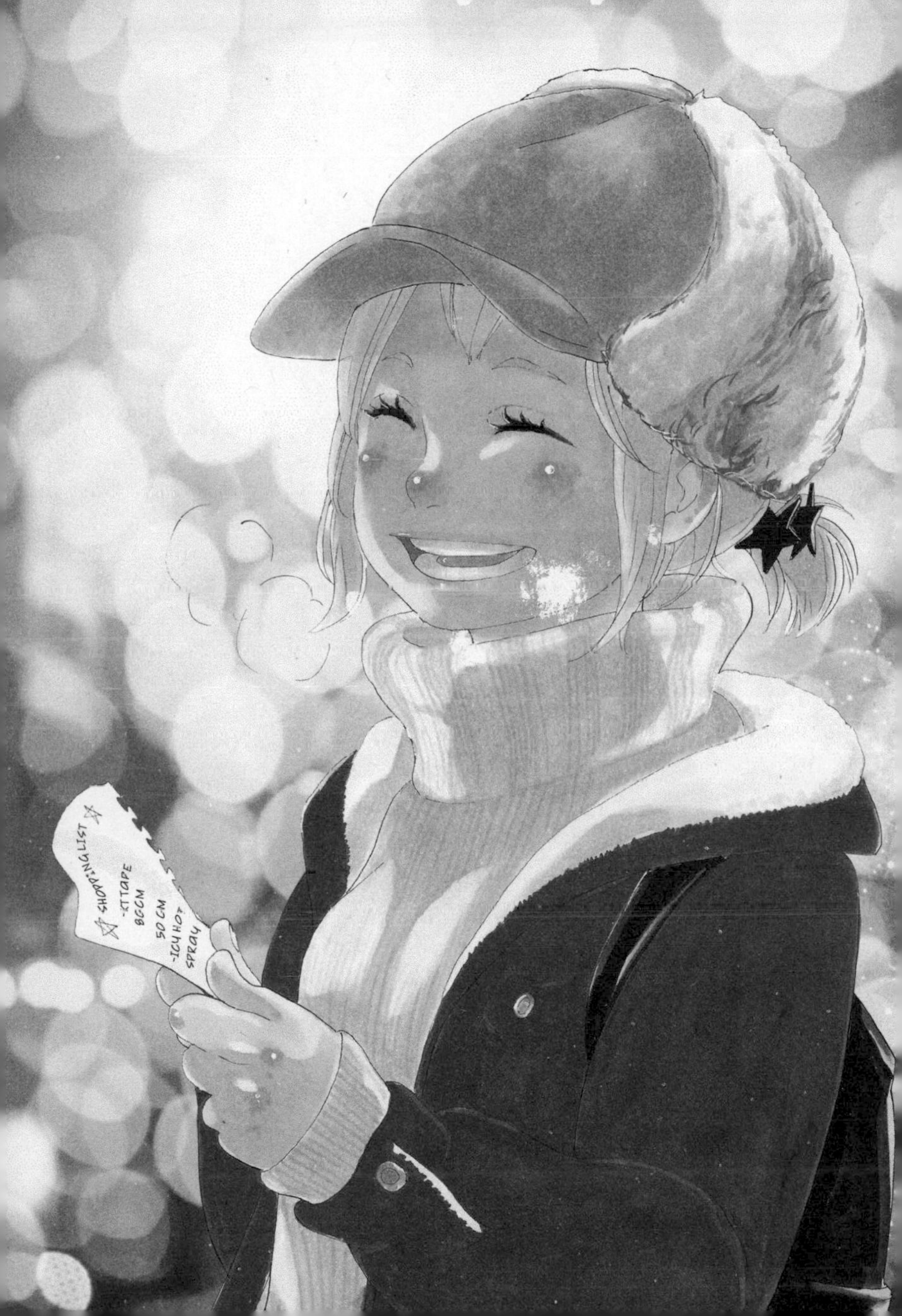
☆SHOPPING LIST☆
-KT TAPE
8CM
50 CM
-ICY HOT SPRAY

HAIKYU!!

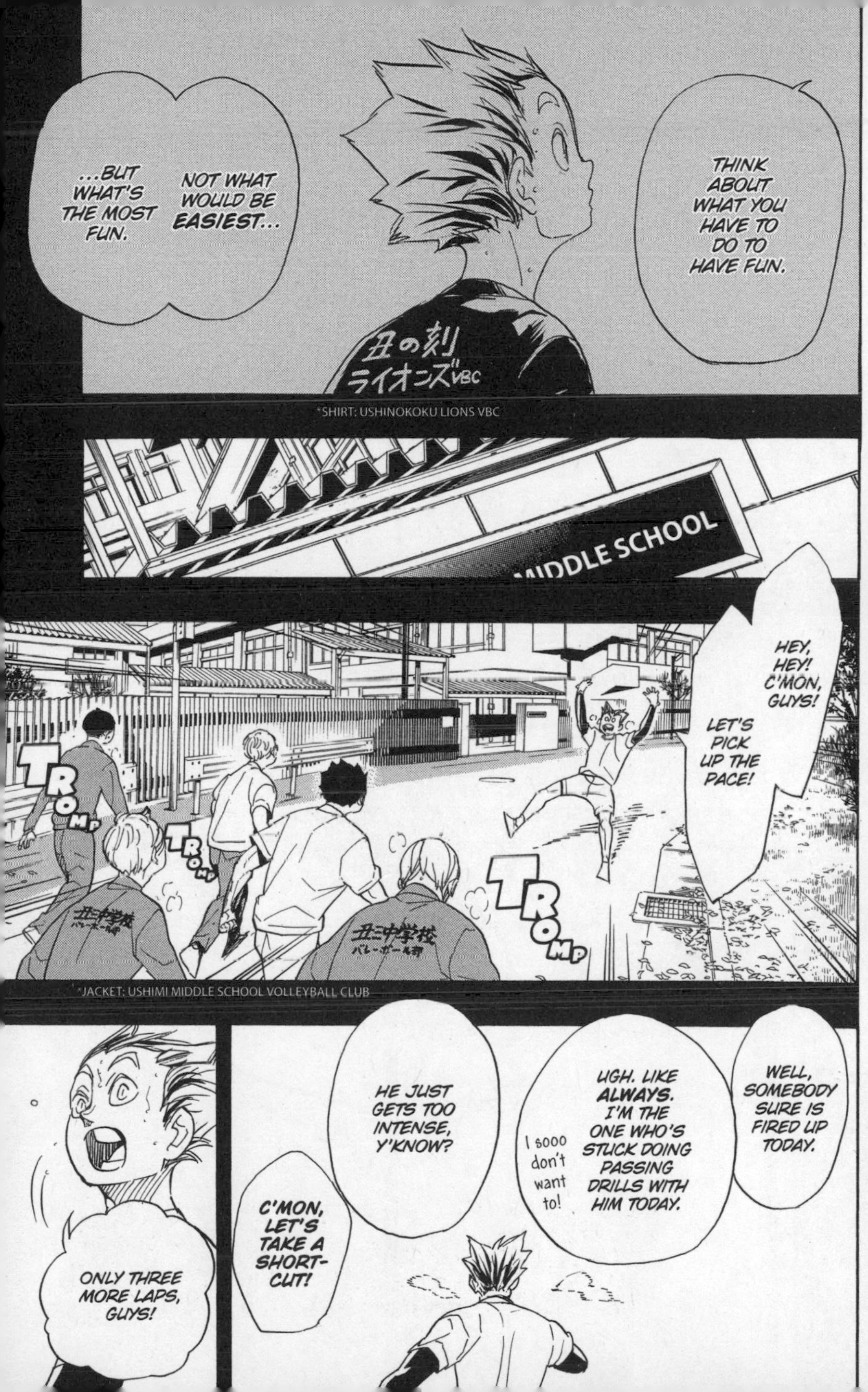
THINK ABOUT WHAT YOU HAVE TO DO TO HAVE FUN.
NOT WHAT WOULD BE EASIEST...
...BUT WHAT'S THE MOST FUN.
丑の刻ライオンズVBC
*SHIRT: USHINOKOKU LIONS VBC
MIDDLE SCHOOL
HEY, HEY! C'MON, GUYS!
LET'S PICK UP THE PACE!
TROMP
TROMP
TROMP
丑三中学校 バレーボール部
*JACKET: USHIMI MIDDLE SCHOOL VOLLEYBALL CLUB
WELL, SOMEBODY SURE IS FIRED UP TODAY.
UGH. LIKE ALWAYS. I'M THE ONE WHO'S STUCK DOING PASSING DRILLS WITH HIM TODAY.
I sooo don't want to!
HE JUST GETS TOO INTENSE, Y'KNOW?
C'MON, LET'S TAKE A SHORT-CUT!
ONLY THREE MORE LAPS, GUYS!

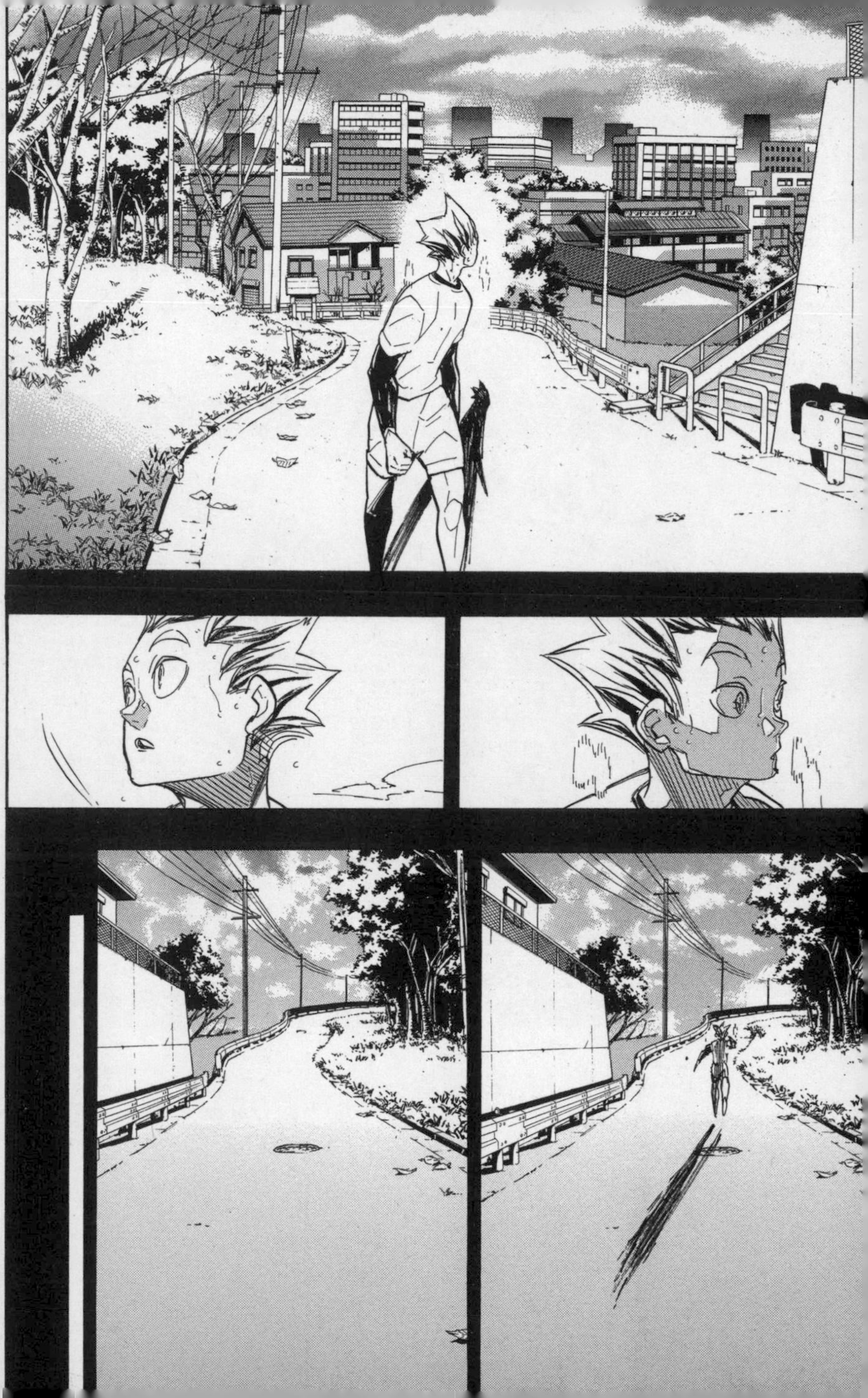

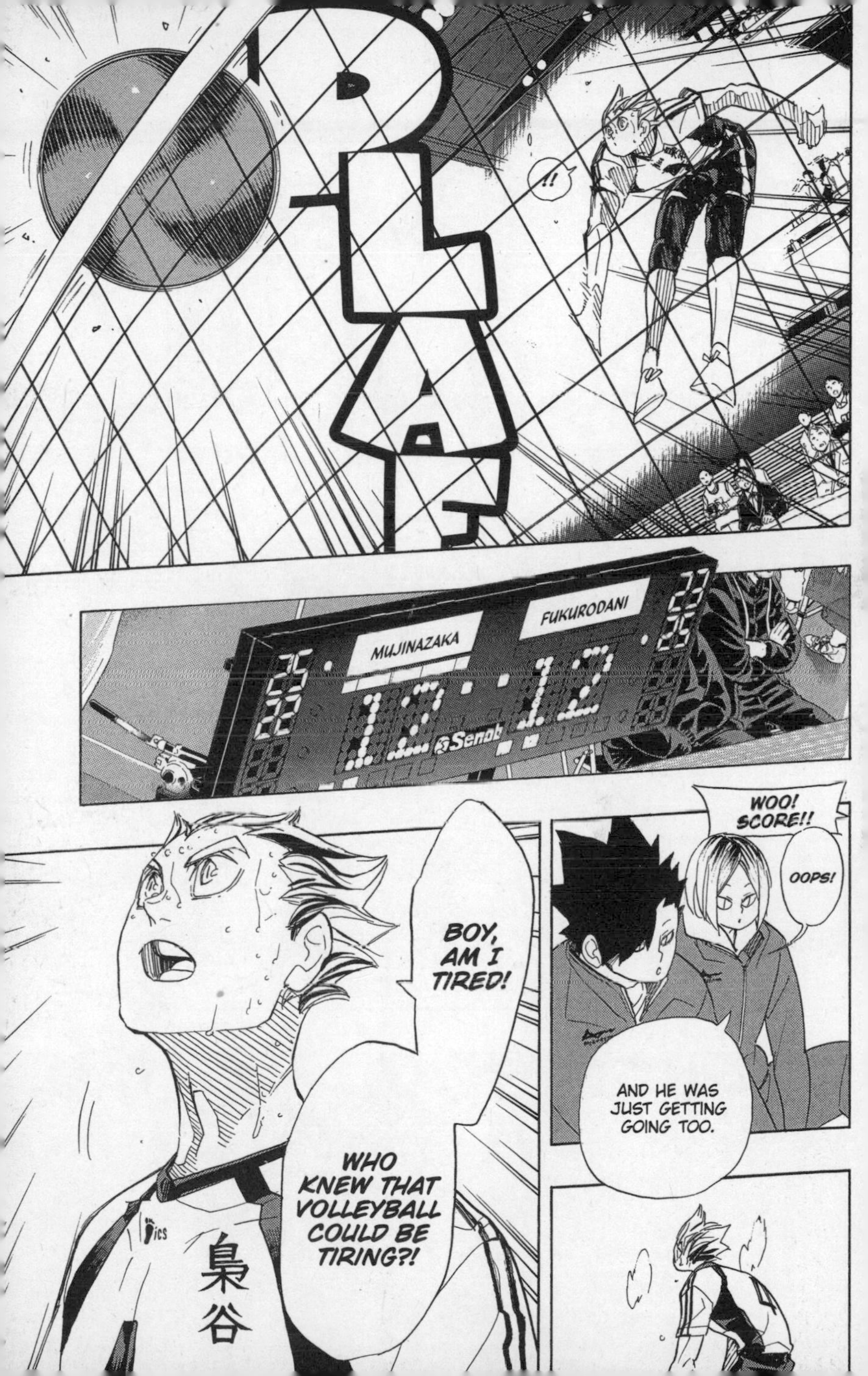
!!
MUJINAZAKA
FUKURODANI
WOO! SCORE!!
OOPS!
AND HE WAS JUST GETTING GOING TOO.
BOY, AM I TIRED!
WHO KNEW THAT VOLLEYBALL COULD BE TIRING?!
梟谷

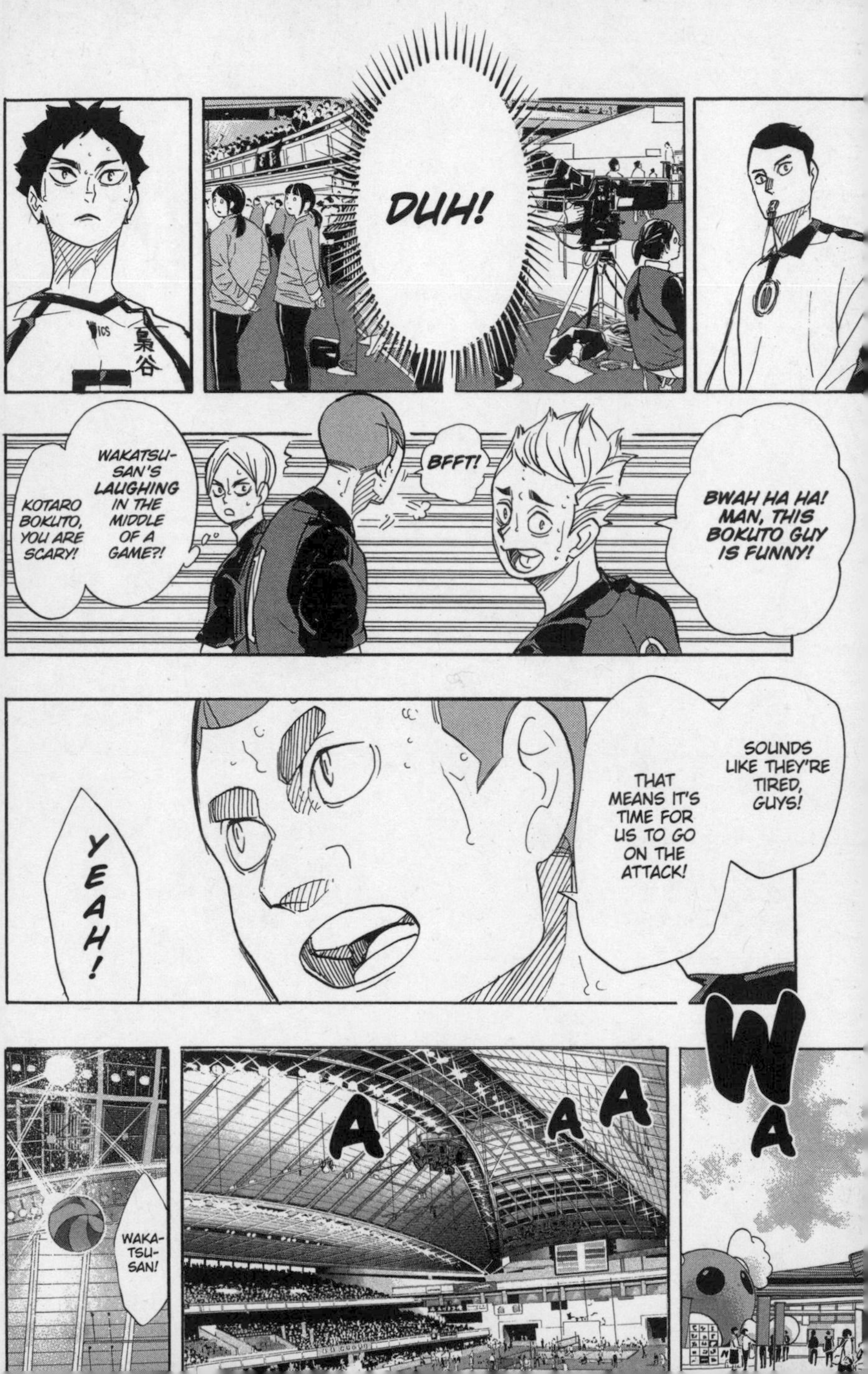
DUH!
BWAH HA HA! MAN, THIS BOKUTO GUY IS FUNNY!
BFFT!
WAKATSU-SAN'S LAUGHING IN THE MIDDLE OF A GAME?!
KOTARO BOKUTO, YOU ARE SCARY!
SOUNDS LIKE THEY'RE TIRED, GUYS!
THAT MEANS IT'S TIME FOR US TO GO ON THE ATTACK!
YEAH!
WA
AAA
WAKA-TSU-SAN!

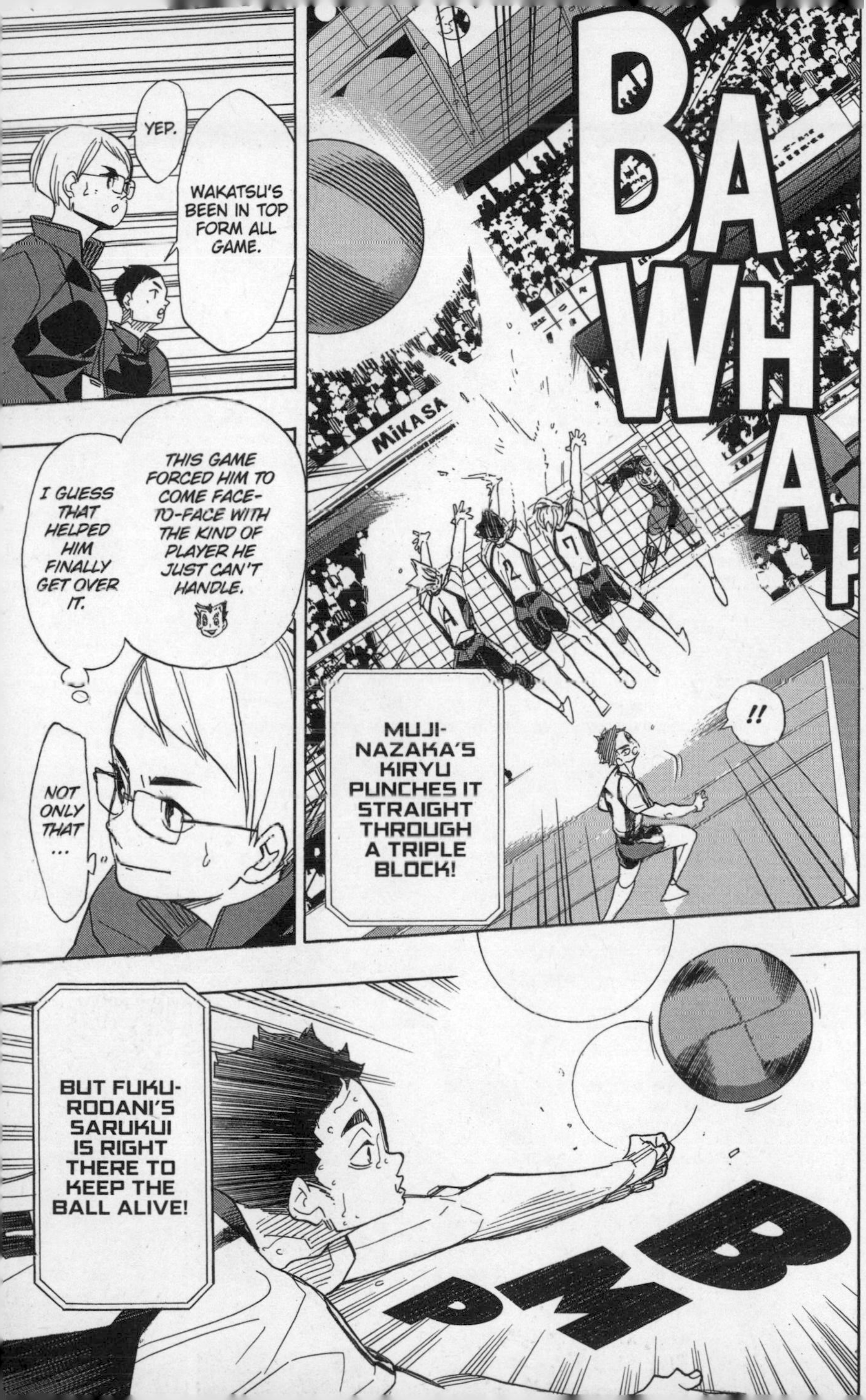
BA WHAP
!!
MUJI-NAZAKA'S KIRYU PUNCHES IT STRAIGHT THROUGH A TRIPLE BLOCK!
YEP.
WAKATSU'S BEEN IN TOP FORM ALL GAME.
THIS GAME FORCED HIM TO COME FACE-TO-FACE WITH THE KIND OF PLAYER HE JUST CAN'T HANDLE.
I GUESS THAT HELPED HIM FINALLY GET OVER IT.
NOT ONLY THAT...
MIKASA
BUT FUKURODANI'S SARUKUI IS RIGHT THERE TO KEEP THE BALL ALIVE!

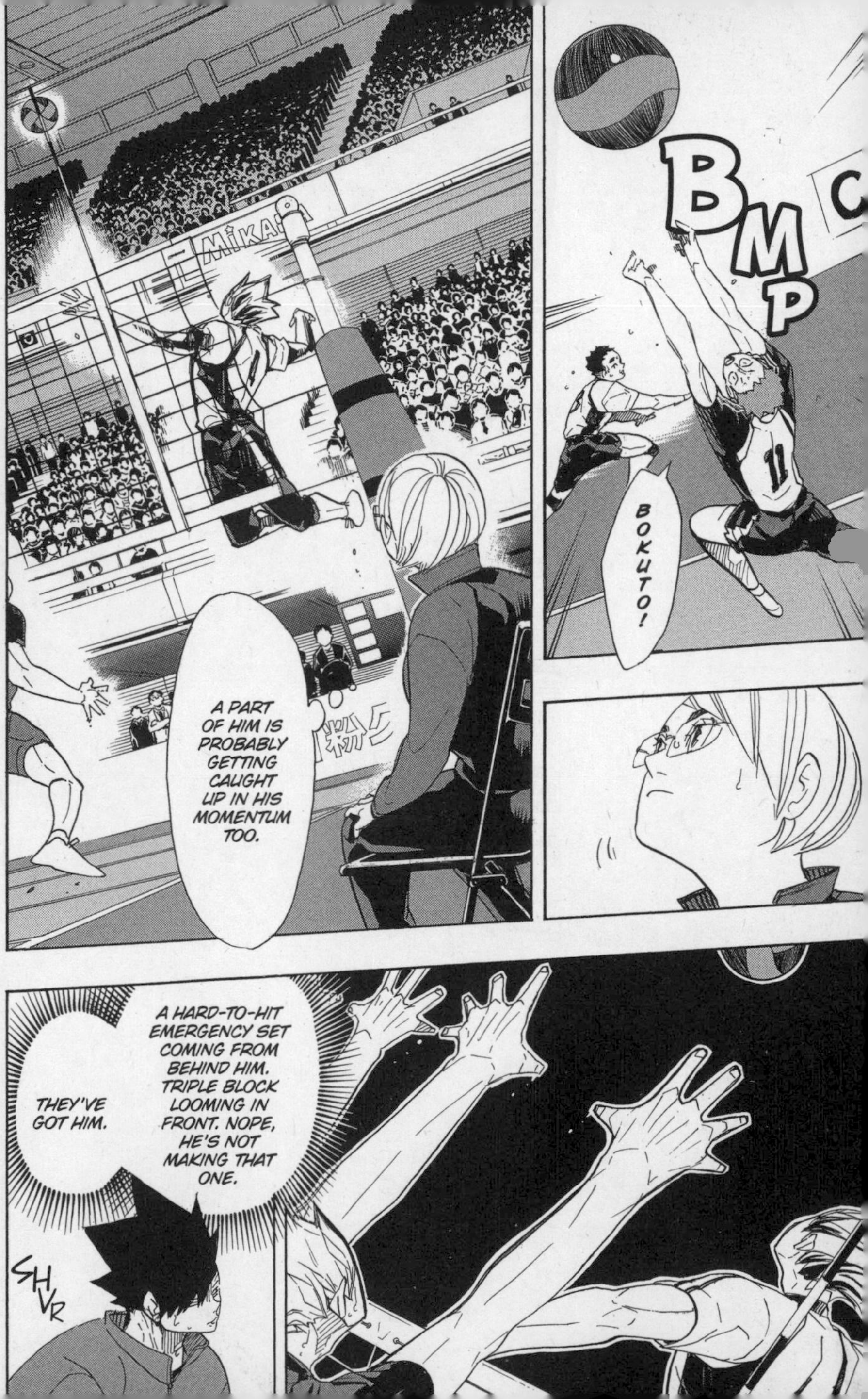
BMP
BOKUTO!
A PART OF HIM IS PROBABLY GETTING CAUGHT UP IN HIS MOMENTUM TOO.
A HARD-TO-HIT EMERGENCY SET COMING FROM BEHIND HIM. TRIPLE BLOCK LOOMING IN FRONT. NOPE, HE'S NOT MAKING THAT ONE.
THEY'VE GOT HIM.
SHVR

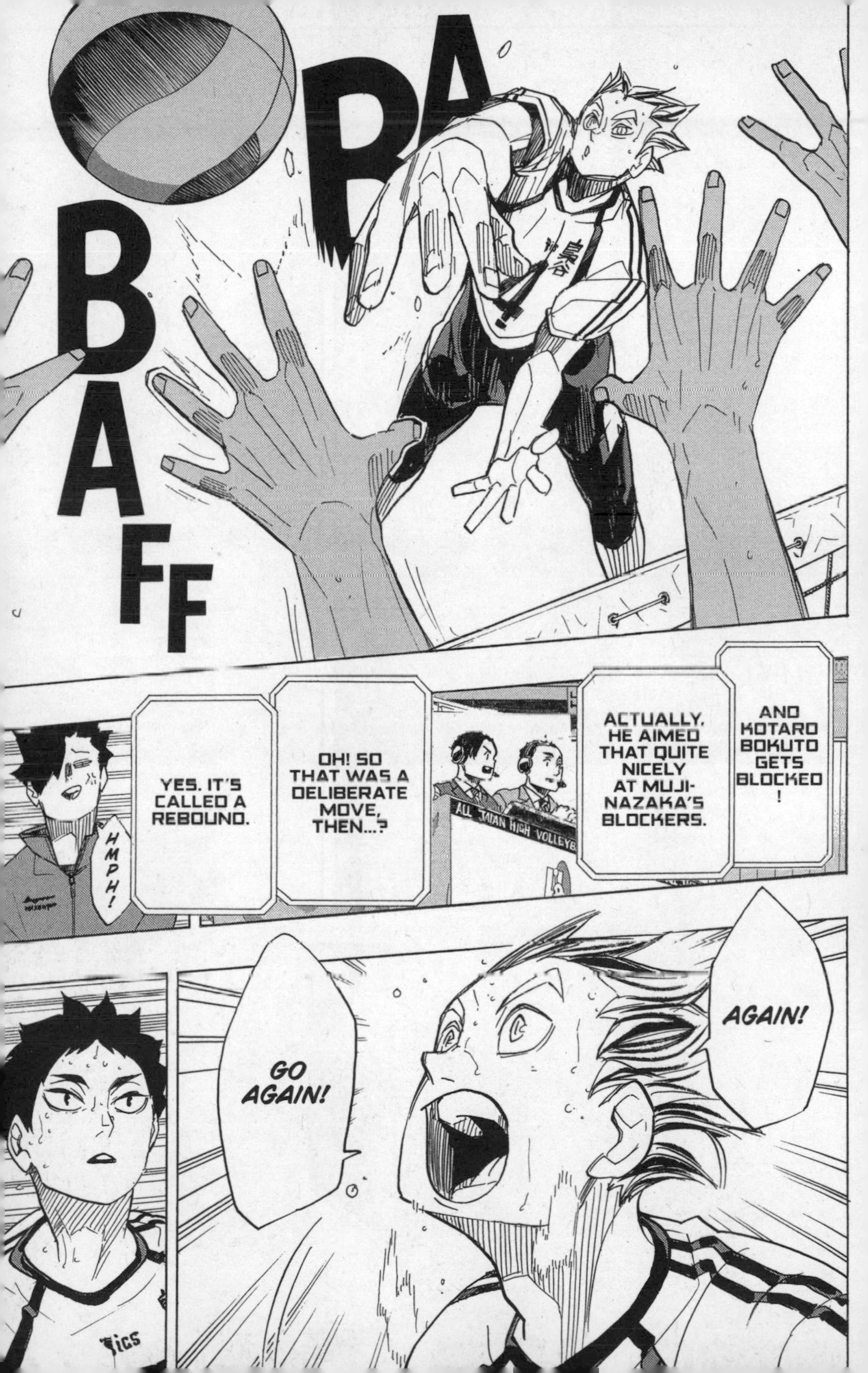
BA
BAFF
AND KOTARO BOKUTO GETS BLOCKED!
ACTUALLY, HE AIMED THAT QUITE NICELY AT MUJI-NAZAKA'S BLOCKERS.
OH! SO THAT WAS A DELIBERATE MOVE, THEN...?
YES. IT'S CALLED A REBOUND.
HMPH!
AGAIN!
GO AGAIN!

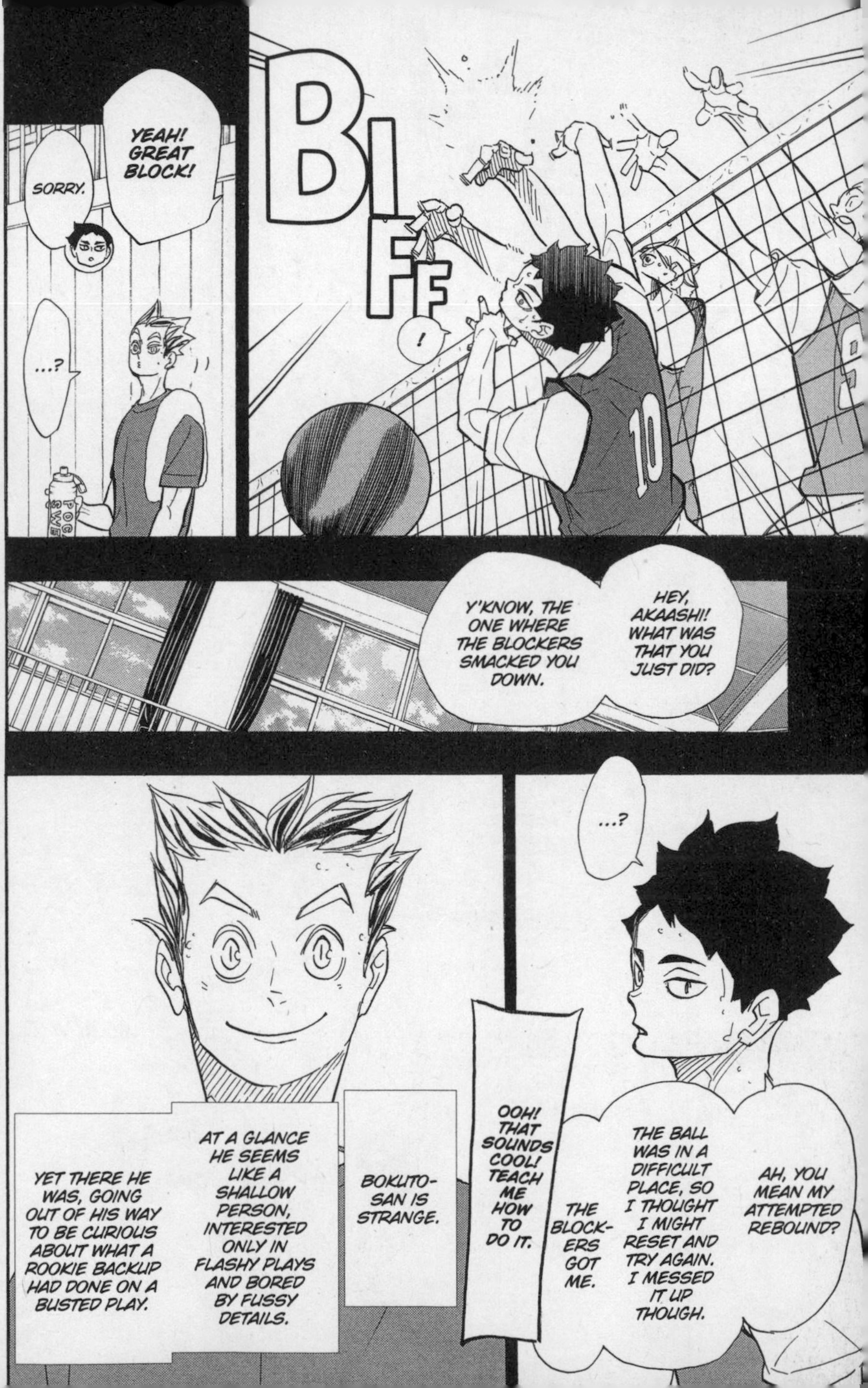
BIFF
!
YEAH! GREAT BLOCK!
SORRY.
...?
HEY, AKAASHI! WHAT WAS THAT YOU JUST DID?
Y'KNOW, THE ONE WHERE THE BLOCKERS SMACKED YOU DOWN.
...?
AH, YOU MEAN MY ATTEMPTED REBOUND?
THE BALL WAS IN A DIFFICULT PLACE, SO I THOUGHT I MIGHT RESET AND TRY AGAIN. I MESSED IT UP THOUGH.
THE BLOCKERS GOT ME.
OOH! THAT SOUNDS COOL! TEACH ME HOW TO DO IT.
BOKUTO-SAN IS STRANGE.
AT A GLANCE HE SEEMS LIKE A SHALLOW PERSON, INTERESTED ONLY IN FLASHY PLAYS AND BORED BY FUSSY DETAILS.
YET THERE HE WAS, GOING OUT OF HIS WAY TO BE CURIOUS ABOUT WHAT A ROOKIE BACKUP HAD DONE ON A BUSTED PLAY.

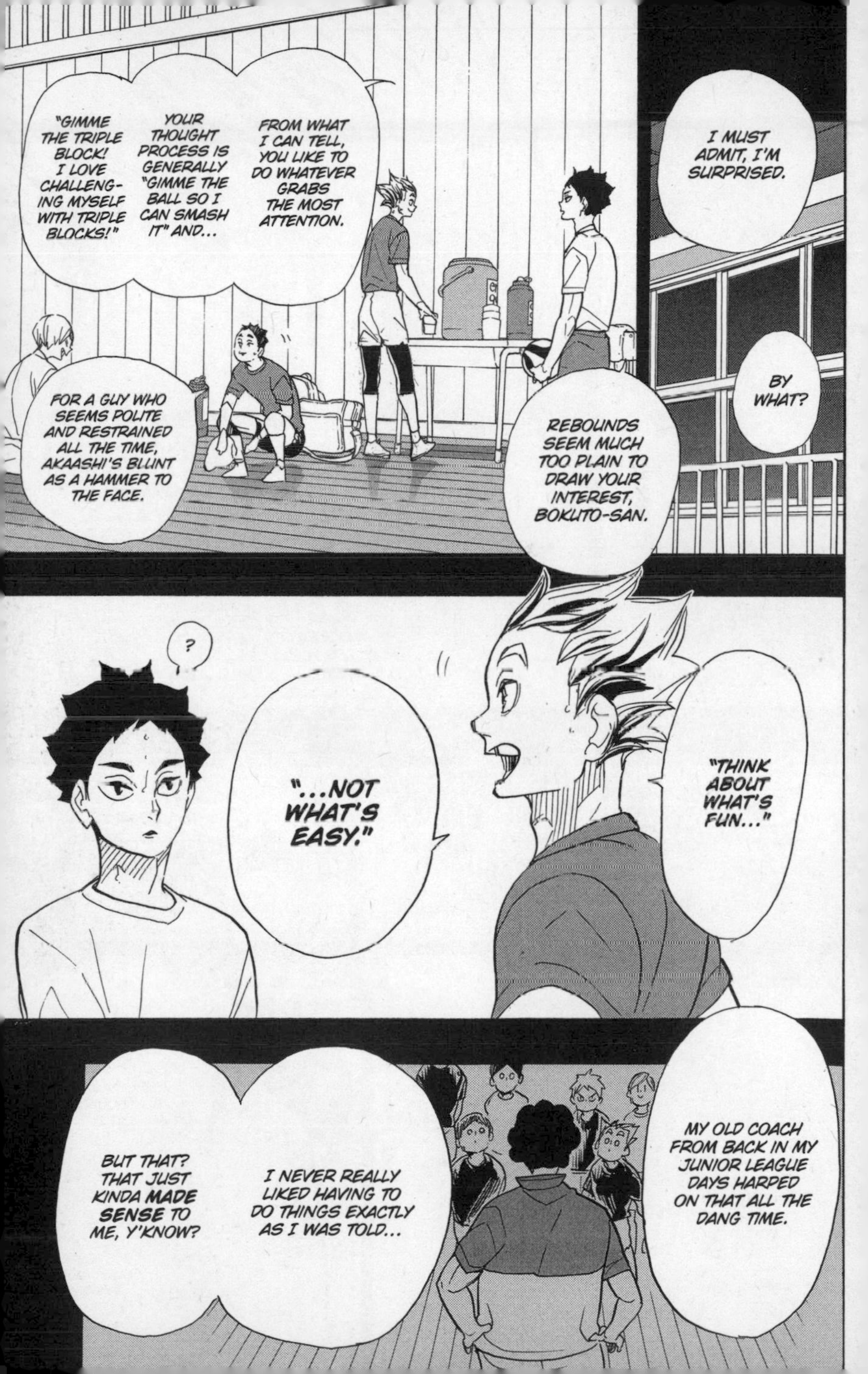
I MUST ADMIT, I'M SURPRISED.
BY WHAT?
REBOUNDS SEEM MUCH TOO PLAIN TO DRAW YOUR INTEREST, BOKUTO-SAN.
FROM WHAT I CAN TELL, YOU LIKE TO DO WHATEVER GRABS THE MOST ATTENTION.
YOUR THOUGHT PROCESS IS GENERALLY "GIMME THE BALL SO I CAN SMASH IT" AND...
"GIMME THE TRIPLE BLOCK! I LOVE CHALLENG-ING MYSELF WITH TRIPLE BLOCKS!"
FOR A GUY WHO SEEMS POLITE AND RESTRAINED ALL THE TIME, AKAASHI'S BLUNT AS A HAMMER TO THE FACE.
"THINK ABOUT WHAT'S FUN..."
"...NOT WHAT'S EASY."
?
MY OLD COACH FROM BACK IN MY JUNIOR LEAGUE DAYS HARPED ON THAT ALL THE DANG TIME.
I NEVER REALLY LIKED HAVING TO DO THINGS EXACTLY AS I WAS TOLD...
BUT THAT? THAT JUST KINDA MADE SENSE TO ME, Y'KNOW?

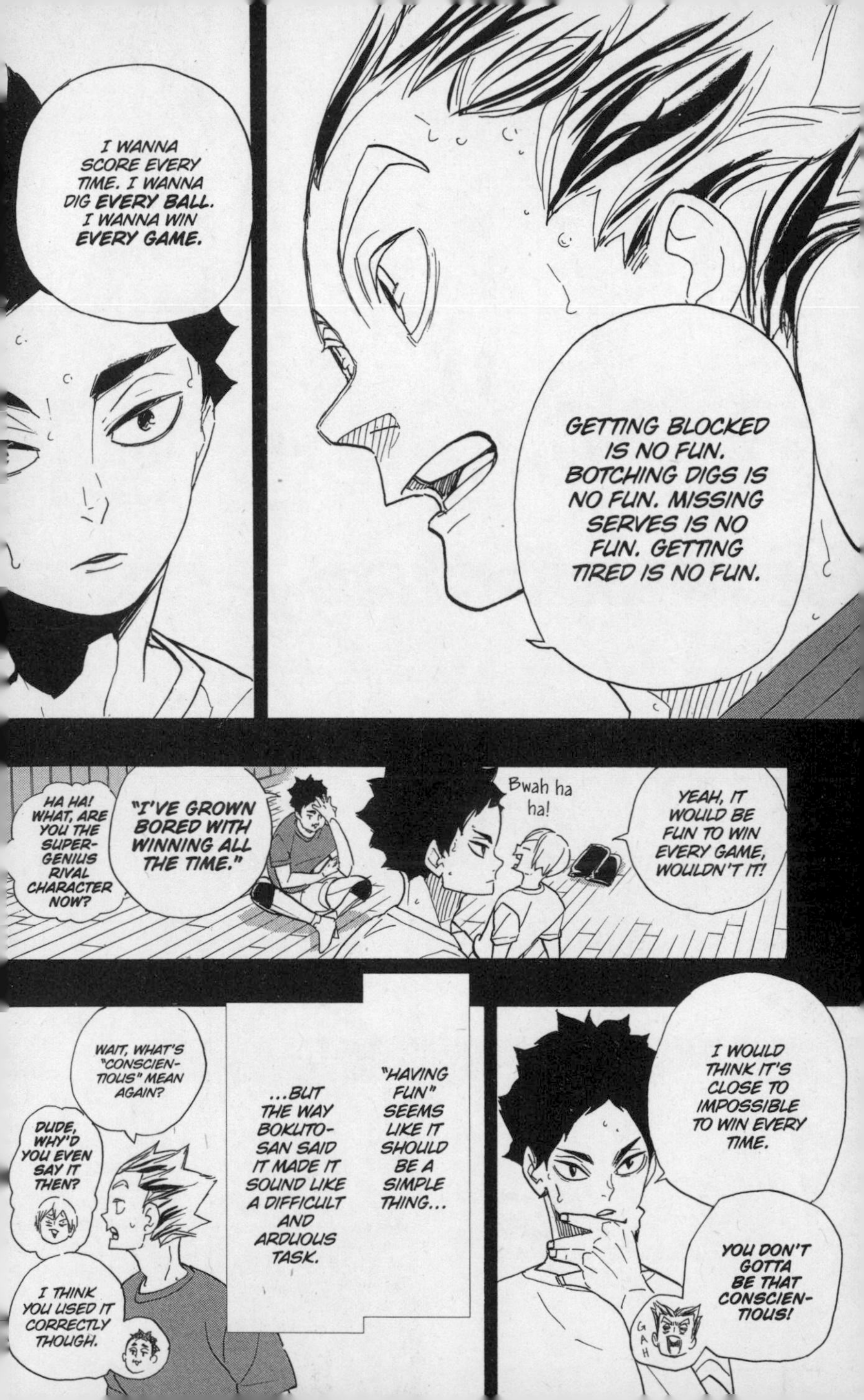
GETTING BLOCKED IS NO FUN. BOTCHING DIGS IS NO FUN. MISSING SERVES IS NO FUN. GETTING TIRED IS NO FUN.
I WANNA SCORE EVERY TIME. I WANNA DIG EVERY BALL. I WANNA WIN EVERY GAME.
YEAH, IT WOULD BE FUN TO WIN EVERY GAME, WOULDN'T IT!
Bwah ha ha!
"I'VE GROWN BORED WITH WINNING ALL THE TIME."
HA HA! WHAT, ARE YOU THE SUPER-GENIUS RIVAL CHARACTER NOW?
I WOULD THINK IT'S CLOSE TO IMPOSSIBLE TO WIN EVERY TIME.
YOU DON'T GOTTA BE THAT CONSCIEN-TIOUS!
GAH
"HAVING FUN" SEEMS LIKE IT SHOULD BE A SIMPLE THING...
...BUT THE WAY BOKUTO-SAN SAID IT MADE IT SOUND LIKE A DIFFICULT AND ARDUOUS TASK.
WAIT, WHAT'S "CONSCIEN-TIOUS" MEAN AGAIN?
DUDE, WHY'D YOU EVEN SAY IT THEN?
I THINK YOU USED IT CORRECTLY THOUGH.

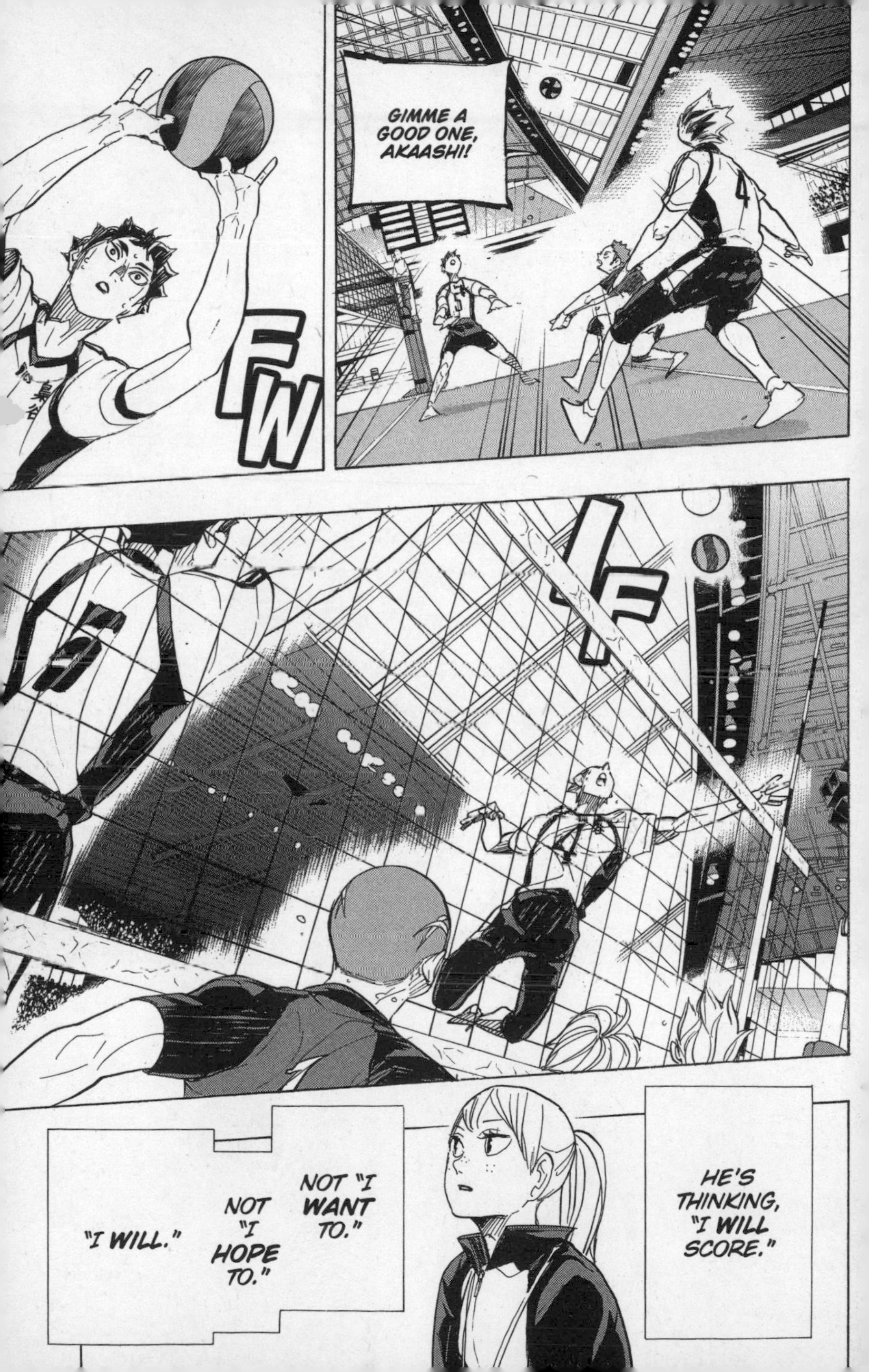
GIMME A GOOD ONE, AKAASHI!
FW
HE'S THINKING, "I WILL SCORE."
NOT "I WANT TO."
NOT "I HOPE TO."
"I WILL."

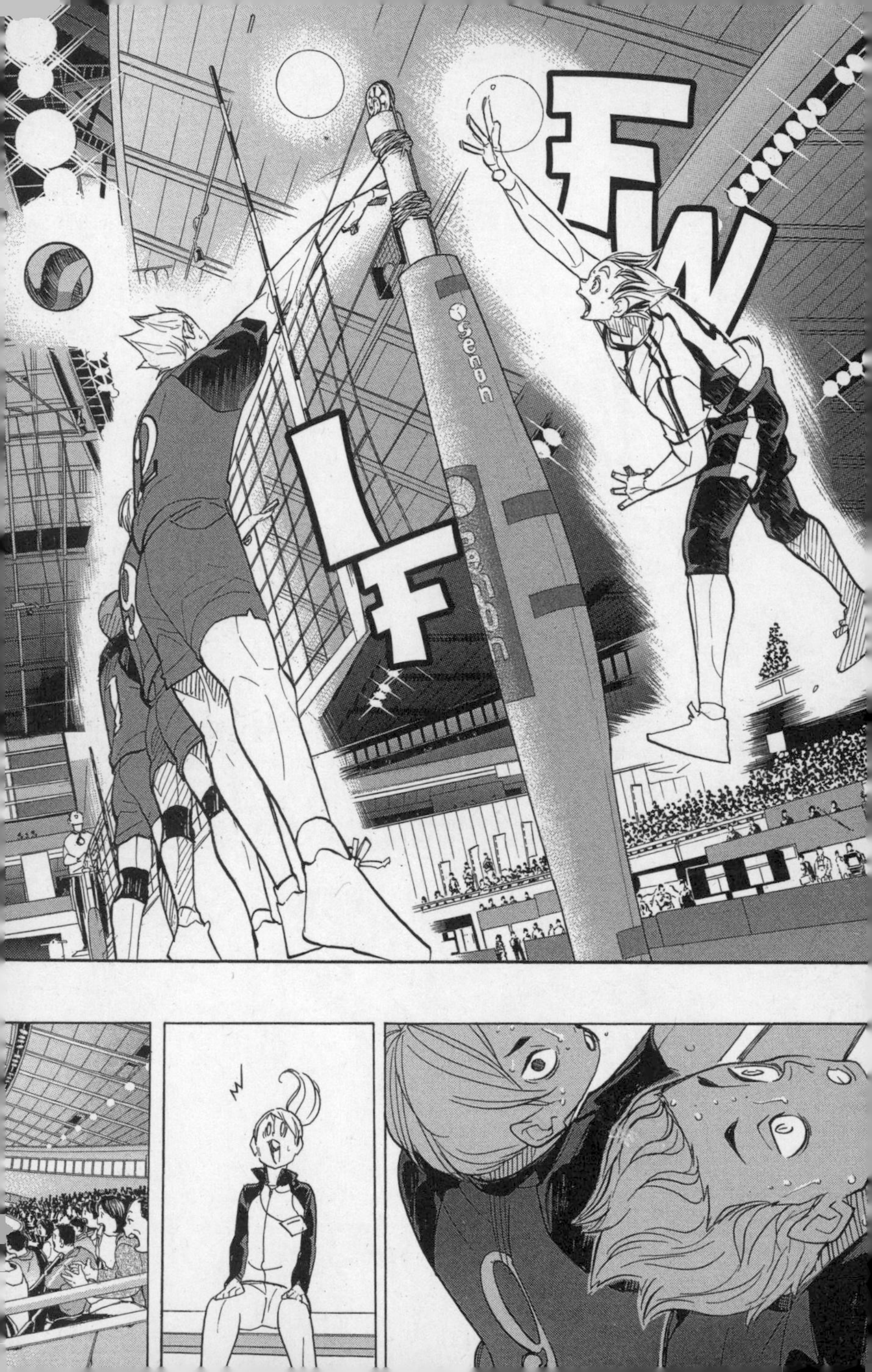
FWIF

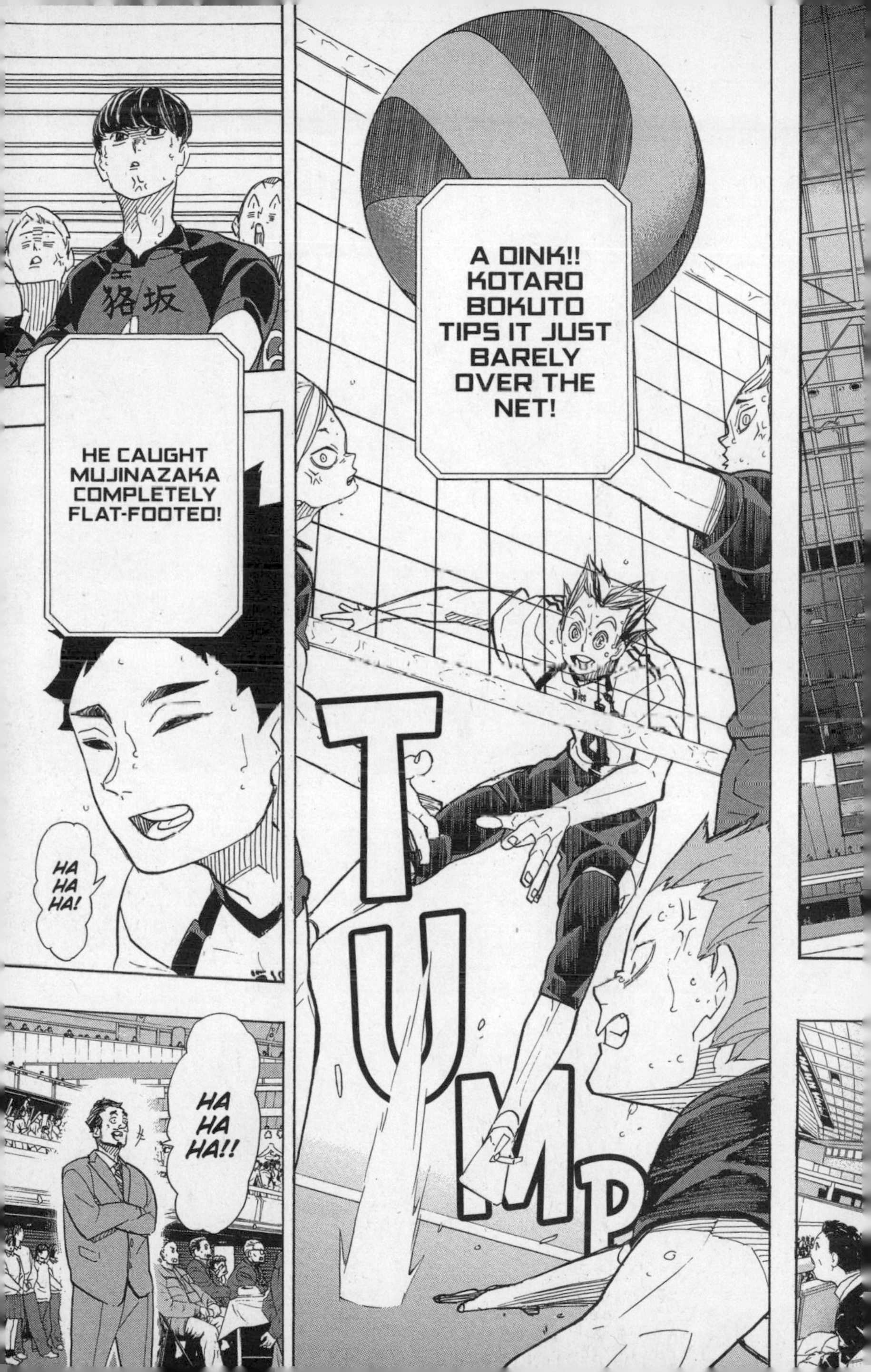
A DINK!! KOTARO BOKUTO TIPS IT JUST BARELY OVER THE NET!
TUMP
HE CAUGHT MUJINAZAKA COMPLETELY FLAT-FOOTED!
HA HA HA!
HA HA HA!!

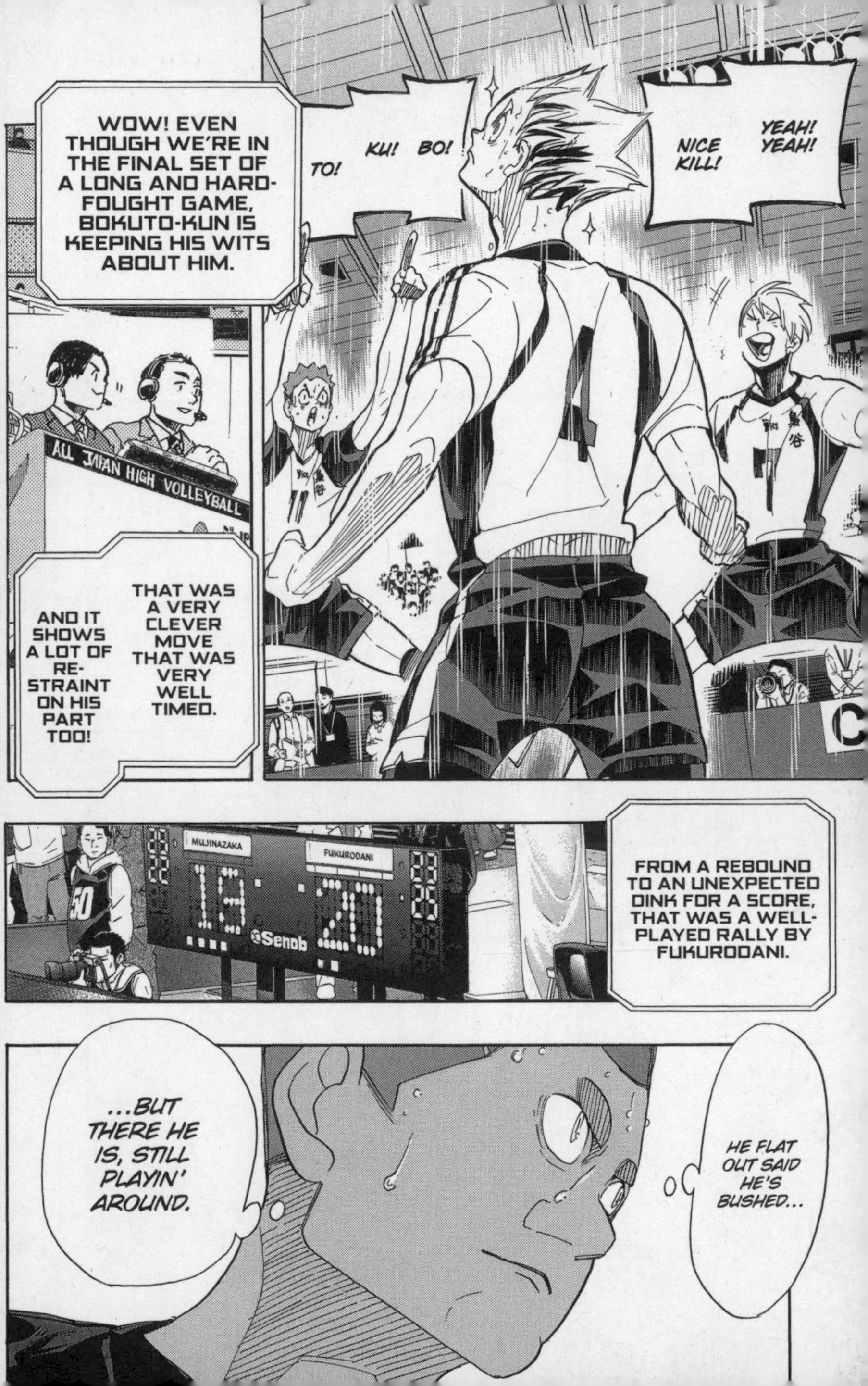
YEAH! YEAH!
NICE KILL!
BO!
KU!
TO!
WOW! EVEN THOUGH WE'RE IN THE FINAL SET OF A LONG AND HARD-FOUGHT GAME, BOKUTO-KUN IS KEEPING HIS WITS ABOUT HIM.
ALL JAPAN HIGH VOLLEYBALL
THAT WAS A VERY CLEVER MOVE THAT WAS VERY WELL TIMED.
AND IT SHOWS A LOT OF RE-STRAINT ON HIS PART TOO!
FROM A REBOUND TO AN UNEXPECTED DINK FOR A SCORE, THAT WAS A WELL-PLAYED RALLY BY FUKURODANI.
MUJINAZAKA
FUKURODANI
Senob
HE FLAT OUT SAID HE'S BUSHED...
...BUT THERE HE IS, STILL PLAYIN' AROUND.

SERVE

*CURRENT ROTATION

BOKUTO | AKAASHI | ONAGA (KOMI)

WASHIO | KONOHA | SARUKUI

NET

USURI | MAMI | KIRYU

HONDO | UNNAN (BISHIN) | EZOTA

BO! KU! TO!

BO! KU! TO!

TMP

TMP

TMP

FWEEEE

WAM

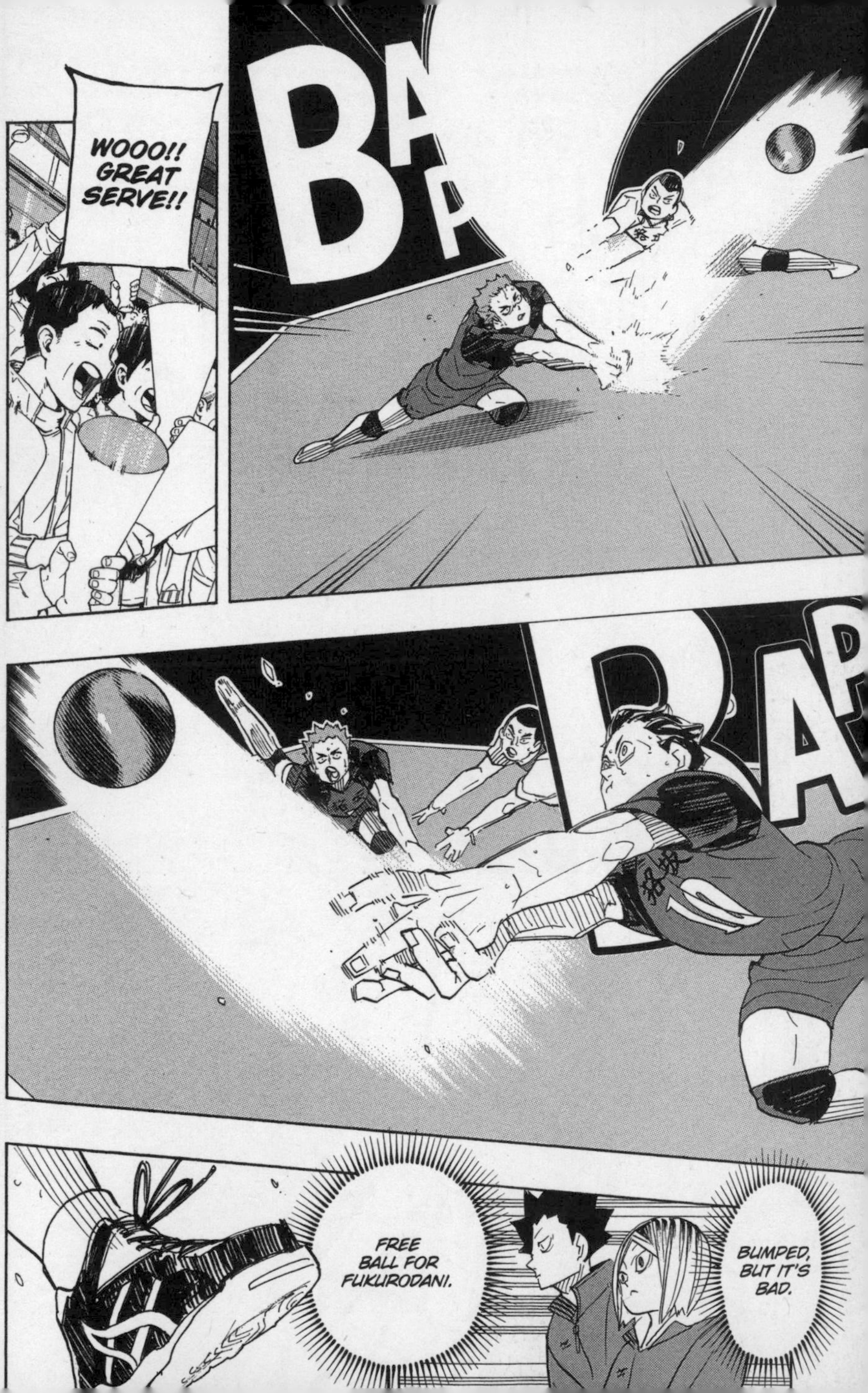
BAP
WOOO!! GREAT SERVE!!
BAP
BUMPED, BUT IT'S BAD.
FREE BALL FOR FUKURODANI.

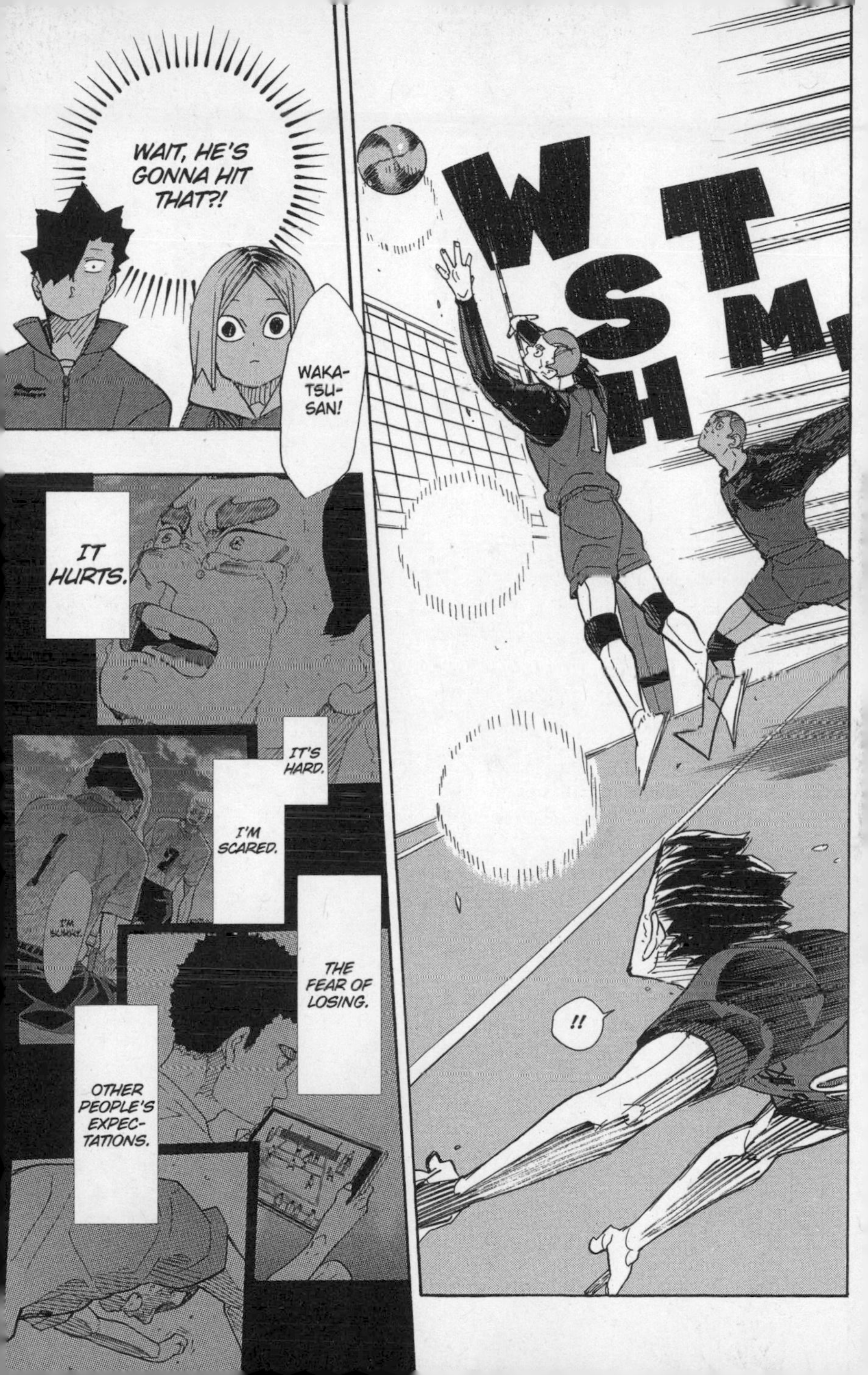
!!
WAIT, HE'S GONNA HIT THAT?!
WAKA-TSU-SAN!
IT HURTS.
IT'S HARD.
I'M SCARED.
THE FEAR OF LOSING.
OTHER PEOPLE'S EXPECTA-TIONS.

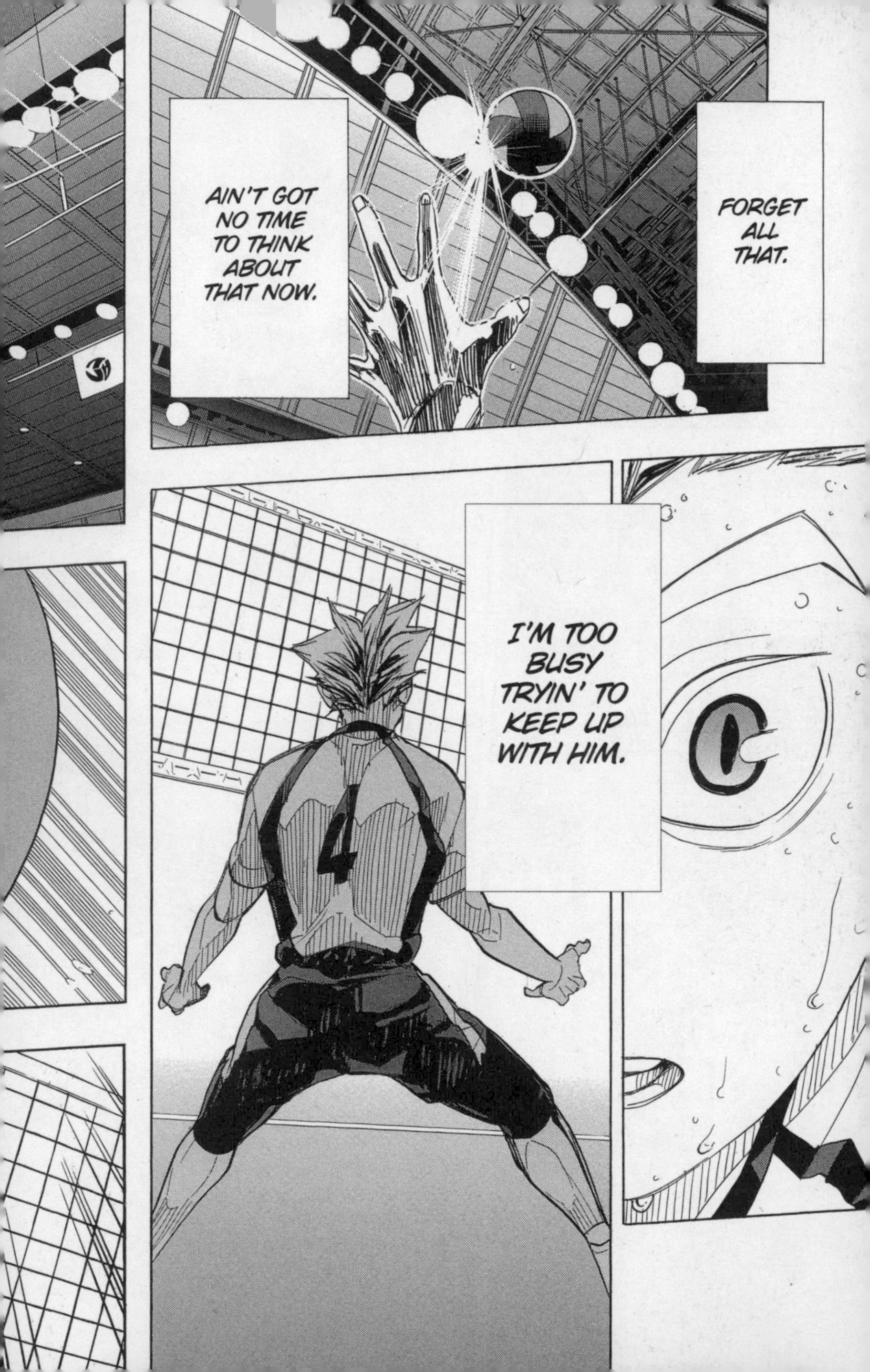
FORGET ALL THAT.
AIN'T GOT NO TIME TO THINK ABOUT THAT NOW.
I'M TOO BUSY TRYIN' TO KEEP UP WITH HIM.

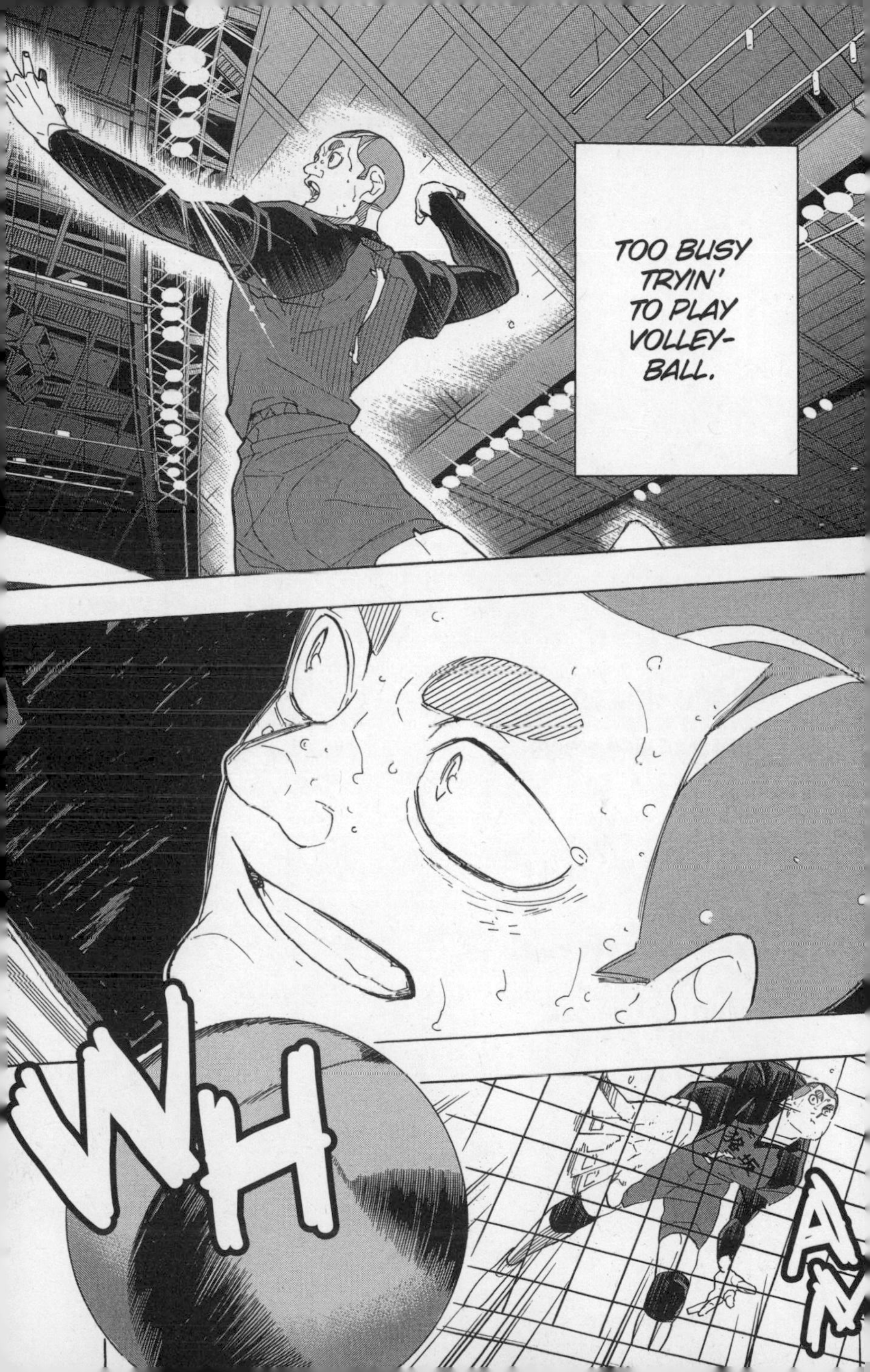
TOO BUSY TRYIN' TO PLAY VOLLEY-BALL.
WH

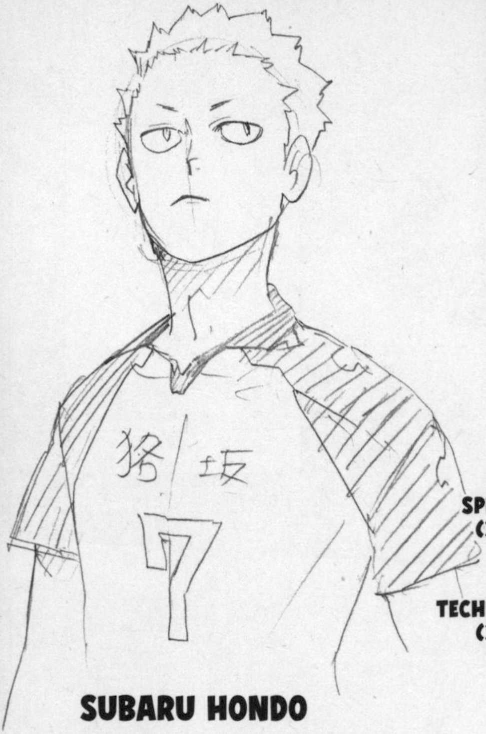

猪坂
7

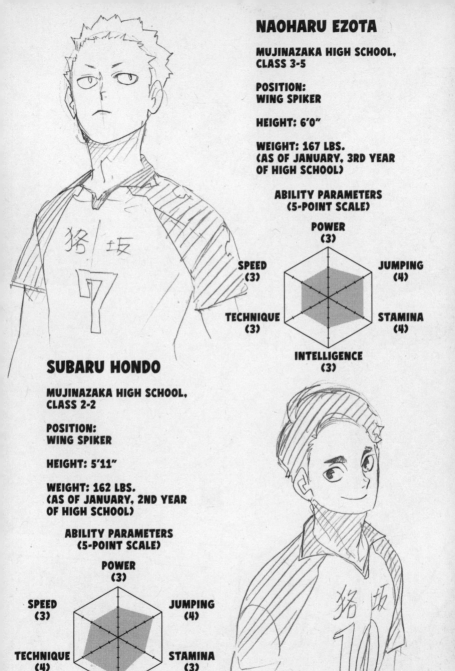

NAOHARU EZOTA

MUJINAZAKA HIGH SCHOOL,
CLASS 3-5

POSITION:
WING SPIKER

HEIGHT: 6'0"

WEIGHT: 167 LBS.
(AS OF JANUARY, 3RD YEAR
OF HIGH SCHOOL)

ABILITY PARAMETERS
(5-POINT SCALE)

POWER
(3)

SPEED
(3)

JUMPING
(4)

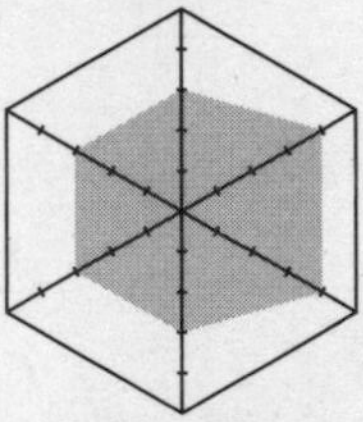

TECHNIQUE
(3)

STAMINA
(4)

INTELLIGENCE
(3)

SUBARU HONDO

MUJINAZAKA HIGH SCHOOL,
CLASS 2-2

POSITION:
WING SPIKER

HEIGHT: 5'11"

WEIGHT: 162 LBS.
(AS OF JANUARY, 2ND YEAR
OF HIGH SCHOOL)

ABILITY PARAMETERS
(5-POINT SCALE)

POWER
(3)

SPEED
(3)

JUMPING
(4)

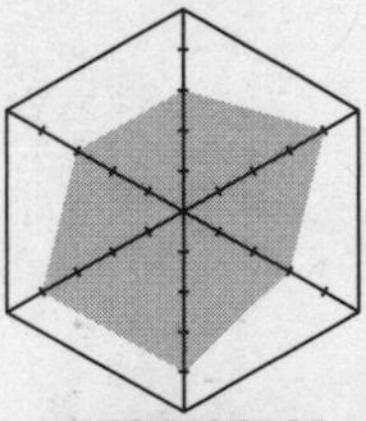

TECHNIQUE
(4)

STAMINA
(3)

INTELLIGENCE
(4)

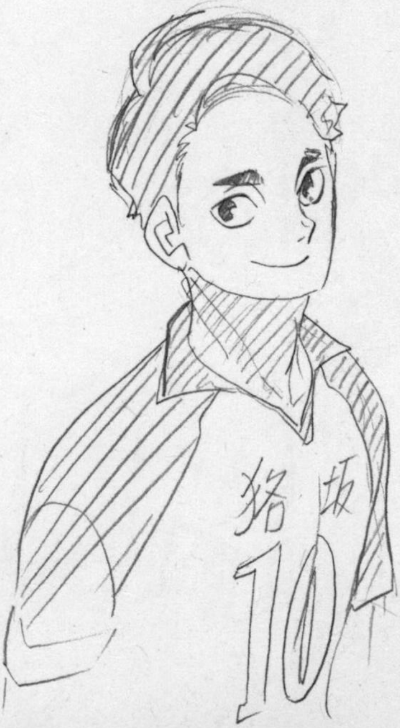

猪坂
10

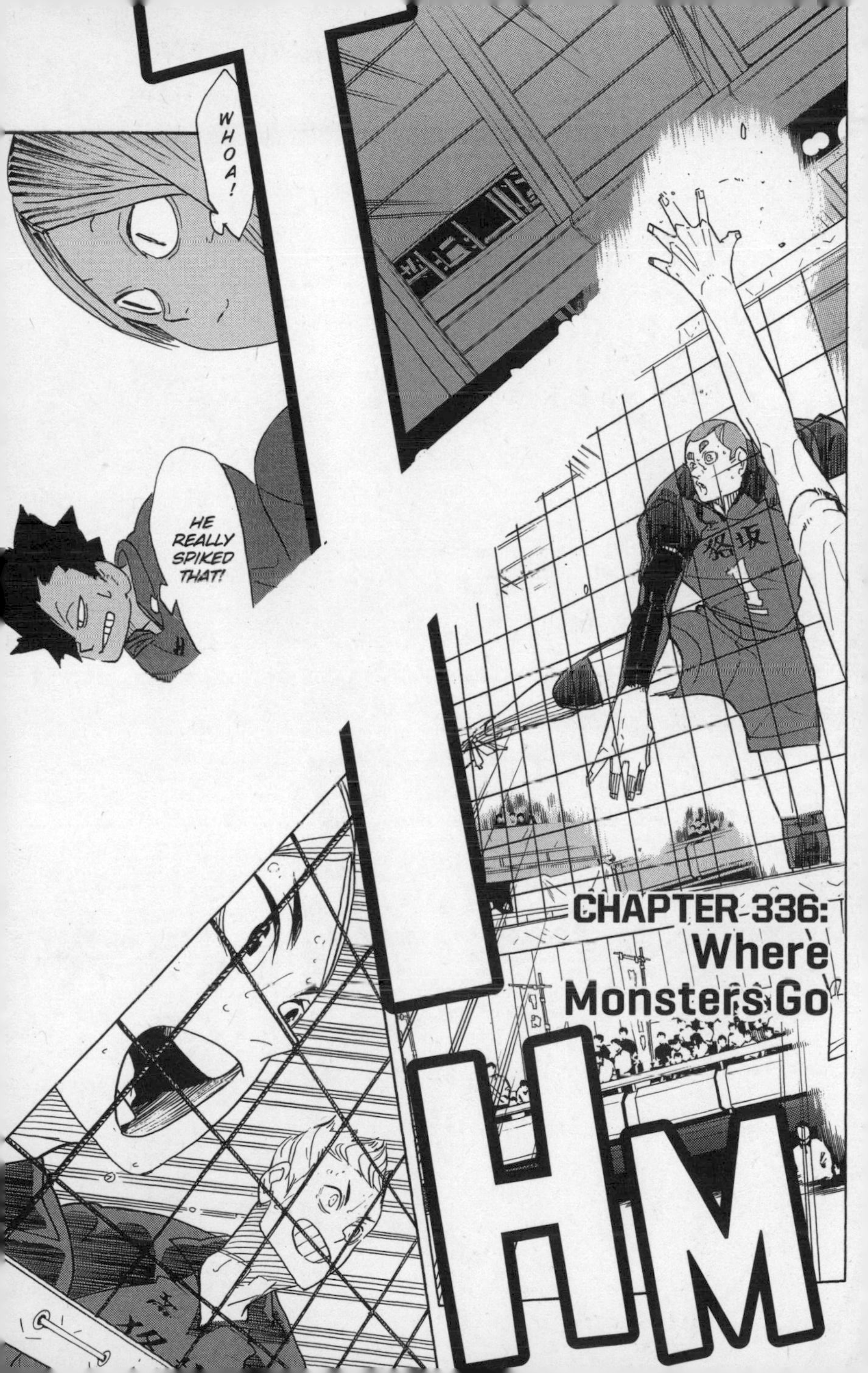
CHAPTER 336: Where Monsters Go
HM
WHOA!
HE REALLY SPIKED THAT!

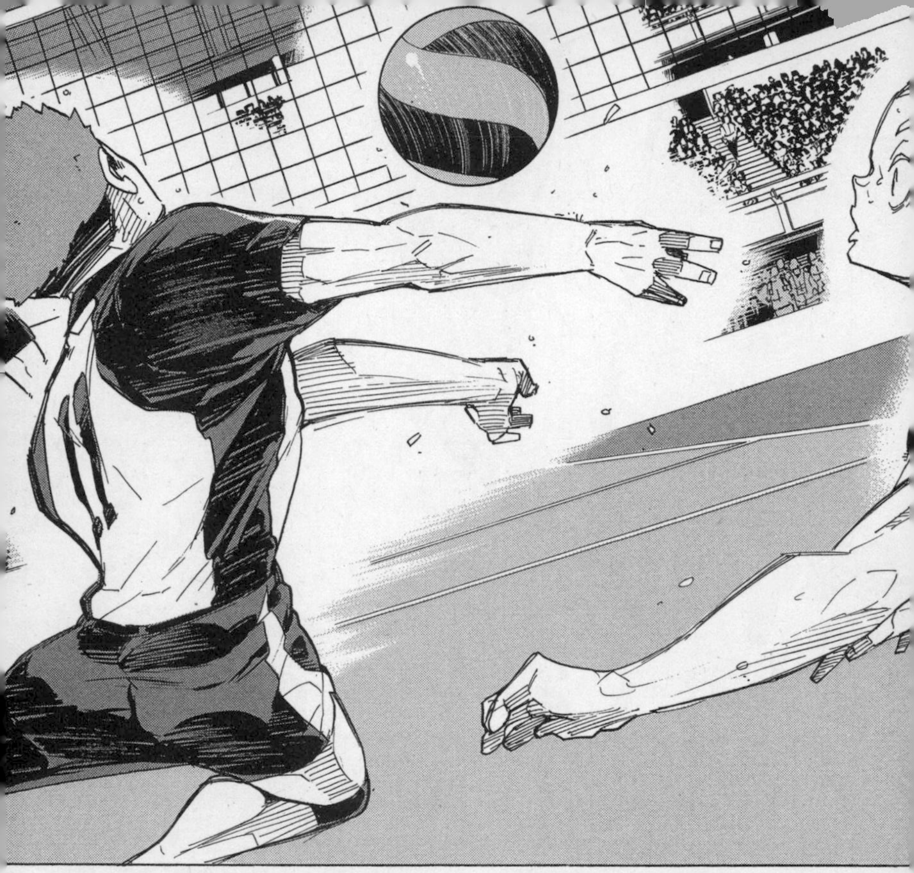

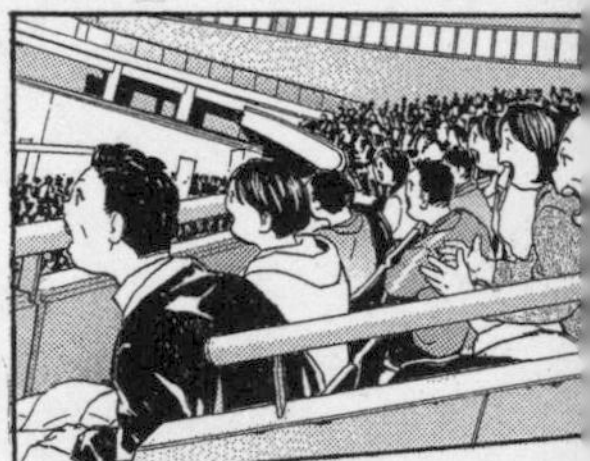

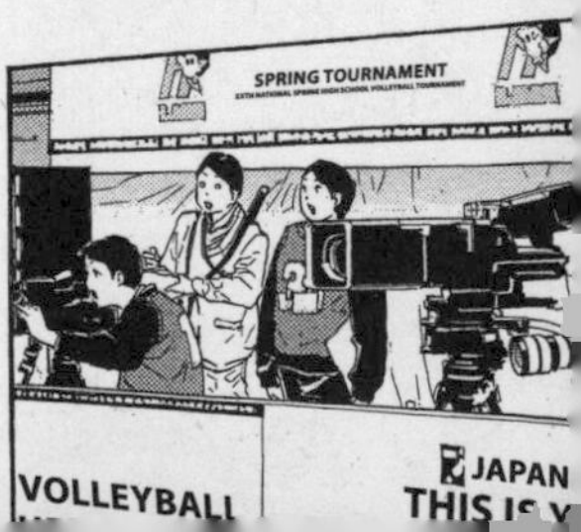
SPRING TOURNAMENT
JAPAN
VOLLEYBALL

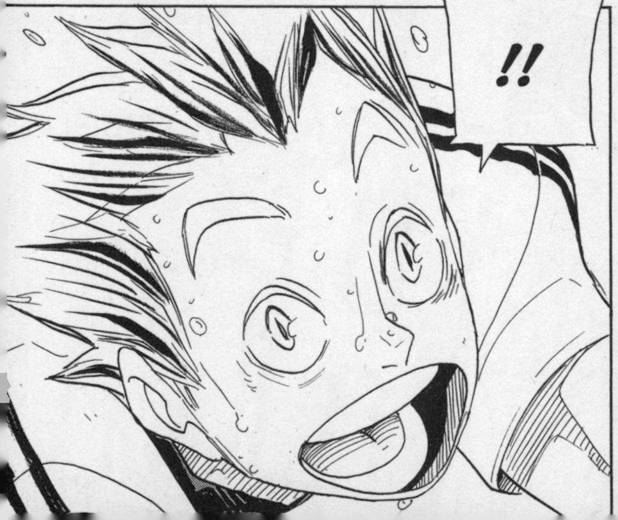
!!

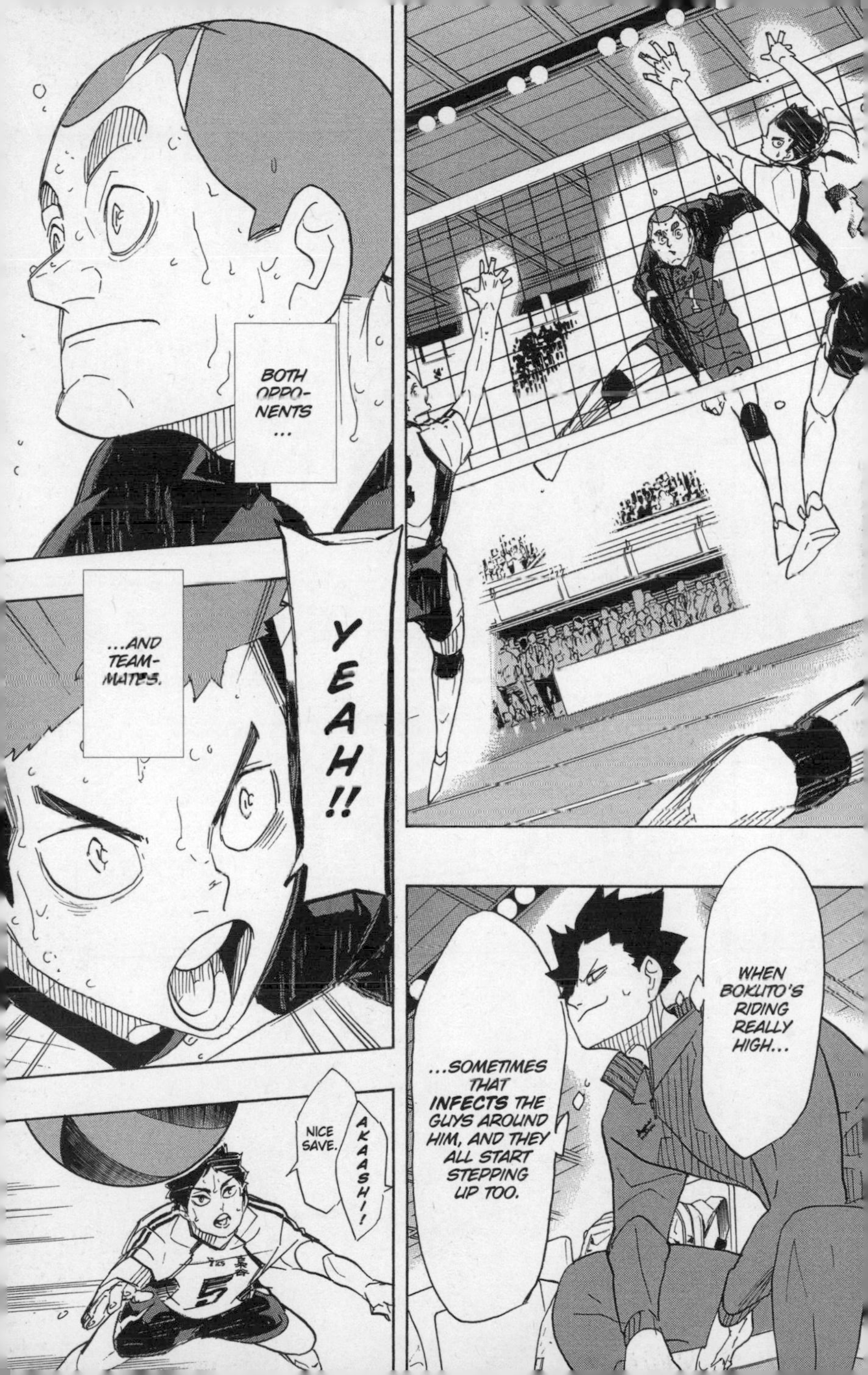
BOTH OPPONENTS...
...AND TEAMMATES.
YEAH!!
WHEN BOKUTO'S RIDING REALLY HIGH...
...SOMETIMES THAT INFECTS THE GUYS AROUND HIM, AND THEY ALL START STEPPING UP TOO.
AKAASHI!
NICE SAVE.

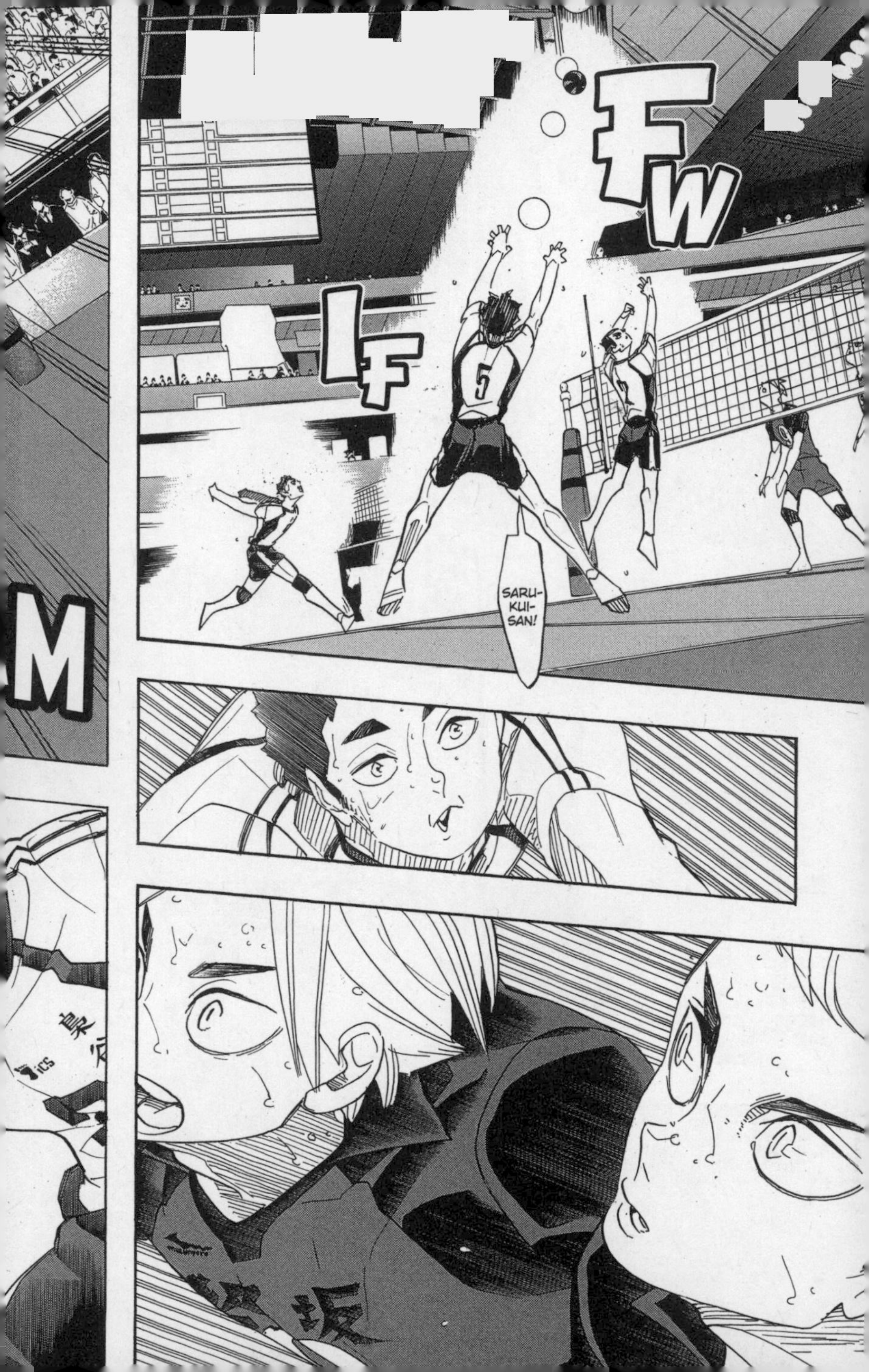
FW
IF
M
SARU-KUI-SAN!

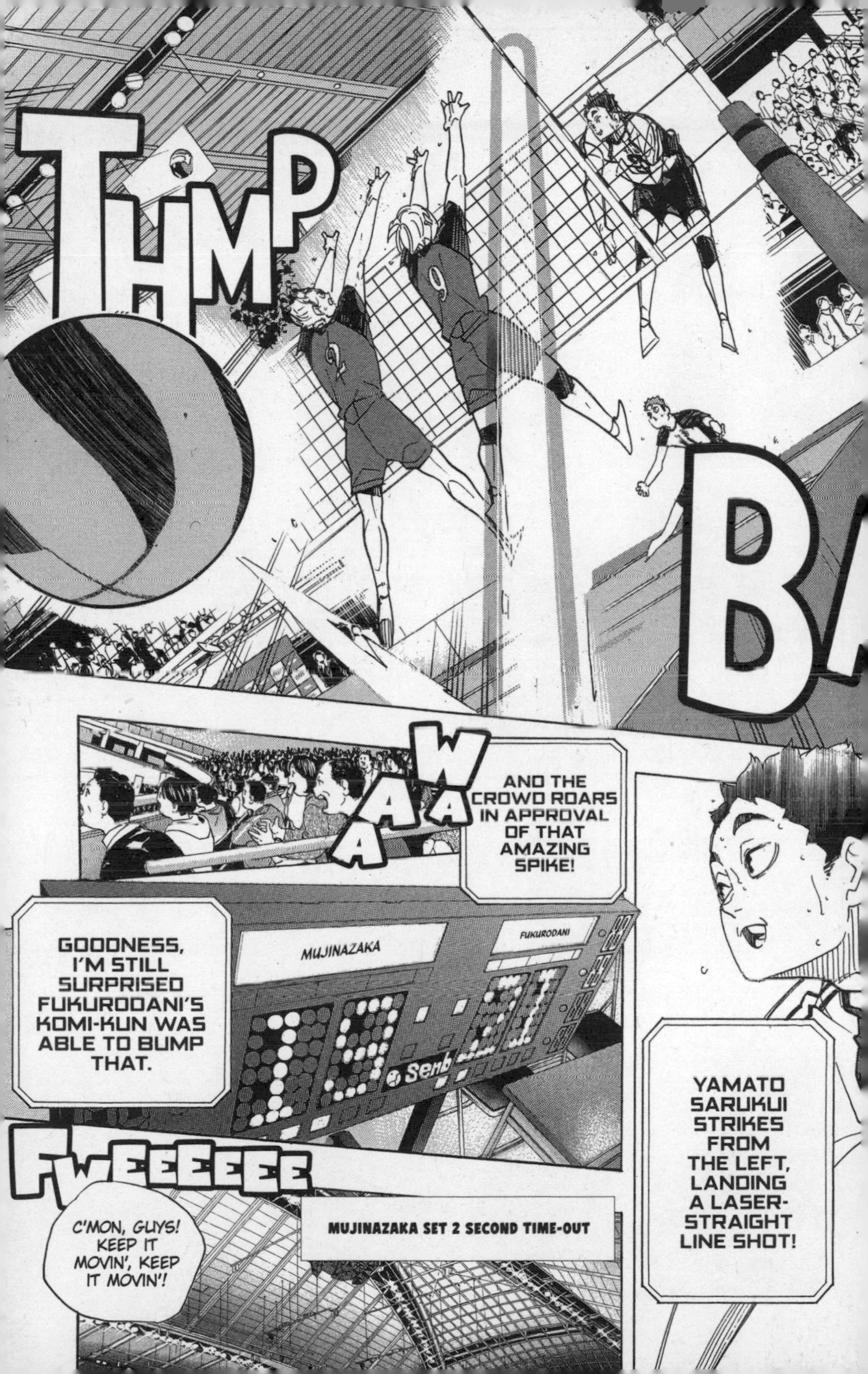
THMP
BA
YAMATO SARUKUI STRIKES FROM THE LEFT, LANDING A LASER-STRAIGHT LINE SHOT!
AND THE CROWD ROARS IN APPROVAL OF THAT AMAZING SPIKE!
WAAA
FUKURODANI
MUJINAZAKA
GOODNESS, I'M STILL SURPRISED FUKURODANI'S KOMI-KUN WAS ABLE TO BUMP THAT.
FWEEEEEE
MUJINAZAKA SET 2 SECOND TIME-OUT
C'MON, GUYS! KEEP IT MOVIN', KEEP IT MOVIN'!

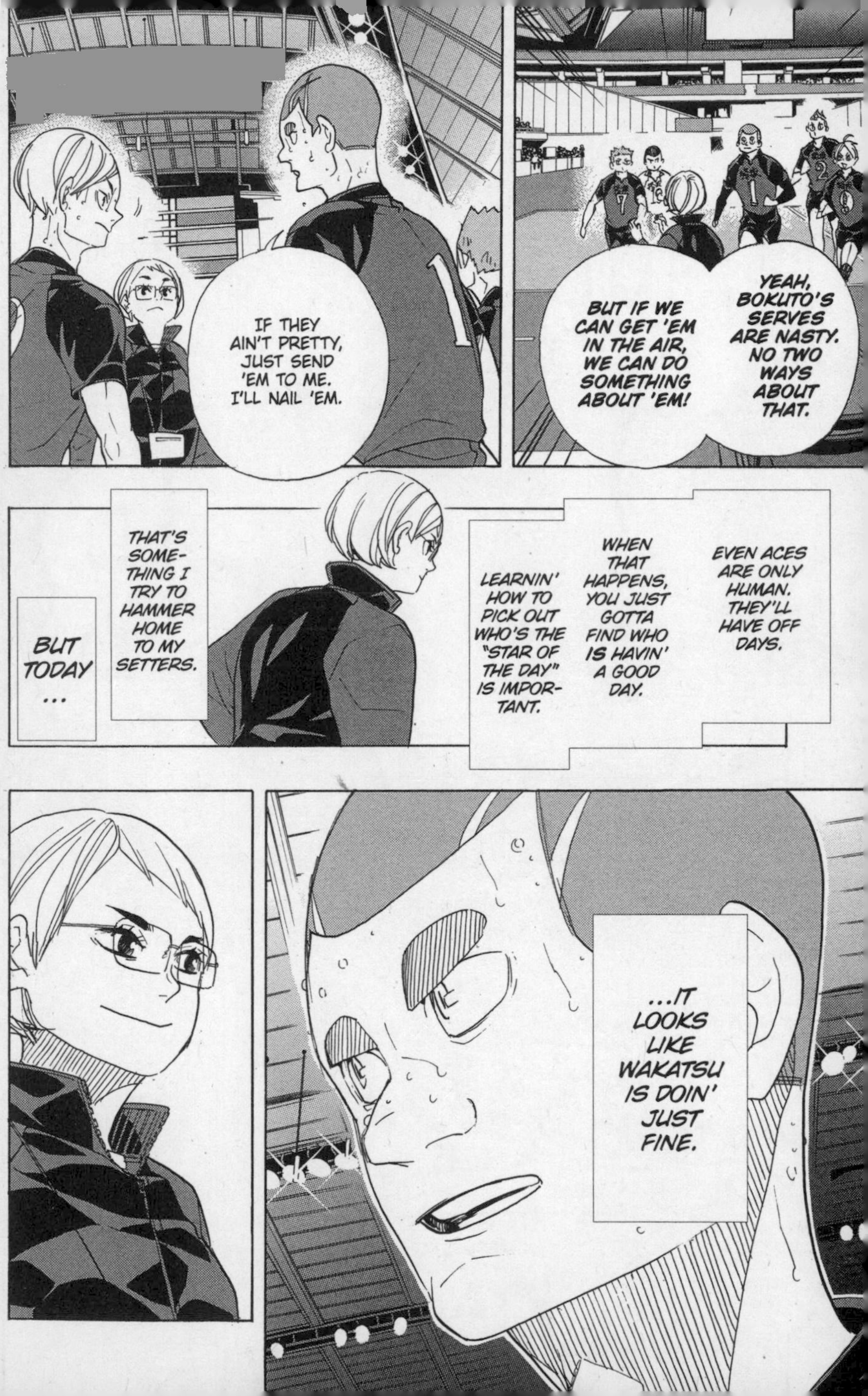
YEAH, BOKUTO'S SERVES ARE NASTY. NO TWO WAYS ABOUT THAT.
BUT IF WE CAN GET 'EM IN THE AIR, WE CAN DO SOMETHING ABOUT 'EM!
IF THEY AIN'T PRETTY, JUST SEND 'EM TO ME. I'LL NAIL 'EM.
EVEN ACES ARE ONLY HUMAN. THEY'LL HAVE OFF DAYS.
WHEN THAT HAPPENS, YOU JUST GOTTA FIND WHO IS HAVIN' A GOOD DAY.
LEARNIN' HOW TO PICK OUT WHO'S THE "STAR OF THE DAY" IS IMPOR-TANT.
THAT'S SOME-THING I TRY TO HAMMER HOME TO MY SETTERS.
BUT TODAY...
...IT LOOKS LIKE WAKATSU IS DOIN' JUST FINE.

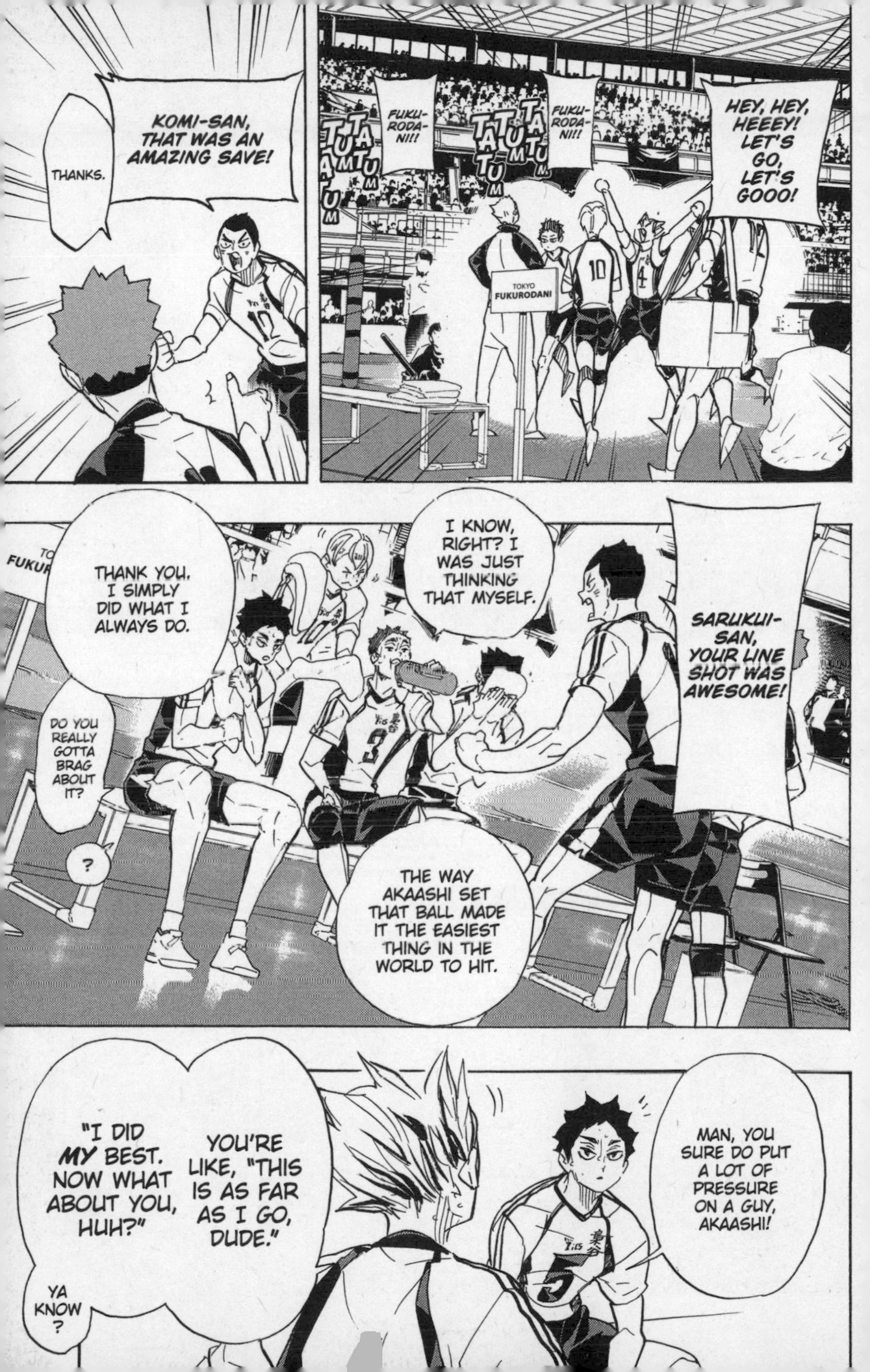
HEY, HEY, HEEEY! LET'S GO, LET'S GOOO!
FUKU-RODA-NI!!!
TA TUM TUM
FUKU-RODA-NI!!!
TA TUM TUM
TOKYO FUKURODANI
KOMI-SAN, THAT WAS AN AMAZING SAVE!
THANKS.
SARUKUI-SAN, YOUR LINE SHOT WAS AWESOME!
I KNOW, RIGHT? I WAS JUST THINKING THAT MYSELF.
THE WAY AKAASHI SET THAT BALL MADE IT THE EASIEST THING IN THE WORLD TO HIT.
THANK YOU. I SIMPLY DID WHAT I ALWAYS DO.
DO YOU REALLY GOTTA BRAG ABOUT IT?
?
MAN, YOU SURE DO PUT A LOT OF PRESSURE ON A GUY, AKAASHI!
YOU'RE LIKE, "THIS IS AS FAR AS I GO, DUDE."
"I DID MY BEST. NOW WHAT ABOUT YOU, HUH?"
YA KNOW?

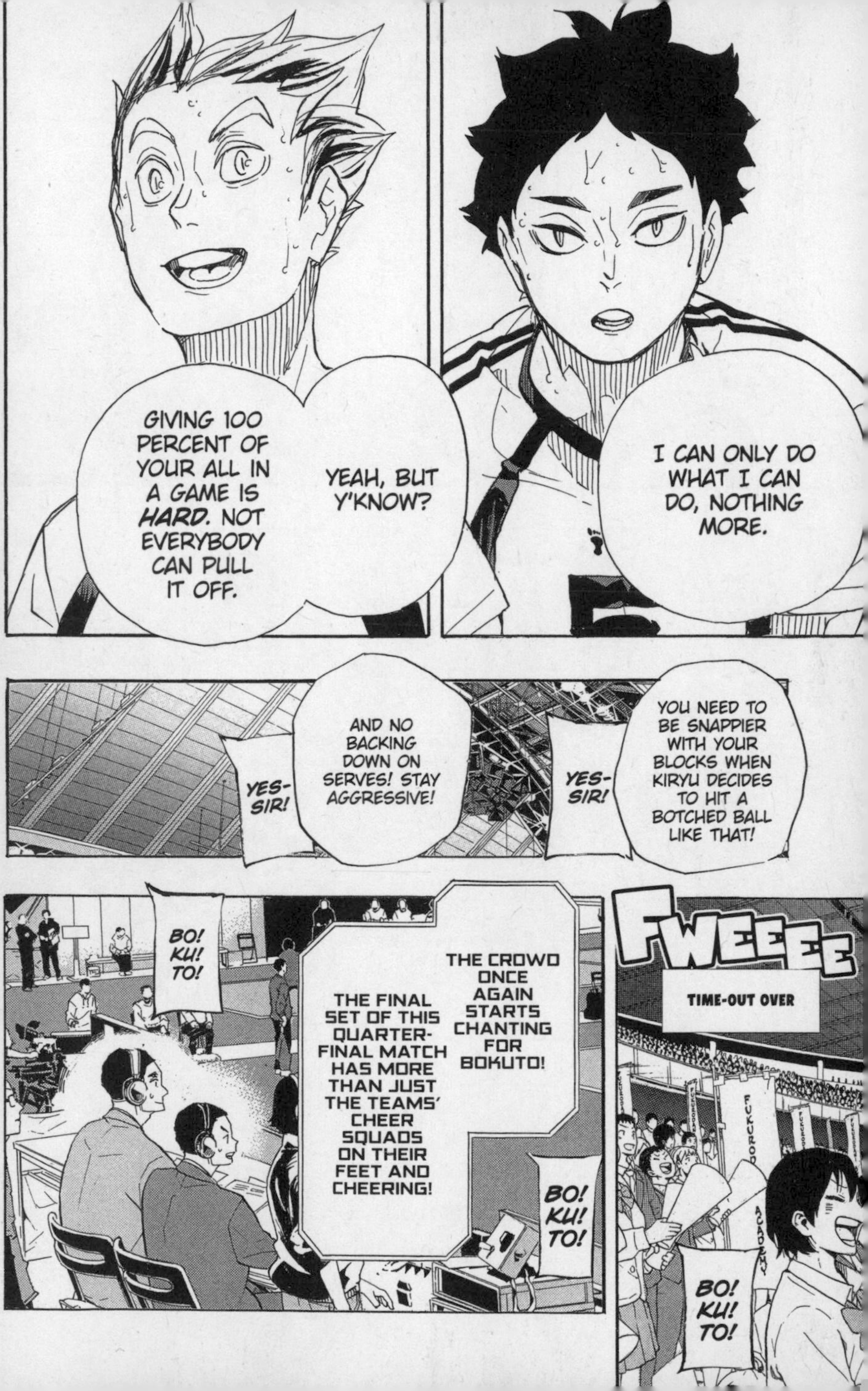
I CAN ONLY DO WHAT I CAN DO, NOTHING MORE.
YEAH, BUT Y'KNOW?
GIVING 100 PERCENT OF YOUR ALL IN A GAME IS *HARD*. NOT EVERYBODY CAN PULL IT OFF.
YOU NEED TO BE SNAPPIER WITH YOUR BLOCKS WHEN KIRYU DECIDES TO HIT A BOTCHED BALL LIKE THAT!
YES-SIR!
AND NO BACKING DOWN ON SERVES! STAY AGGRESSIVE!
YES-SIR!
FWEEEE
TIME-OUT OVER
BO! KU! TO!
THE CROWD ONCE AGAIN STARTS CHANTING FOR BOKUTO!
THE FINAL SET OF THIS QUARTER-FINAL MATCH HAS MORE THAN JUST THE TEAMS' CHEER SQUADS ON THEIR FEET AND CHEERING!
BO! KU! TO!
BO! KU! TO!

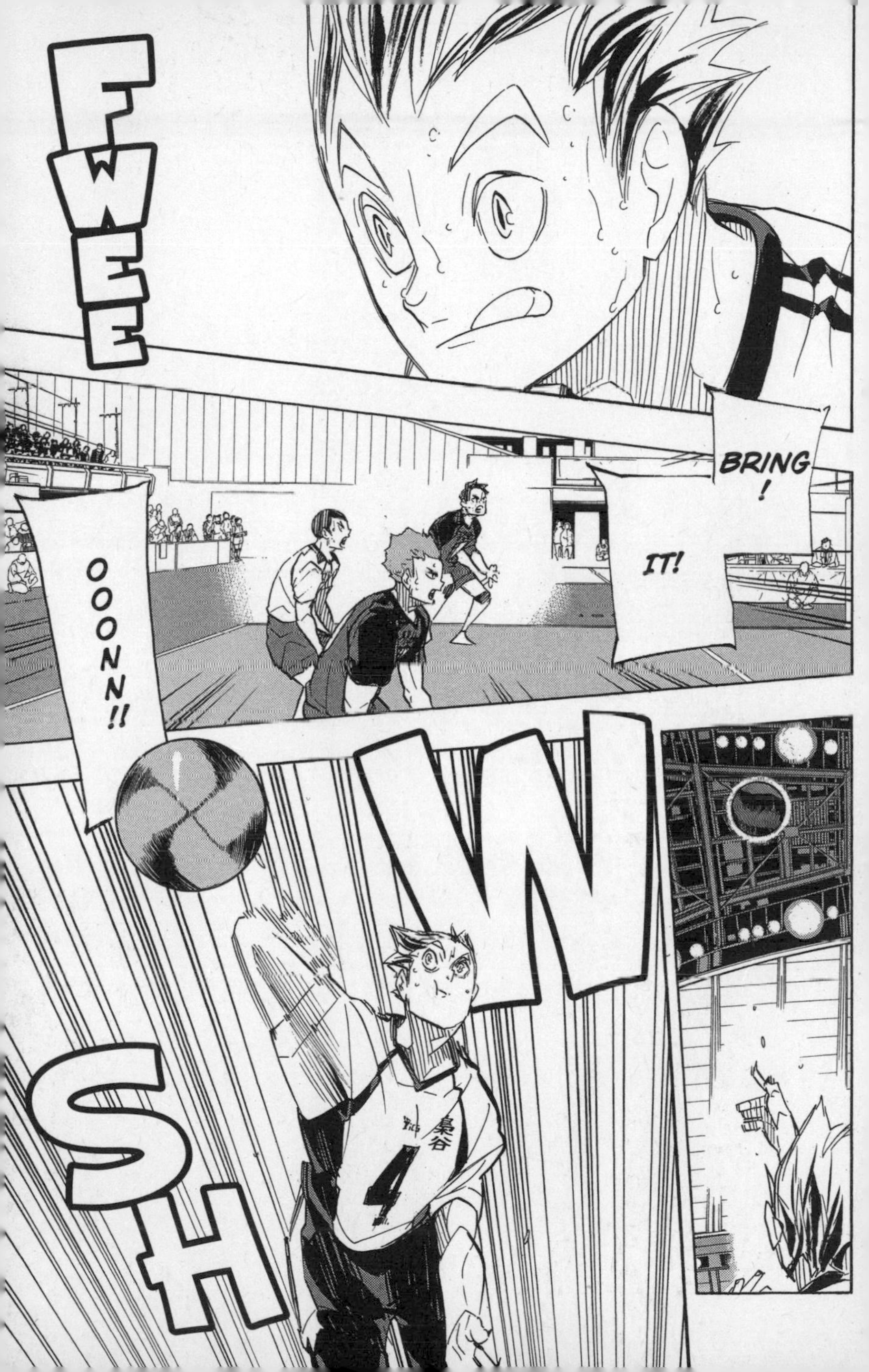
FWEE
BRING
!
IT!
OOOONN!!
WSH
梟谷
4

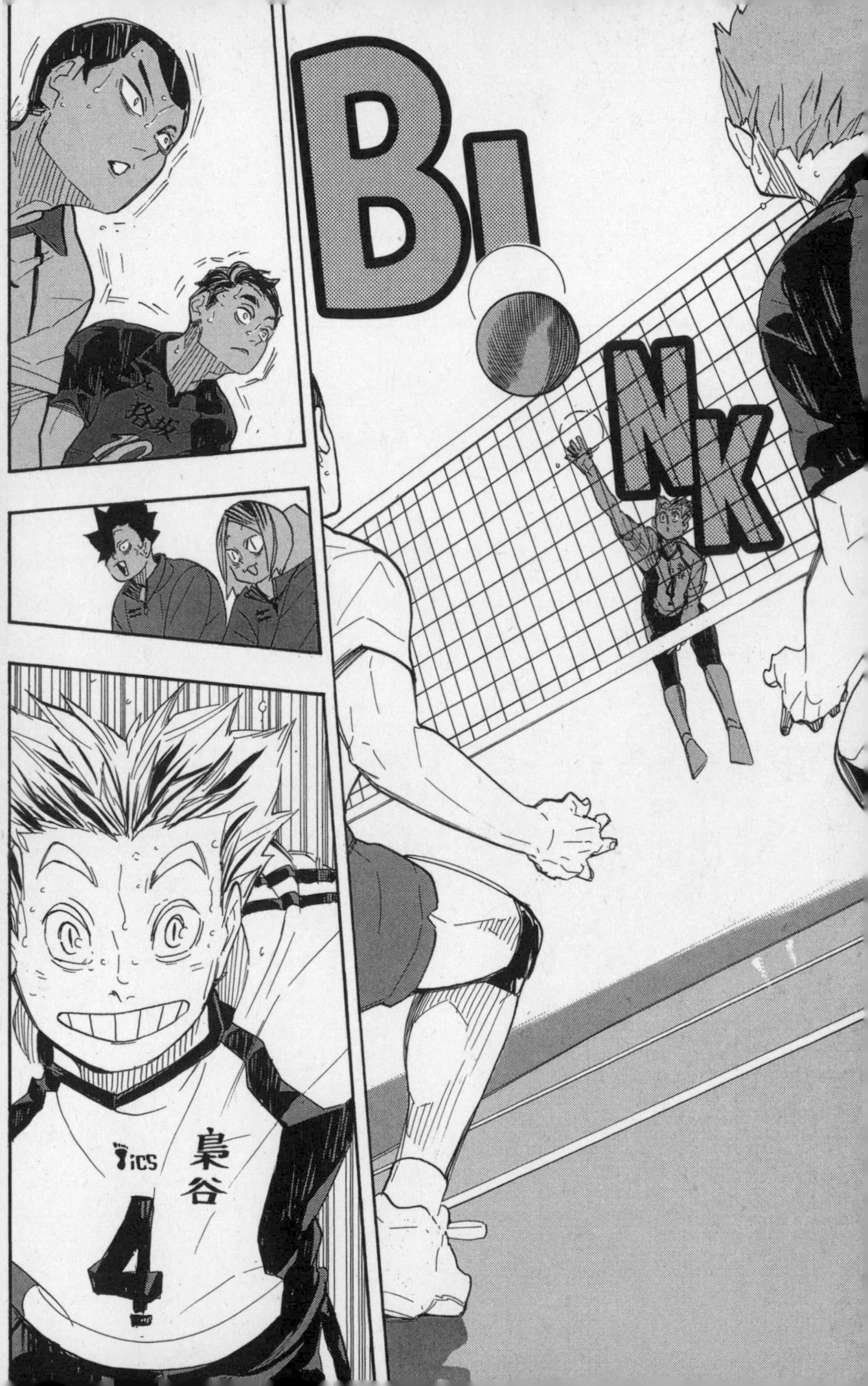

B!
NK
梟谷
4

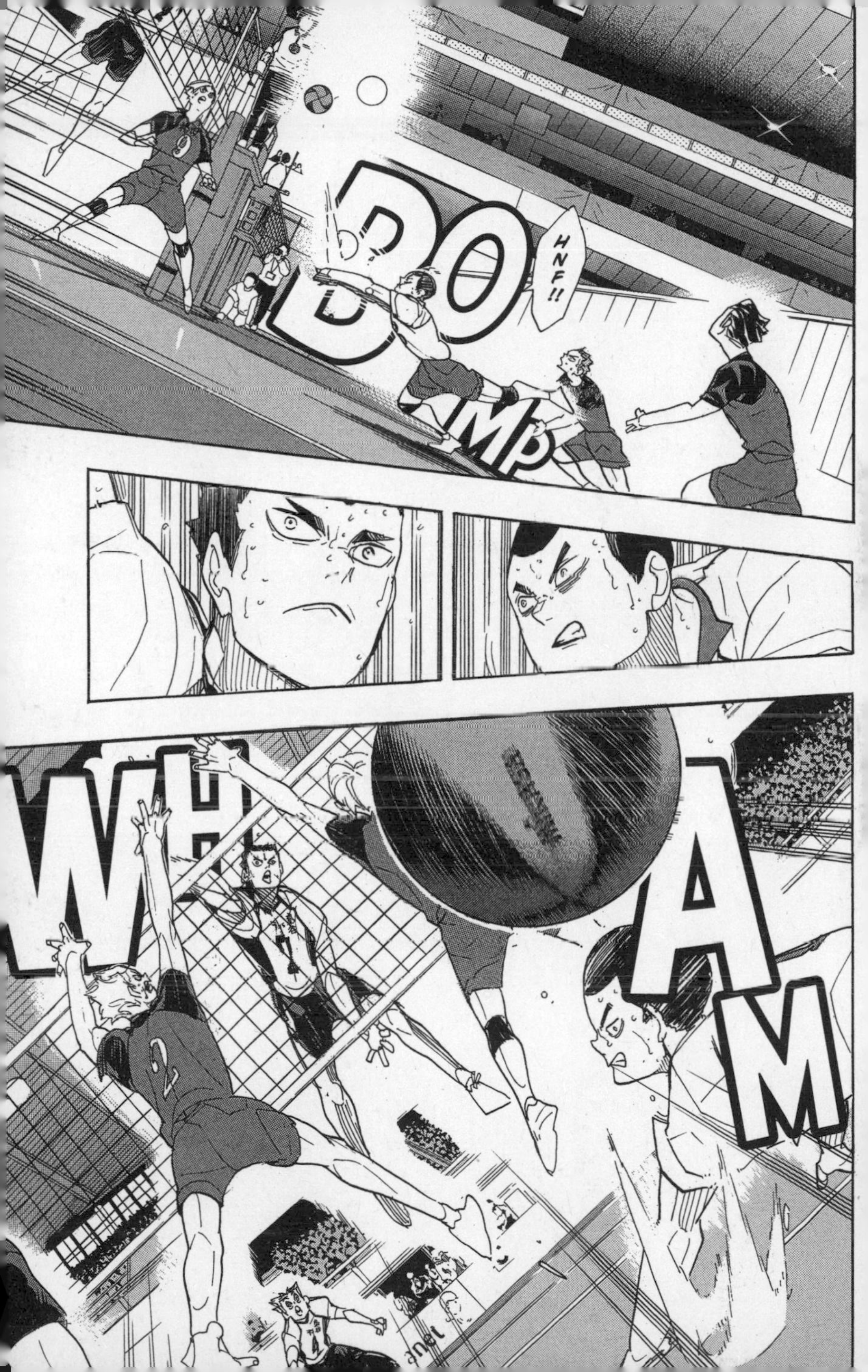
HNF!!
DOMP
WHAM

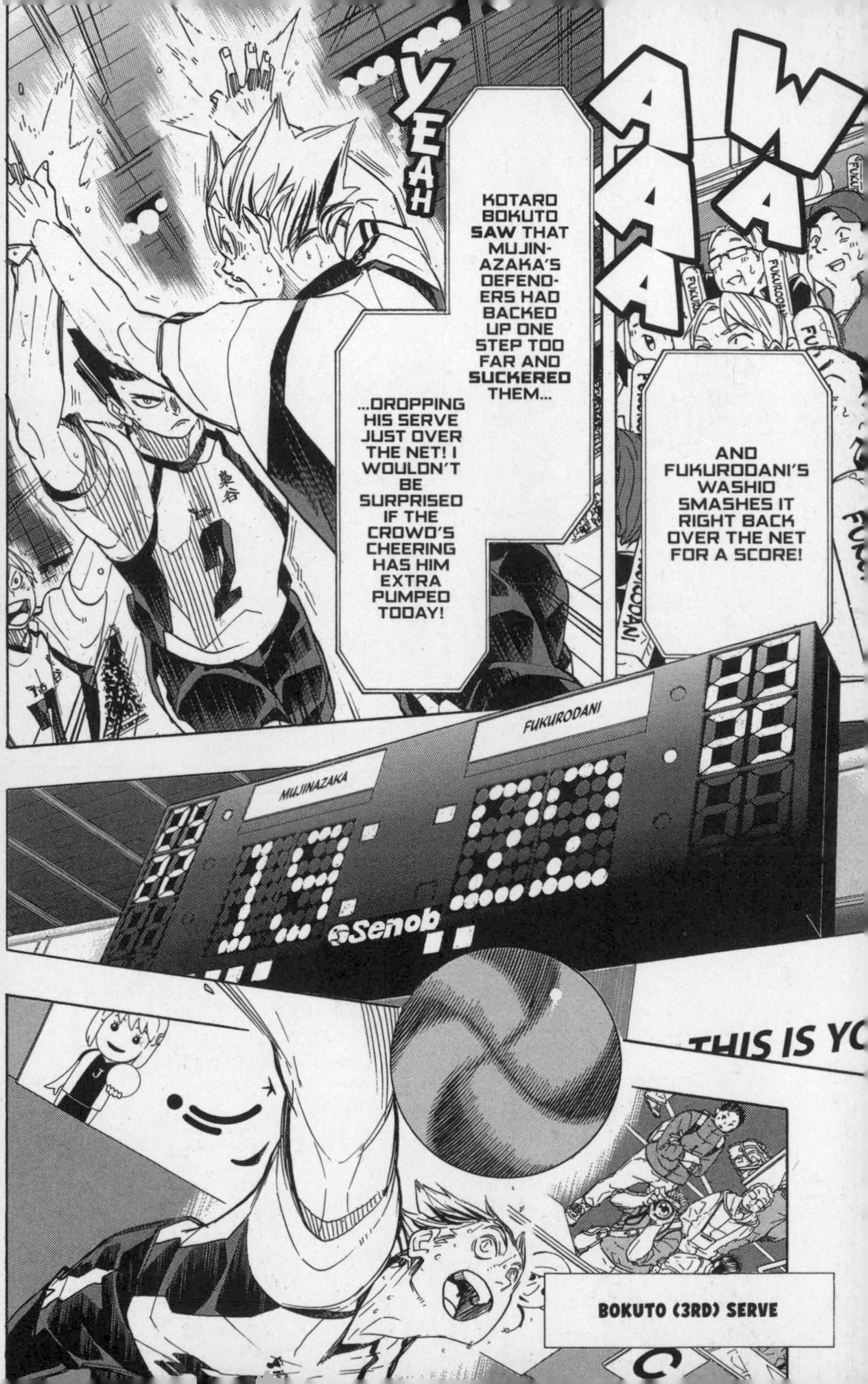
WAAAA
AND FUKURODANI'S WASHIO SMASHES IT RIGHT BACK OVER THE NET FOR A SCORE!
KOTARO BOKUTO SAW THAT MUJIN-AZAKA'S DEFENDERS HAD BACKED UP ONE STEP TOO FAR AND SUCKERED THEM...
...DROPPING HIS SERVE JUST OVER THE NET! I WOULDN'T BE SURPRISED IF THE CROWD'S CHEERING HAS HIM EXTRA PUMPED TODAY!
YEAH
FUKURODANI
MUJINAZAKA
19
22
Senob
THIS IS Y
BOKUTO (3RD) SERVE

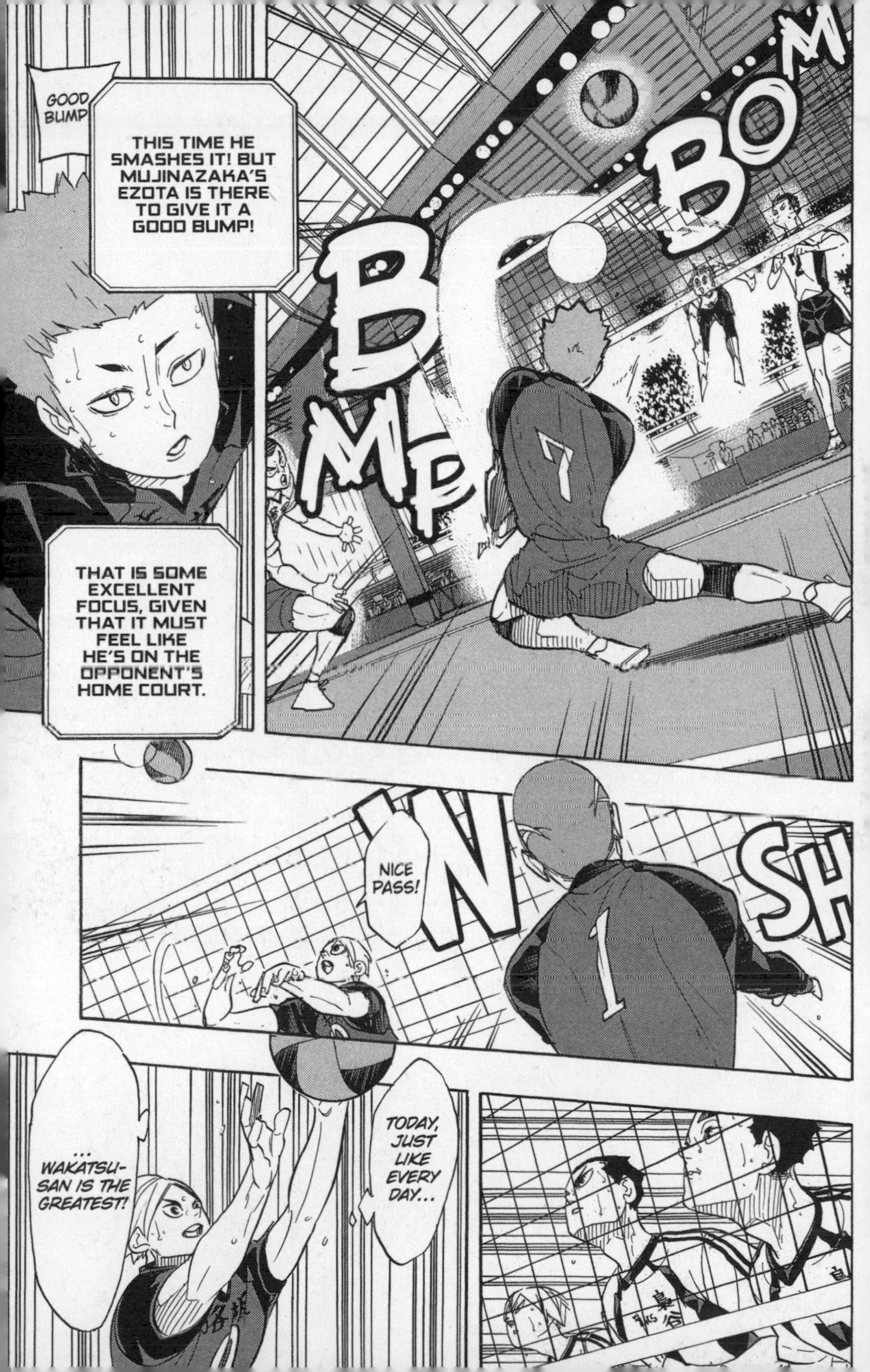
THIS TIME HE SMASHES IT! BUT MUJINAZAKA'S EZOTA IS THERE TO GIVE IT A GOOD BUMP!
GOOD BUMP
THAT IS SOME EXCELLENT FOCUS, GIVEN THAT IT MUST FEEL LIKE HE'S ON THE OPPONENT'S HOME COURT.
NICE PASS!
TODAY, JUST LIKE EVERY DAY...
...WAKATSU-SAN IS THE GREATEST!

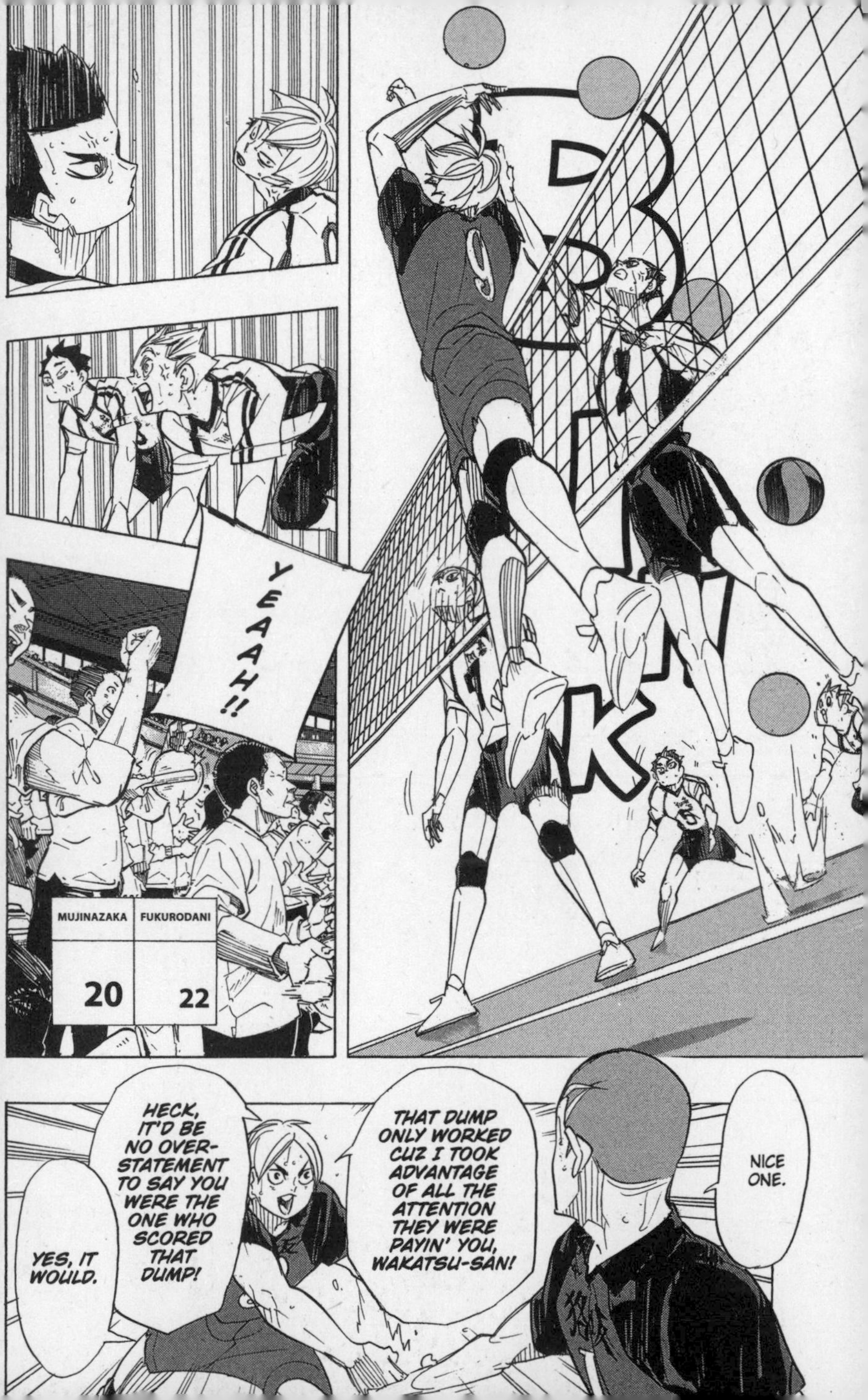
YEAAAH!!
MUJINAZAKA
20
FUKURODANI
22
NICE ONE.
THAT DUMP ONLY WORKED CUZ I TOOK ADVANTAGE OF ALL THE ATTENTION THEY WERE PAYIN' YOU, WAKATSU-SAN!
HECK, IT'D BE NO OVER-STATEMENT TO SAY YOU WERE THE ONE WHO SCORED THAT DUMP!
YES, IT WOULD.

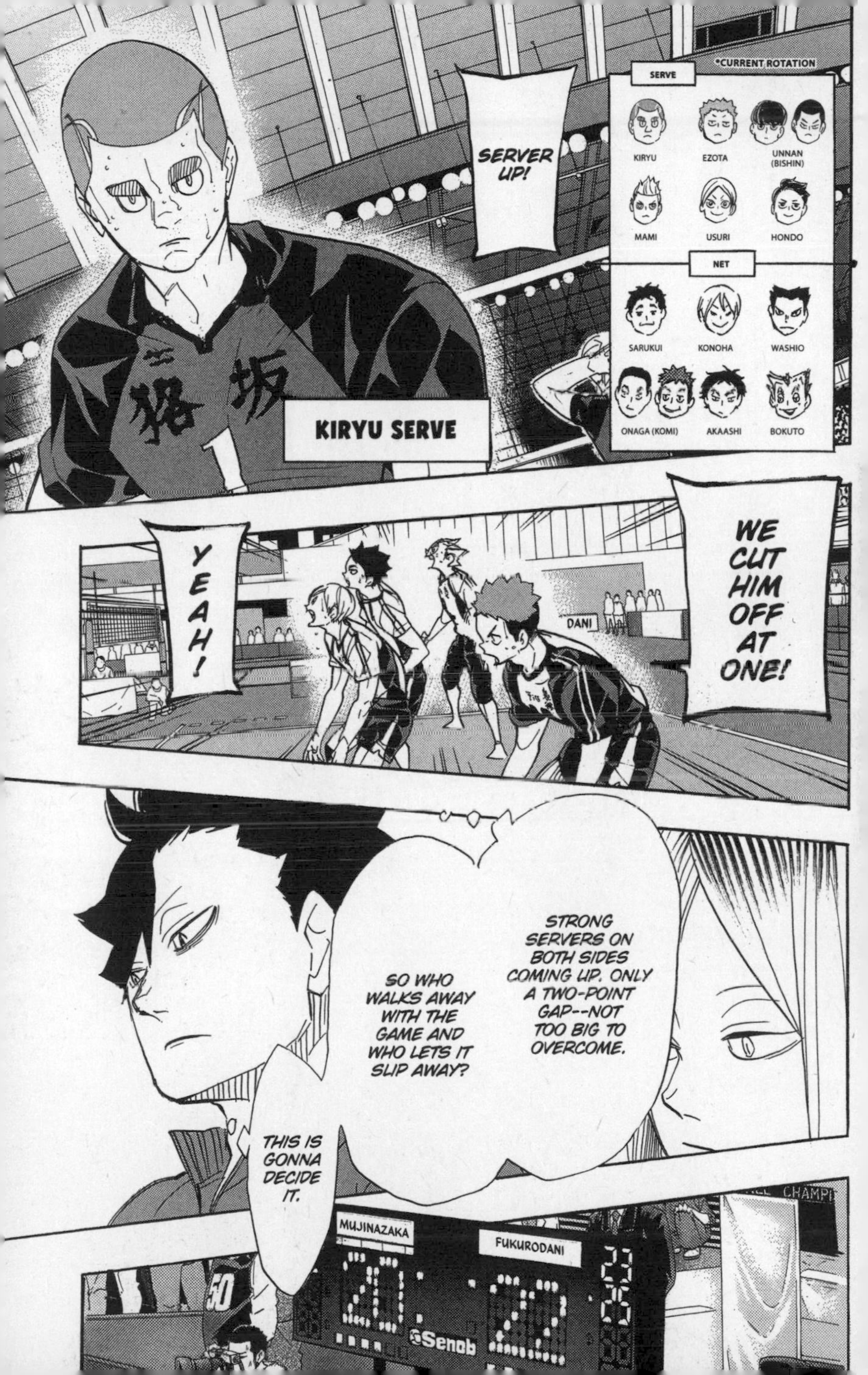
*CURRENT ROTATION
SERVE
KIRYU
EZOTA
UNNAN (BISHIN)
MAMI
USURI
HONDO
NET
SARUKUI
KONOHA
WASHIO
ONAGA (KOMI)
AKAASHI
BOKUTO
SERVER UP!
KIRYU SERVE
WE CUT HIM OFF AT ONE!
DANI
YEAH!
STRONG SERVERS ON BOTH SIDES COMING UP. ONLY A TWO-POINT GAP--NOT TOO BIG TO OVERCOME.
SO WHO WALKS AWAY WITH THE GAME AND WHO LETS IT SLIP AWAY?
THIS IS GONNA DECIDE IT.
MUJINAZAKA
FUKURODANI

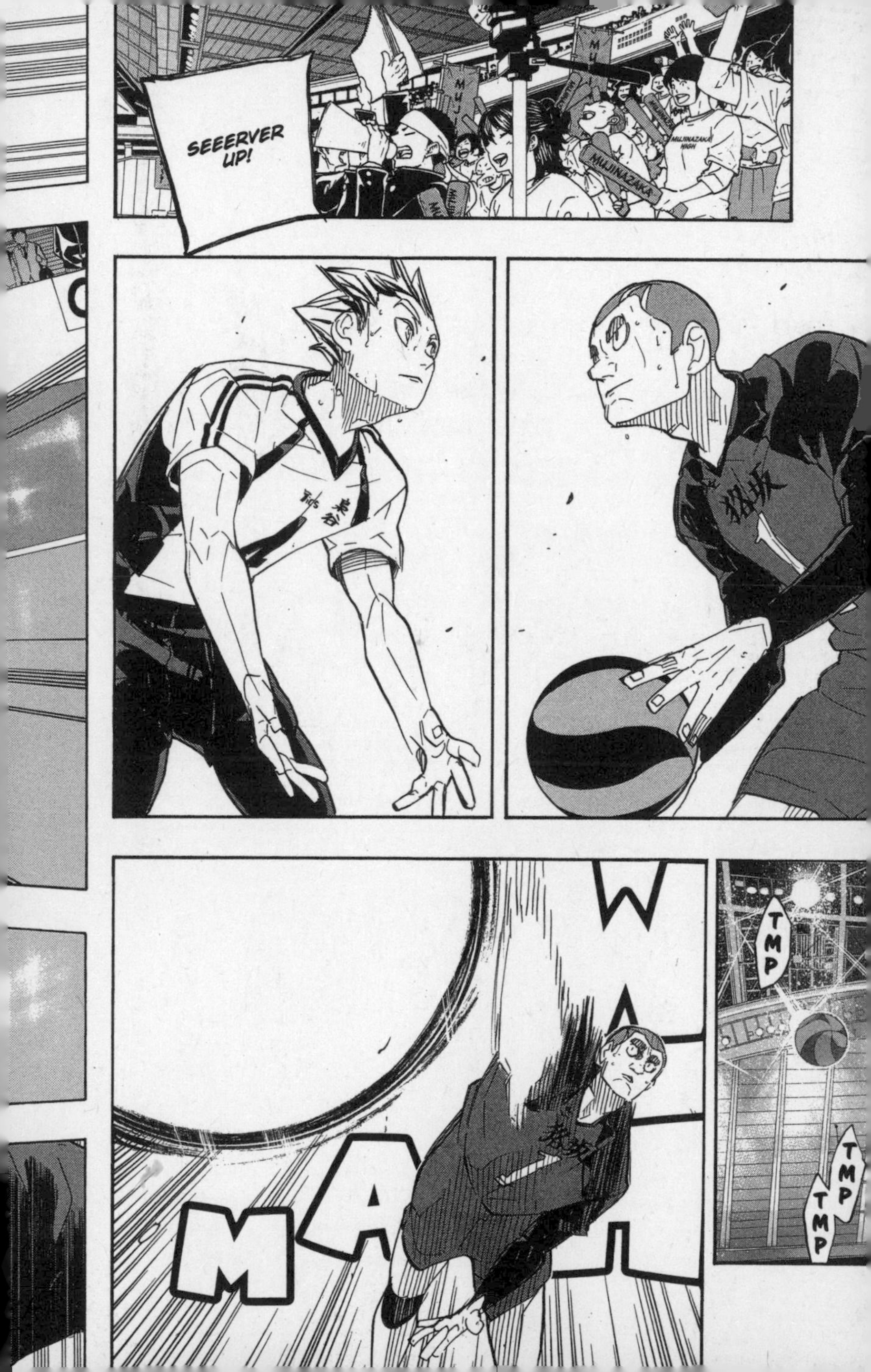
MUJINAZAKA HIGH
MUJINAZAKA
SEEERVER UP!
TMP
TMP
TMP
TMP

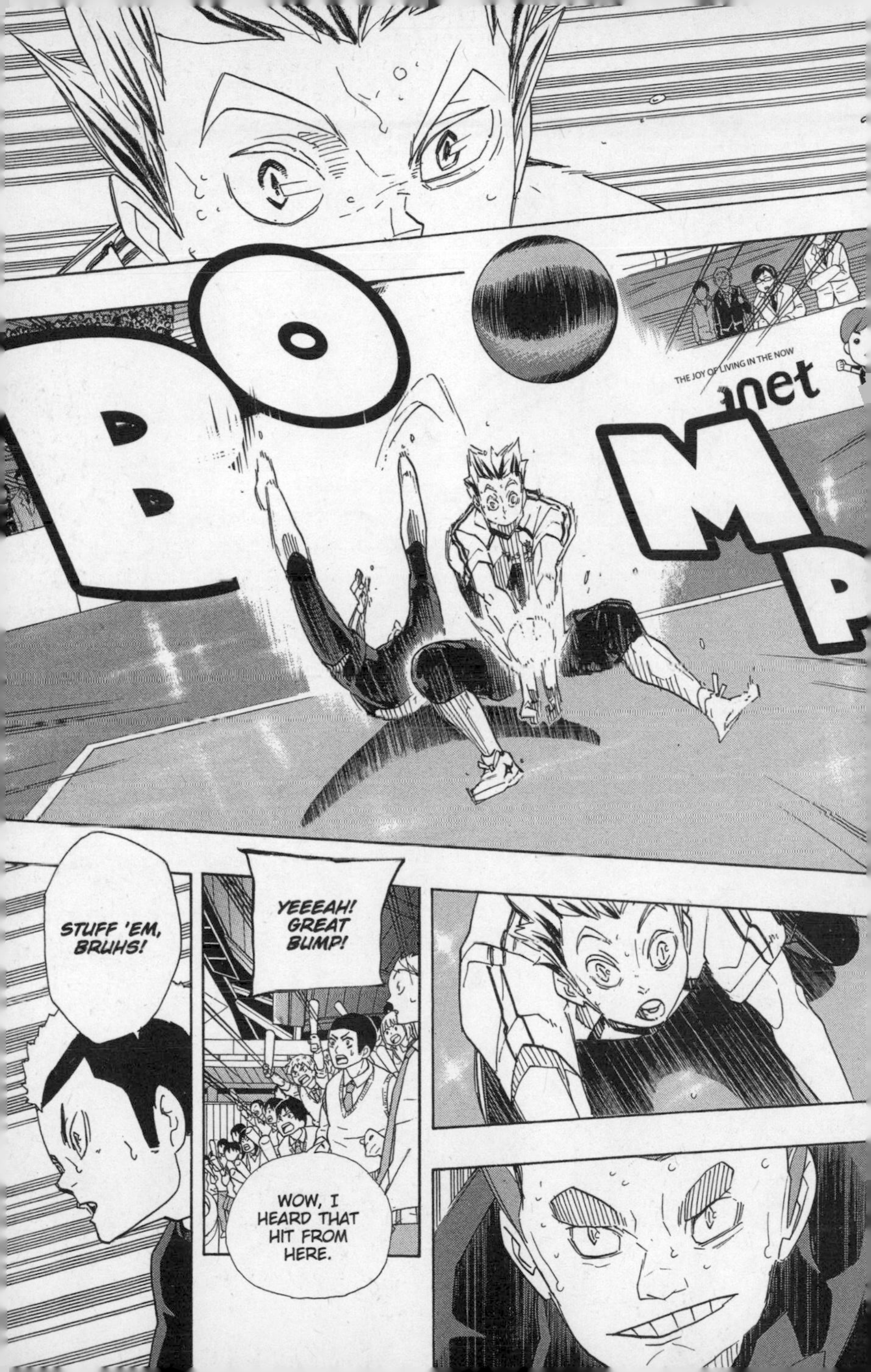
THE JOY OF LIVING IN THE NOW
YEEEAH! GREAT BUMP!
WOW, I HEARD THAT HIT FROM HERE.
STUFF 'EM, BRUHS!

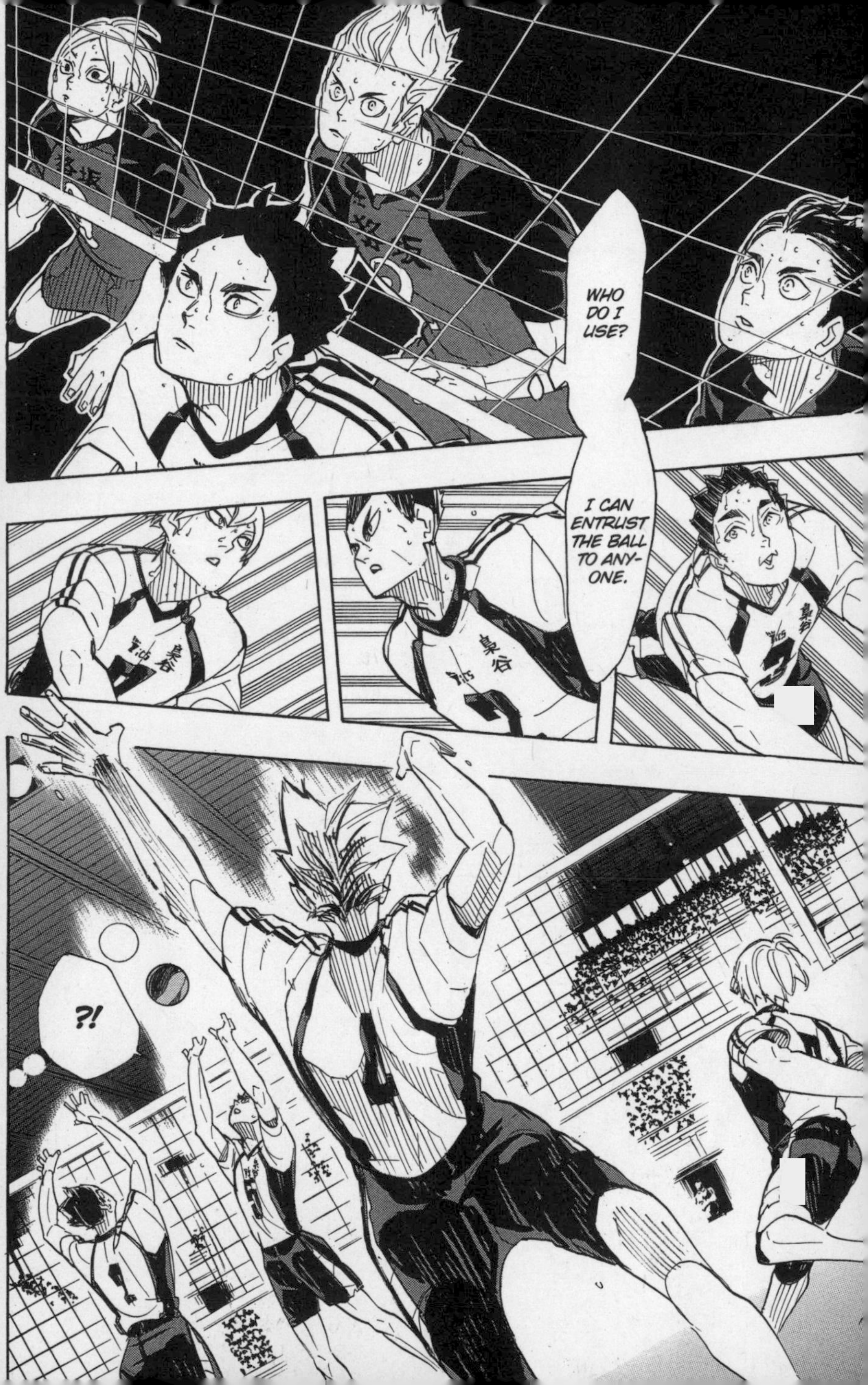
WHO DO I USE?
I CAN ENTRUST THE BALL TO ANYONE.
?!

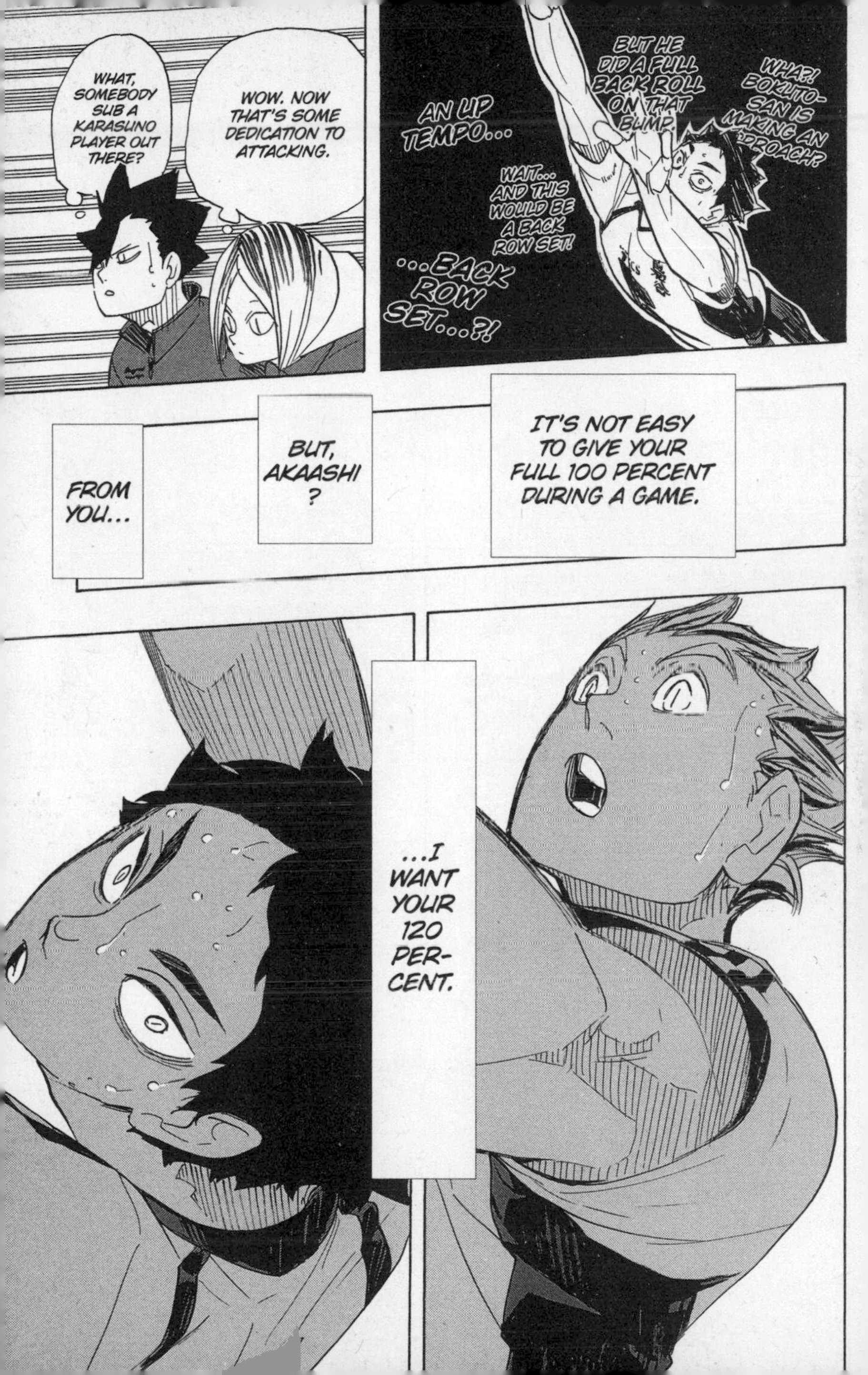
WHA?! BOKUTO-SAN IS MAKING AN APPROACH?
BUT HE DID A FULL BACK ROLL ON THAT BUMP.
AN UP TEMPO...
WAIT... AND THIS WOULD BE A BACK ROW SET!
...BACK ROW SET...?!
WOW. NOW THAT'S SOME DEDICATION TO ATTACKING.
WHAT, SOMEBODY SUB A KARASUNO PLAYER OUT THERE?
IT'S NOT EASY TO GIVE YOUR FULL 100 PERCENT DURING A GAME.
BUT, AKAASHI?
FROM YOU...
...I WANT YOUR 120 PER-CENT.

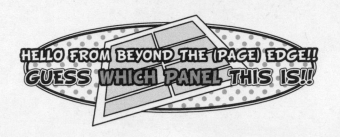

HELLO FROM BEYOND THE (PAGE) EDGE!!
GUESS WHICH PANEL THIS IS!!

FROM CHAPTER 336

THERE WERE SO MANY PUPPIES THIS WEEK.

CHAPTER 337: Next

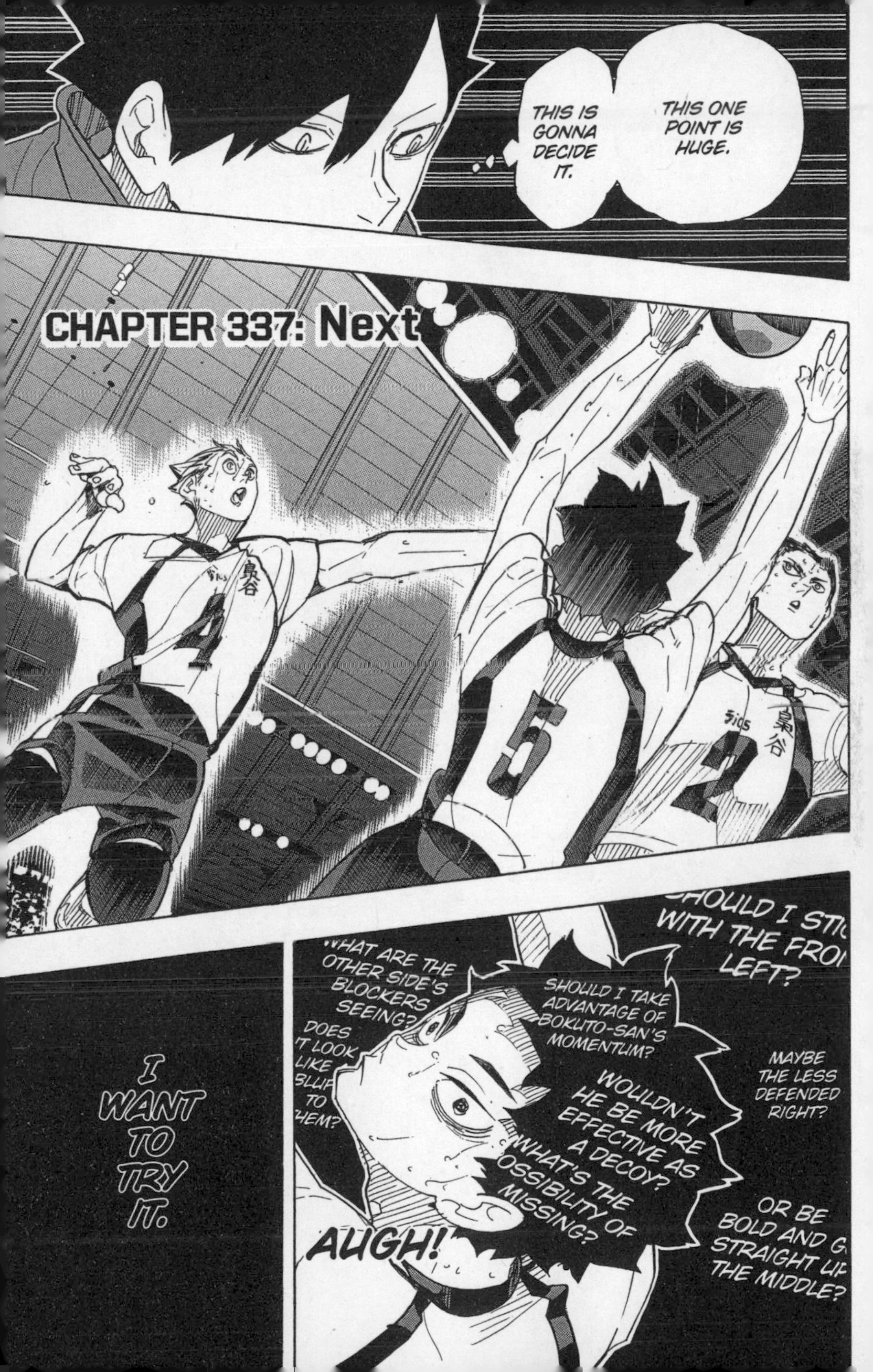
THIS ONE POINT IS HUGE.
THIS IS GONNA DECIDE IT.
SHOULD I STIC WITH THE FRON LEFT?
MAYBE THE LESS DEFENDED RIGHT?
OR BE BOLD AND G STRAIGHT UP THE MIDDLE?
SHOULD I TAKE ADVANTAGE OF BOKUTO-SAN'S MOMENTUM?
WOULDN'T HE BE MORE EFFECTIVE AS A DECOY?
WHAT ARE THE OTHER SIDE'S BLOCKERS SEEING?
DOES IT LOOK LIKE BLUF TO HEM?
WHAT'S THE OSSIBILITY OF MISSING?
AUGH!
I WANT TO TRY IT.

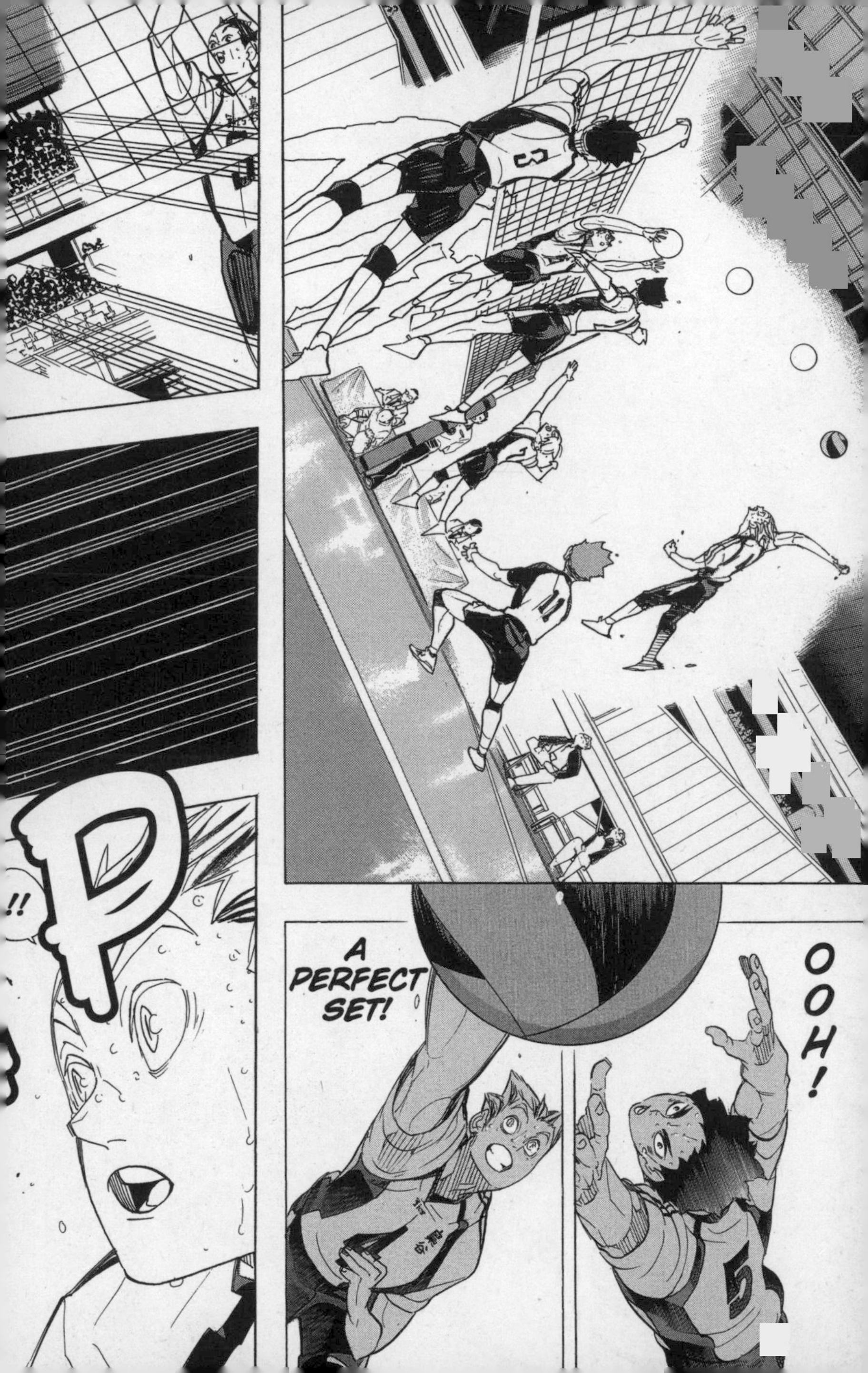
OOH!
A PERFECT SET!
P
!!

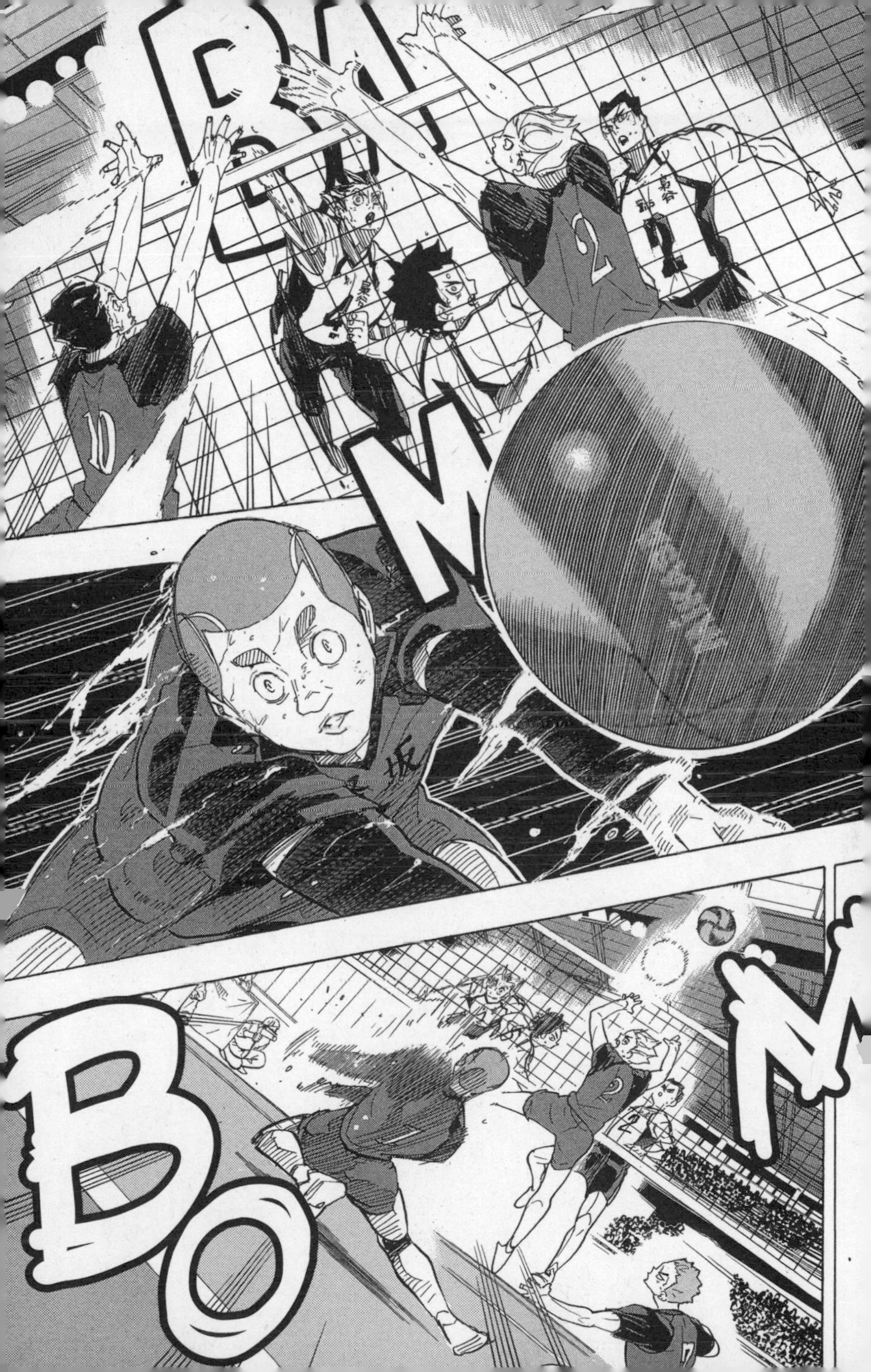
BAM
BOM

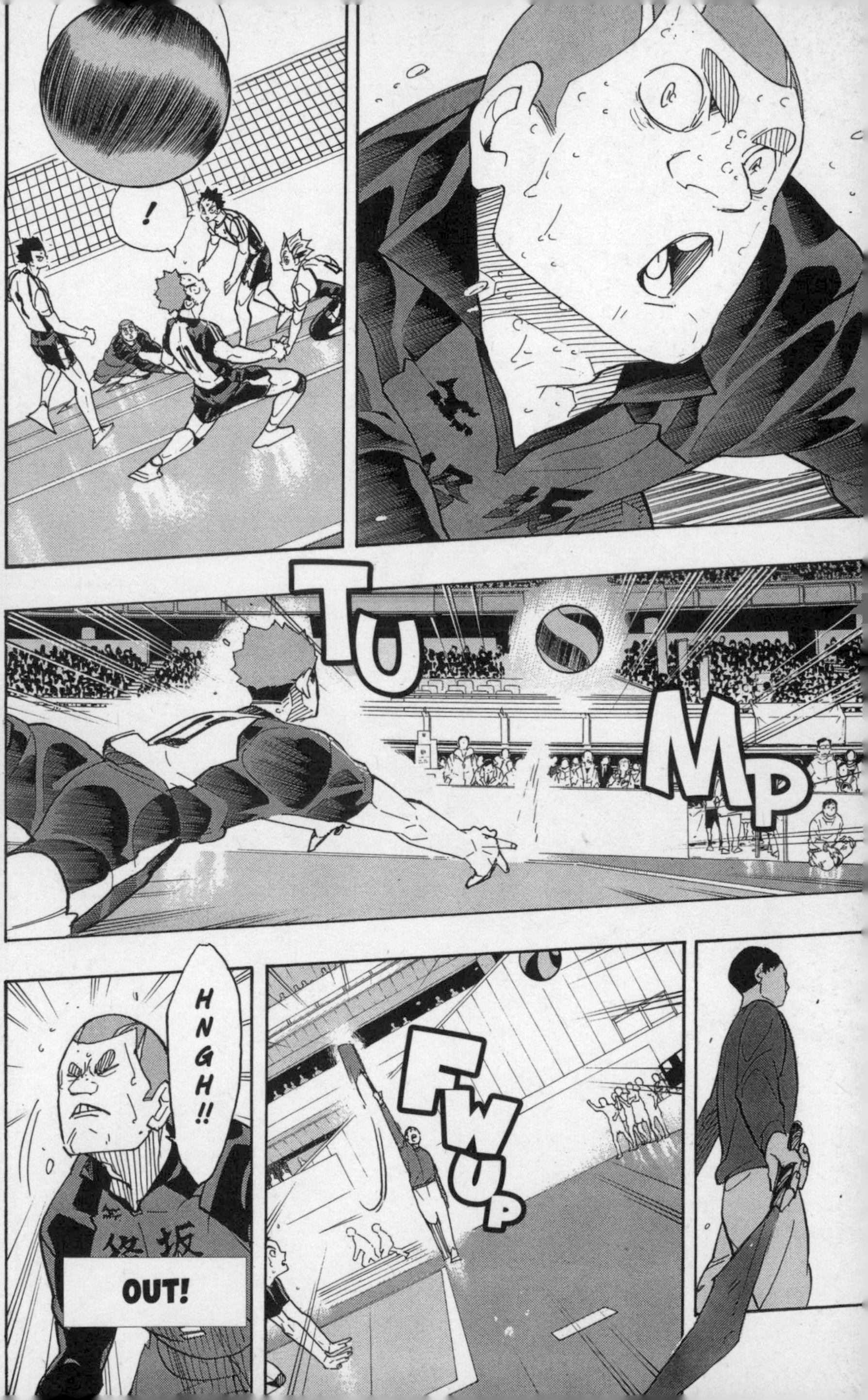
!
TU
MP
FWUP
HNGH!!
OUT!

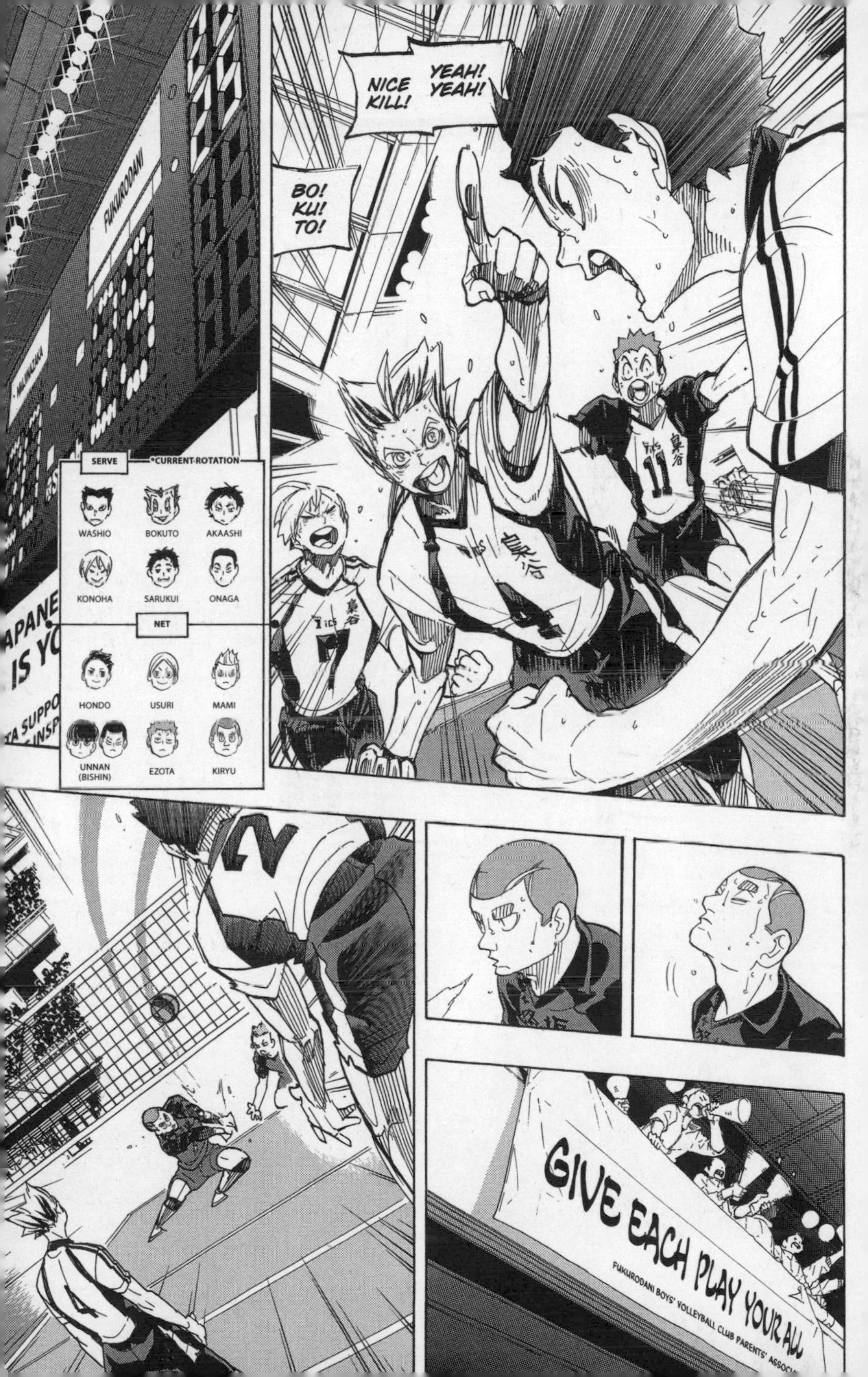
YEAH! YEAH!
NICE KILL!
BO! KU! TO!
FUKURODANI
SERVE
*CURRENT ROTATION
WASHIO
BOKUTO
AKAASHI
KONOHA
SARUKUI
ONAGA
NET
HONDO
USURI
MAMI
UNNAN (BISHIN)
EZOTA
KIRYU
GIVE EACH PLAY YOUR ALL
FUKURODANI BOYS' VOLLEYBALL CLUB PARENTS'

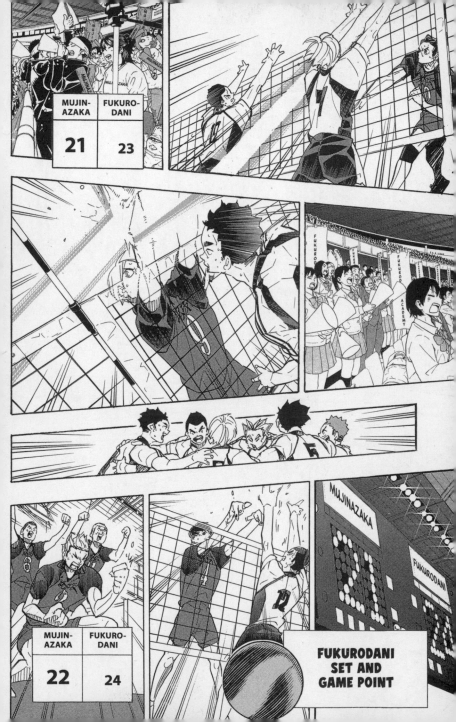

MUJIN-AZAKA	FUKURO-DANI
21	23

MUJIN-AZAKA	FUKURO-DANI
22	24

FUKURODANI SET AND GAME POINT

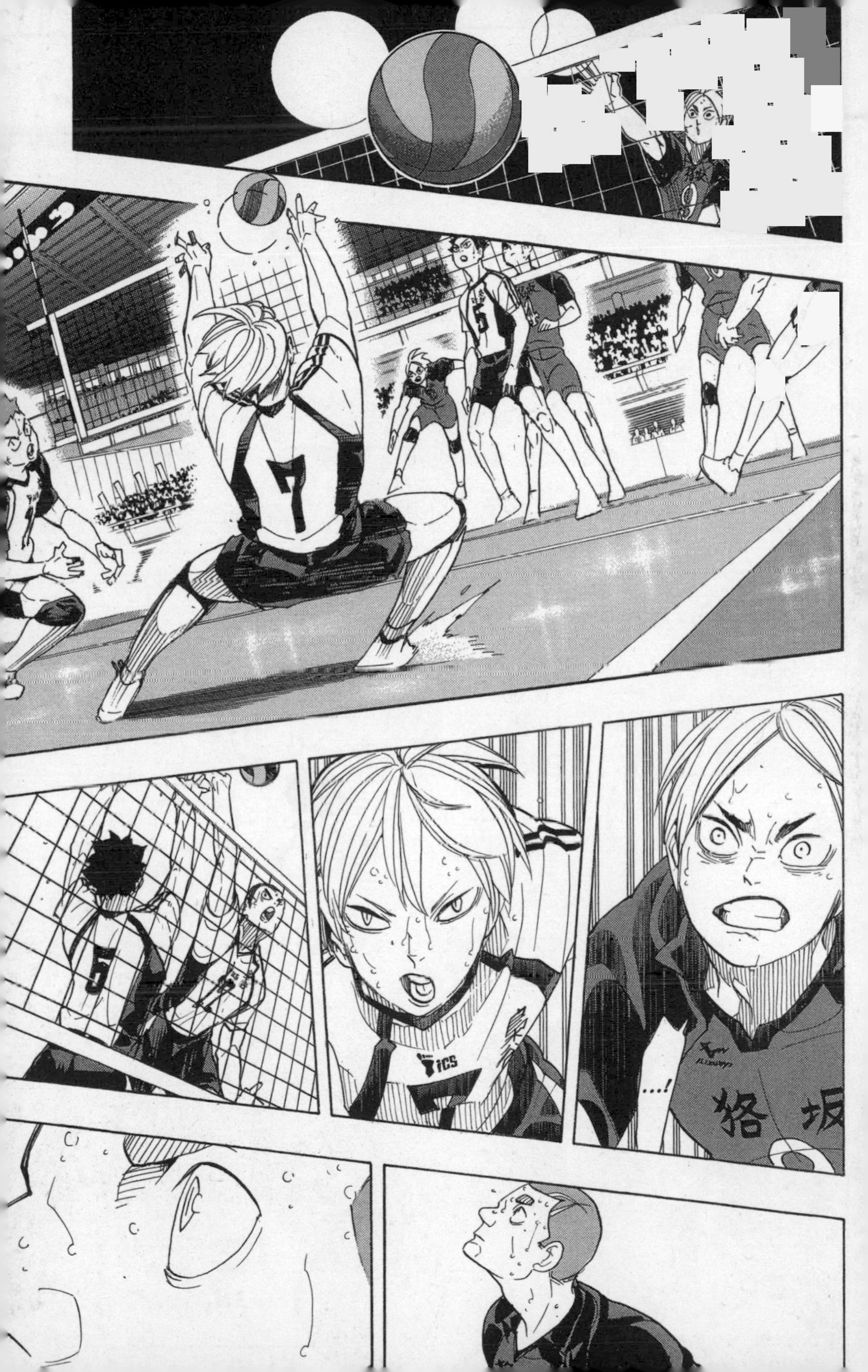
...!
狢坂

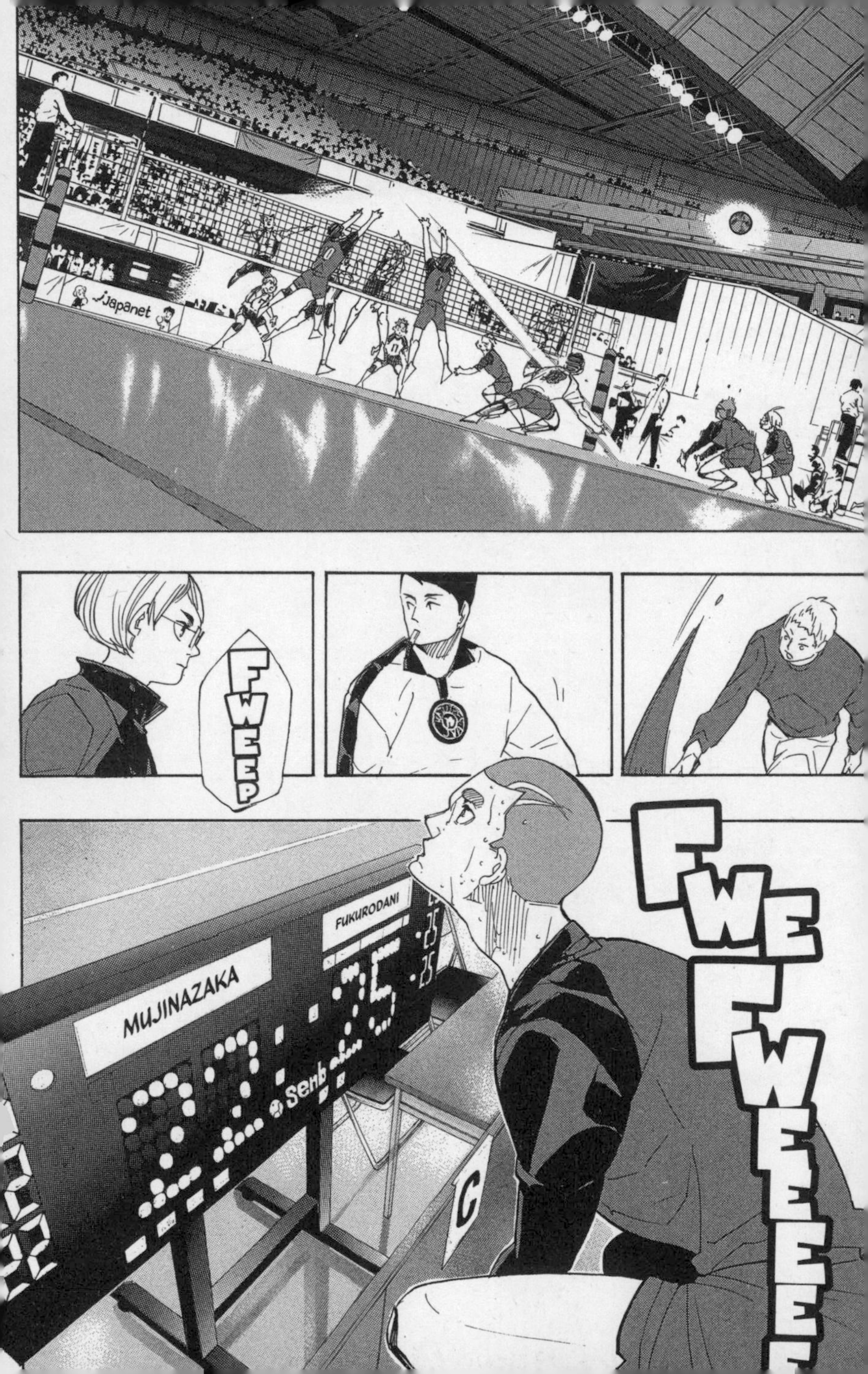
Japanet
FWEEP
FUKURODANI
MUJINAZAKA
FWE-FWEEEEE

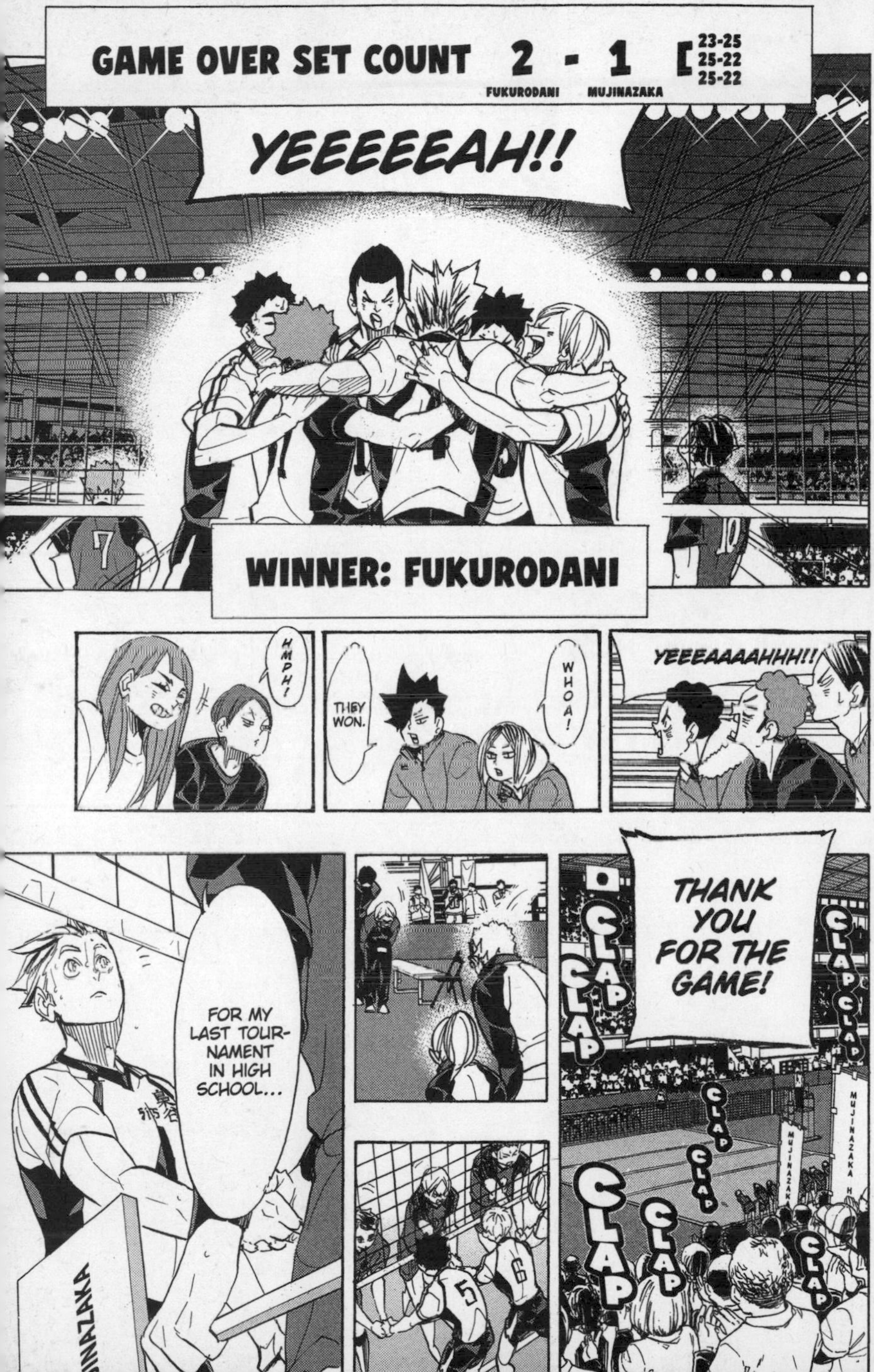
GAME OVER SET COUNT 2 - 1 [23-25 25-22 25-22
FUKURODANI MUJINAZAKA
YEEEEEEAH!!
WINNER: FUKURODANI
YEEEAAAAHHH!!
WHOA!
THEY WON.
HMPH!
THANK YOU FOR THE GAME!
CLAP
CLAP
CLAP
CLAP
CLAP
CLAP
CLAP
CLAP
CLAP
CLAP
MUJINAZAKA
MUJINAZAKA
FOR MY LAST TOURNAMENT IN HIGH SCHOOL...
MUJINAZAKA

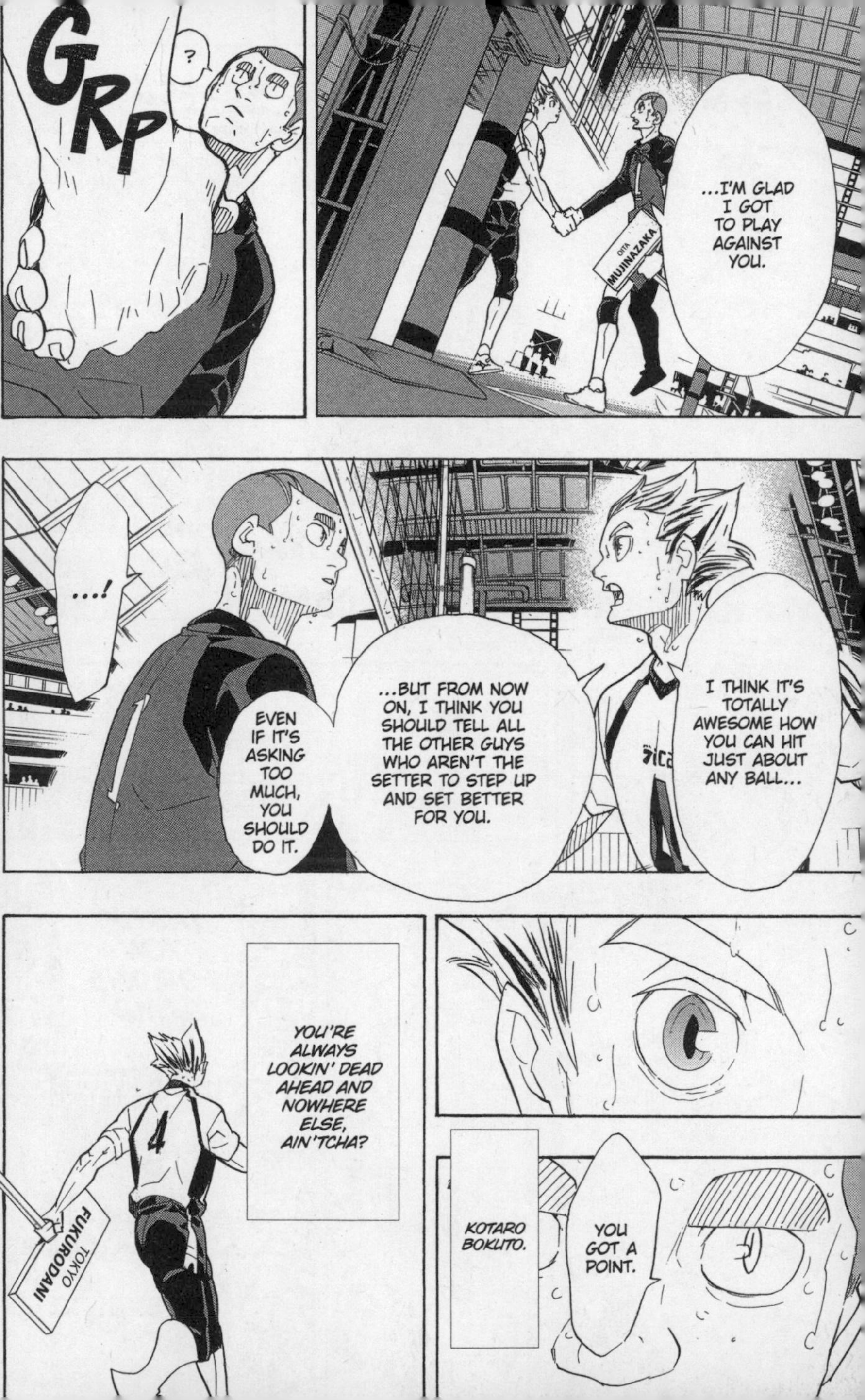
...I'M GLAD I GOT TO PLAY AGAINST YOU.
OITA MUJINAZAKA
?
GRP
I THINK IT'S TOTALLY AWESOME HOW YOU CAN HIT JUST ABOUT ANY BALL...
...BUT FROM NOW ON, I THINK YOU SHOULD TELL ALL THE OTHER GUYS WHO AREN'T THE SETTER TO STEP UP AND SET BETTER FOR YOU.
EVEN IF IT'S ASKING TOO MUCH, YOU SHOULD DO IT.
...!
YOU GOT A POINT.
KOTARO BOKUTO.
YOU'RE ALWAYS LOOKIN' DEAD AHEAD AND NOWHERE ELSE, AIN'TCHA?
TOKYO FUKURODANI

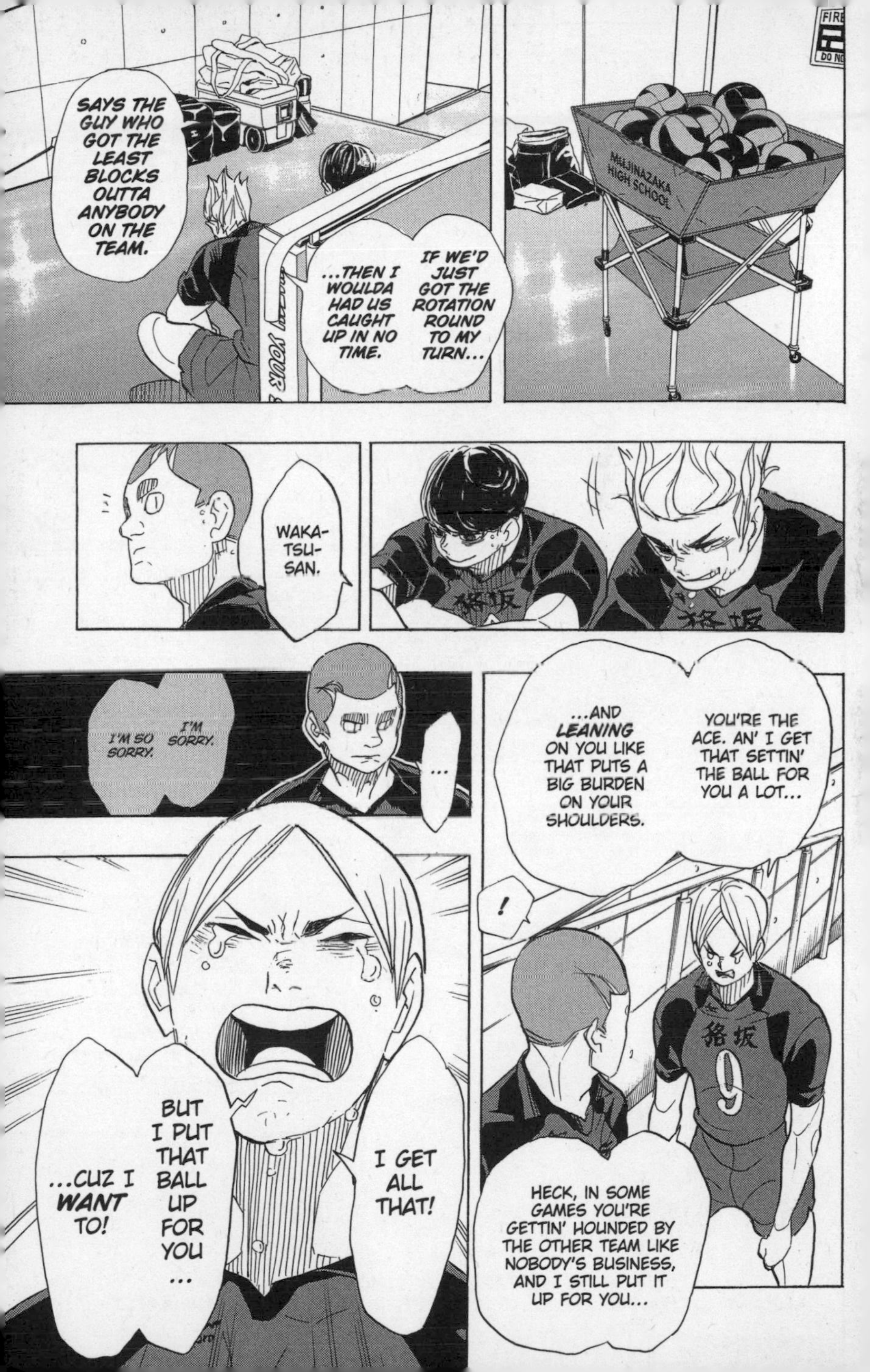
MUJINAZAKA HIGH SCHOOL
IF WE'D JUST GOT THE ROTATION ROUND TO MY TURN...
...THEN I WOULDA HAD US CAUGHT UP IN NO TIME.
SAYS THE GUY WHO GOT THE LEAST BLOCKS OUTTA ANYBODY ON THE TEAM.
WAKATSU-SAN.
YOU'RE THE ACE. AN' I GET THAT SETTIN' THE BALL FOR YOU A LOT...
...AND LEANING ON YOU LIKE THAT PUTS A BIG BURDEN ON YOUR SHOULDERS.
!
HECK, IN SOME GAMES YOU'RE GETTIN' HOUNDED BY THE OTHER TEAM LIKE NOBODY'S BUSINESS, AND I STILL PUT IT UP FOR YOU...
...
I'M SORRY.
I'M SO SORRY.
I GET ALL THAT!
BUT I PUT THAT BALL UP FOR YOU...
...CUZ I WANT TO!

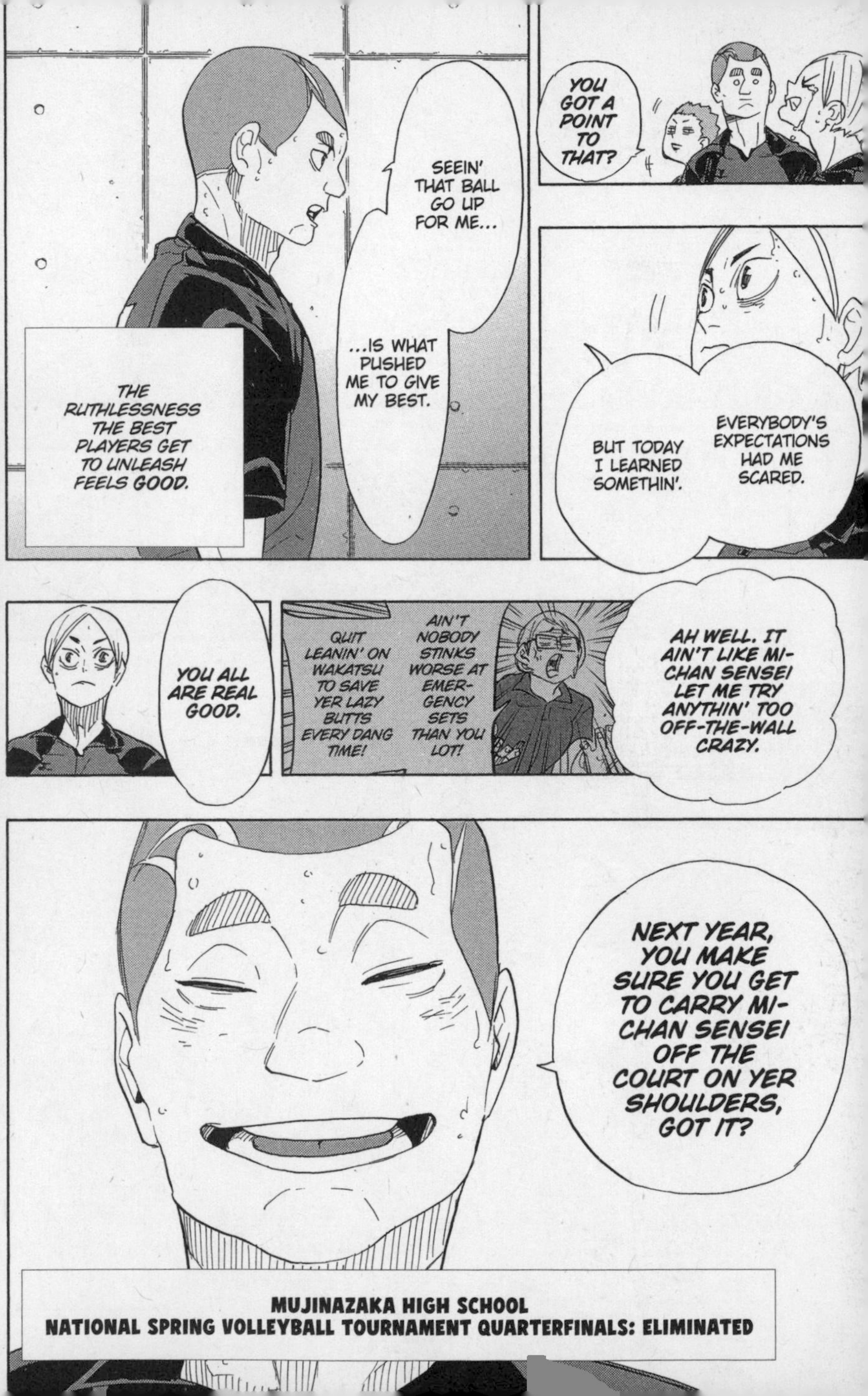
YOU GOT A POINT TO THAT?
EVERYBODY'S EXPECTATIONS HAD ME SCARED.
BUT TODAY I LEARNED SOMETHIN'.
SEEIN' THAT BALL GO UP FOR ME...
...IS WHAT PUSHED ME TO GIVE MY BEST.
THE RUTHLESSNESS THE BEST PLAYERS GET TO UNLEASH FEELS GOOD.
AH WELL. IT AIN'T LIKE MI-CHAN SENSEI LET ME TRY ANYTHIN' TOO OFF-THE-WALL CRAZY.
AIN'T NOBODY STINKS WORSE AT EMERGENCY SETS THAN YOU LOT!
QUIT LEANIN' ON WAKATSU TO SAVE YER LAZY BUTTS EVERY DANG TIME!
YOU ALL ARE REAL GOOD.
NEXT YEAR, YOU MAKE SURE YOU GET TO CARRY MI-CHAN SENSEI OFF THE COURT ON YER SHOULDERS, GOT IT?
MUJINAZAKA HIGH SCHOOL
NATIONAL SPRING VOLLEYBALL TOURNAMENT QUARTERFINALS: ELIMINATED

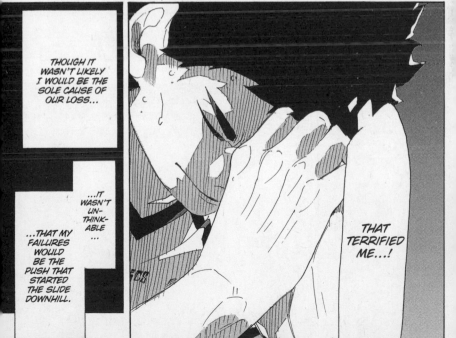

THOUGH IT WASN'T LIKELY I WOULD BE THE SOLE CAUSE OF OUR LOSS...

...IT WASN'T UN-THINK-ABLE...

...THAT MY FAILURES WOULD BE THE PUSH THAT STARTED THE SLIDE DOWNHILL.

THAT TERRIFIED ME...!

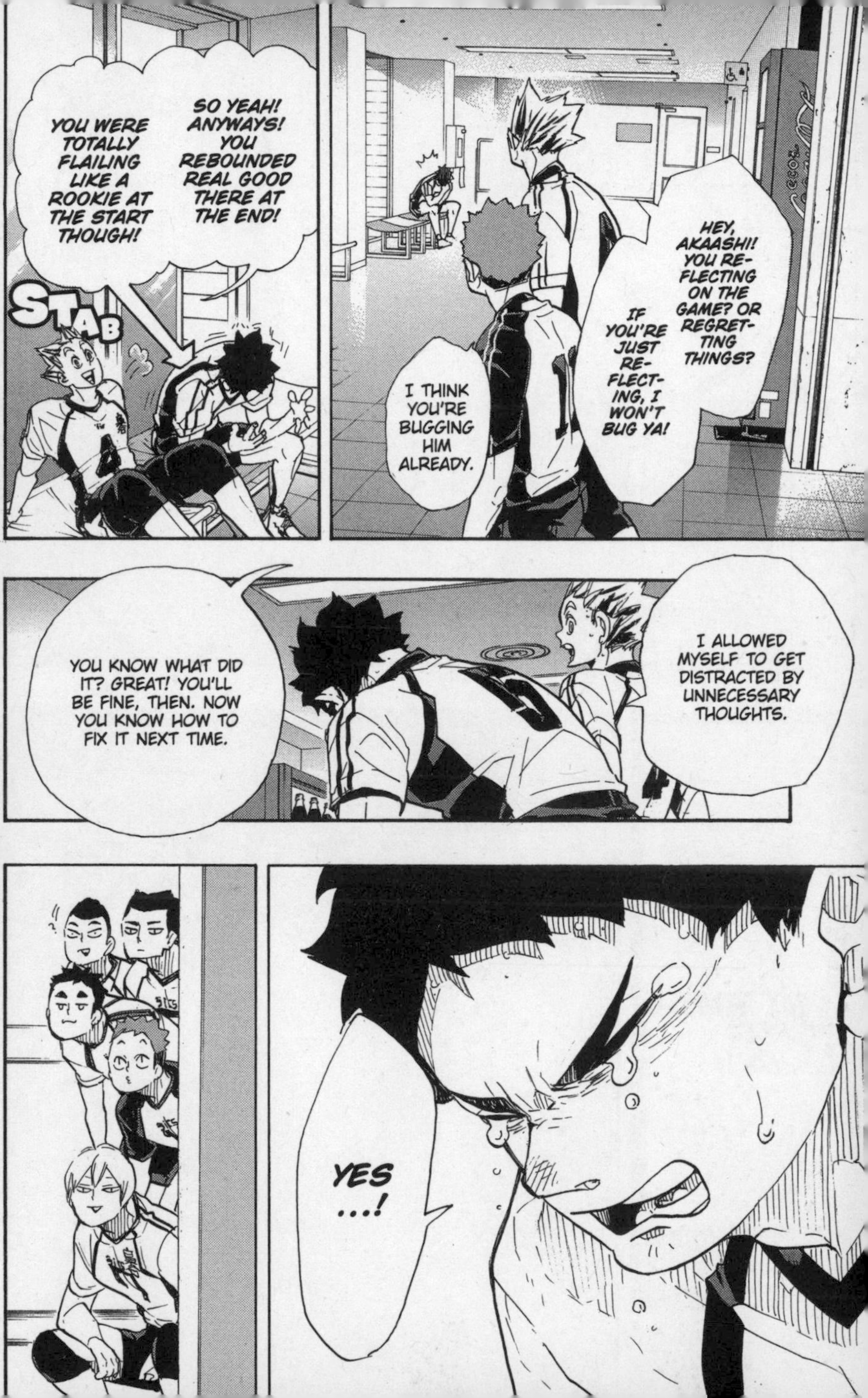
HEY, AKAASHI! YOU RE-FLECTING ON THE GAME? OR REGRET-TING THINGS?
IF YOU'RE JUST RE-FLECT-ING, I WON'T BUG YA!
I THINK YOU'RE BUGGING HIM ALREADY.
SO YEAH! ANYWAYS! YOU REBOUNDED REAL GOOD THERE AT THE END!
YOU WERE TOTALLY FLAILING LIKE A ROOKIE AT THE START THOUGH!
STAB
I ALLOWED MYSELF TO GET DISTRACTED BY UNNECESSARY THOUGHTS.
YOU KNOW WHAT DID IT? GREAT! YOU'LL BE FINE, THEN. NOW YOU KNOW HOW TO FIX IT NEXT TIME.
YES ...!

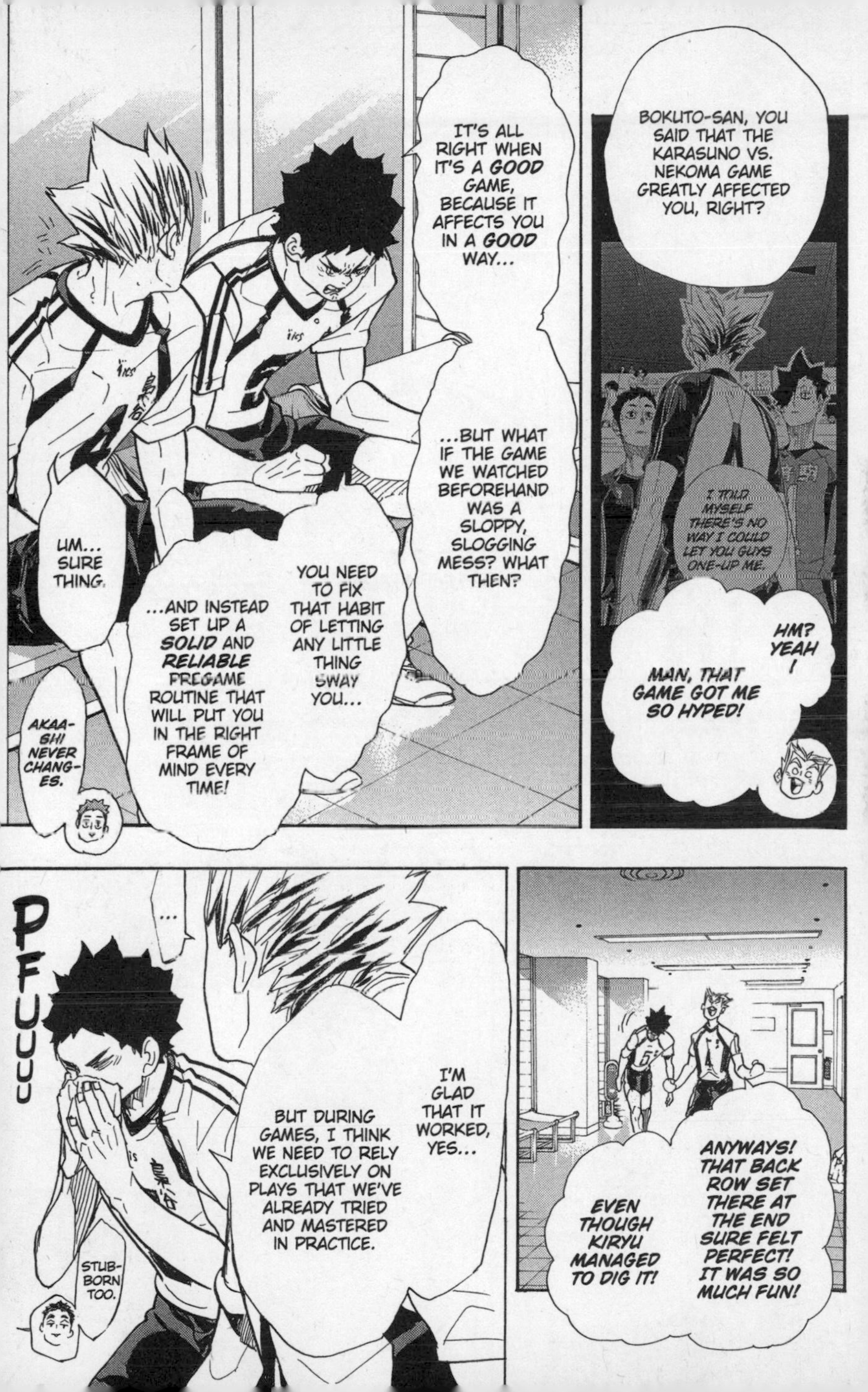
BOKUTO-SAN, YOU SAID THAT THE KARASUNO VS. NEKOMA GAME GREATLY AFFECTED YOU, RIGHT?
I TOLD MYSELF THERE'S NO WAY I COULD LET YOU GUYS ONE-UP ME.
HM? YEAH!
MAN, THAT GAME GOT ME SO HYPED!
IT'S ALL RIGHT WHEN IT'S A GOOD GAME, BECAUSE IT AFFECTS YOU IN A GOOD WAY...
...BUT WHAT IF THE GAME WE WATCHED BEFOREHAND WAS A SLOPPY, SLOGGING MESS? WHAT THEN?
YOU NEED TO FIX THAT HABIT OF LETTING ANY LITTLE THING SWAY YOU...
...AND INSTEAD SET UP A SOLID AND RELIABLE PREGAME ROUTINE THAT WILL PUT YOU IN THE RIGHT FRAME OF MIND EVERY TIME!
UM... SURE THING.
AKAASHI NEVER CHANGES.
ANYWAYS! THAT BACK ROW SET THERE AT THE END SURE FELT PERFECT! IT WAS SO MUCH FUN!
EVEN THOUGH KIRYU MANAGED TO DIG IT!
...
I'M GLAD THAT IT WORKED, YES...
BUT DURING GAMES, I THINK WE NEED TO RELY EXCLUSIVELY ON PLAYS THAT WE'VE ALREADY TRIED AND MASTERED IN PRACTICE.
PFUUUU
STUBBORN TOO.

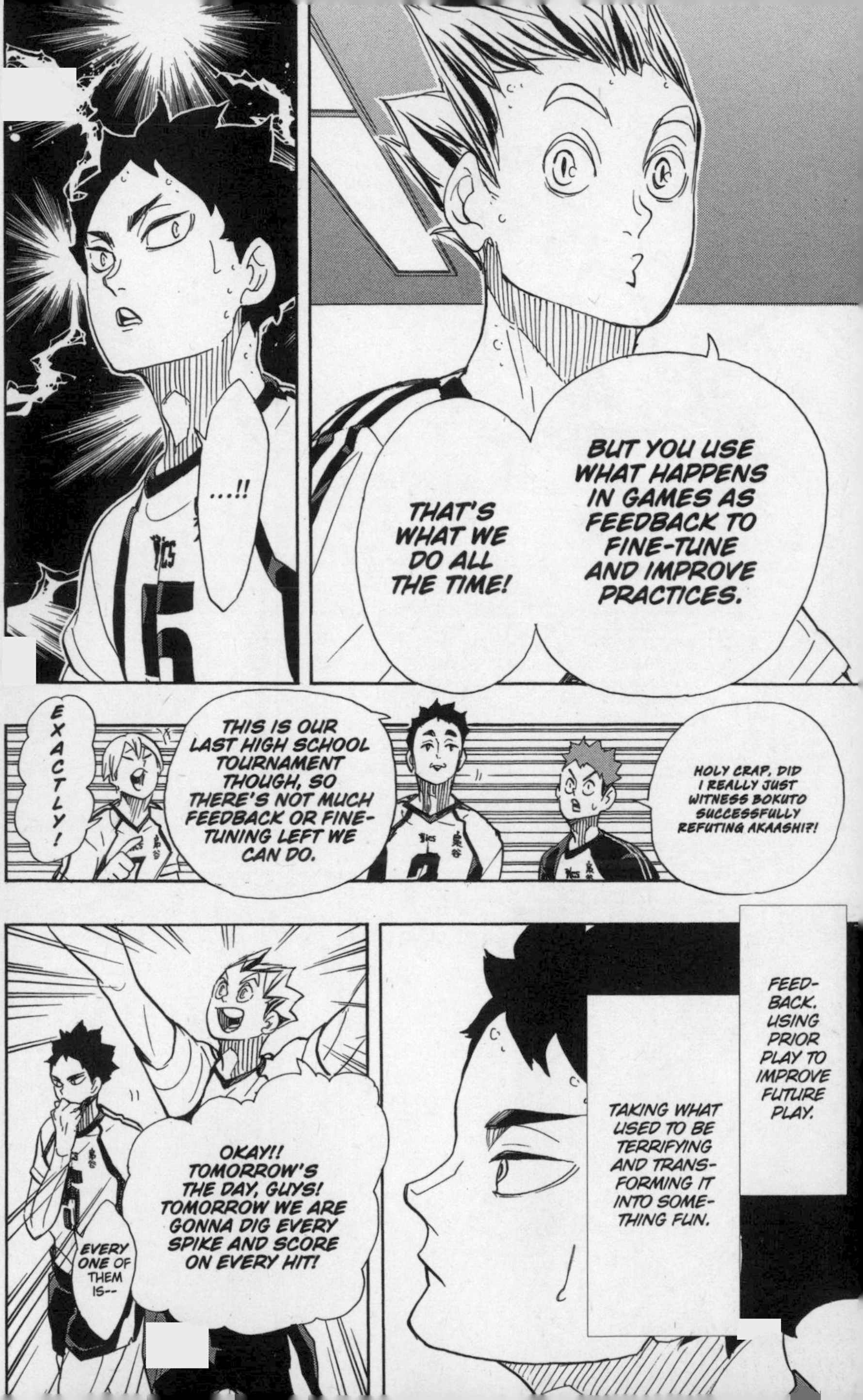
BUT YOU USE WHAT HAPPENS IN GAMES AS FEEDBACK TO FINE-TUNE AND IMPROVE PRACTICES.
THAT'S WHAT WE DO ALL THE TIME!
...!!
HOLY CRAP, DID I REALLY JUST WITNESS BOKUTO SUCCESSFULLY REFUTING AKAASHI?!
THIS IS OUR LAST HIGH SCHOOL TOURNAMENT THOUGH, SO THERE'S NOT MUCH FEEDBACK OR FINE-TUNING LEFT WE CAN DO.
EXACTLY!
FEED-BACK. USING PRIOR PLAY TO IMPROVE FUTURE PLAY.
TAKING WHAT USED TO BE TERRIFYING AND TRANS-FORMING IT INTO SOME-THING FUN.
OKAY!! TOMORROW'S THE DAY, GUYS! TOMORROW WE ARE GONNA DIG EVERY SPIKE AND SCORE ON EVERY HIT!
EVERY ONE OF THEM IS--

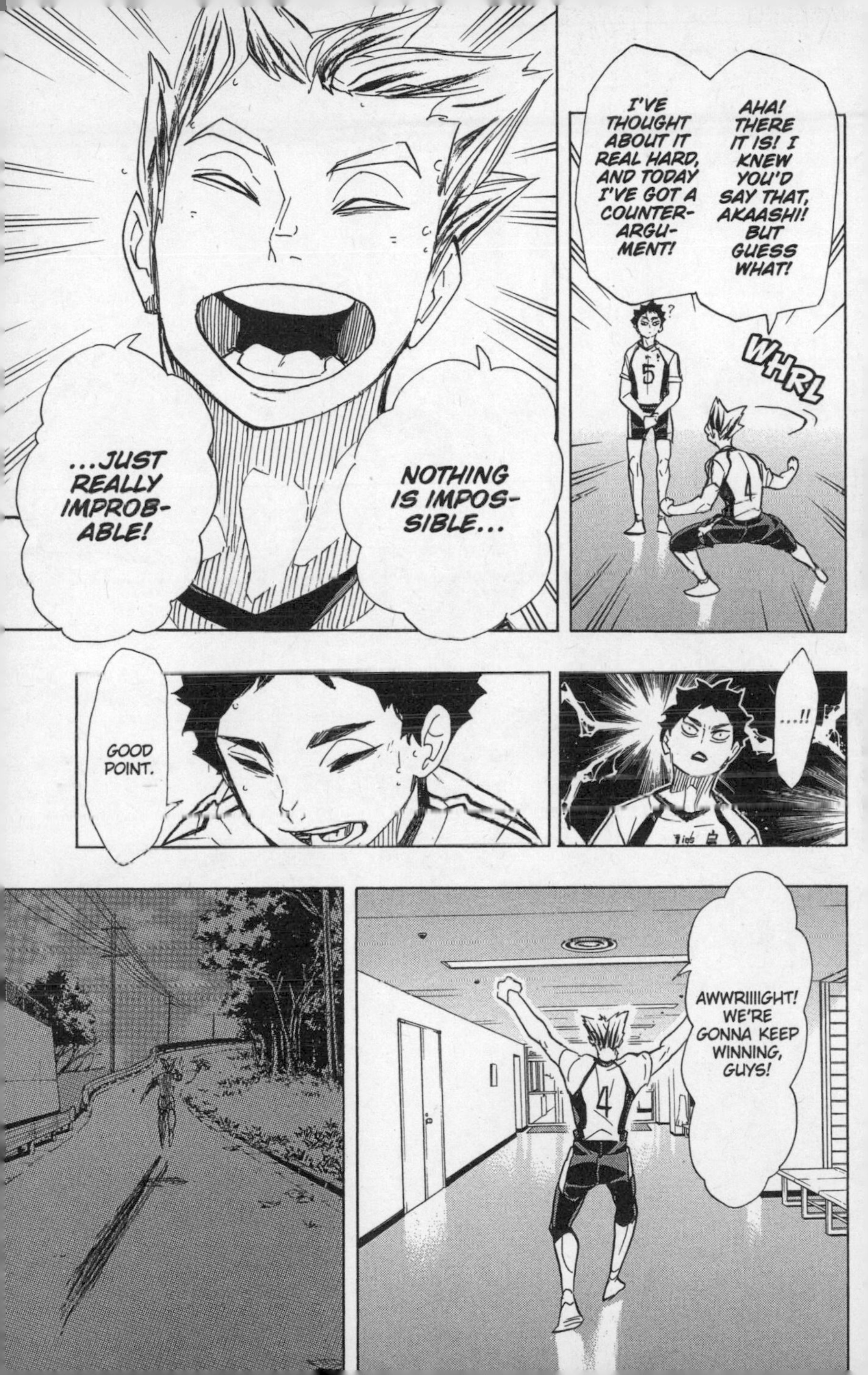
AHA! THERE IT IS! I KNEW YOU'D SAY THAT, AKAASHI! BUT GUESS WHAT!
I'VE THOUGHT ABOUT IT REAL HARD, AND TODAY I'VE GOT A COUNTER-ARGUMENT!
WHRL
NOTHING IS IMPOSSIBLE...
...JUST REALLY IMPROBABLE!
...!!
GOOD POINT.
AWWRIIIIGHT! WE'RE GONNA KEEP WINNING, GUYS!

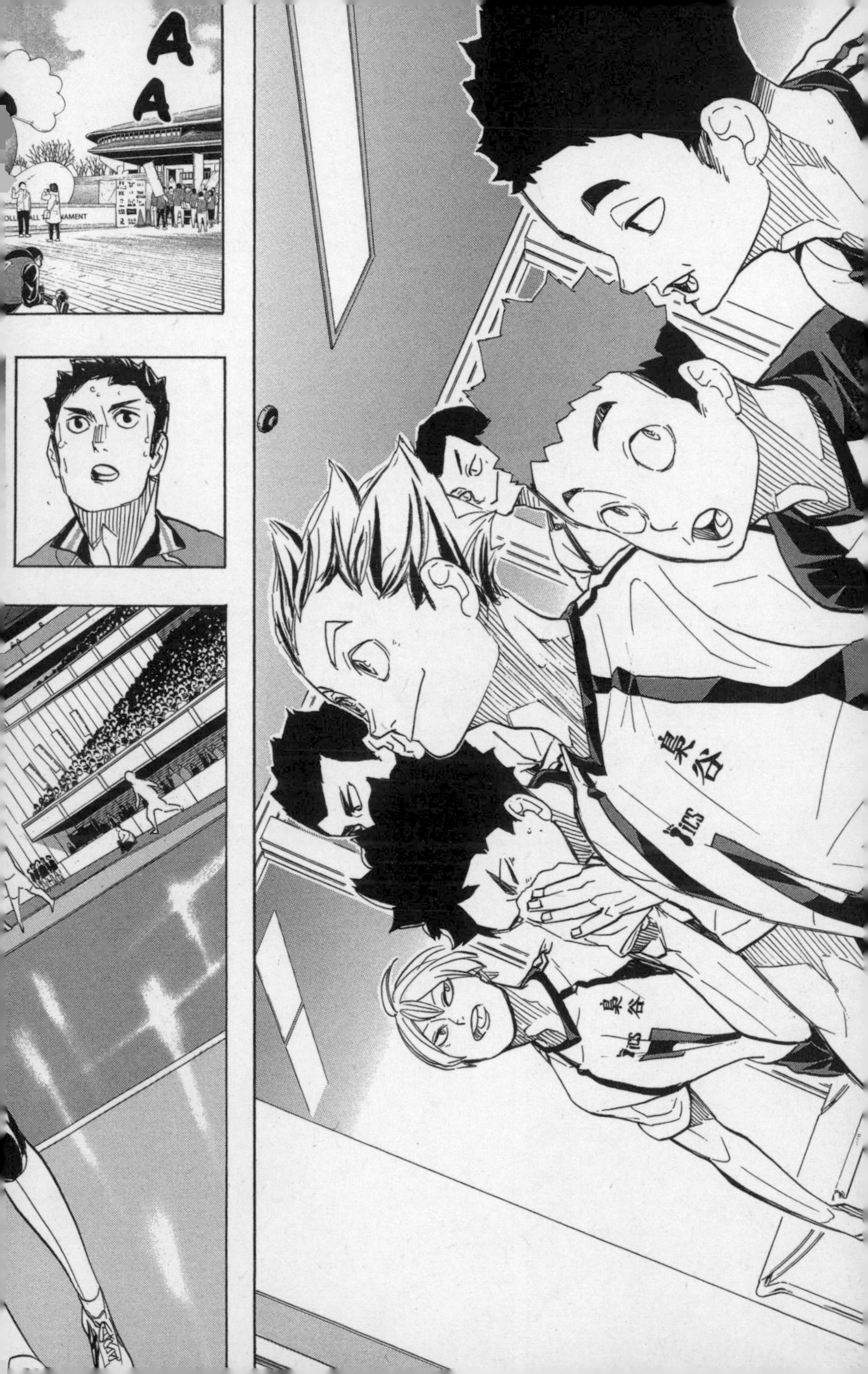
A
A

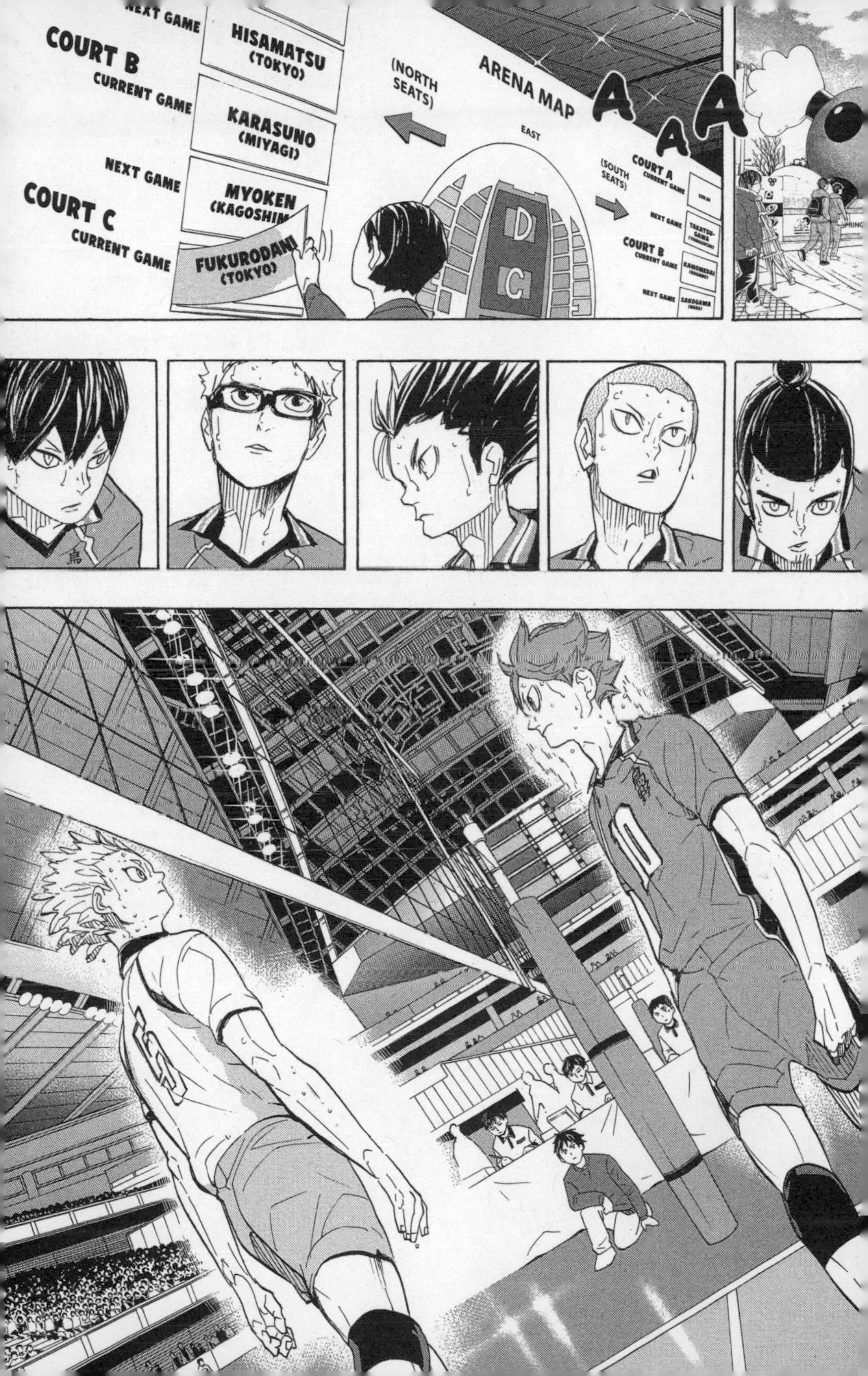
AAA
ARENA MAP
EAST
(NORTH SEATS)
(SOUTH SEATS)
COURT A
CURRENT GAME
SENJU
NEXT GAME
TAKATSU-GAWA
COURT B
CURRENT GAME
KAMOMEDAI
NEXT GAME
SAKOGAWA (NARA)
D
C
NEXT GAME
HISAMATSU (TOKYO)
COURT B
CURRENT GAME
KARASUNO (MIYAGI)
NEXT GAME
MYOKEN (KAGOSHIM
COURT C
CURRENT GAME
FUKURODANI (TOKYO)

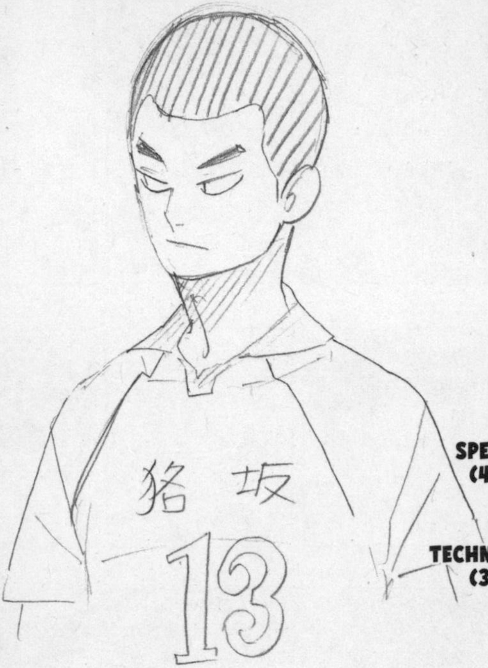

狢 坂
13

HARUMA BISHIN

MUJINAZAKA HIGH SCHOOL, CLASS 2-1

POSITION:
LIBERO

HEIGHT: 5'8"

WEIGHT: 151 LBS.
(AS OF JANUARY, 2ND YEAR OF HIGH SCHOOL)

ABILITY PARAMETERS
(5-POINT SCALE)

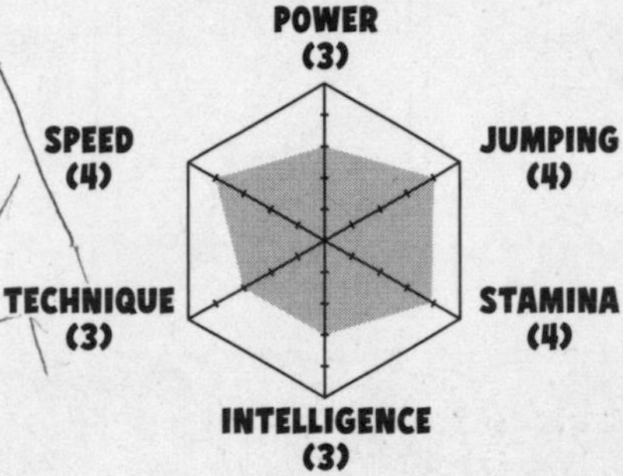

POWER (3)
JUMPING (4)
STAMINA (4)
INTELLIGENCE (3)
TECHNIQUE (3)
SPEED (4)

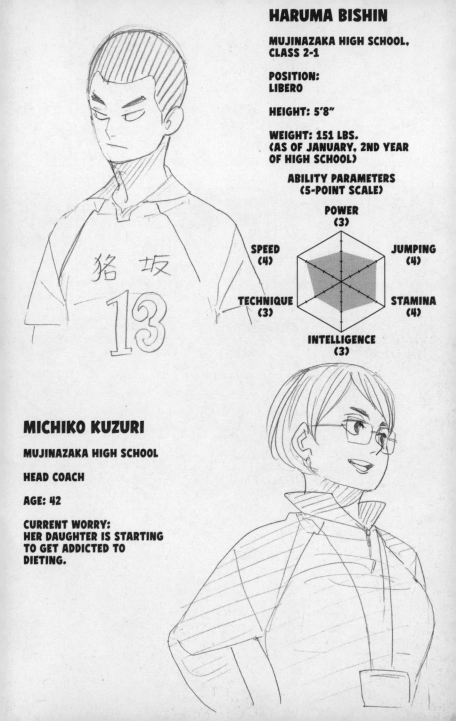

MICHIKO KUZURI

MUJINAZAKA HIGH SCHOOL

HEAD COACH

AGE: 42

CURRENT WORRY:
HER DAUGHTER IS STARTING TO GET ADDICTED TO DIETING.

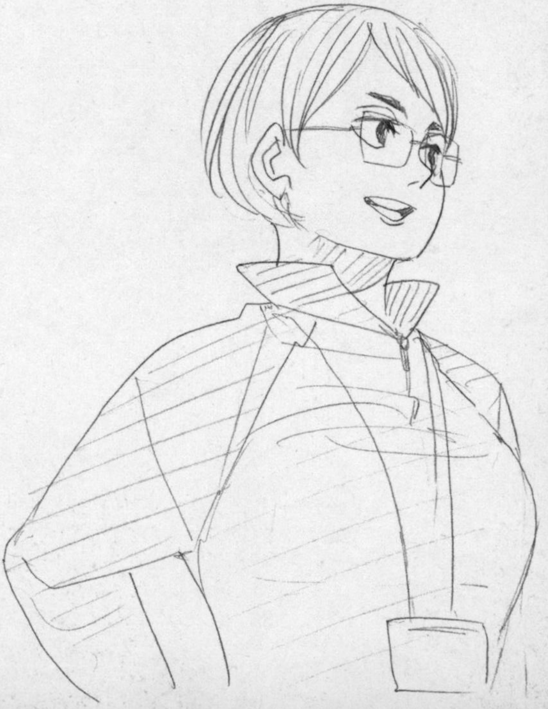

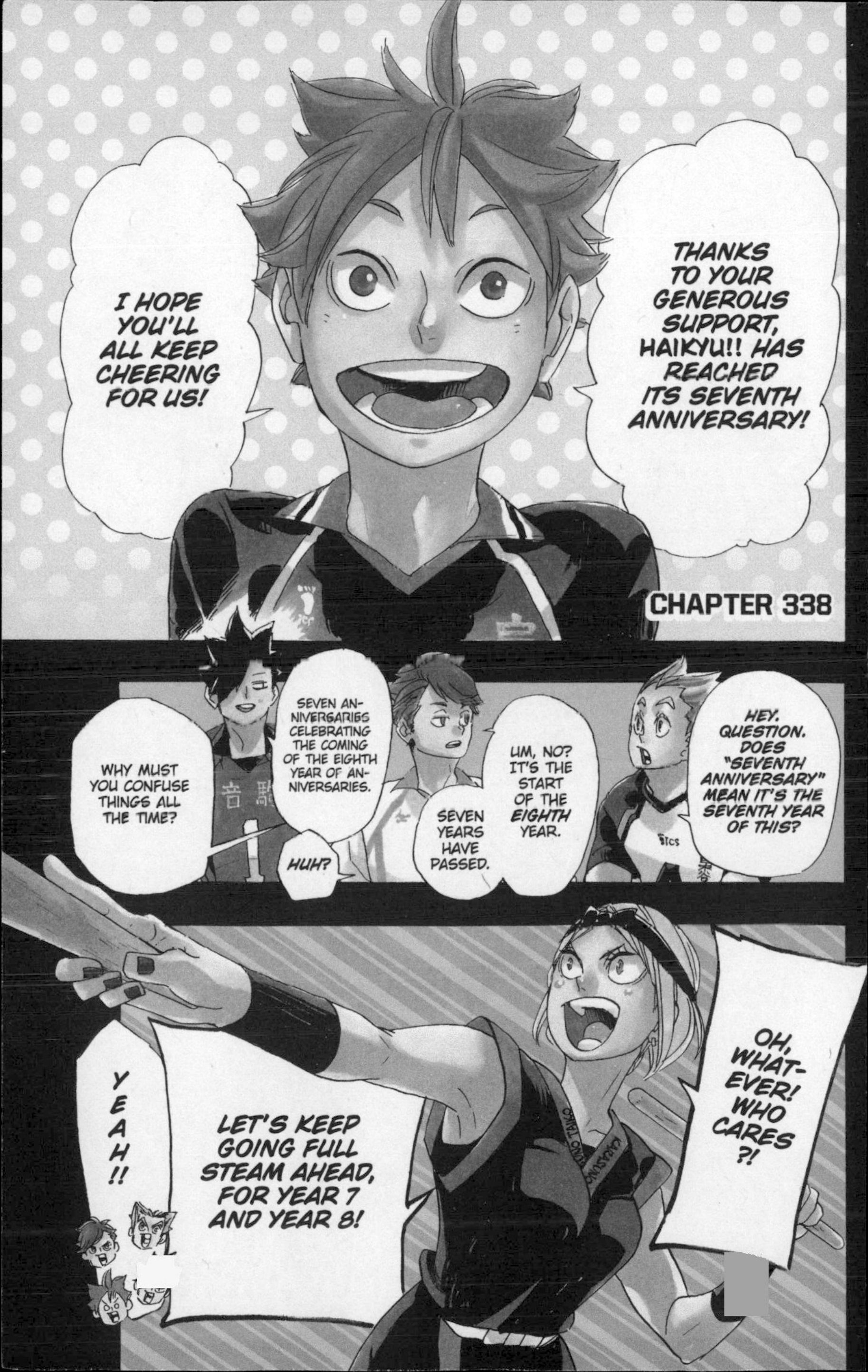
THANKS TO YOUR GENEROUS SUPPORT, HAIKYU!! HAS REACHED ITS SEVENTH ANNIVERSARY!
I HOPE YOU'LL ALL KEEP CHEERING FOR US!
CHAPTER 338
HEY. QUESTION. DOES "SEVENTH ANNIVERSARY" MEAN IT'S THE SEVENTH YEAR OF THIS?
UM, NO? IT'S THE START OF THE EIGHTH YEAR.
SEVEN YEARS HAVE PASSED.
SEVEN ANNIVERSARIES CELEBRATING THE COMING OF THE EIGHTH YEAR OF ANNIVERSARIES.
HUH?
WHY MUST YOU CONFUSE THINGS ALL THE TIME?
OH, WHATEVER! WHO CARES?!
LET'S KEEP GOING FULL STEAM AHEAD, FOR YEAR 7 AND YEAR 8!
YEAH!!

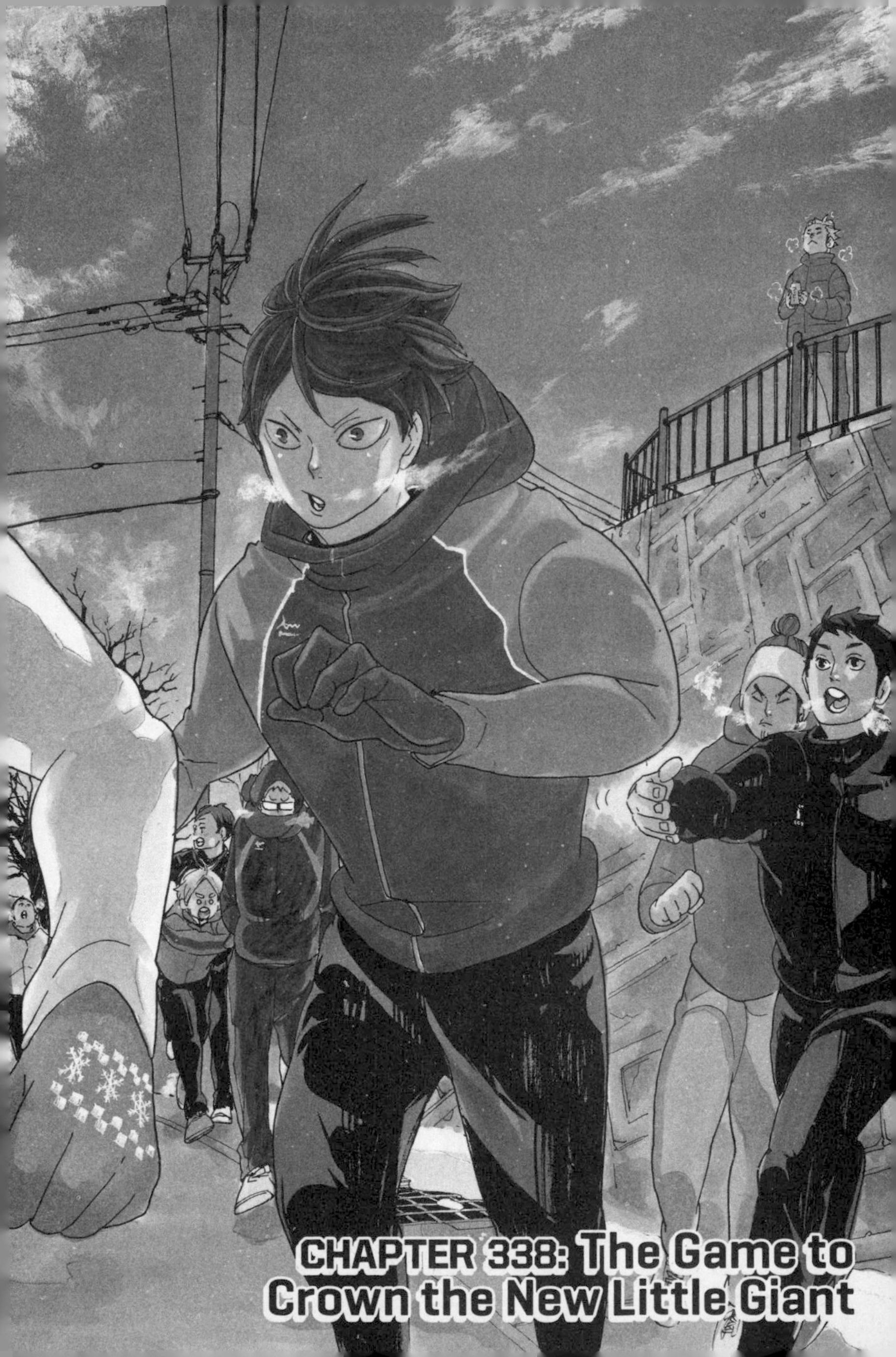
CHAPTER 338: The Game to Crown the New Little Giant

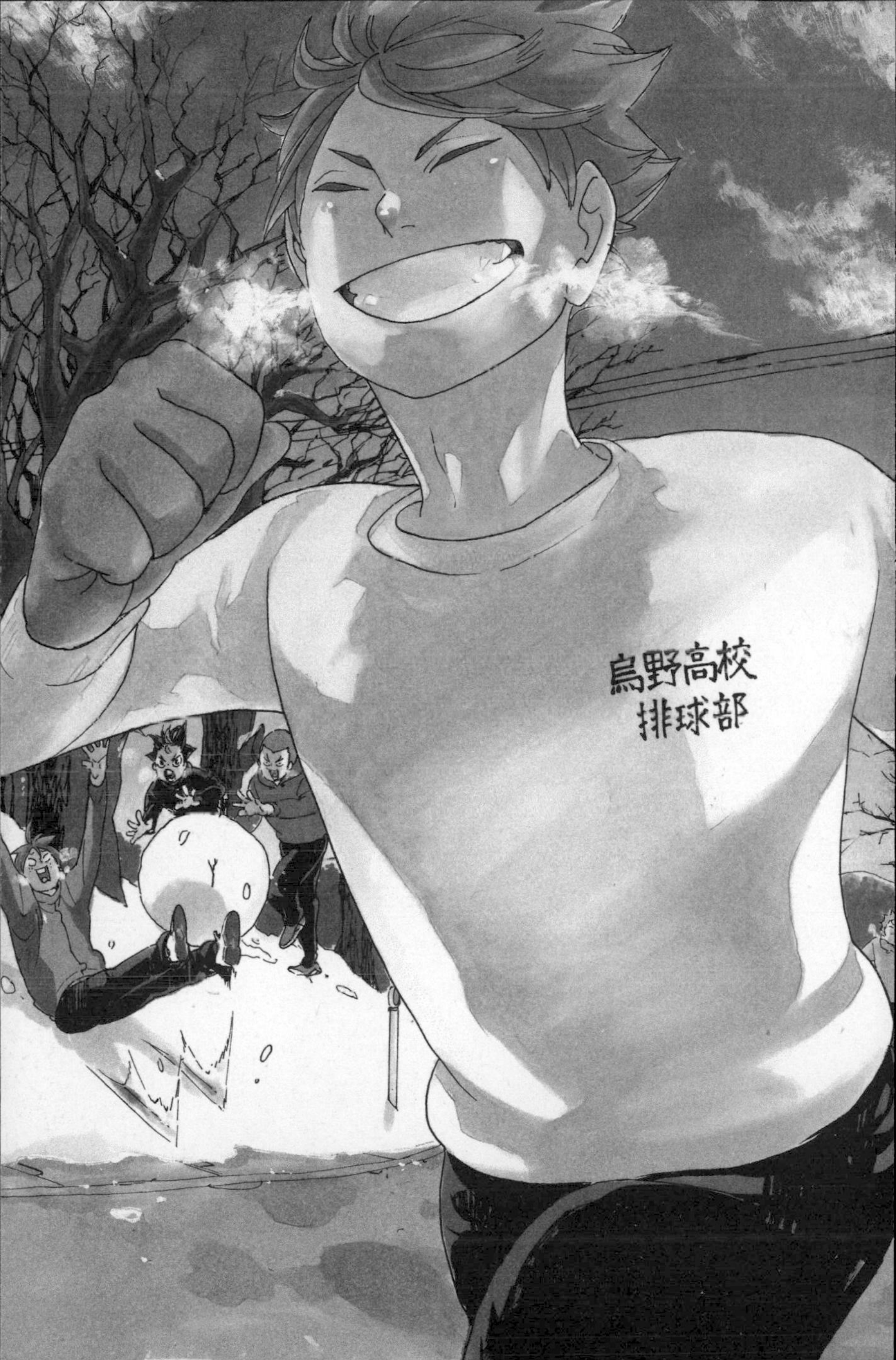
烏野高校
排球部

HAIKYU!!

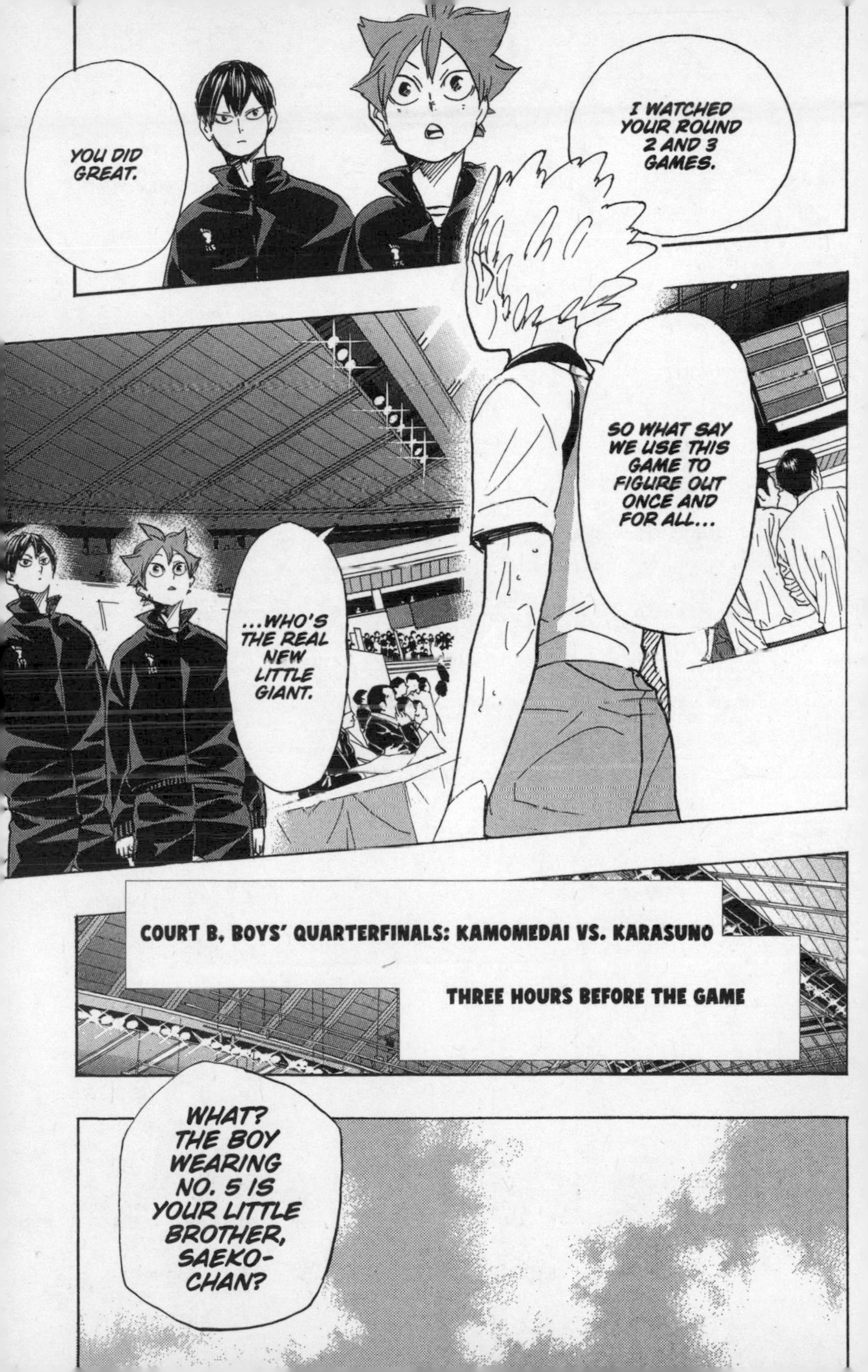
I WATCHED YOUR ROUND 2 AND 3 GAMES.
YOU DID GREAT.
SO WHAT SAY WE USE THIS GAME TO FIGURE OUT ONCE AND FOR ALL...
...WHO'S THE REAL NEW LITTLE GIANT.
COURT B, BOYS' QUARTERFINALS: KAMOMEDAI VS. KARASUNO
THREE HOURS BEFORE THE GAME
WHAT? THE BOY WEARING NO. 5 IS YOUR LITTLE BROTHER, SAEKO-CHAN?

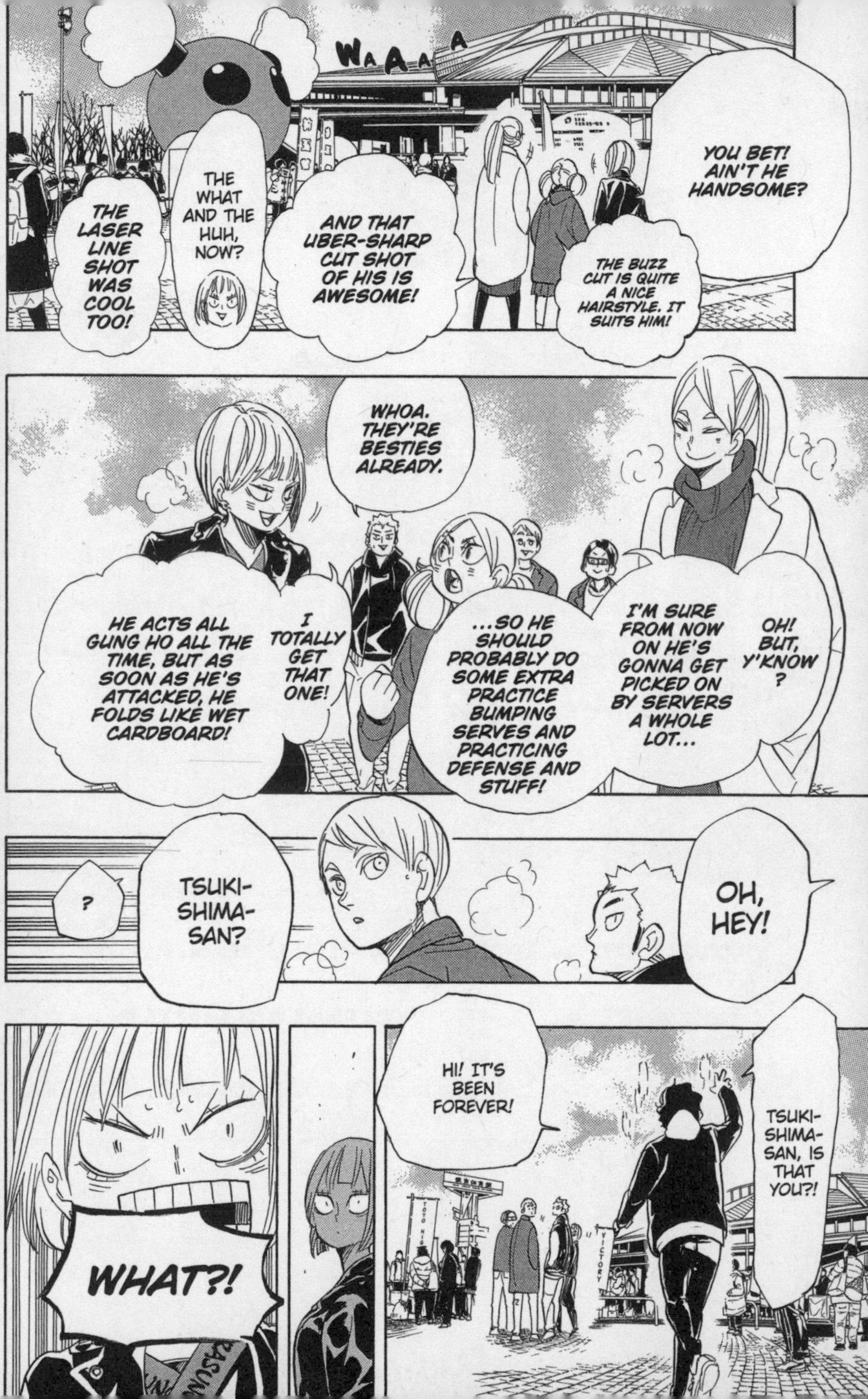
WAAAAA
YOU BET! AIN'T HE HANDSOME?
THE BUZZ CUT IS QUITE A NICE HAIRSTYLE. IT SUITS HIM!
AND THAT UBER-SHARP CUT SHOT OF HIS IS AWESOME!
THE WHAT AND THE HUH, NOW?
THE LASER LINE SHOT WAS COOL TOO!
OH! BUT, Y'KNOW?
I'M SURE FROM NOW ON HE'S GONNA GET PICKED ON BY SERVERS A WHOLE LOT...
...SO HE SHOULD PROBABLY DO SOME EXTRA PRACTICE BUMPING SERVES AND PRACTICING DEFENSE AND STUFF!
WHOA. THEY'RE BESTIES ALREADY.
I TOTALLY GET THAT ONE!
HE ACTS ALL GUNG HO ALL THE TIME, BUT AS SOON AS HE'S ATTACKED, HE FOLDS LIKE WET CARDBOARD!
OH, HEY!
TSUKI-SHIMA-SAN?
?
TSUKI-SHIMA-SAN, IS THAT YOU?!
HI! IT'S BEEN FOREVER!
VICTORY
WHAT?!

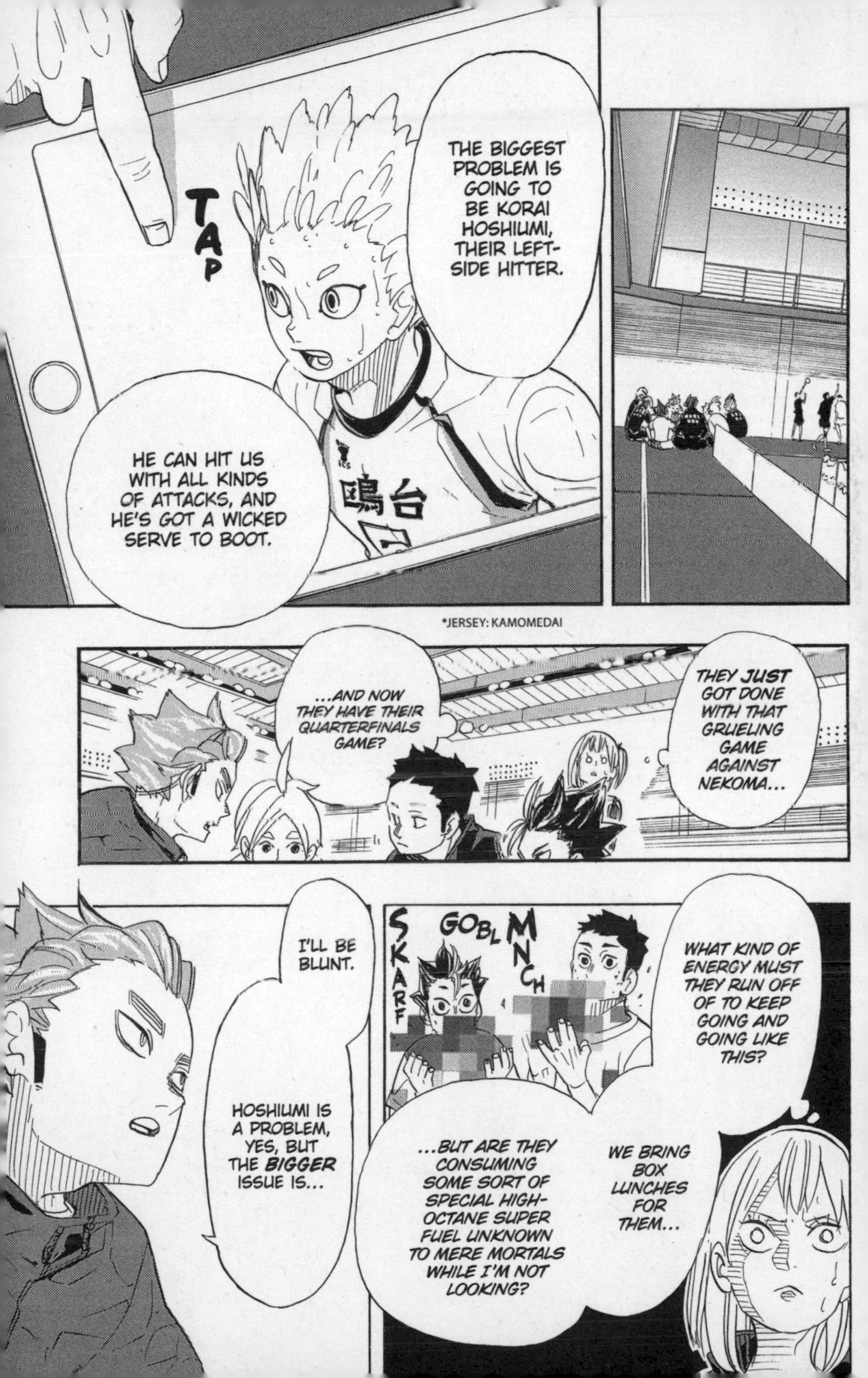
TAP
THE BIGGEST PROBLEM IS GOING TO BE KORAI HOSHIUMI, THEIR LEFT-SIDE HITTER.
HE CAN HIT US WITH ALL KINDS OF ATTACKS, AND HE'S GOT A WICKED SERVE TO BOOT.
鴎台
THEY JUST GOT DONE WITH THAT GRUELING GAME AGAINST NEKOMA...
...AND NOW THEY HAVE THEIR QUARTERFINALS GAME?
WHAT KIND OF ENERGY MUST THEY RUN OFF OF TO KEEP GOING AND GOING LIKE THIS?
MNCH
GOBL
SKARF
WE BRING BOX LUNCHES FOR THEM...
...BUT ARE THEY CONSUMING SOME SORT OF SPECIAL HIGH-OCTANE SUPER FUEL UNKNOWN TO MERE MORTALS WHILE I'M NOT LOOKING?
I'LL BE BLUNT.
HOSHIUMI IS A PROBLEM, YES, BUT THE BIGGER ISSUE IS...

*JERSEY: KAMOMEDAI

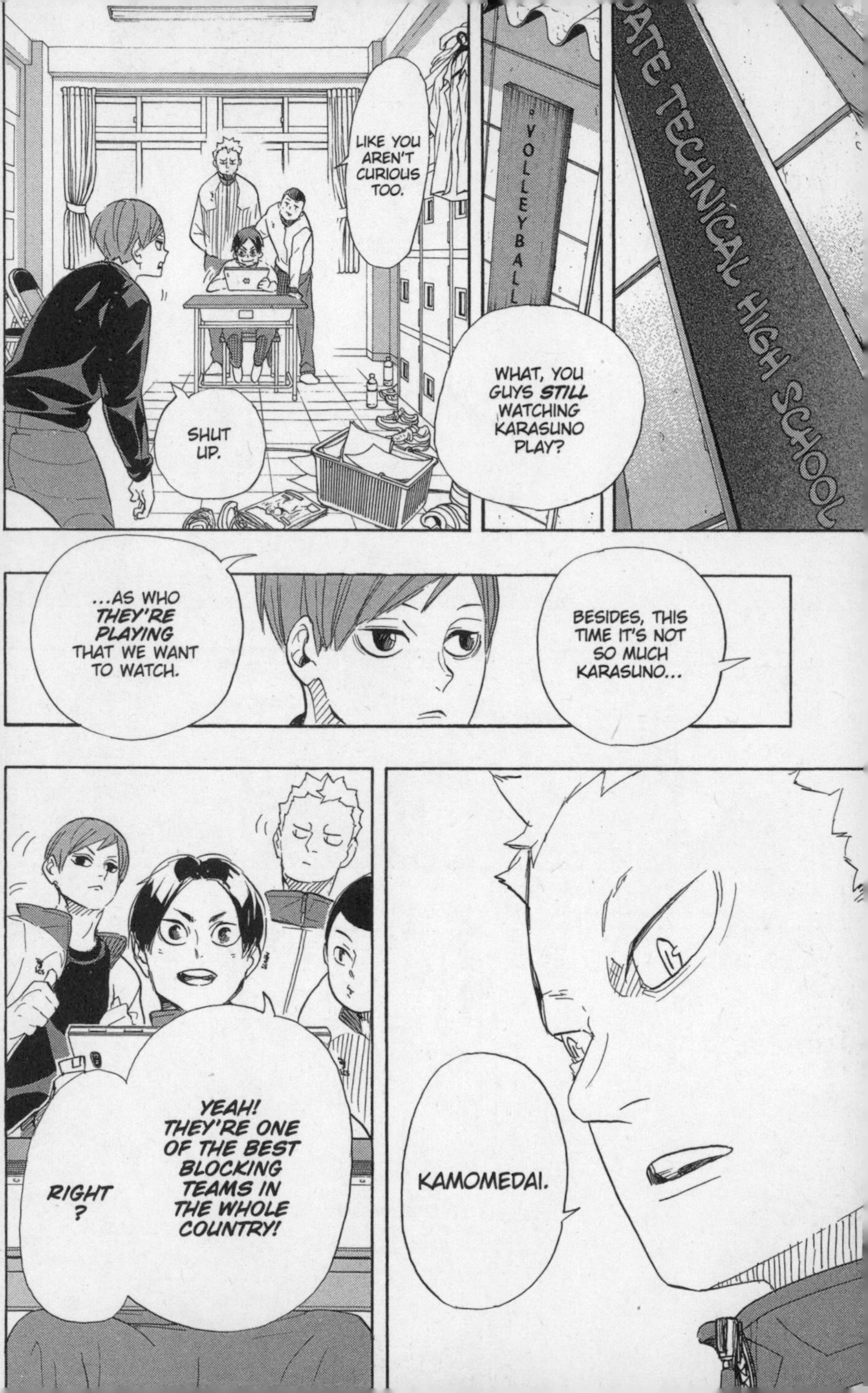
DATE TECHNICAL HIGH SCHOOL
VOLLEYBALL
WHAT, YOU GUYS *STILL* WATCHING KARASUNO PLAY?
LIKE YOU AREN'T CURIOUS TOO.
SHUT UP.
BESIDES, THIS TIME IT'S NOT SO MUCH KARASUNO...
...AS WHO *THEY'RE PLAYING* THAT WE WANT TO WATCH.
KAMOMEDAI.
YEAH! THEY'RE ONE OF THE BEST BLOCKING TEAMS IN THE WHOLE COUNTRY!
RIGHT?

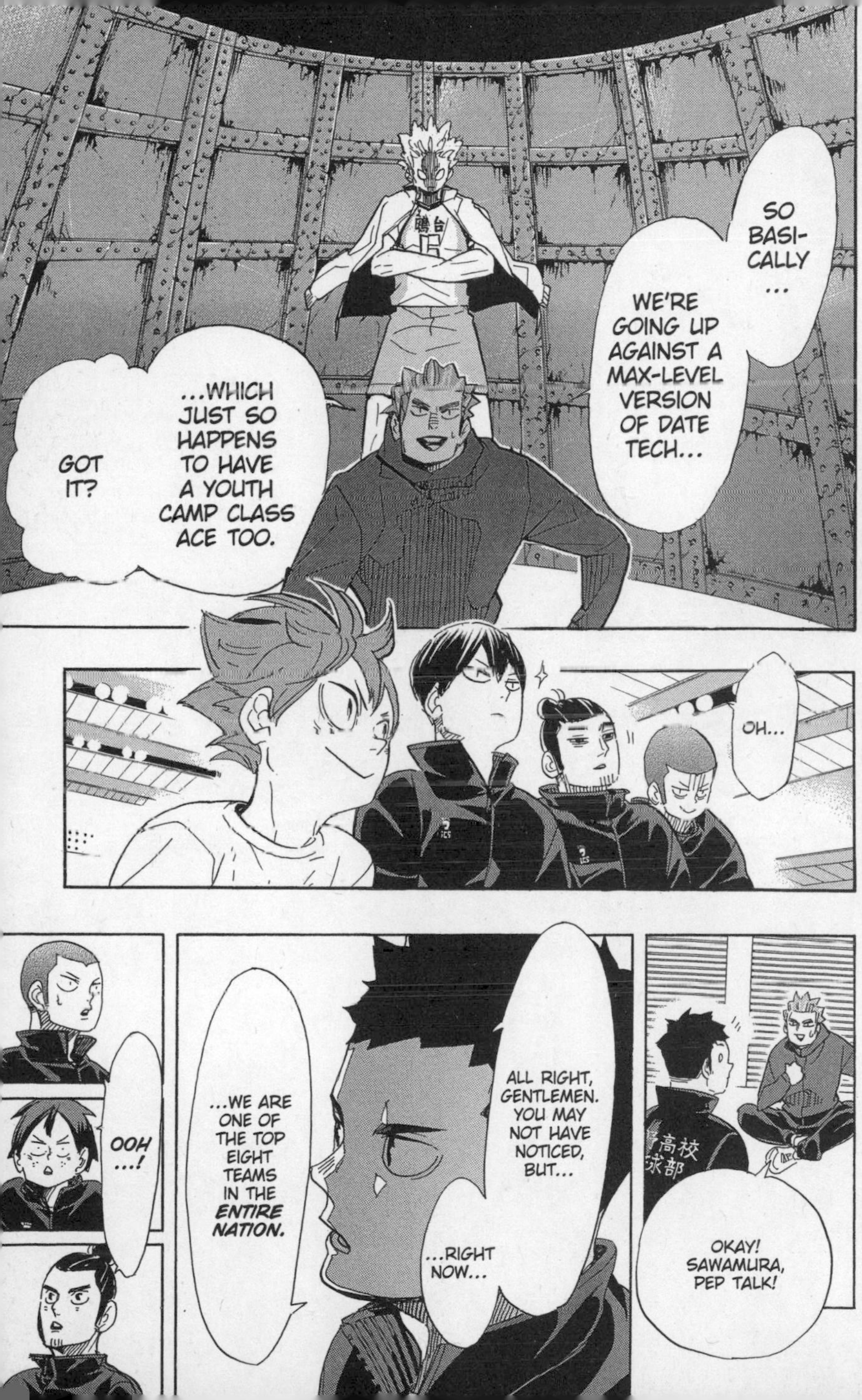
SO BASI-CALLY...
WE'RE GOING UP AGAINST A MAX-LEVEL VERSION OF DATE TECH...
...WHICH JUST SO HAPPENS TO HAVE A YOUTH CAMP CLASS ACE TOO.
GOT IT?
OH...
OKAY! SAWAMURA, PEP TALK!
ALL RIGHT, GENTLEMEN. YOU MAY NOT HAVE NOTICED, BUT...
...RIGHT NOW...
...WE ARE ONE OF THE TOP EIGHT TEAMS IN THE *ENTIRE NATION.*
OOH...!

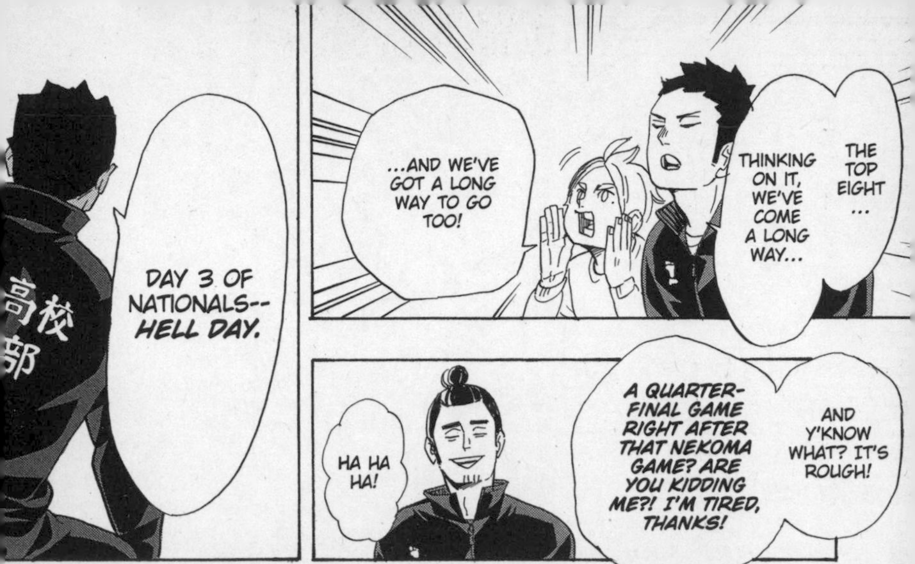
THE TOP EIGHT...
THINKING ON IT, WE'VE COME A LONG WAY...
...AND WE'VE GOT A LONG WAY TO GO TOO!
AND Y'KNOW WHAT? IT'S ROUGH!
A QUARTER-FINAL GAME RIGHT AFTER THAT NEKOMA GAME? ARE YOU KIDDING ME?! I'M TIRED, THANKS!
HA HA HA!
DAY 3 OF NATIONALS-- *HELL DAY.*

*JACKET: KARASUNO HIGH VOLLEYBALL

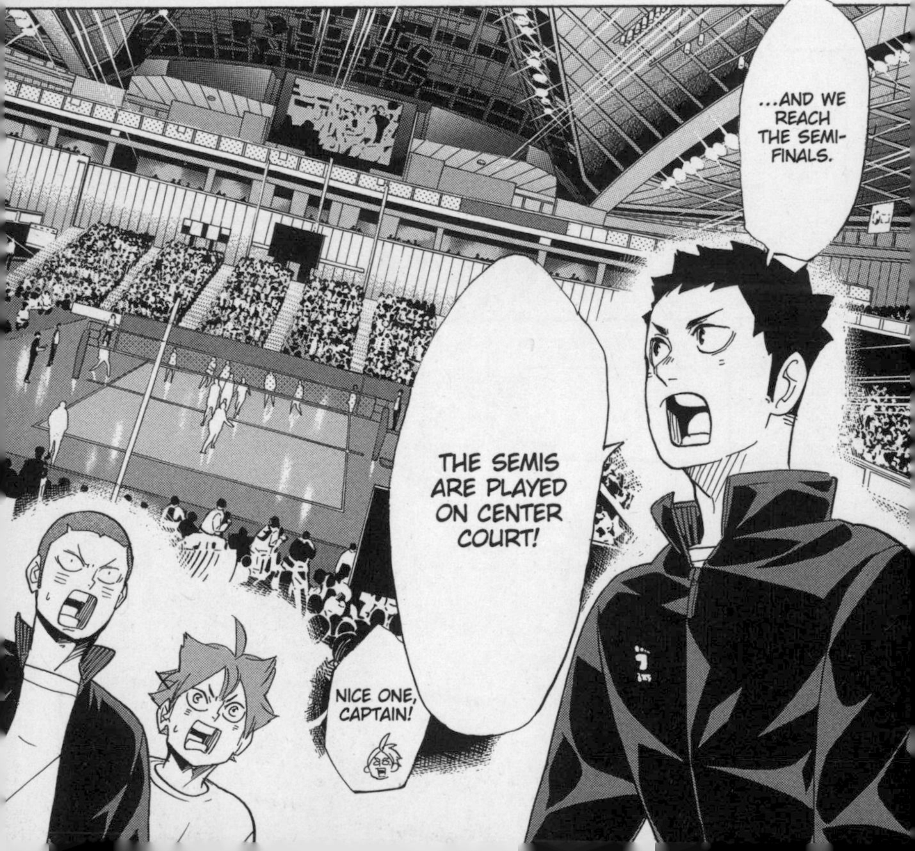
...AND WE REACH THE SEMI-FINALS.
THE SEMIS ARE PLAYED ON CENTER COURT!
NICE ONE, CAPTAIN!

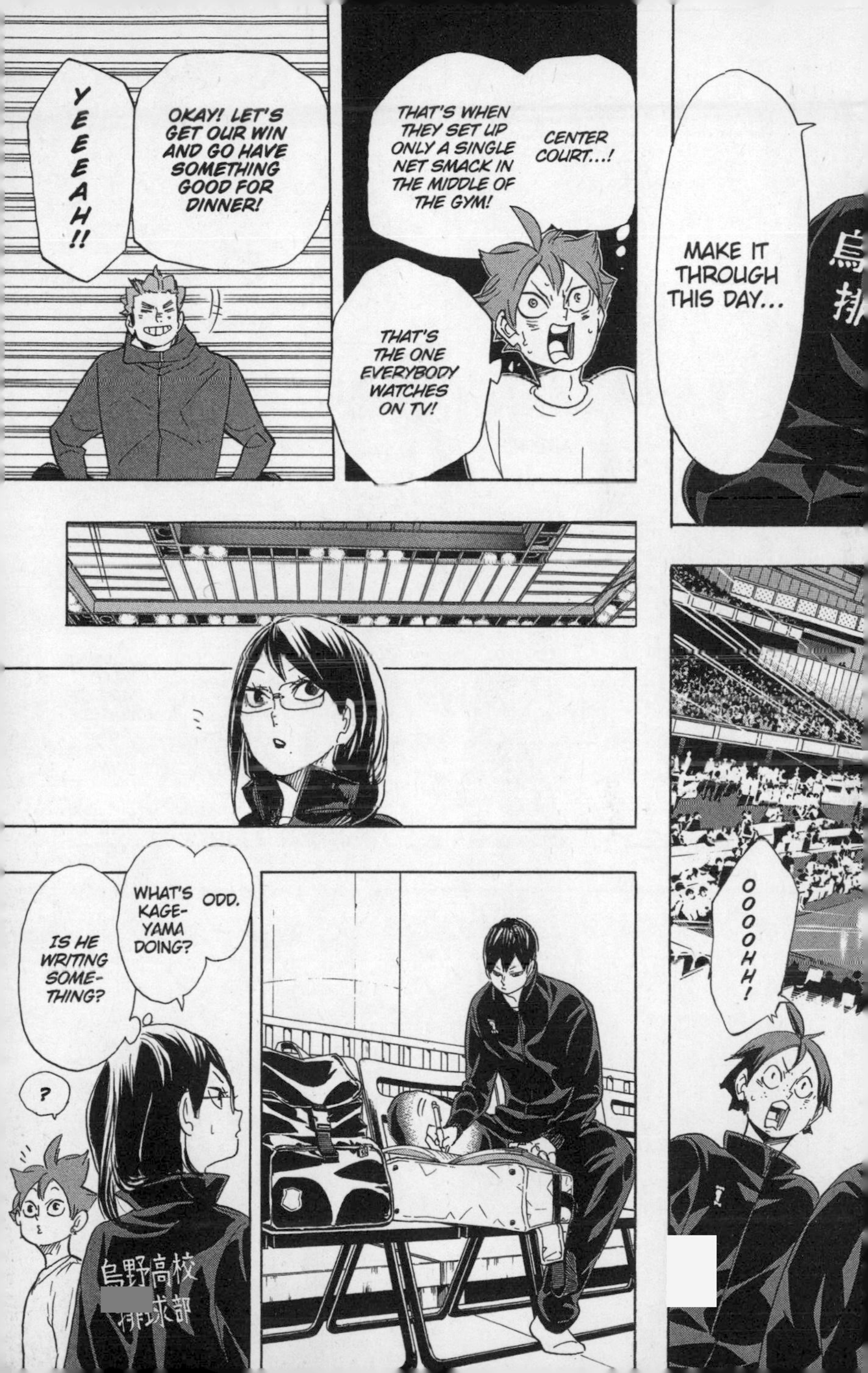
MAKE IT THROUGH THIS DAY...
CENTER COURT...!
THAT'S WHEN THEY SET UP ONLY A SINGLE NET SMACK IN THE MIDDLE OF THE GYM!
THAT'S THE ONE EVERYBODY WATCHES ON TV!
OKAY! LET'S GET OUR WIN AND GO HAVE SOMETHING GOOD FOR DINNER!
YEEEAH!!
OOOOOHH!
ODD.
WHAT'S KAGE-YAMA DOING?
IS HE WRITING SOME-THING?
?
烏野高校
排球部

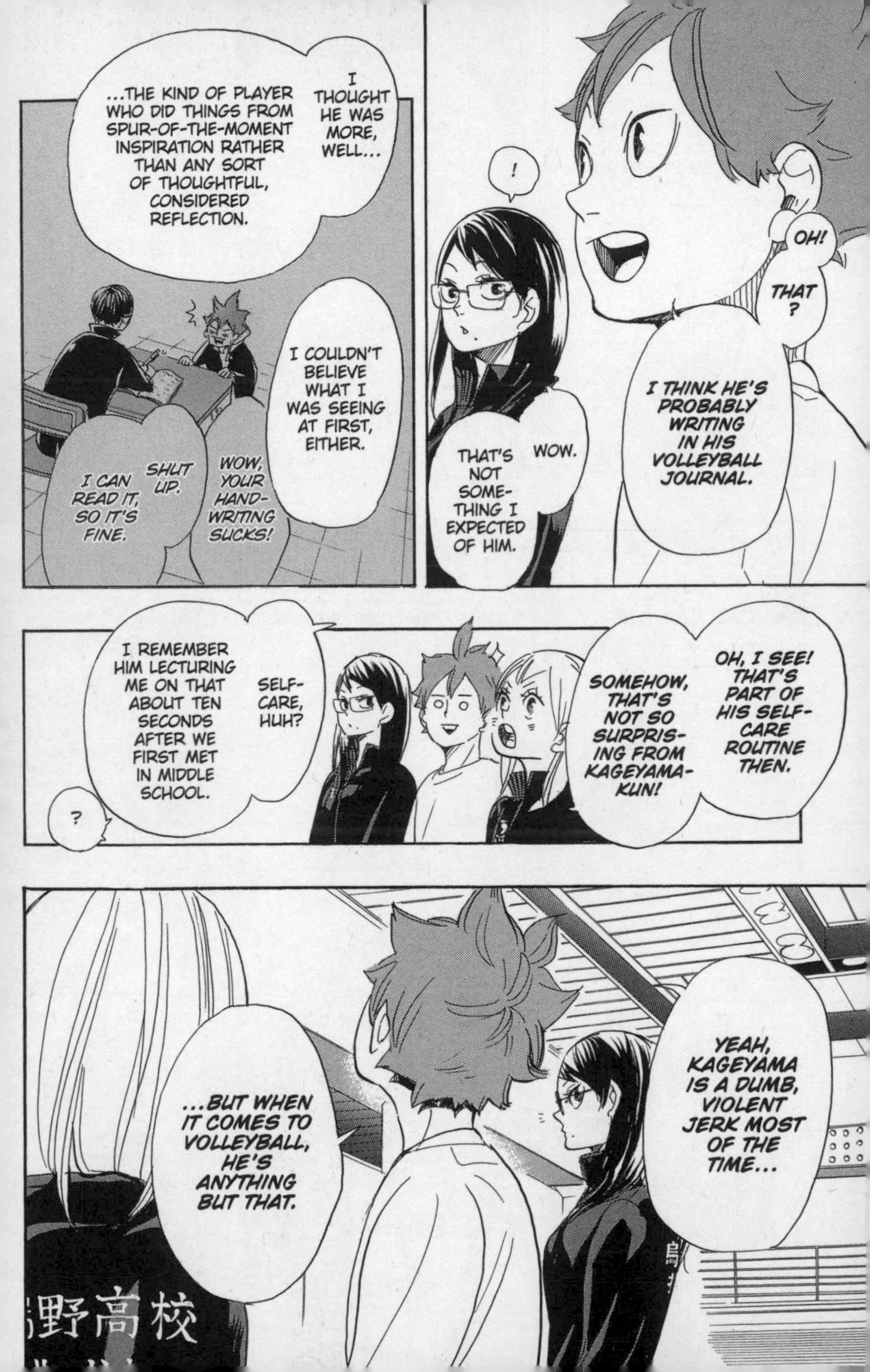
OH!
THAT?
I THINK HE'S PROBABLY WRITING IN HIS VOLLEYBALL JOURNAL.
!
WOW.
THAT'S NOT SOME-THING I EXPECTED OF HIM.
I THOUGHT HE WAS MORE, WELL...
...THE KIND OF PLAYER WHO DID THINGS FROM SPUR-OF-THE-MOMENT INSPIRATION RATHER THAN ANY SORT OF THOUGHTFUL, CONSIDERED REFLECTION.
I COULDN'T BELIEVE WHAT I WAS SEEING AT FIRST, EITHER.
WOW, YOUR HAND-WRITING SUCKS!
SHUT UP.
I CAN READ IT, SO IT'S FINE.
OH, I SEE! THAT'S PART OF HIS SELF-CARE ROUTINE THEN.
SOMEHOW, THAT'S NOT SO SURPRIS-ING FROM KAGEYAMA-KUN!
SELF-CARE, HUH?
I REMEMBER HIM LECTURING ME ON THAT ABOUT TEN SECONDS AFTER WE FIRST MET IN MIDDLE SCHOOL.
?
YEAH, KAGEYAMA IS A DUMB, VIOLENT JERK MOST OF THE TIME...
...BUT WHEN IT COMES TO VOLLEYBALL, HE'S ANYTHING BUT THAT.
野高校

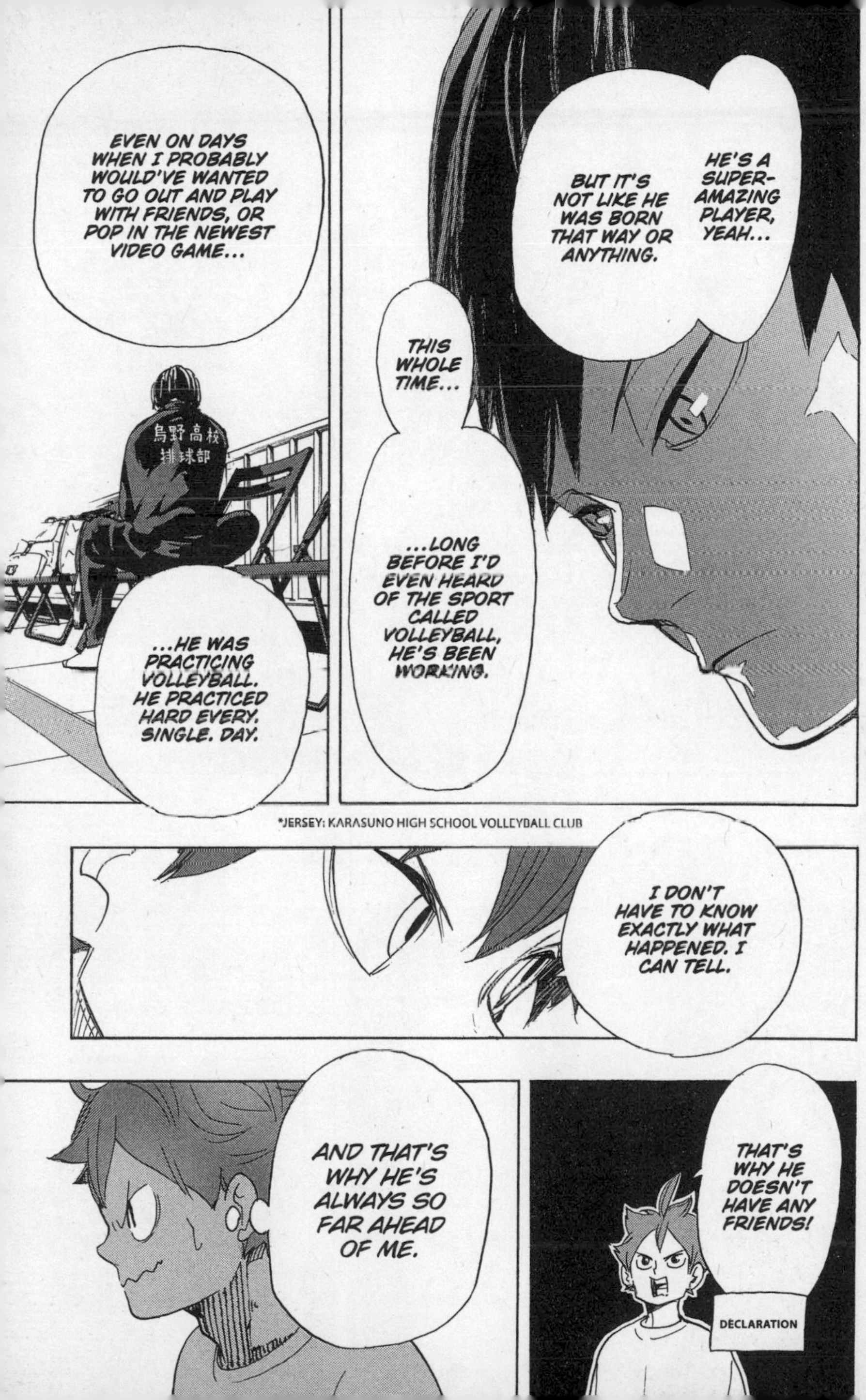
HE'S A SUPER-AMAZING PLAYER, YEAH...
BUT IT'S NOT LIKE HE WAS BORN THAT WAY OR ANYTHING.
THIS WHOLE TIME...
...LONG BEFORE I'D EVEN HEARD OF THE SPORT CALLED VOLLEYBALL, HE'S BEEN WORKING.
EVEN ON DAYS WHEN I PROBABLY WOULD'VE WANTED TO GO OUT AND PLAY WITH FRIENDS, OR POP IN THE NEWEST VIDEO GAME...
烏野高校 排球部
...HE WAS PRACTICING VOLLEYBALL. HE PRACTICED HARD EVERY. SINGLE. DAY.
*JERSEY: KARASUNO HIGH SCHOOL VOLLEYBALL CLUB
I DON'T HAVE TO KNOW EXACTLY WHAT HAPPENED. I CAN TELL.
THAT'S WHY HE DOESN'T HAVE ANY FRIENDS!
DECLARATION
AND THAT'S WHY HE'S ALWAYS SO FAR AHEAD OF ME.

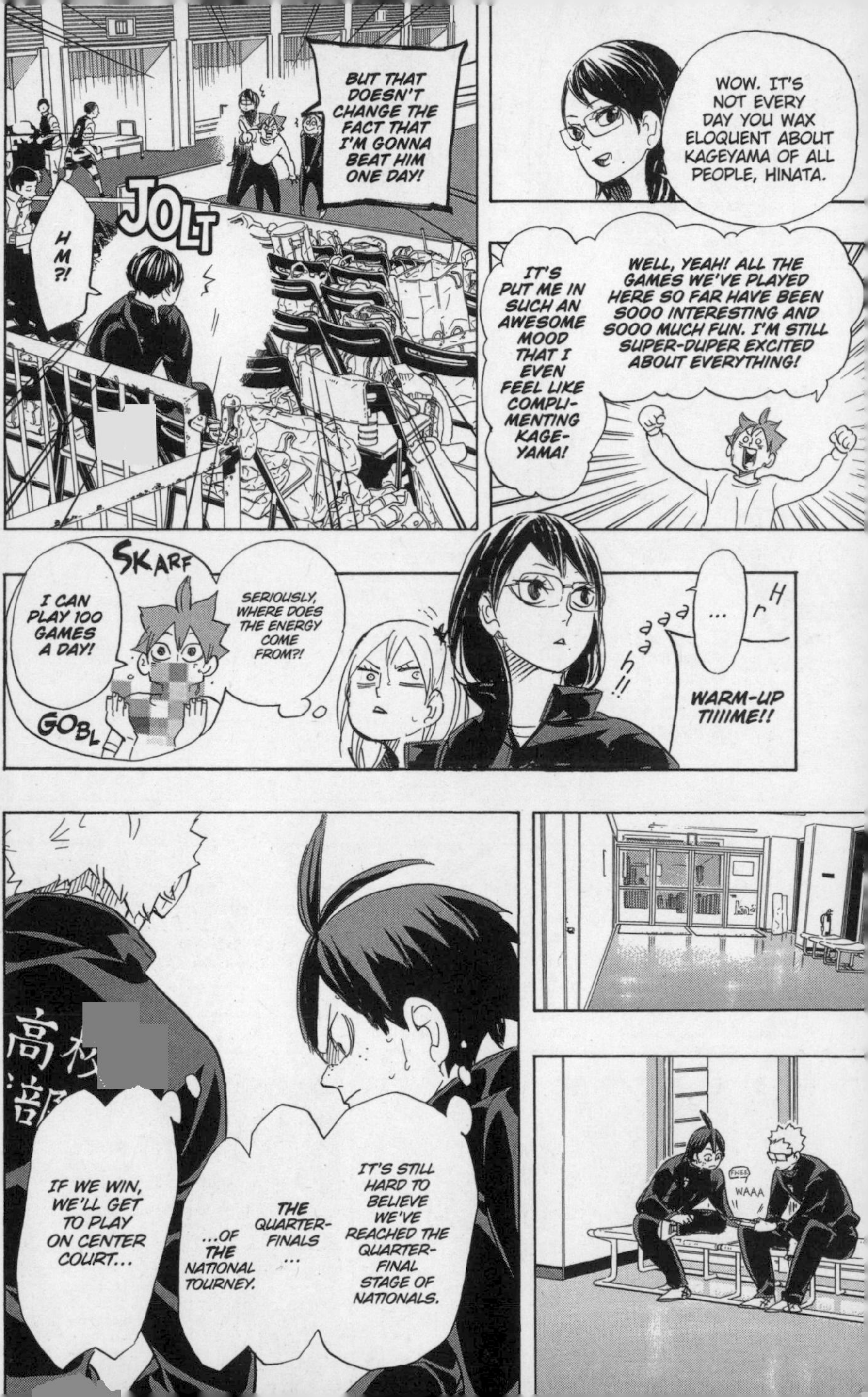
WOW. IT'S NOT EVERY DAY YOU WAX ELOQUENT ABOUT KAGEYAMA OF ALL PEOPLE, HINATA.
WELL, YEAH! ALL THE GAMES WE'VE PLAYED HERE SO FAR HAVE BEEN SOOO INTERESTING AND SOOO MUCH FUN. I'M STILL SUPER-DUPER EXCITED ABOUT EVERYTHING!
IT'S PUT ME IN SUCH AN AWESOME MOOD THAT I EVEN FEEL LIKE COMPLI-MENTING KAGE-YAMA!
BUT THAT DOESN'T CHANGE THE FACT THAT I'M GONNA BEAT HIM ONE DAY!
JOLT
HM?!
...
Hrraaaaah!!
WARM-UP TIIIIME!!
SERIOUSLY, WHERE DOES THE ENERGY COME FROM?!
SKARF
I CAN PLAY 100 GAMES A DAY!
GOBL
FNEE
WAAA
IT'S STILL HARD TO BELIEVE WE'VE REACHED THE QUARTER-FINAL STAGE OF NATIONALS.
THE QUARTER-FINALS...
...OF THE NATIONAL TOURNEY.
IF WE WIN, WE'LL GET TO PLAY ON CENTER COURT...

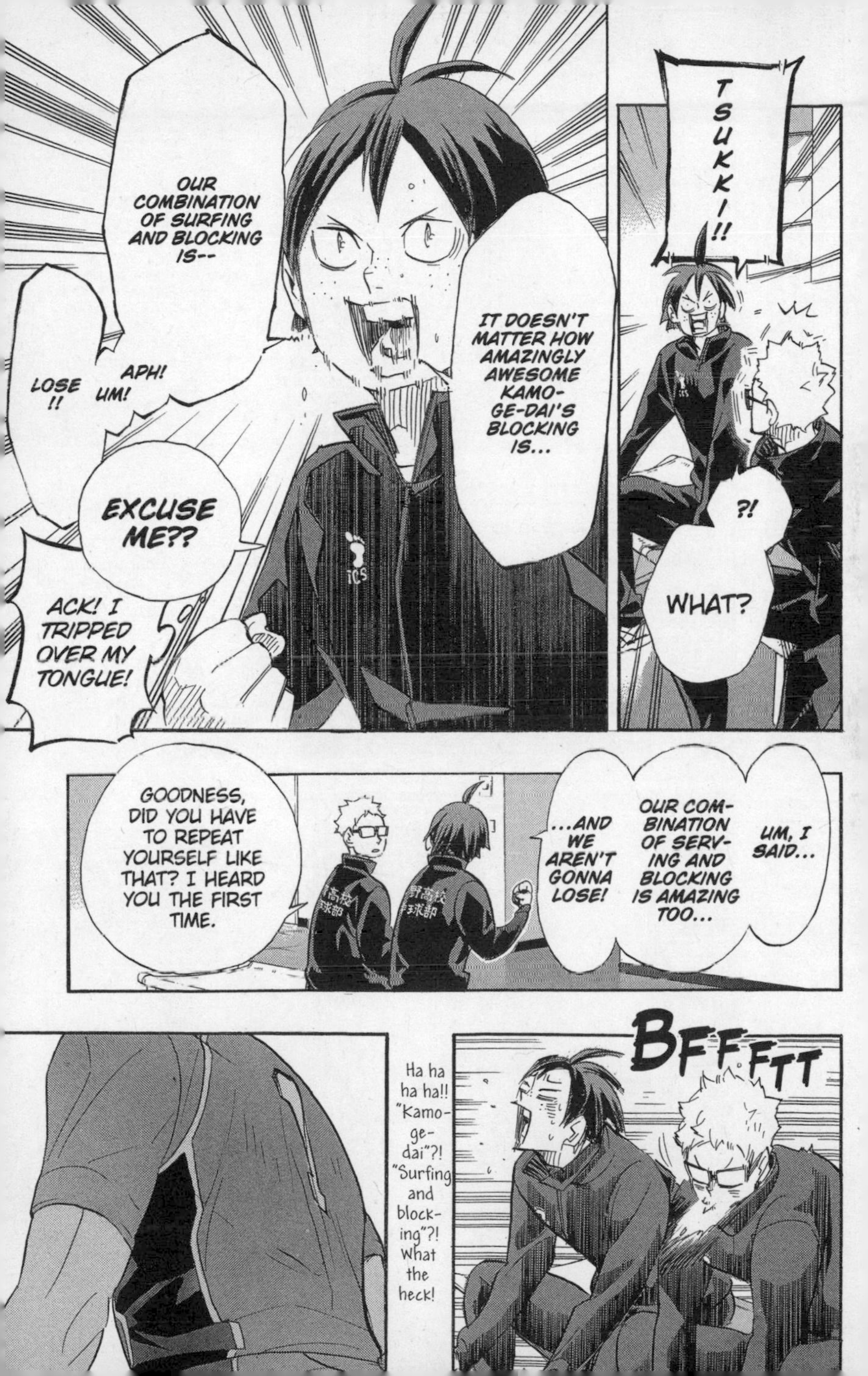
TSUKKI!!
?!
WHAT?
IT DOESN'T MATTER HOW AMAZINGLY AWESOME KAMO-GE-DAI'S BLOCKING IS...
OUR COMBINATION OF SURFING AND BLOCKING IS--
APH! UM!
LOSE !!
EXCUSE ME??
ACK! I TRIPPED OVER MY TONGUE!
UM, I SAID...
OUR COM-BINATION OF SERV-ING AND BLOCKING IS AMAZING TOO...
...AND WE AREN'T GONNA LOSE!
GOODNESS, DID YOU HAVE TO REPEAT YOURSELF LIKE THAT? I HEARD YOU THE FIRST TIME.
BFFFFTT
Ha ha ha ha!! "Kamo-ge-dai"?! "Surfing and block-ing"?! What the heck!

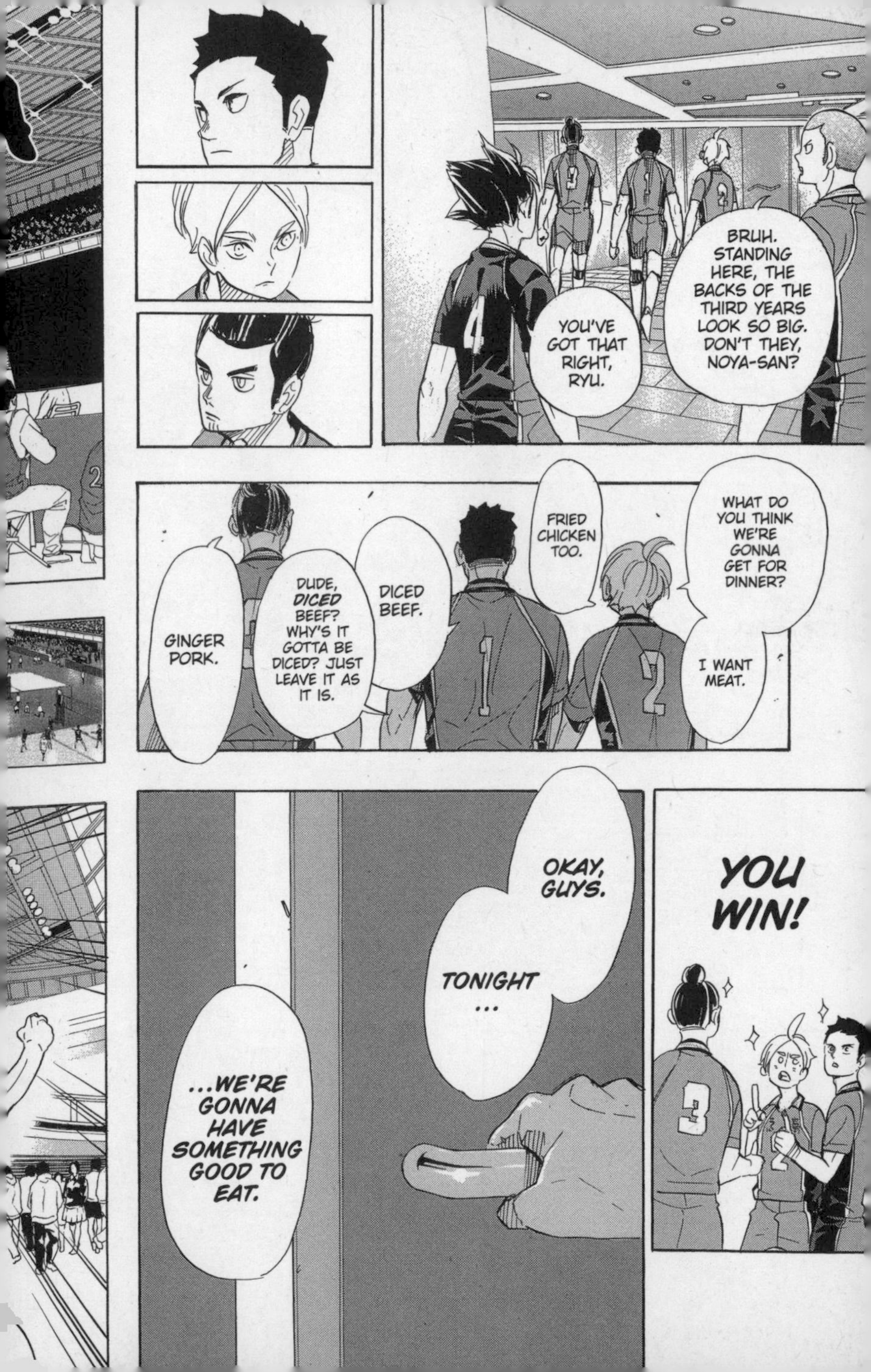
BRUH. STANDING HERE, THE BACKS OF THE THIRD YEARS LOOK SO BIG. DON'T THEY, NOYA-SAN?
YOU'VE GOT THAT RIGHT, RYU.
WHAT DO YOU THINK WE'RE GONNA GET FOR DINNER?
I WANT MEAT.
FRIED CHICKEN TOO.
DICED BEEF.
DUDE, ***DICED*** BEEF? WHY'S IT GOTTA BE DICED? JUST LEAVE IT AS IT IS.
GINGER PORK.
YOU WIN!
OKAY, GUYS.
TONIGHT ...
...WE'RE GONNA HAVE SOMETHING GOOD TO EAT.

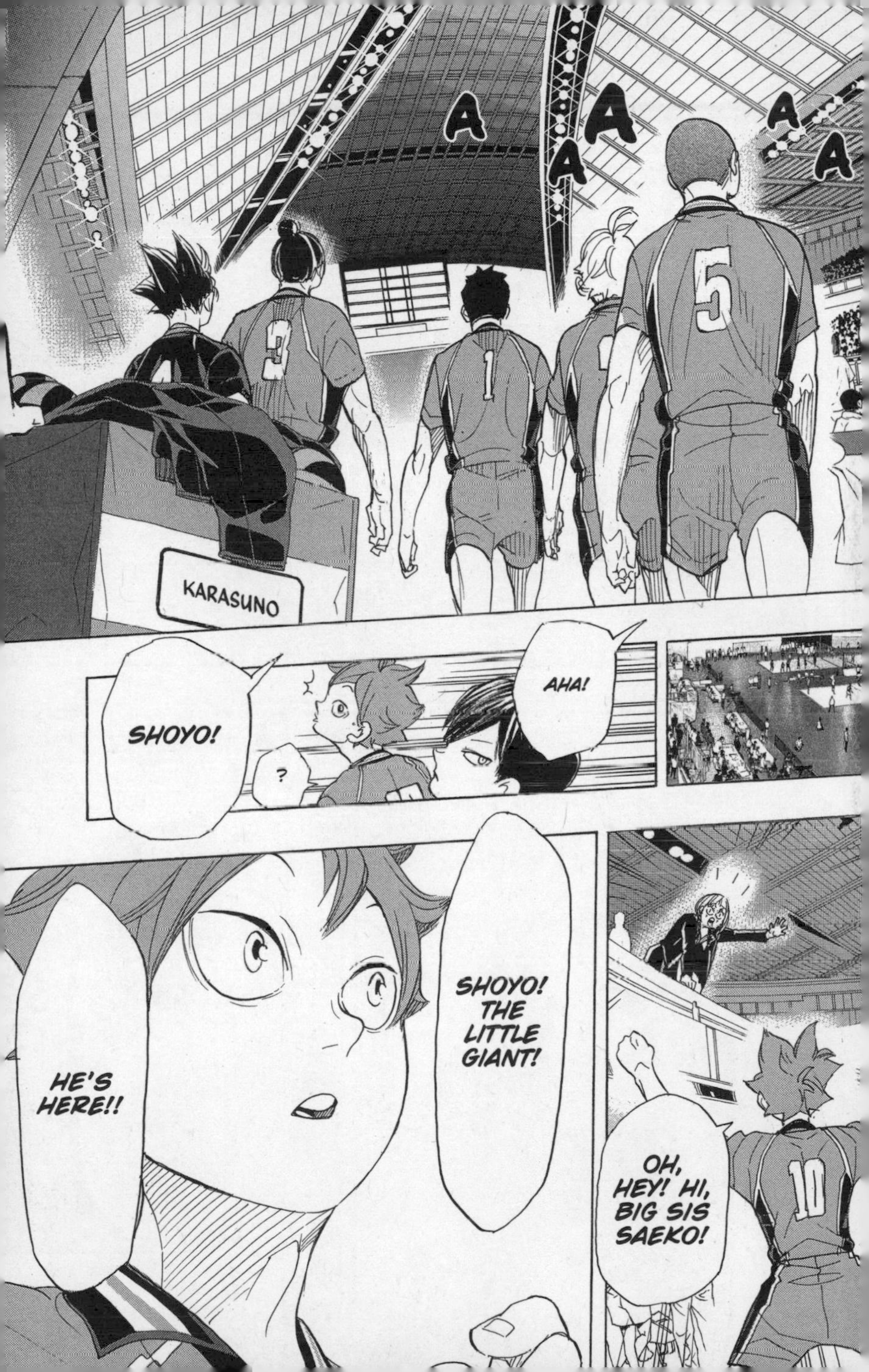
A A A A A A
KARASUNO
AHA!
SHOYO!
?
OH, HEY! HI, BIG SIS SAEKO!
SHOYO! THE LITTLE GIANT!
HE'S HERE!!

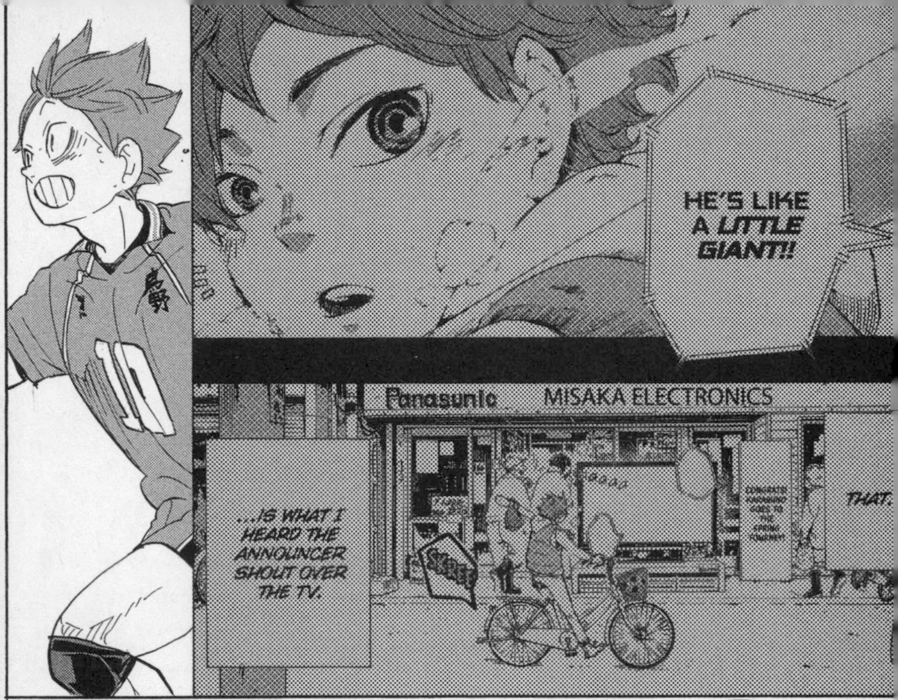
HE'S LIKE A *LITTLE GIANT!!*
THAT.
Panasunic
MISAKA ELECTRONICS
CONGRATS! KARASUNO GOES TO THE SPRING TOURNEY!
...IS WHAT I HEARD THE ANNOUNCER SHOUT OVER THE TV.

*JERSEY: KARASUNO

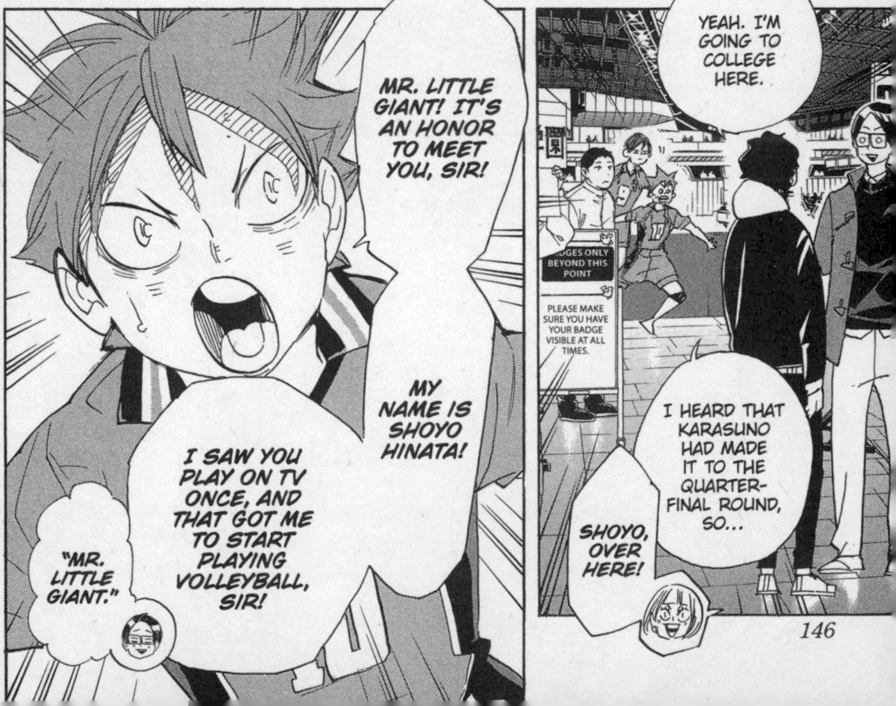
YEAH. I'M GOING TO COLLEGE HERE.
DGES ONLY BEYOND THIS POINT
PLEASE MAKE SURE YOU HAVE YOUR BADGE VISIBLE AT ALL TIMES.
I HEARD THAT KARASUNO HAD MADE IT TO THE QUARTER-FINAL ROUND, SO...
SHOYO, OVER HERE!
MR. LITTLE GIANT! IT'S AN HONOR TO MEET YOU, SIR!
MY NAME IS SHOYO HINATA!
I SAW YOU PLAY ON TV ONCE, AND THAT GOT ME TO START PLAYING VOLLEYBALL, SIR!
"MR. LITTLE GIANT."

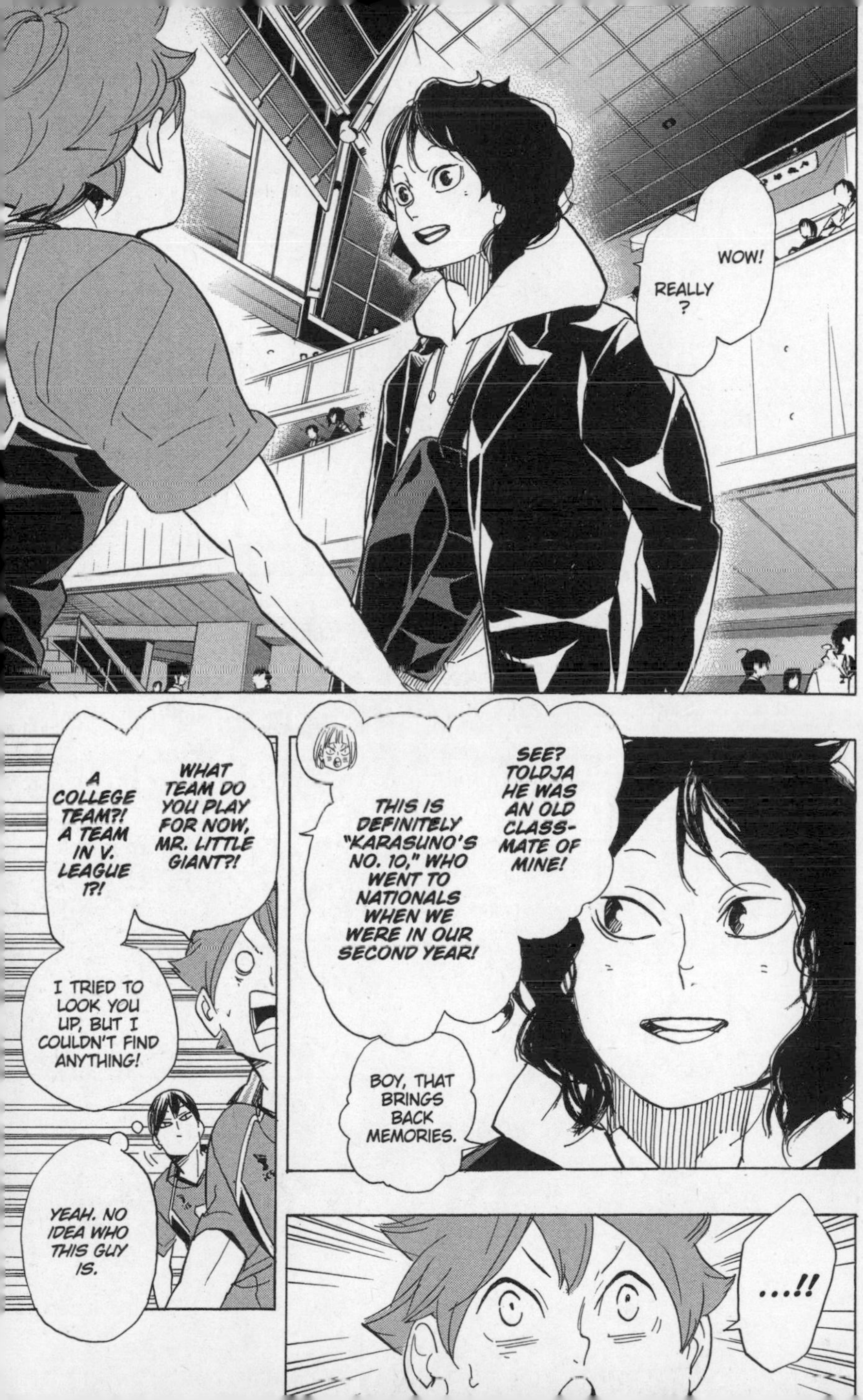
WOW!
REALLY?
SEE? TOLDJA HE WAS AN OLD CLASSMATE OF MINE!
THIS IS DEFINITELY "KARASUNO'S NO. 10," WHO WENT TO NATIONALS WHEN WE WERE IN OUR SECOND YEAR!
BOY, THAT BRINGS BACK MEMORIES.
...!!
WHAT TEAM DO YOU PLAY FOR NOW, MR. LITTLE GIANT?!
A COLLEGE TEAM?! A TEAM IN V. LEAGUE!?!
I TRIED TO LOOK YOU UP, BUT I COULDN'T FIND ANYTHING!
YEAH. NO IDEA WHO THIS GUY IS.

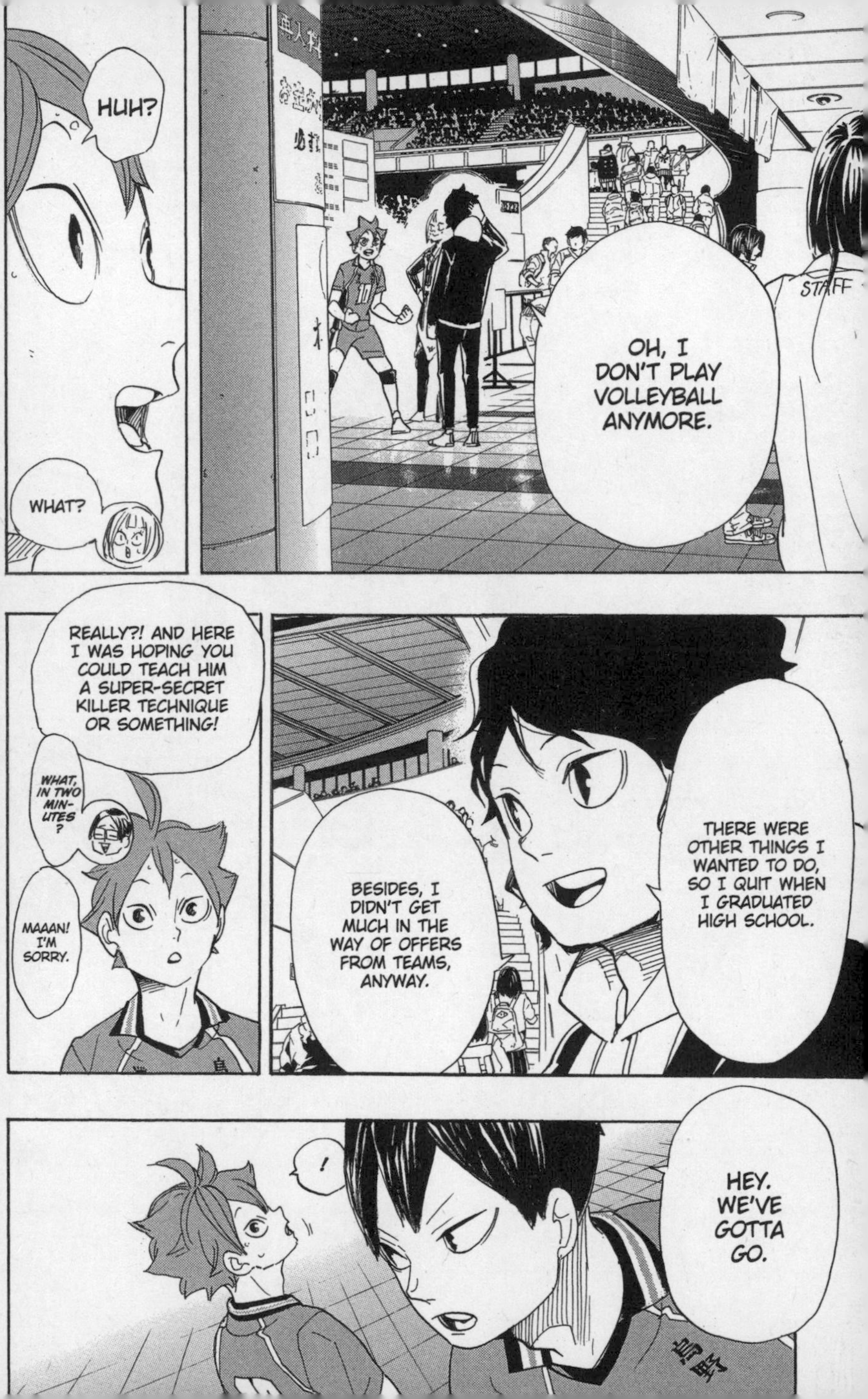
STAFF
OH, I DON'T PLAY VOLLEYBALL ANYMORE.
HUH?
WHAT?
THERE WERE OTHER THINGS I WANTED TO DO, SO I QUIT WHEN I GRADUATED HIGH SCHOOL.
BESIDES, I DIDN'T GET MUCH IN THE WAY OF OFFERS FROM TEAMS, ANYWAY.
REALLY?! AND HERE I WAS HOPING YOU COULD TEACH HIM A SUPER-SECRET KILLER TECHNIQUE OR SOMETHING!
WHAT, IN TWO MIN-UTES?
MAAAN! I'M SORRY.
HEY. WE'VE GOTTA GO.
!

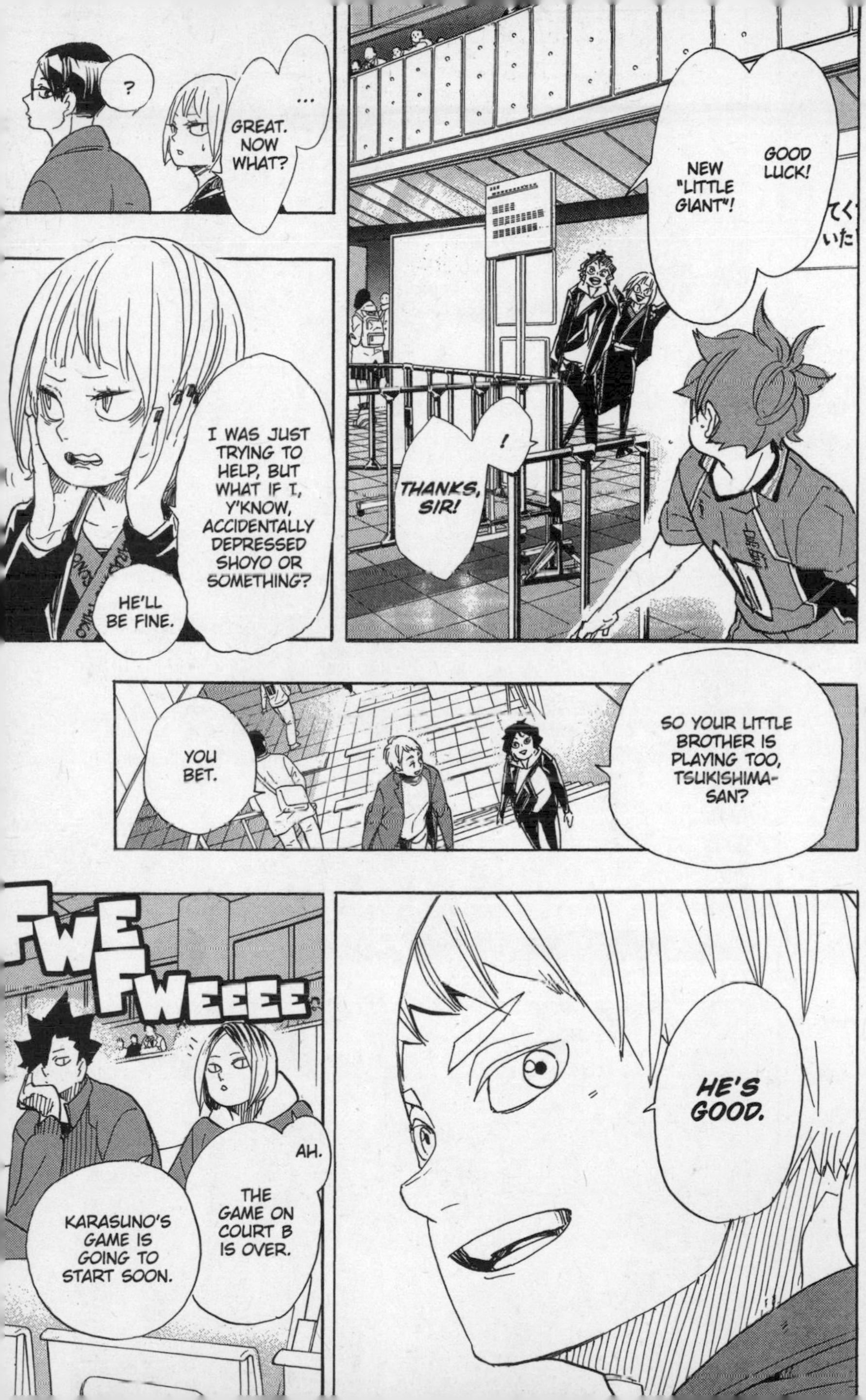
GOOD LUCK!
NEW "LITTLE GIANT"!
!
THANKS, SIR!
?
...
GREAT. NOW WHAT?
I WAS JUST TRYING TO HELP, BUT WHAT IF I, Y'KNOW, ACCIDENTALLY DEPRESSED SHOYO OR SOMETHING?
HE'LL BE FINE.
SO YOUR LITTLE BROTHER IS PLAYING TOO, TSUKISHIMA-SAN?
YOU BET.
HE'S GOOD.
FWE FWEEEE
AH.
THE GAME ON COURT B IS OVER.
KARASUNO'S GAME IS GOING TO START SOON.

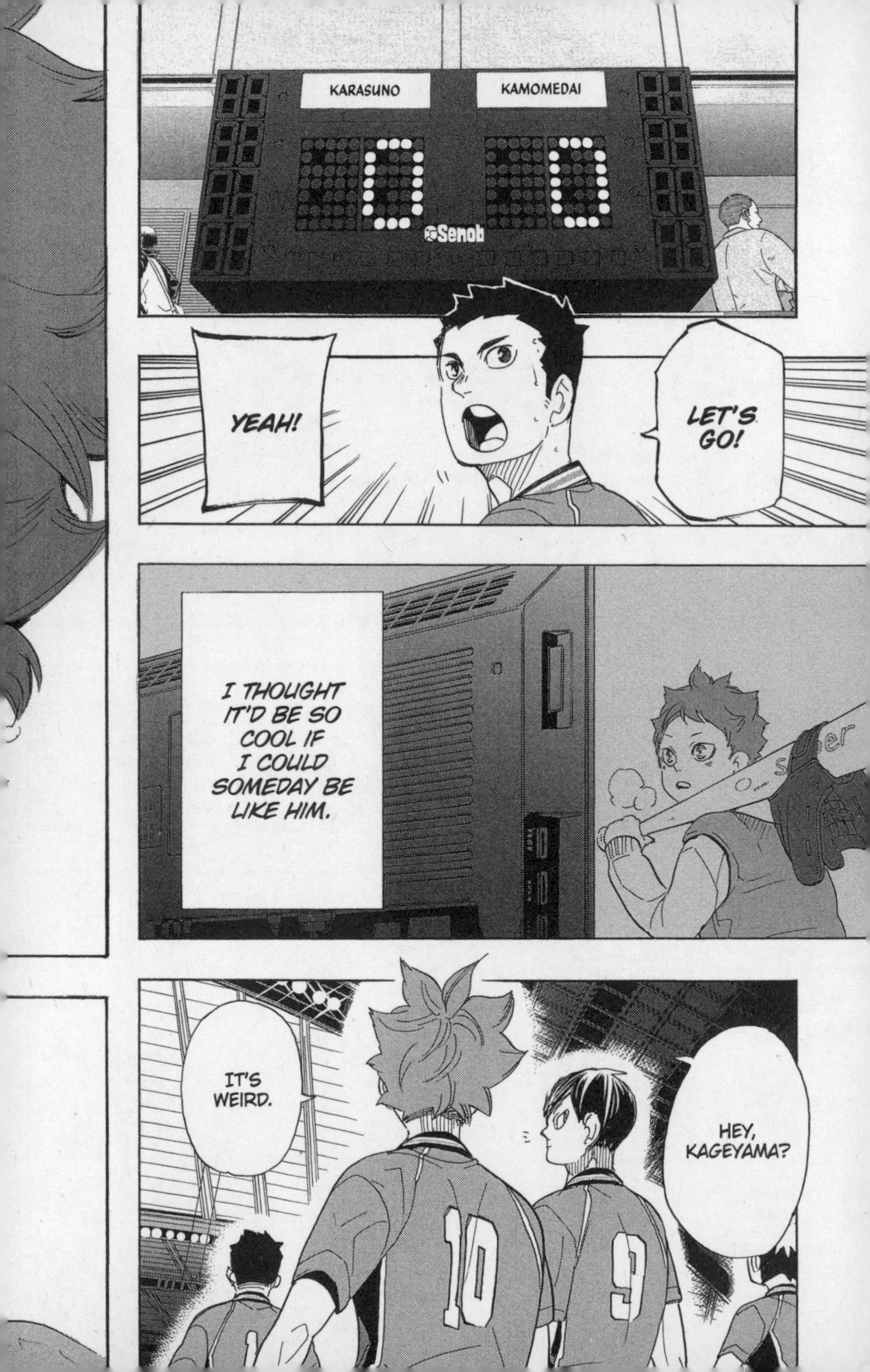
KARASUNO
KAMOMEDAI
Senob
LET'S GO!
YEAH!
I THOUGHT IT'D BE SO COOL IF I COULD SOMEDAY BE LIKE HIM.
HEY, KAGEYAMA?
IT'S WEIRD.

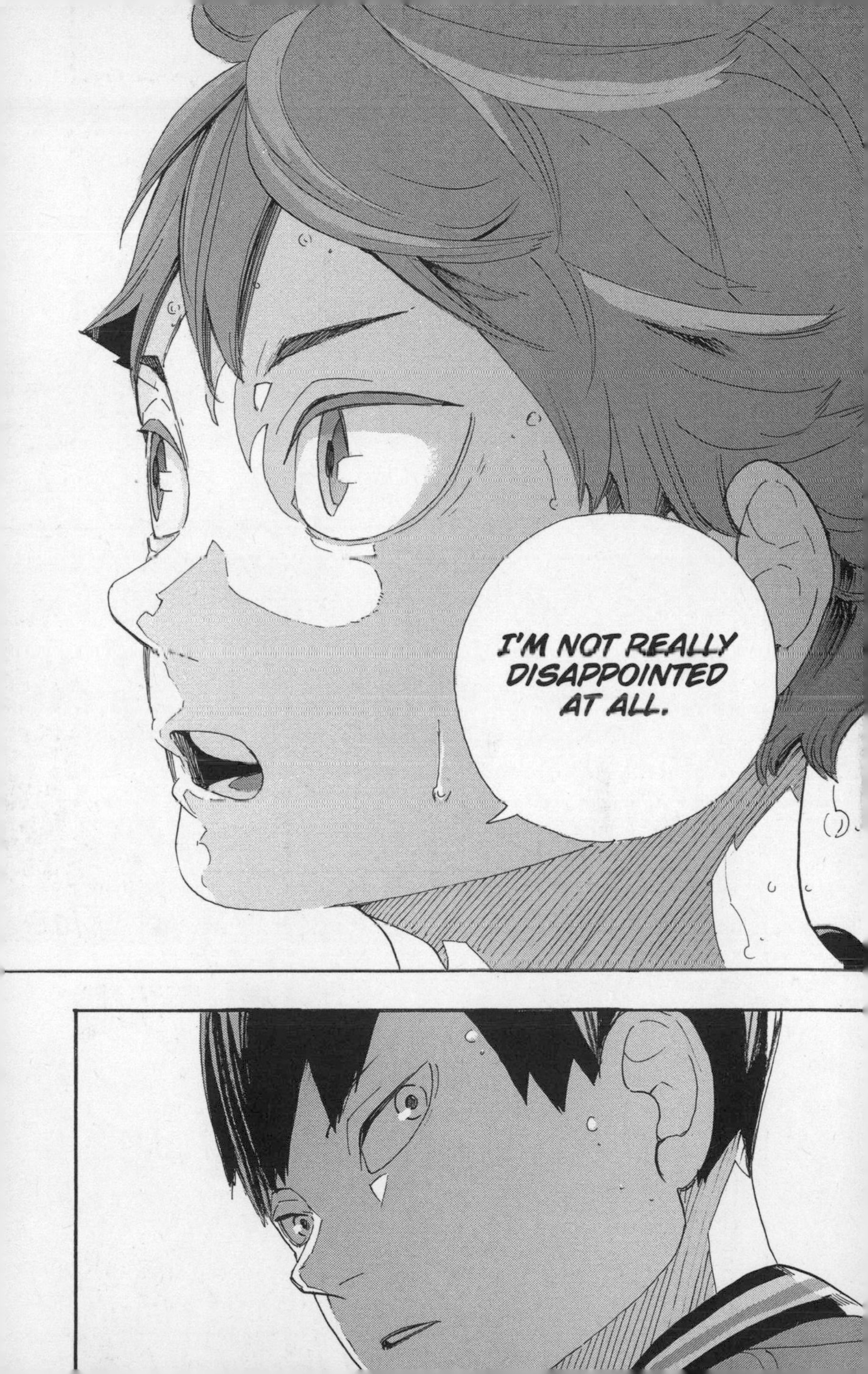
I'M NOT REALLY DISAPPOINTED AT ALL.

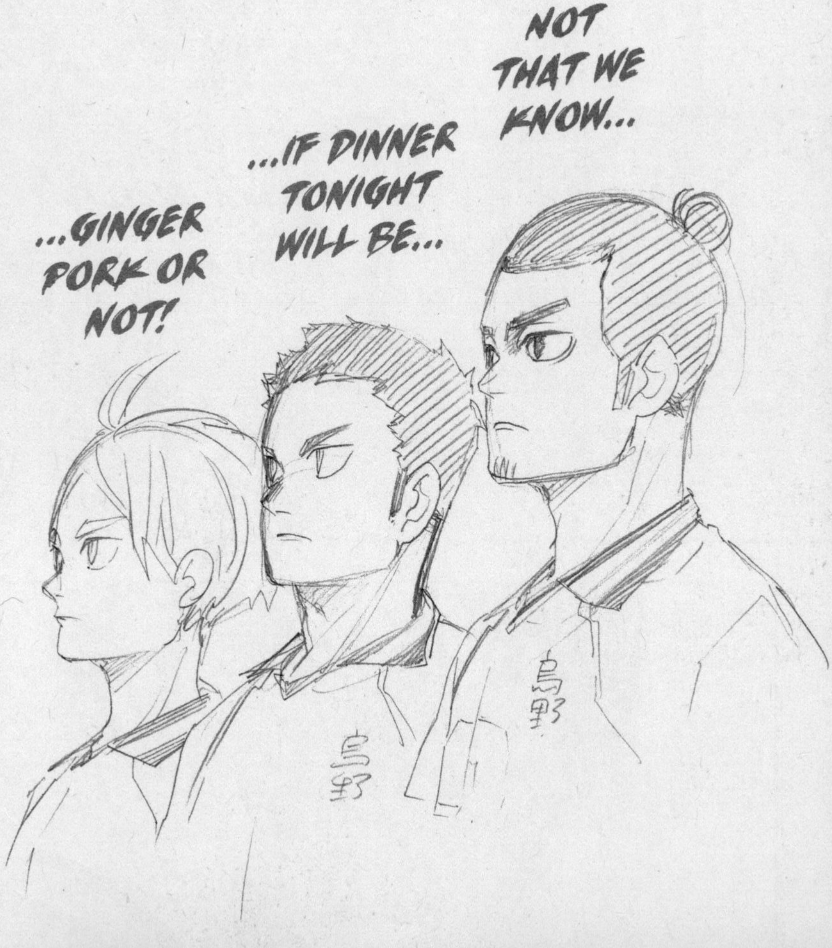
NOT THAT WE KNOW...
...IF DINNER TONIGHT WILL BE...
...GINGER PORK OR NOT!

CHAPTER 339: Acknowledgment

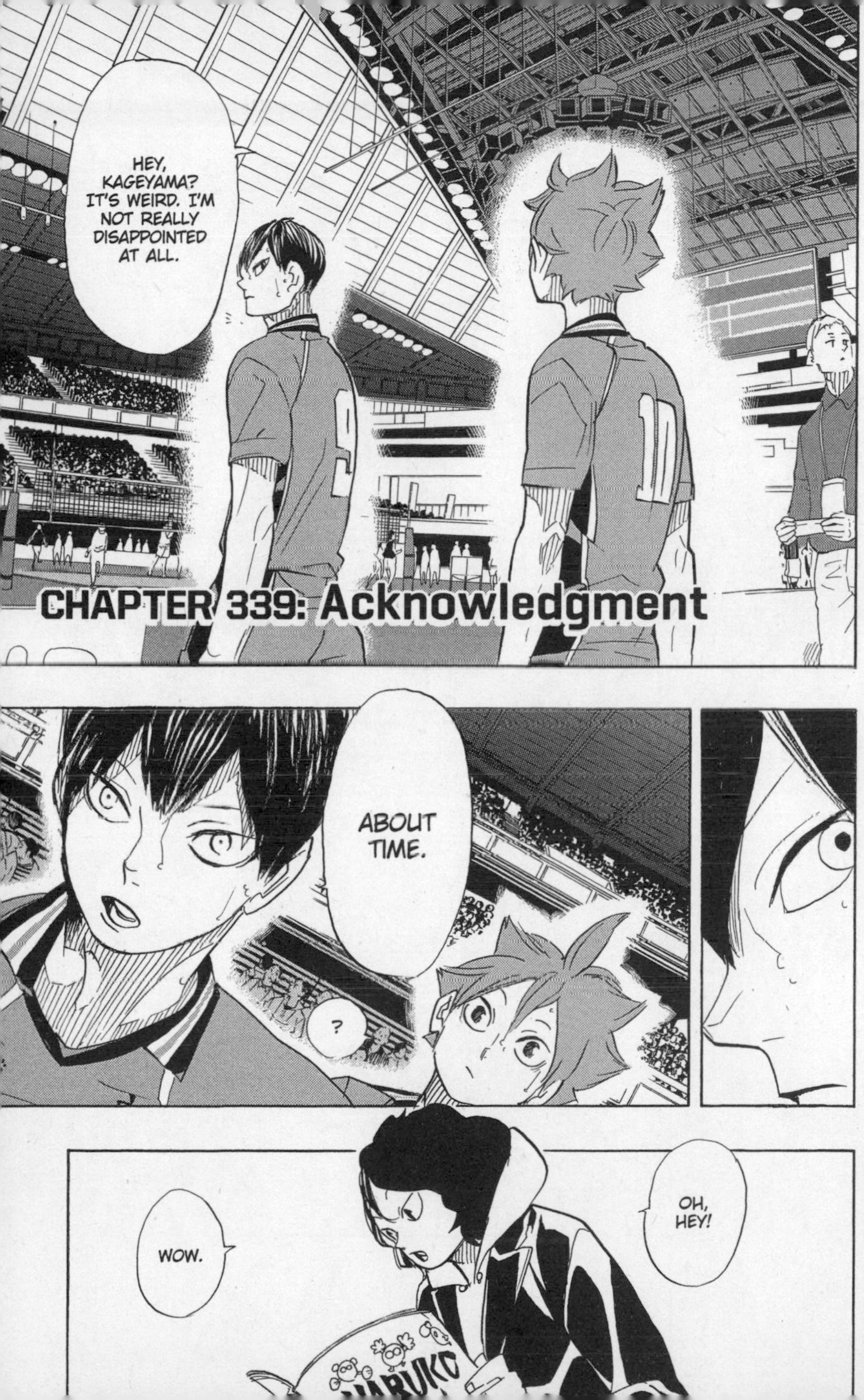
HEY, KAGEYAMA? IT'S WEIRD. I'M NOT REALLY DISAPPOINTED AT ALL.
ABOUT TIME.
?
OH, HEY!
WOW.

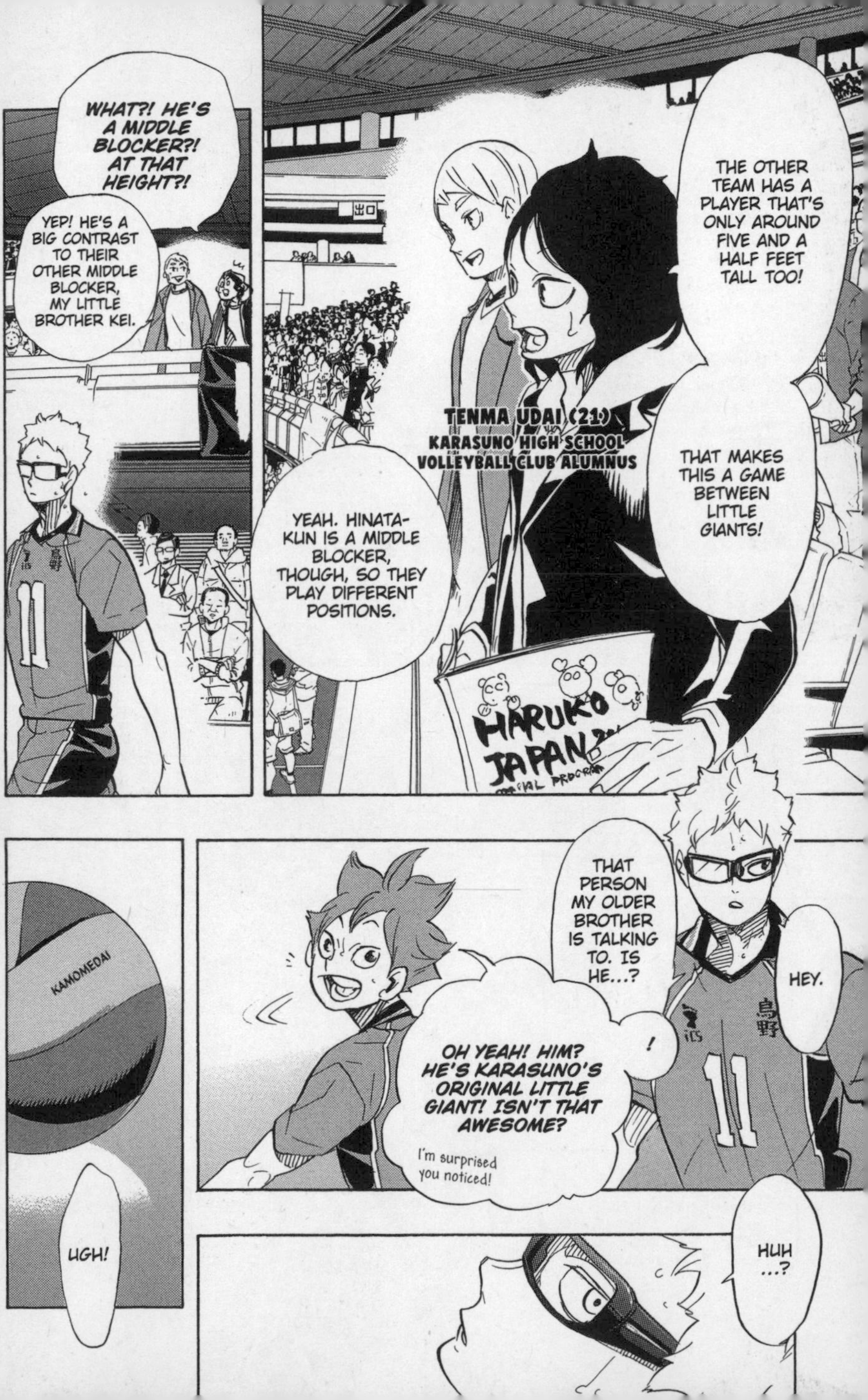
THE OTHER TEAM HAS A PLAYER THAT'S ONLY AROUND FIVE AND A HALF FEET TALL TOO!
THAT MAKES THIS A GAME BETWEEN LITTLE GIANTS!
TENMA UDAI (21) KARASUNO HIGH SCHOOL VOLLEYBALL CLUB ALUMNUS
YEAH. HINATA-KUN IS A MIDDLE BLOCKER, THOUGH, SO THEY PLAY DIFFERENT POSITIONS.
HARUKO JAPAN
WHAT?! HE'S A MIDDLE BLOCKER?! AT THAT HEIGHT?!
YEP! HE'S A BIG CONTRAST TO THEIR OTHER MIDDLE BLOCKER, MY LITTLE BROTHER KEI.
HEY.
THAT PERSON MY OLDER BROTHER IS TALKING TO. IS HE...?
!
OH YEAH! HIM? HE'S KARASUNO'S ORIGINAL LITTLE GIANT! ISN'T THAT AWESOME?
I'm surprised you noticed!
HUH ...?
KAMOMEDAI
UGH!

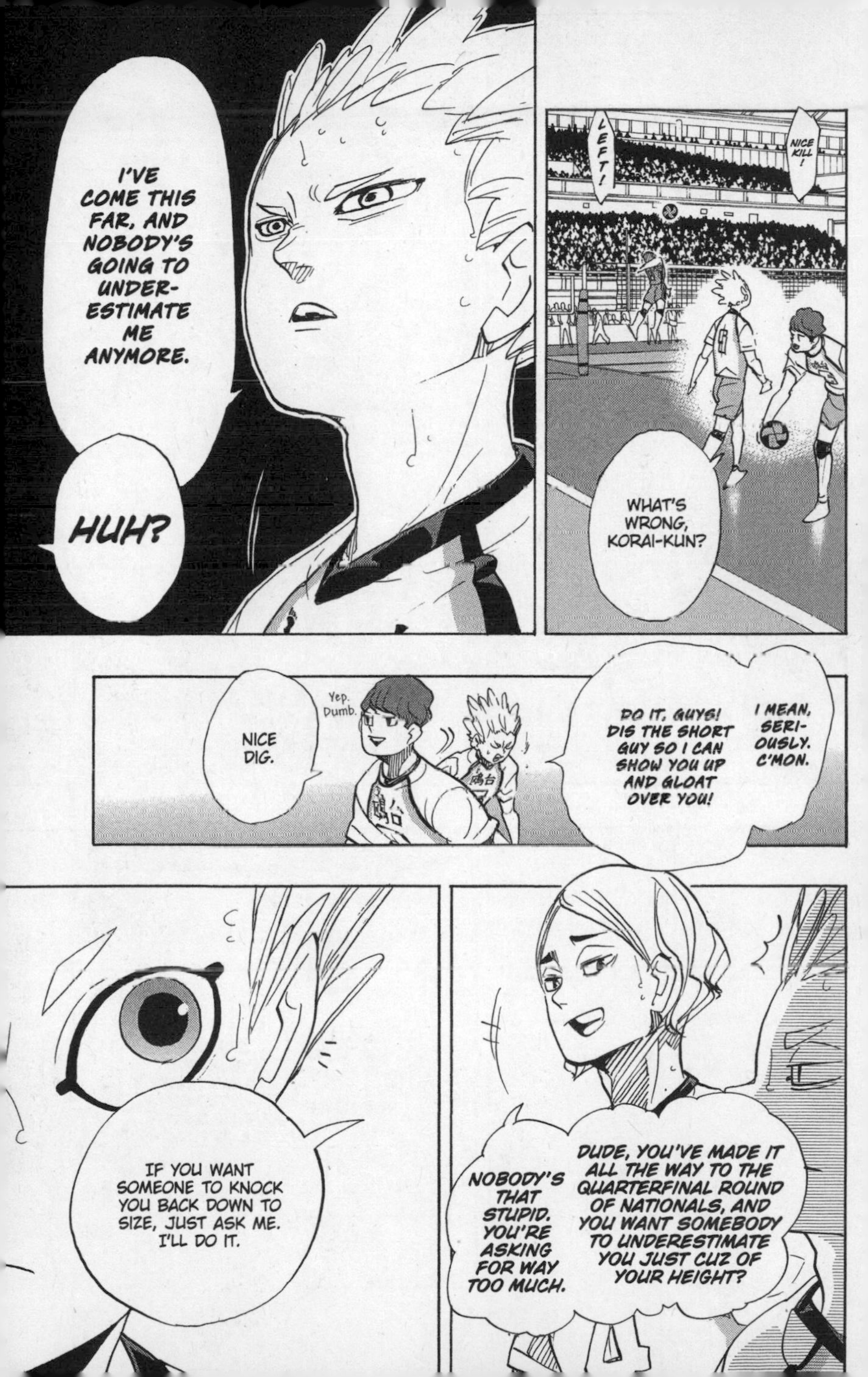
NICE KILL!
LEFT!
WHAT'S WRONG, KORAI-KUN?
I'VE COME THIS FAR, AND NOBODY'S GOING TO UNDER-ESTIMATE ME ANYMORE.
HUH?
I MEAN, SERI-OUSLY. C'MON.
DO IT, GUYS! DIS THE SHORT GUY SO I CAN SHOW YOU UP AND GLOAT OVER YOU!
Yep. Dumb.
NICE DIG.
DUDE, YOU'VE MADE IT ALL THE WAY TO THE QUARTERFINAL ROUND OF NATIONALS, AND YOU WANT SOMEBODY TO UNDERESTIMATE YOU JUST CUZ OF YOUR HEIGHT?
NOBODY'S THAT STUPID. YOU'RE ASKING FOR WAY TOO MUCH.
IF YOU WANT SOMEONE TO KNOCK YOU BACK DOWN TO SIZE, JUST ASK ME. I'LL DO IT.

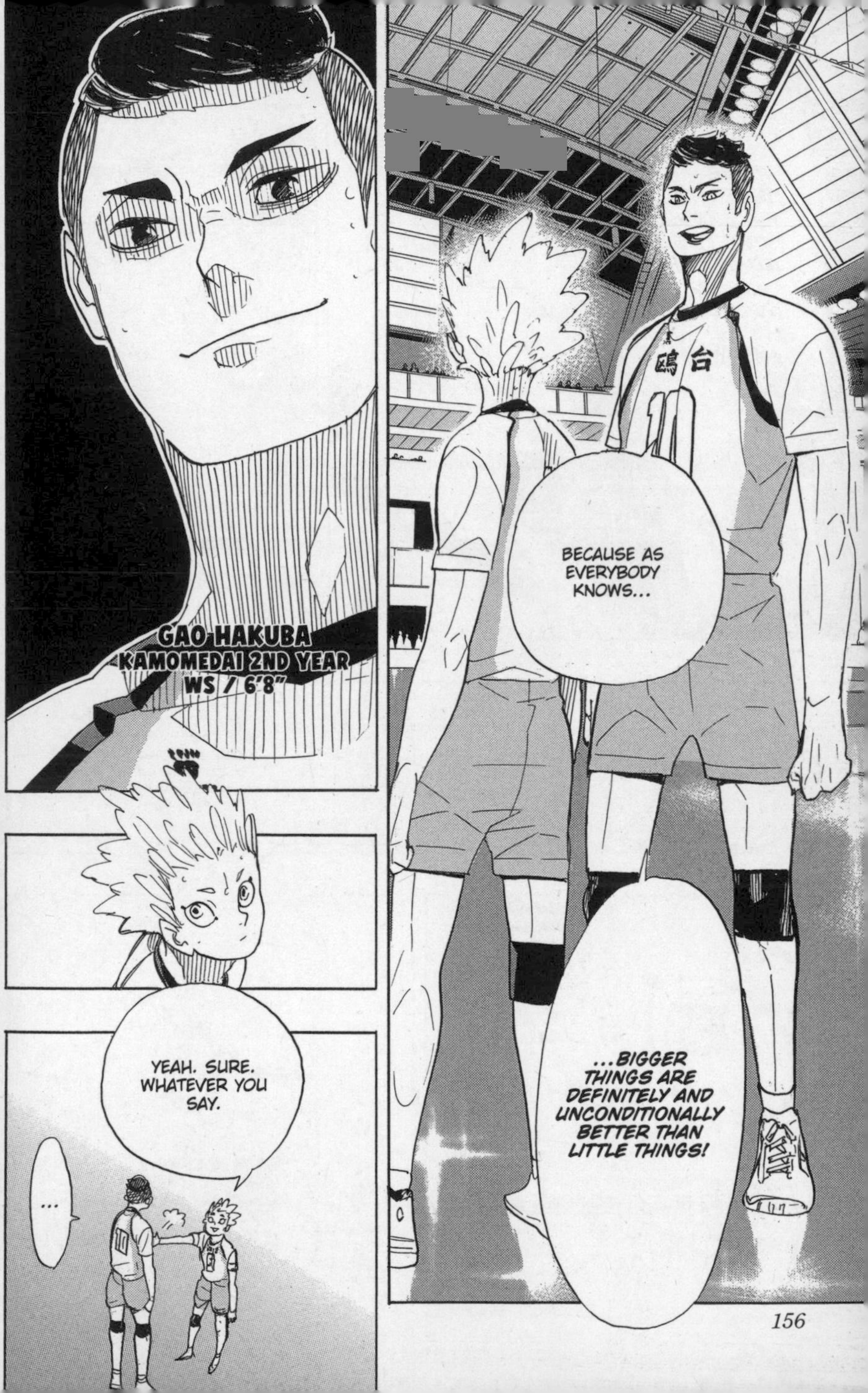
BECAUSE AS EVERYBODY KNOWS...
...BIGGER THINGS ARE DEFINITELY AND UNCONDITIONALLY BETTER THAN LITTLE THINGS!
鴎台
GAO HAKUBA
KAMOMEDAI 2ND YEAR
WS / 6'8"
YEAH. SURE. WHATEVER YOU SAY.
...

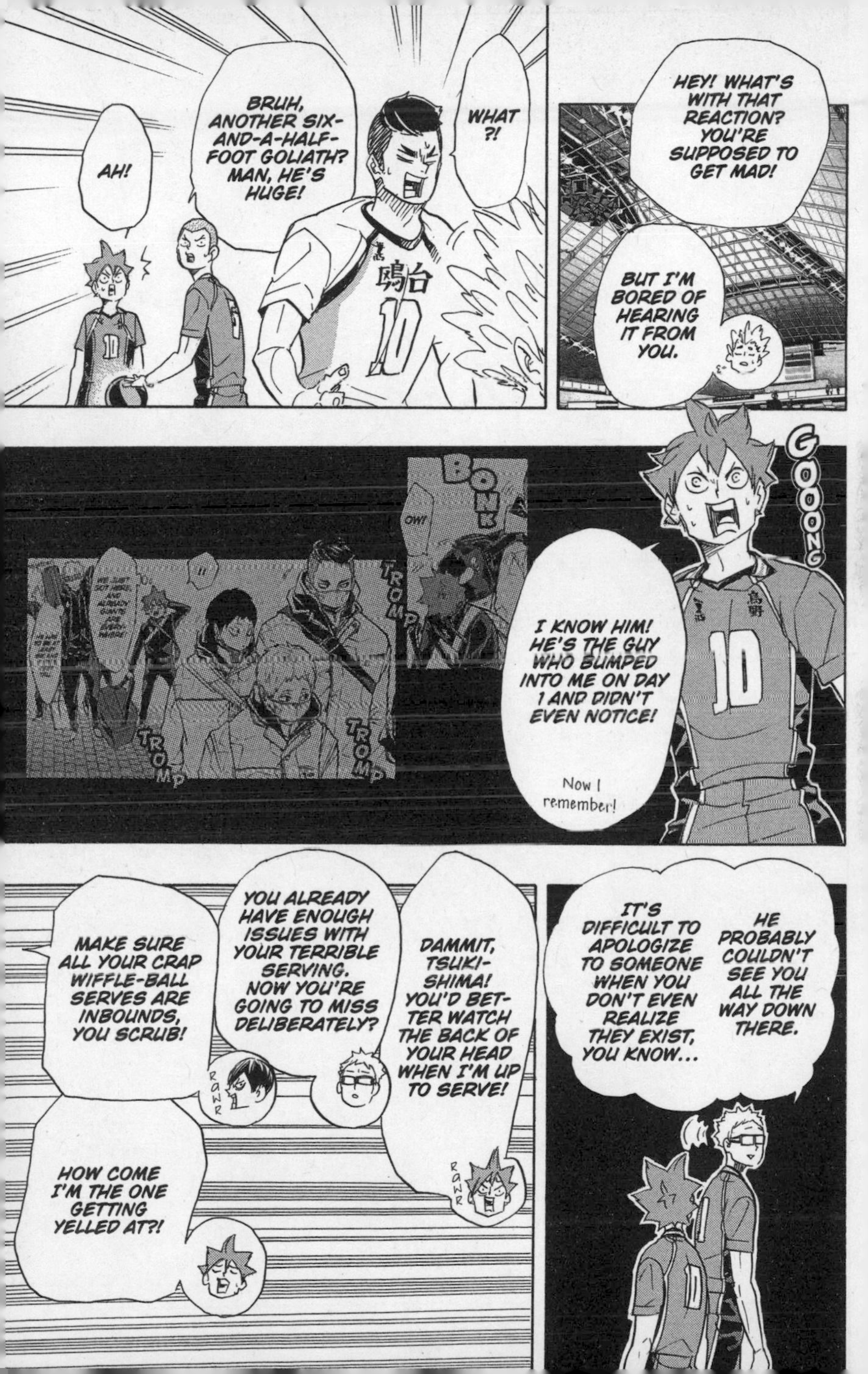
HEY! WHAT'S WITH THAT REACTION? YOU'RE SUPPOSED TO GET MAD!
BUT I'M BORED OF HEARING IT FROM YOU.
WHAT ?!
BRUH, ANOTHER SIX-AND-A-HALF-FOOT GOLIATH? MAN, HE'S HUGE!
AH!
GOOOONG
I KNOW HIM! HE'S THE GUY WHO BUMPED INTO ME ON DAY 1 AND DIDN'T EVEN NOTICE!
Now I remember!
BONK
OW!
TROMP
TROMP
TROMP
HE PROBABLY COULDN'T SEE YOU ALL THE WAY DOWN THERE.
IT'S DIFFICULT TO APOLOGIZE TO SOMEONE WHEN YOU DON'T EVEN REALIZE THEY EXIST, YOU KNOW...
DAMMIT, TSUKISHIMA! YOU'D BETTER WATCH THE BACK OF YOUR HEAD WHEN I'M UP TO SERVE!
RAWR
YOU ALREADY HAVE ENOUGH ISSUES WITH YOUR TERRIBLE SERVING. NOW YOU'RE GOING TO MISS DELIBERATELY?
MAKE SURE ALL YOUR CRAP WIFFLE-BALL SERVES ARE INBOUNDS, YOU SCRUB!
RAWR
HOW COME I'M THE ONE GETTING YELLED AT?!

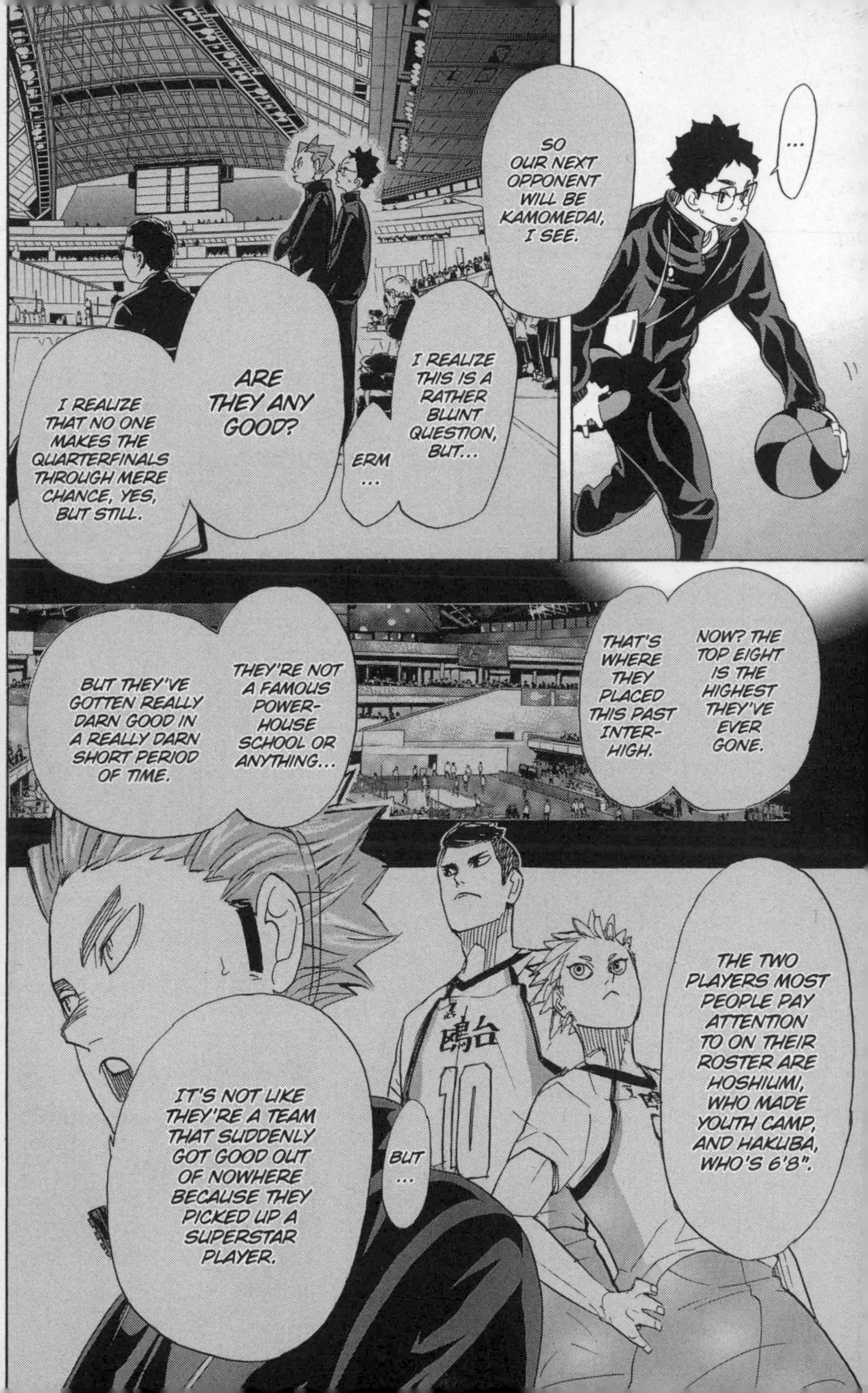
...
SO OUR NEXT OPPONENT WILL BE KAMOMEDAI, I SEE.
I REALIZE THIS IS A RATHER BLUNT QUESTION, BUT...
ERM ...
ARE THEY ANY GOOD?
I REALIZE THAT NO ONE MAKES THE QUARTERFINALS THROUGH MERE CHANCE, YES, BUT STILL.
NOW? THE TOP EIGHT IS THE HIGHEST THEY'VE EVER GONE.
THAT'S WHERE THEY PLACED THIS PAST INTER-HIGH.
THEY'RE NOT A FAMOUS POWER-HOUSE SCHOOL OR ANYTHING...
BUT THEY'VE GOTTEN REALLY DARN GOOD IN A REALLY DARN SHORT PERIOD OF TIME.
THE TWO PLAYERS MOST PEOPLE PAY ATTENTION TO ON THEIR ROSTER ARE HOSHIUMI, WHO MADE YOUTH CAMP, AND HAKUBA, WHO'S 6'8".
BUT ...
IT'S NOT LIKE THEY'RE A TEAM THAT SUDDENLY GOT GOOD OUT OF NOWHERE BECAUSE THEY PICKED UP A SUPERSTAR PLAYER.

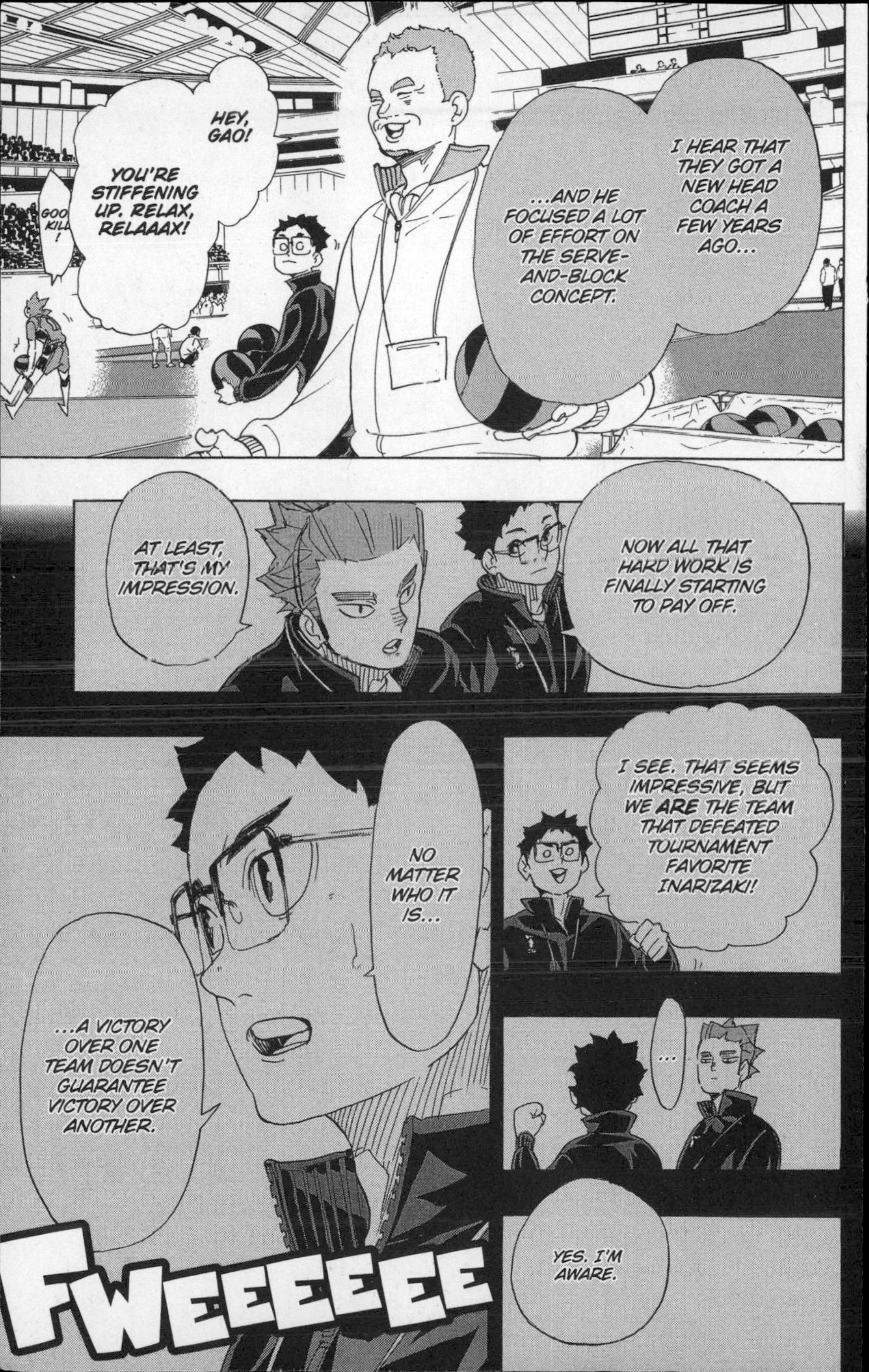
I HEAR THAT THEY GOT A NEW HEAD COACH A FEW YEARS AGO...
...AND HE FOCUSED A LOT OF EFFORT ON THE SERVE-AND-BLOCK CONCEPT.
HEY, GAO! YOU'RE STIFFENING UP. RELAX, RELAAAX!
NOW ALL THAT HARD WORK IS FINALLY STARTING TO PAY OFF.
AT LEAST, THAT'S MY IMPRESSION.
I SEE. THAT SEEMS IMPRESSIVE, BUT WE **ARE** THE TEAM THAT DEFEATED TOURNAMENT FAVORITE INARIZAKI!
...
YES. I'M AWARE.
NO MATTER WHO IT IS...
...A VICTORY OVER ONE TEAM DOESN'T GUARANTEE VICTORY OVER ANOTHER.
FWEEEEEEE

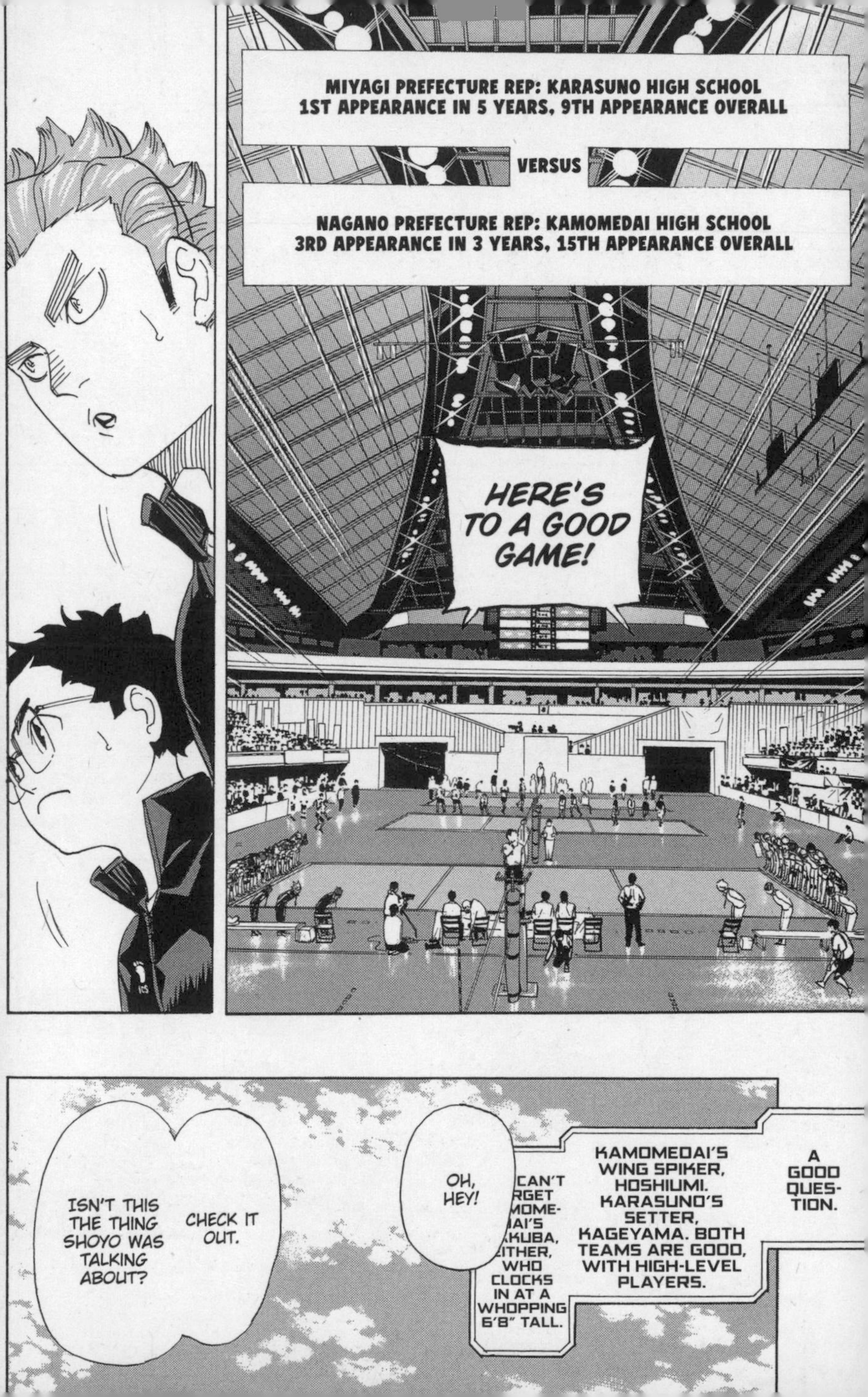
MIYAGI PREFECTURE REP: KARASUNO HIGH SCHOOL 1ST APPEARANCE IN 5 YEARS, 9TH APPEARANCE OVERALL
VERSUS
NAGANO PREFECTURE REP: KAMOMEDAI HIGH SCHOOL 3RD APPEARANCE IN 3 YEARS, 15TH APPEARANCE OVERALL
HERE'S TO A GOOD GAME!
A GOOD QUES-TION.
KAMOMEDAI'S WING SPIKER, HOSHIUMI. KARASUNO'S SETTER, KAGEYAMA. BOTH TEAMS ARE GOOD, WITH HIGH-LEVEL PLAYERS.
CAN'T RGET MOME-AI'S KUBA, ITHER, WHO CLOCKS IN AT A WHOPPING 6'8" TALL.
OH, HEY!
CHECK IT OUT.
ISN'T THIS THE THING SHOYO WAS TALKING ABOUT?

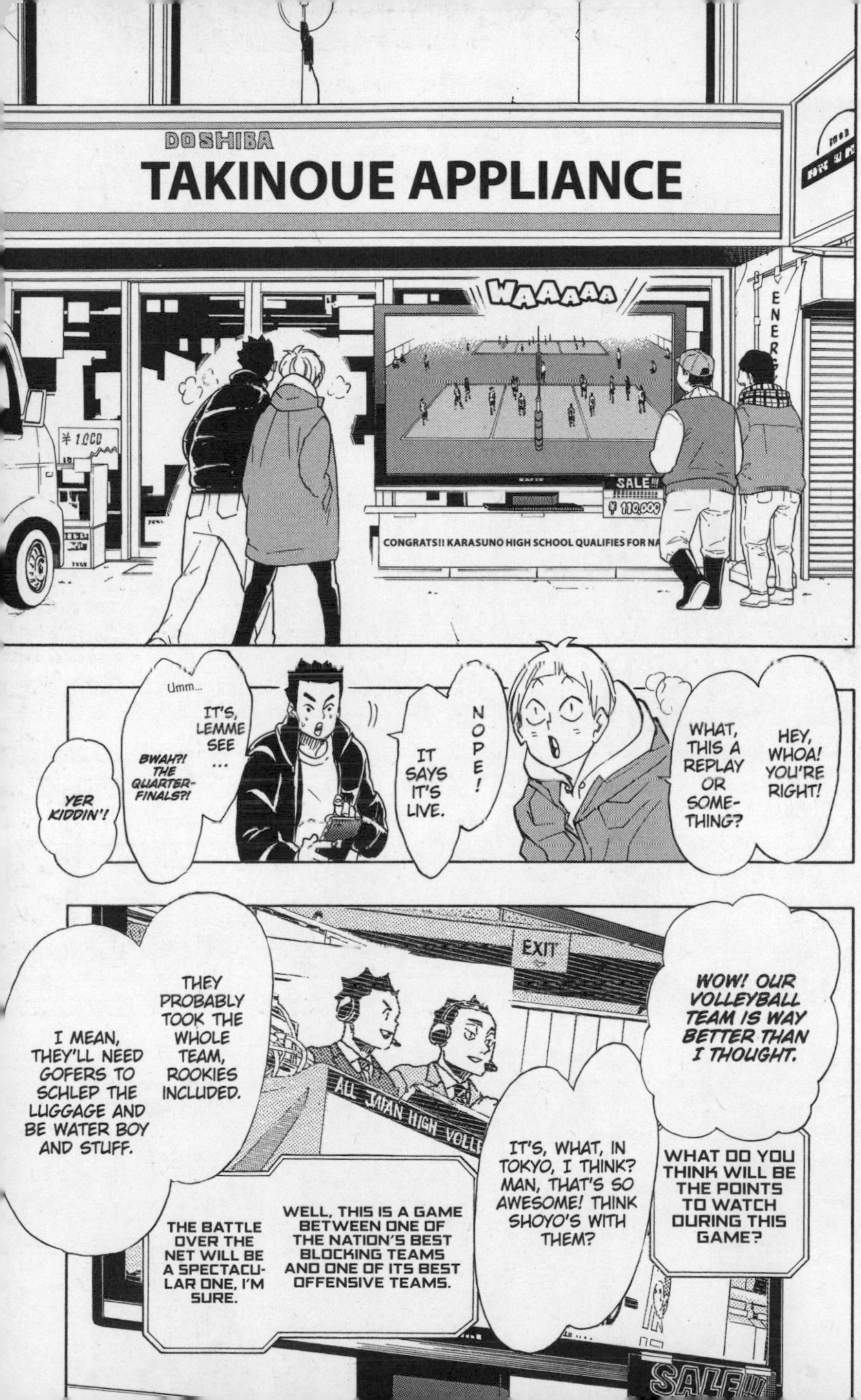
DOSHIBA
TAKINOUE APPLIANCE
WAAAAA
SALE!!!
¥110,000
CONGRATS!! KARASUNO HIGH SCHOOL QUALIFIES FOR
HEY, WHOA! YOU'RE RIGHT!
WHAT, THIS A REPLAY OR SOME-THING?
NOPE!
IT SAYS IT'S LIVE.
Umm... IT'S, LEMME SEE ...
BWAH?! THE QUARTER-FINALS?!
YER KIDDIN'!
EXIT
WOW! OUR VOLLEYBALL TEAM IS WAY BETTER THAN I THOUGHT.
IT'S, WHAT, IN TOKYO, I THINK? MAN, THAT'S SO AWESOME! THINK SHOYO'S WITH THEM?
THEY PROBABLY TOOK THE WHOLE TEAM, ROOKIES INCLUDED.
I MEAN, THEY'LL NEED GOFERS TO SCHLEP THE LUGGAGE AND BE WATER BOY AND STUFF.
WHAT DO YOU THINK WILL BE THE POINTS TO WATCH DURING THIS GAME?
WELL, THIS IS A GAME BETWEEN ONE OF THE NATION'S BEST BLOCKING TEAMS AND ONE OF ITS BEST OFFENSIVE TEAMS.
THE BATTLE OVER THE NET WILL BE A SPECTACU-LAR ONE, I'M SURE.
SALE!!!

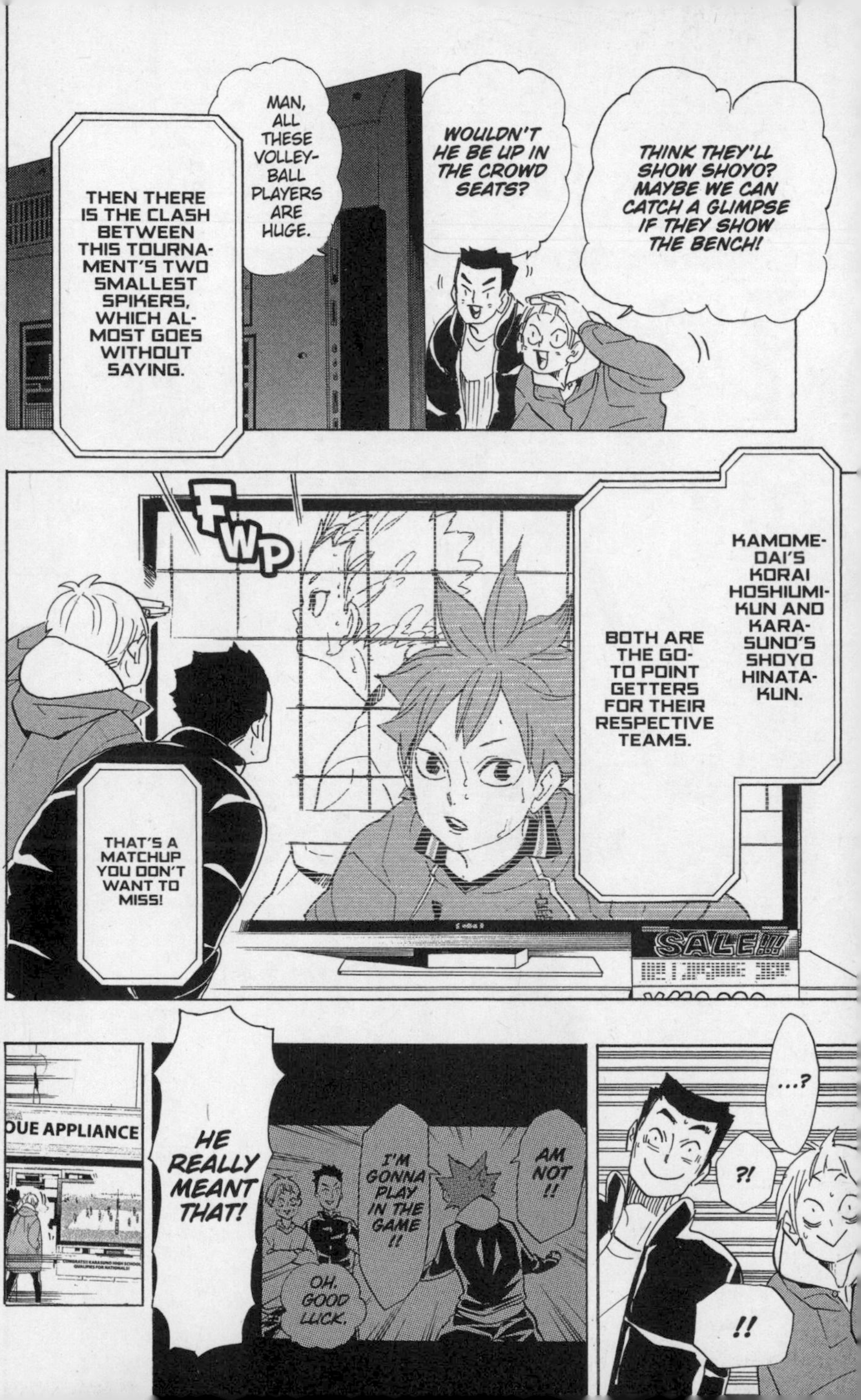
THINK THEY'LL SHOW SHOYO? MAYBE WE CAN CATCH A GLIMPSE IF THEY SHOW THE BENCH!
WOULDN'T HE BE UP IN THE CROWD SEATS?
MAN, ALL THESE VOLLEY-BALL PLAYERS ARE HUGE.
THEN THERE IS THE CLASH BETWEEN THIS TOURNA-MENT'S TWO SMALLEST SPIKERS, WHICH AL-MOST GOES WITHOUT SAYING.
KAMOME-DAI'S KORAI HOSHIUMI-KUN AND KARA-SUNO'S SHOYO HINATA-KUN.
BOTH ARE THE GO-TO POINT GETTERS FOR THEIR RESPECTIVE TEAMS.
FWP
THAT'S A MATCHUP YOU DON'T WANT TO MISS!
SALE!!!
...?
?!
!!
AM NOT!!
I'M GONNA PLAY IN THE GAME!!
OH. GOOD LUCK.
HE REALLY MEANT THAT!
OUE APPLIANCE

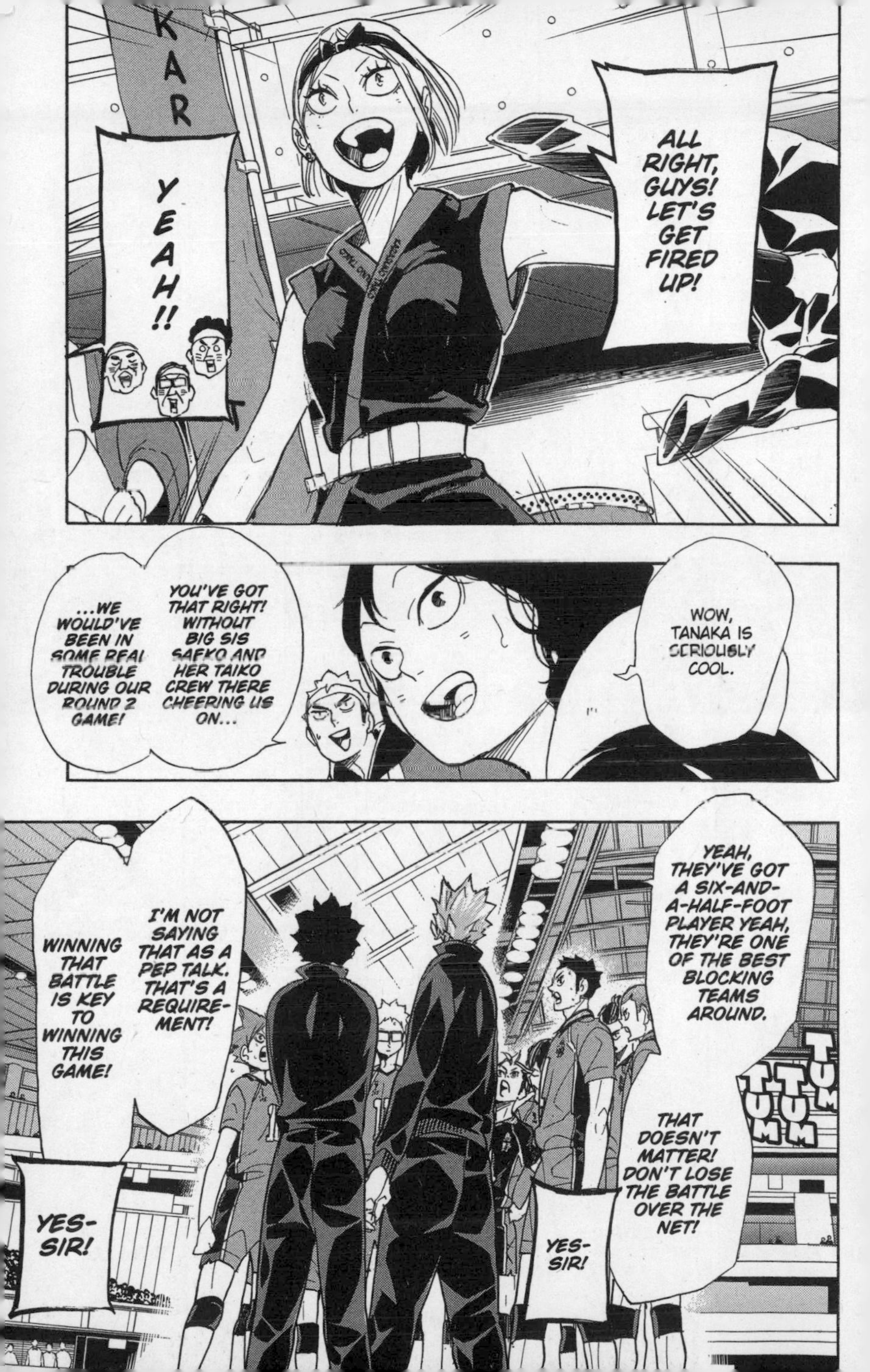
KAR
ALL RIGHT, GUYS! LET'S GET FIRED UP!
YEAH!!
WOW, TANAKA IS SERIOUSLY COOL.
YOU'VE GOT THAT RIGHT! WITHOUT BIG SIS SAEKO AND HER TAIKO CREW THERE CHEERING US ON...
...WE WOULD'VE BEEN IN SOME REAL TROUBLE DURING OUR ROUND 2 GAME!
YEAH, THEY'VE GOT A SIX-AND-A-HALF-FOOT PLAYER YEAH, THEY'RE ONE OF THE BEST BLOCKING TEAMS AROUND.
TUM TUM TUM
THAT DOESN'T MATTER! DON'T LOSE THE BATTLE OVER THE NET!
YES-SIR!
I'M NOT SAYING THAT AS A PEP TALK. THAT'S A REQUIREMENT!
WINNING THAT BATTLE IS KEY TO WINNING THIS GAME!
YES-SIR!

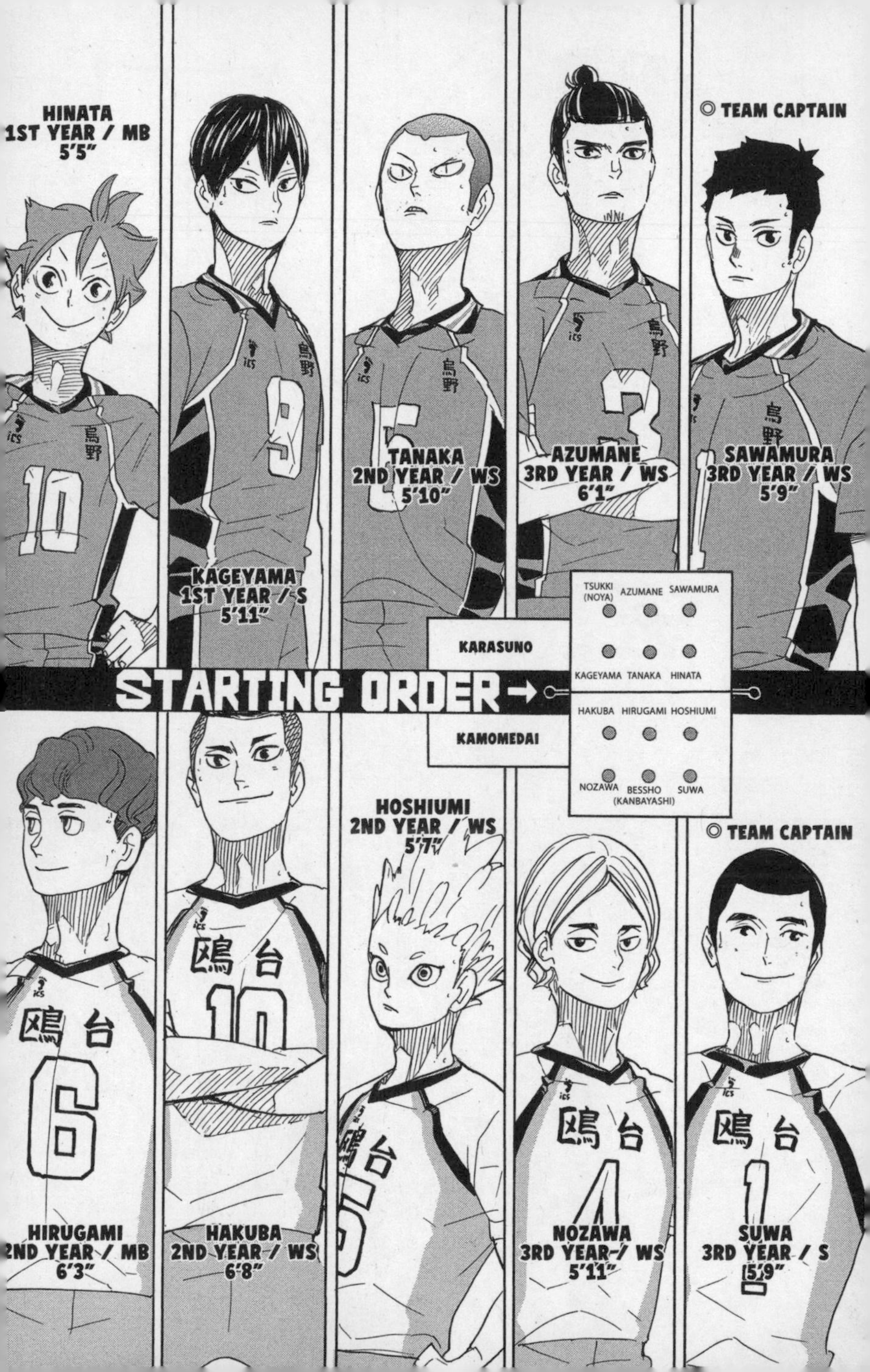
◎ TEAM CAPTAIN
SAWAMURA
3RD YEAR / WS
5'9"
AZUMANE
3RD YEAR / WS
6'1"
TANAKA
2ND YEAR / WS
5'10"
KAGEYAMA
1ST YEAR / S
5'11"
HINATA
1ST YEAR / MB
5'5"
STARTING ORDER →
KARASUNO
TSUKKI (NOYA) AZUMANE SAWAMURA
KAGEYAMA TANAKA HINATA
KAMOMEDAI
HAKUBA HIRUGAMI HOSHIUMI
NOZAWA BESSHO (KANBAYASHI) SUWA
◎ TEAM CAPTAIN
SUWA
3RD YEAR / S
5'9"
NOZAWA
3RD YEAR / WS
5'11"
HOSHIUMI
2ND YEAR / WS
5'7"
HAKUBA
2ND YEAR / WS
6'8"
HIRUGAMI
2ND YEAR / MB
6'3"

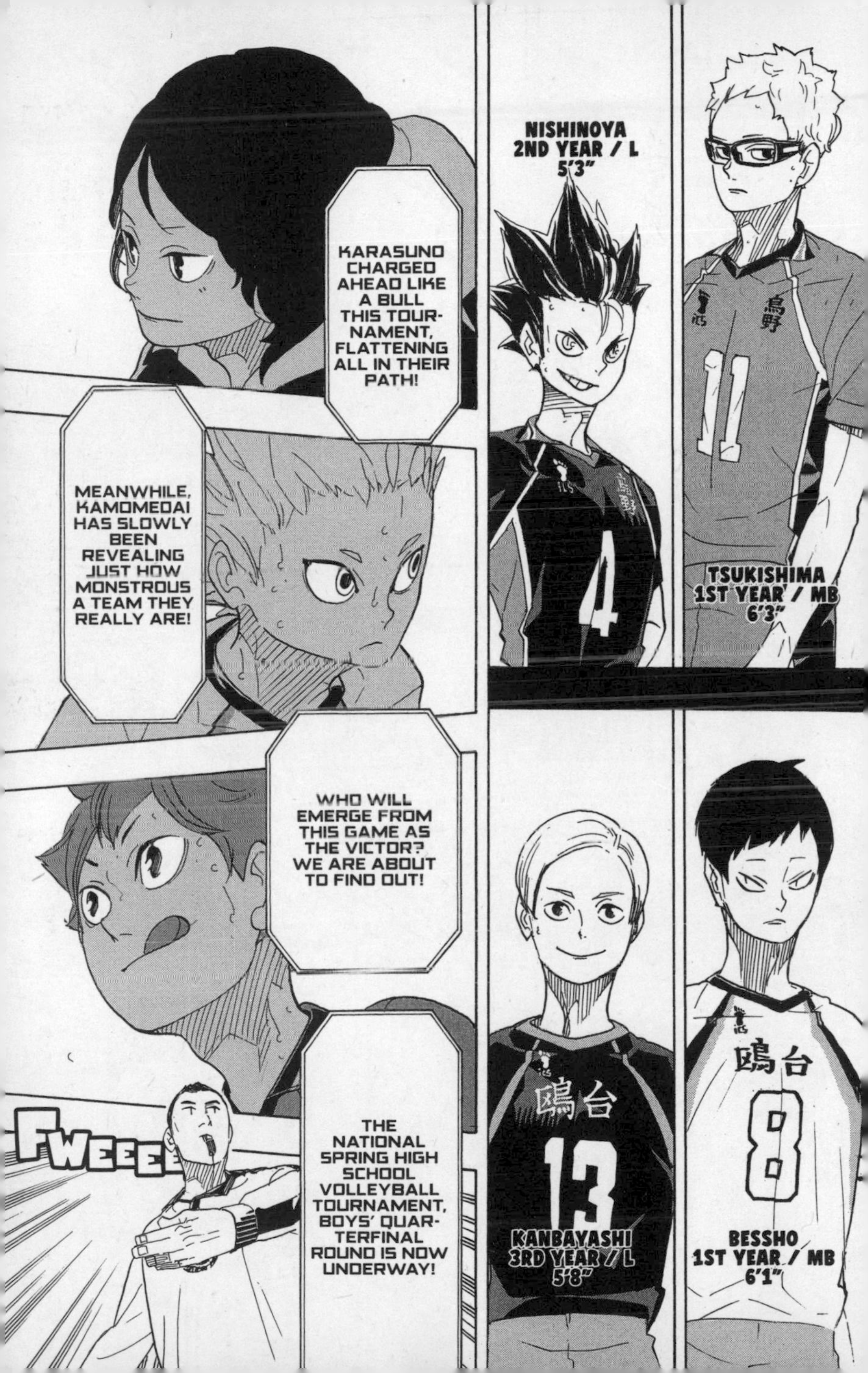
烏野
TSUKISHIMA
1ST YEAR / MB
6'3"
NISHINOYA
2ND YEAR / L
5'3"
鴎台
BESSHO
1ST YEAR / MB
6'1"
鴎台
KANBAYASHI
3RD YEAR / L
5'8"
KARASUNO CHARGED AHEAD LIKE A BULL THIS TOURNAMENT, FLATTENING ALL IN THEIR PATH!
MEANWHILE, KAMOMEDAI HAS SLOWLY BEEN REVEALING JUST HOW MONSTROUS A TEAM THEY REALLY ARE!
WHO WILL EMERGE FROM THIS GAME AS THE VICTOR? WE ARE ABOUT TO FIND OUT!
THE NATIONAL SPRING HIGH SCHOOL VOLLEYBALL TOURNAMENT, BOYS' QUARTERFINAL ROUND IS NOW UNDERWAY!
FWEEEE

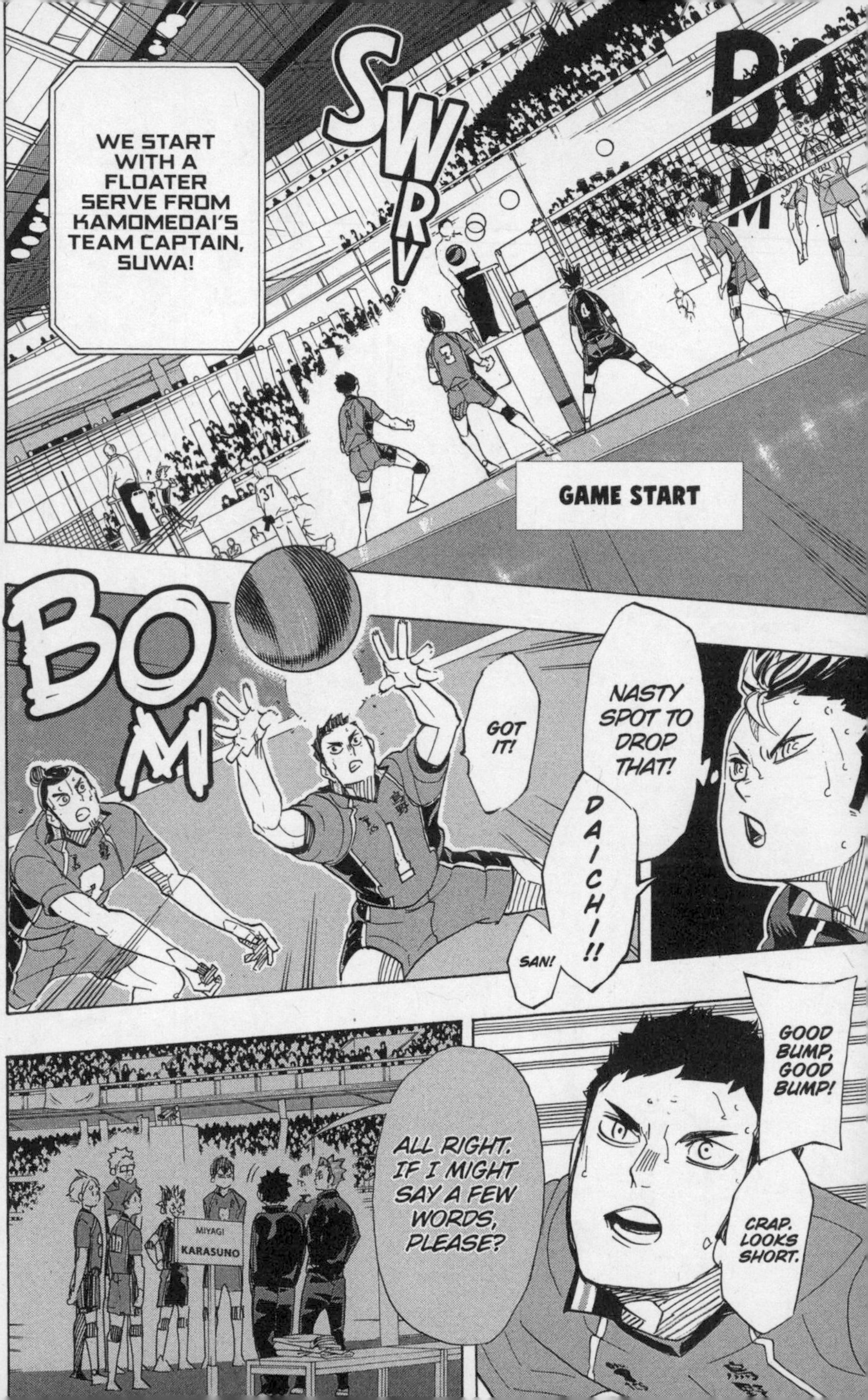
BOOM
SWRV
WE START WITH A FLOATER SERVE FROM KAMOMEDAI'S TEAM CAPTAIN, SUWA!
GAME START
NASTY SPOT TO DROP THAT!
DAICHI!! SAN!
GOT IT!
BOOM
GOOD BUMP, GOOD BUMP!
CRAP. LOOKS SHORT.
ALL RIGHT. IF I MIGHT SAY A FEW WORDS, PLEASE?
MIYAGI
KARASUNO

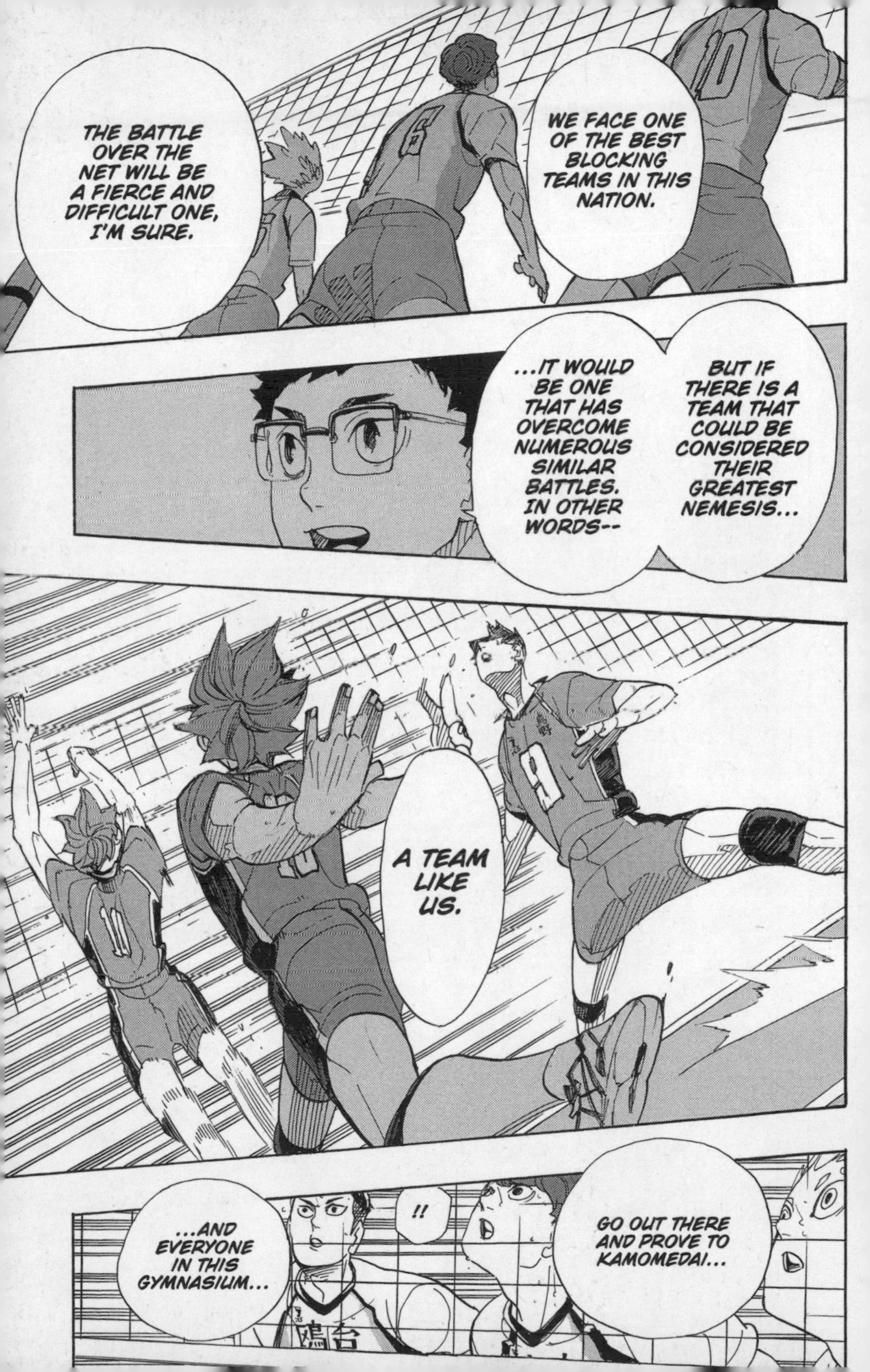
WE FACE ONE OF THE BEST BLOCKING TEAMS IN THIS NATION.
THE BATTLE OVER THE NET WILL BE A FIERCE AND DIFFICULT ONE, I'M SURE.
BUT IF THERE IS A TEAM THAT COULD BE CONSIDERED THEIR GREATEST NEMESIS...
...IT WOULD BE ONE THAT HAS OVERCOME NUMEROUS SIMILAR BATTLES. IN OTHER WORDS--
A TEAM LIKE US.
GO OUT THERE AND PROVE TO KAMOMEDAI...
!!
...AND EVERYONE IN THIS GYMNASIUM...

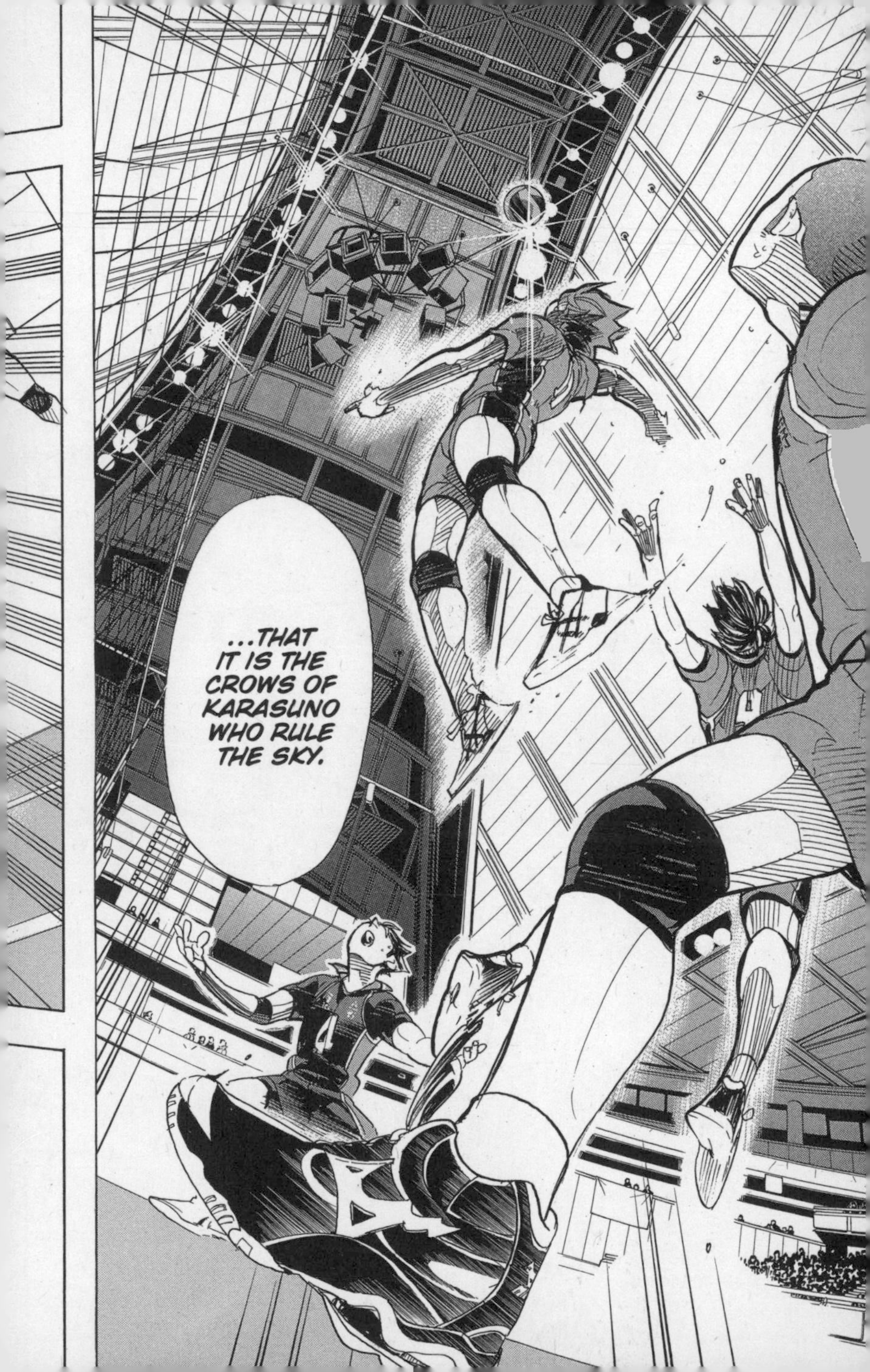
...THAT IT IS THE CROWS OF KARASUNO WHO RULE THE SKY.

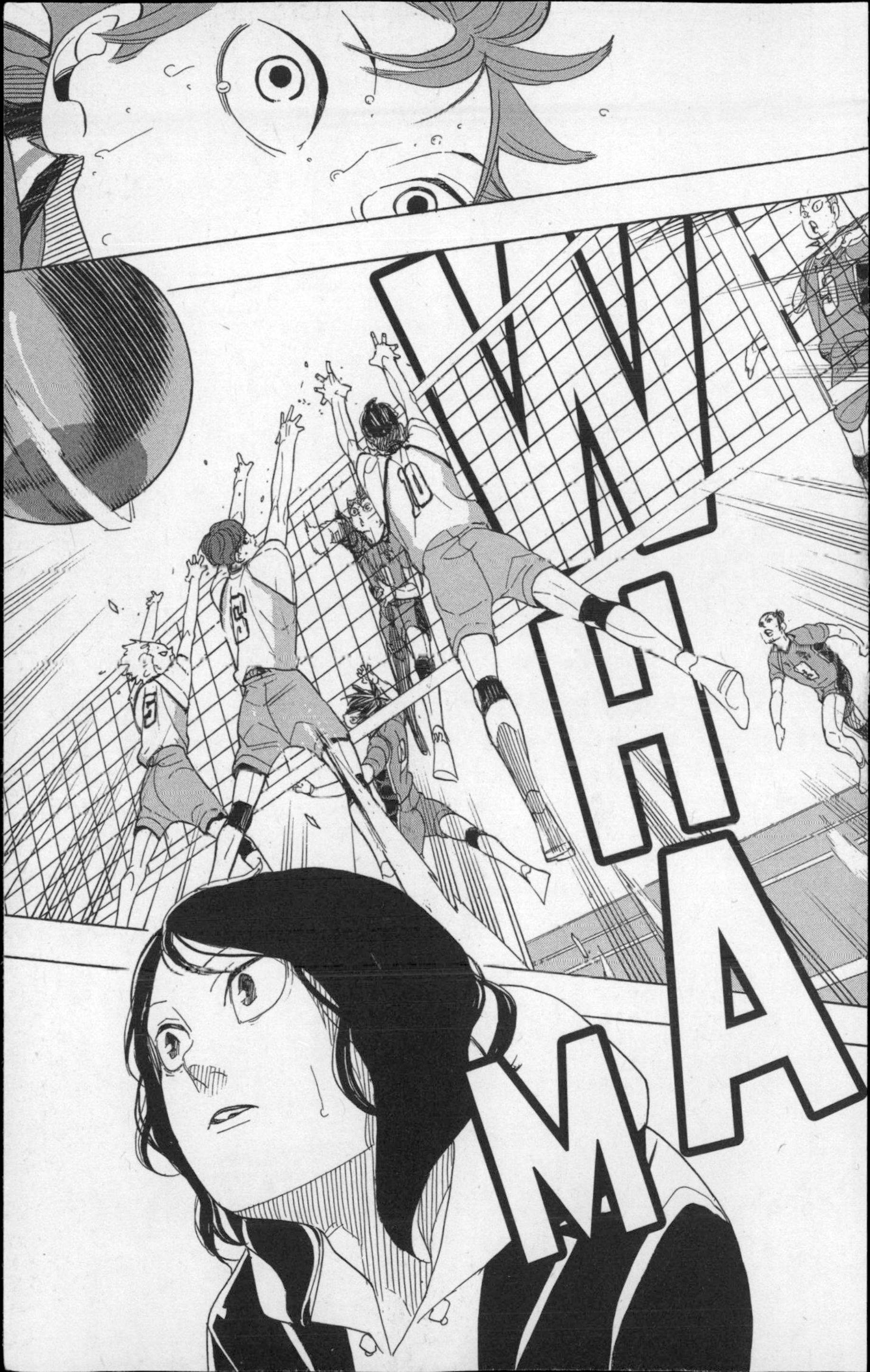
WHAM

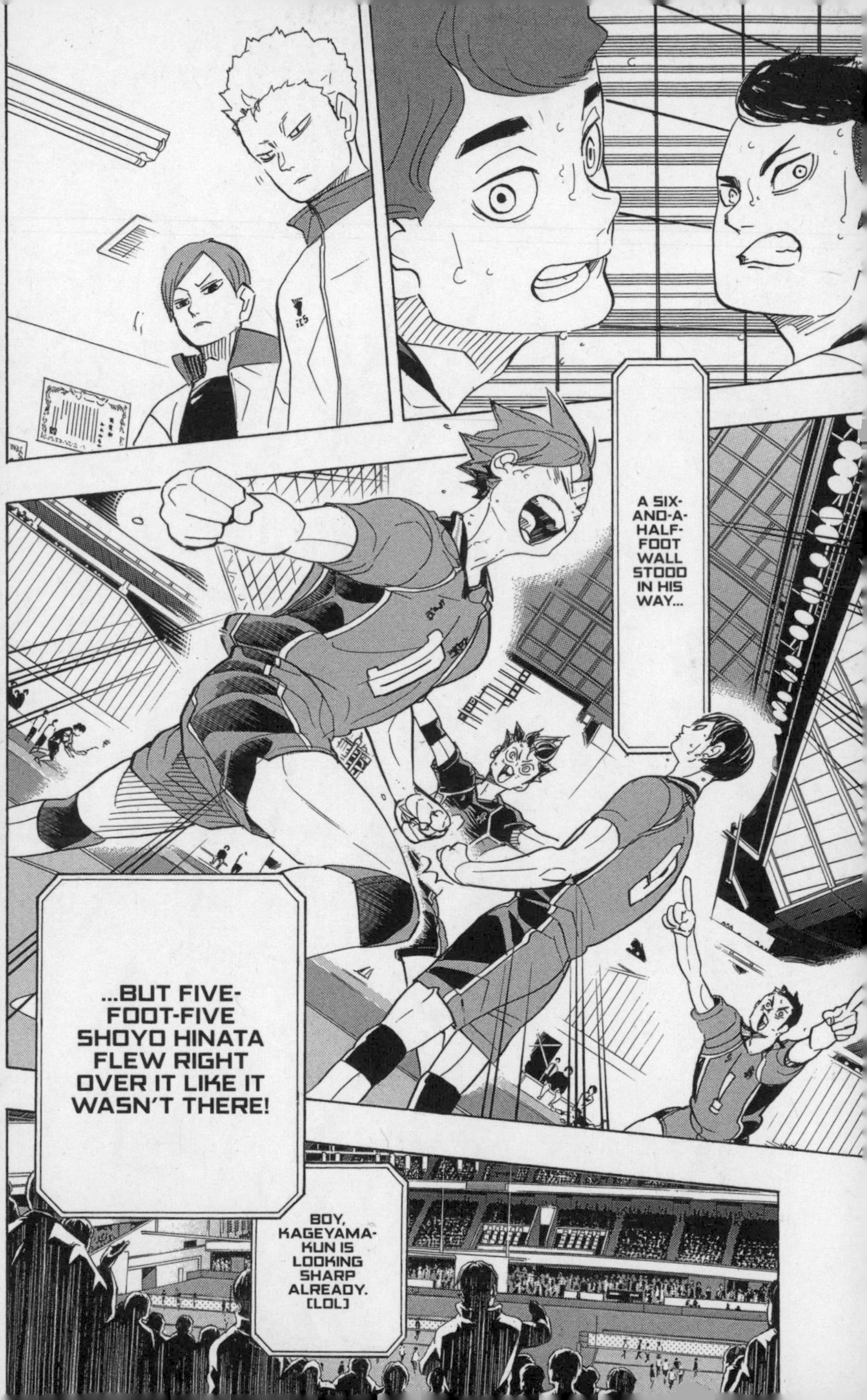
A SIX-AND-A-HALF-FOOT WALL STOOD IN HIS WAY...
...BUT FIVE-FOOT-FIVE SHOYO HINATA FLEW RIGHT OVER IT LIKE IT WASN'T THERE!
BOY, KAGEYAMA-KUN IS LOOKING SHARP ALREADY. [LOL]

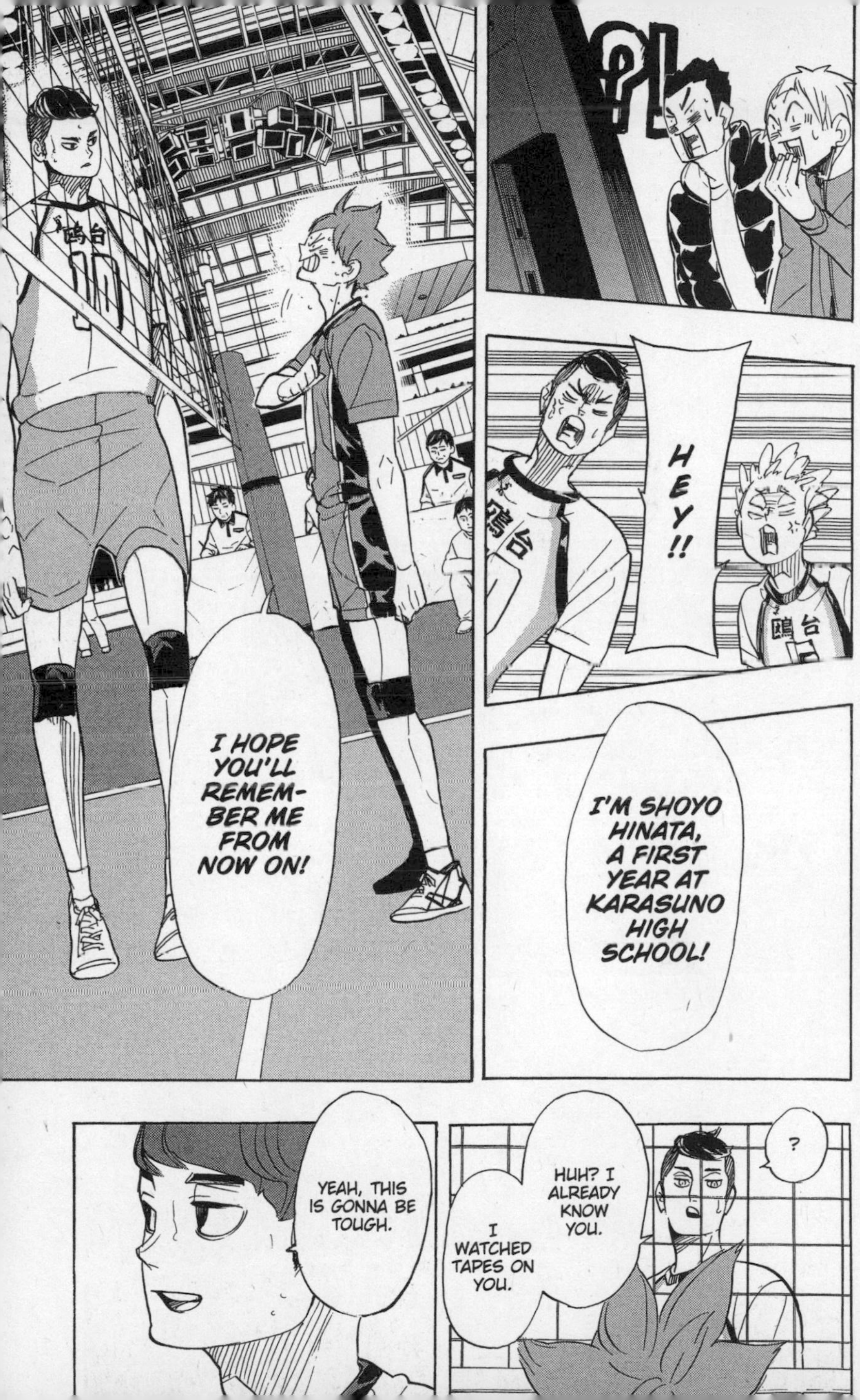
?!
HEY!!
I'M SHOYO HINATA, A FIRST YEAR AT KARASUNO HIGH SCHOOL!
I HOPE YOU'LL REMEM-BER ME FROM NOW ON!
?
HUH? I ALREADY KNOW YOU.
I WATCHED TAPES ON YOU.
YEAH, THIS IS GONNA BE TOUGH.

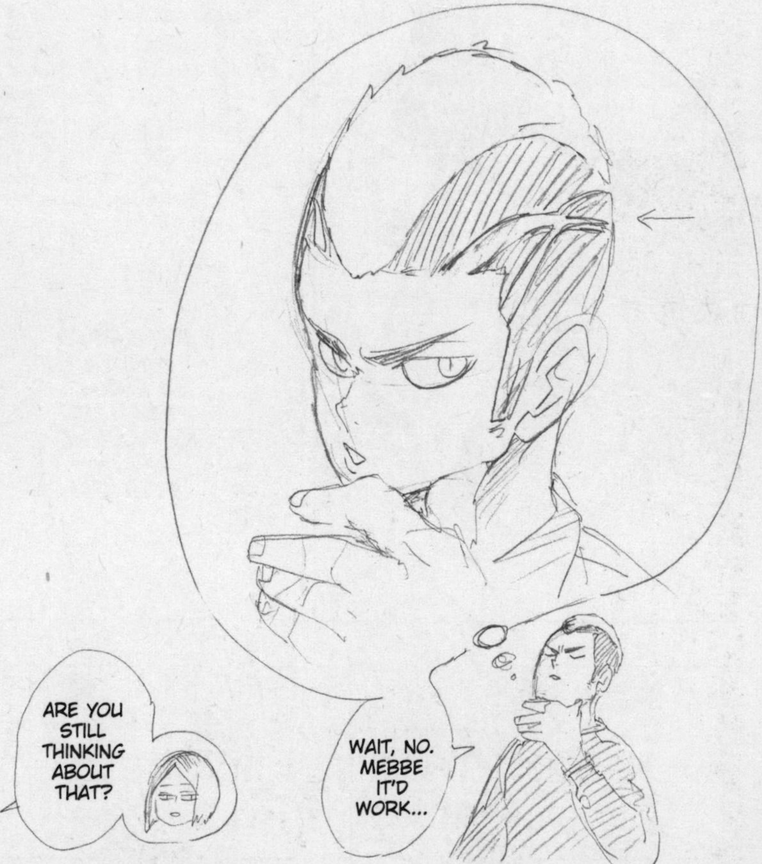
WAIT, NO. MEBBE IT'D WORK...
ARE YOU STILL THINKING ABOUT THAT?

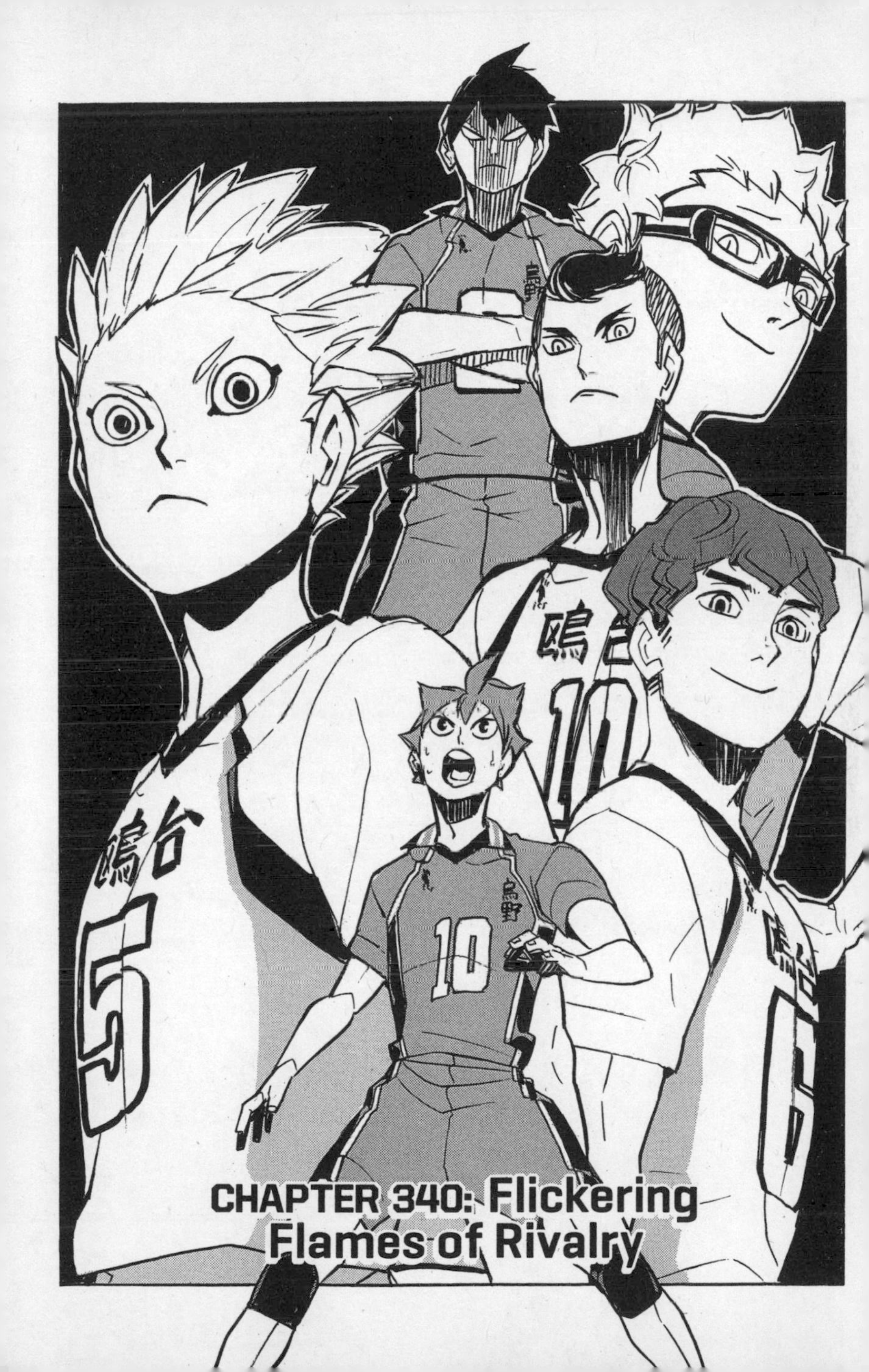
CHAPTER 340: Flickering Flames of Rivalry

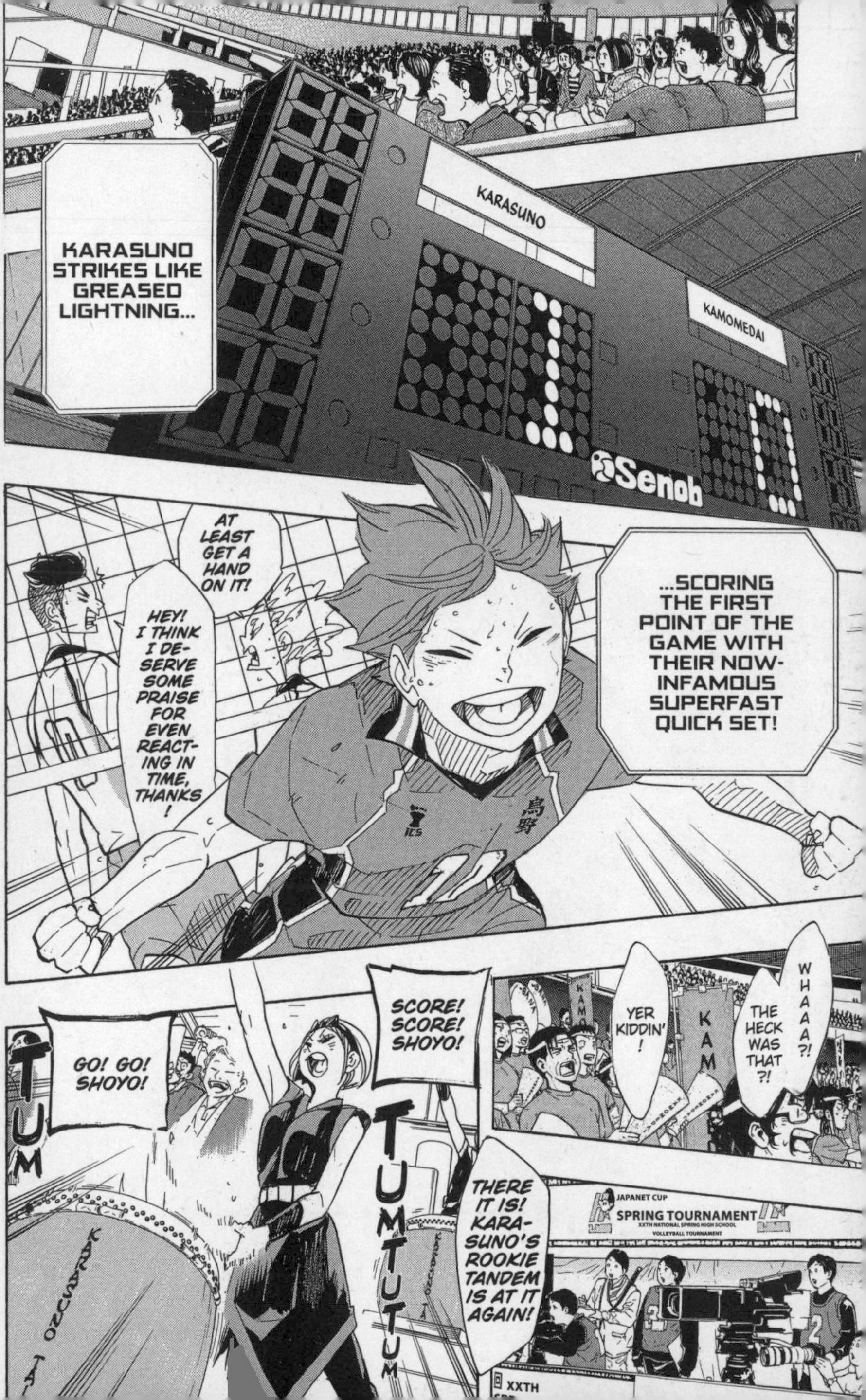
KARASUNO STRIKES LIKE GREASED LIGHTNING...
KARASUNO
KAMOMEDAI
Senob
...SCORING THE FIRST POINT OF THE GAME WITH THEIR NOW-INFAMOUS SUPERFAST QUICK SET!
AT LEAST GET A HAND ON IT!
HEY! I THINK I DE-SERVE SOME PRAISE FOR EVEN REACT-ING IN TIME, THANKS!
WHAAAA?!
THE HECK WAS THAT?!
YER KIDDIN'!
KAM
SCORE! SCORE! SHOYO!
GO! GO! SHOYO!
TUM
TUMTUTUM
THERE IT IS! KARA-SUNO'S ROOKIE TANDEM IS AT IT AGAIN!
JAPANET CUP
SPRING TOURNAMENT
XXTH NATIONAL SPRING HIGH SCHOOL
VOLLEYBALL TOURNAMENT
XXTH

TMP
TMP
TMP

鴎台 6

YEP! WE FIGURED THEY'D COME RIGHT OVER THE MIDDLE FIRST. STILL, EVEN KNOWING IT WAS COMING, THAT SURE WAS FAST!

NOD

THAT'S THE FIRST TIME THEY'VE SEEN SHOYO HINATA'S QUICK SET. *ALL THREE BLOCKERS* REACTED.

THAT AGAIN!

NOT JUST THAT...

HE KNEW THAT WE KNEW IT WAS COMING... AND HE DID IT ANYWAY.

TMP

*CURRENT ROTATION

SERVE

KAGEYAMA | TSUKKI (NOYA) | AZUMANE

TANAKA | HINATA | SAWAMURA

NET

HAKUBA | HIRUGAMI | HOSHIUMI

NOZAWA | BESSHO (KANBAYASHI) | SUWA

YEP, THAT FIRST ONE WAS A THREAT.

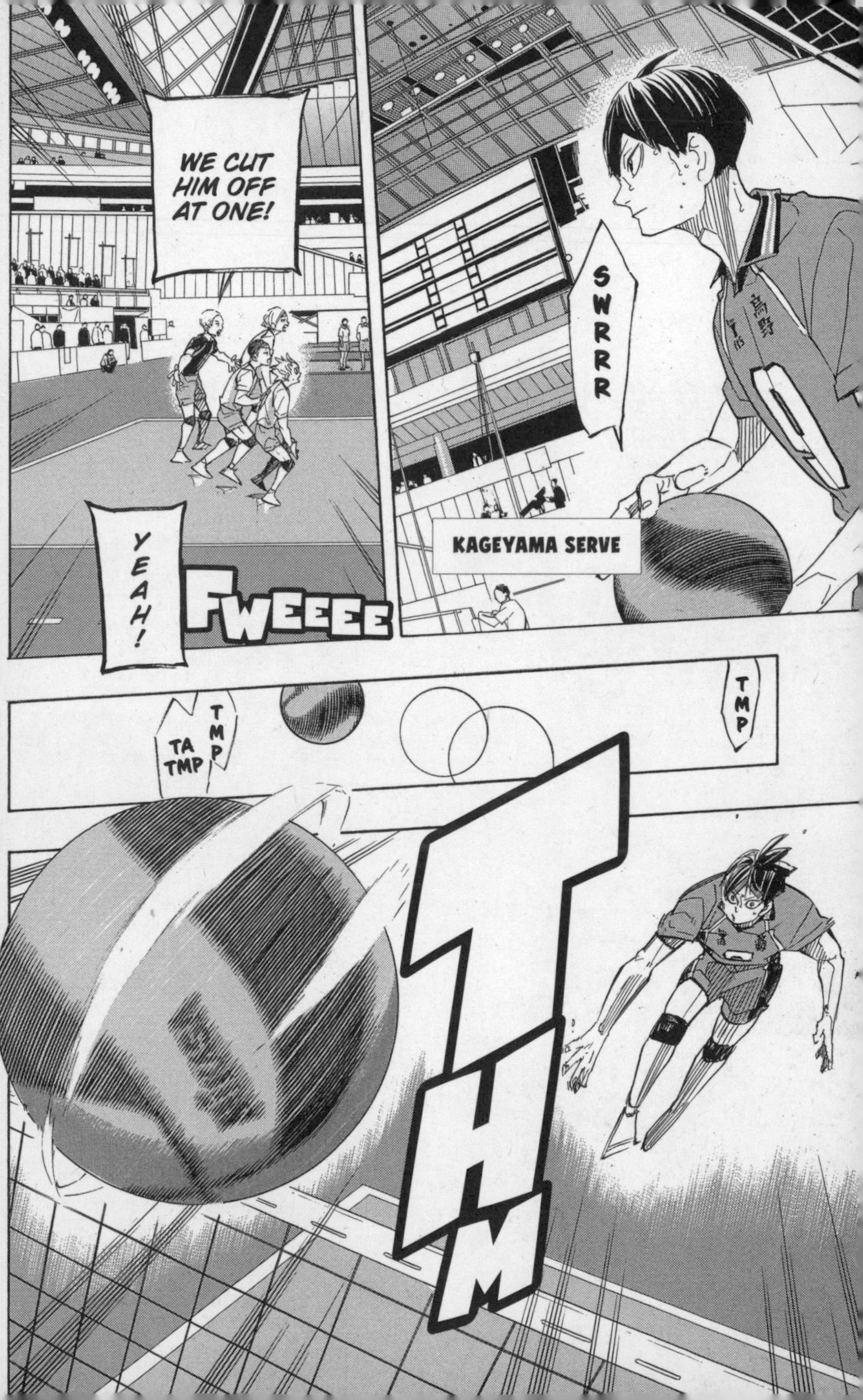
SWRRR
KAGEYAMA SERVE
WE CUT HIM OFF AT ONE!
YEAH!
FWEEEE
TMP
TMP TMP
TA TMP
THM

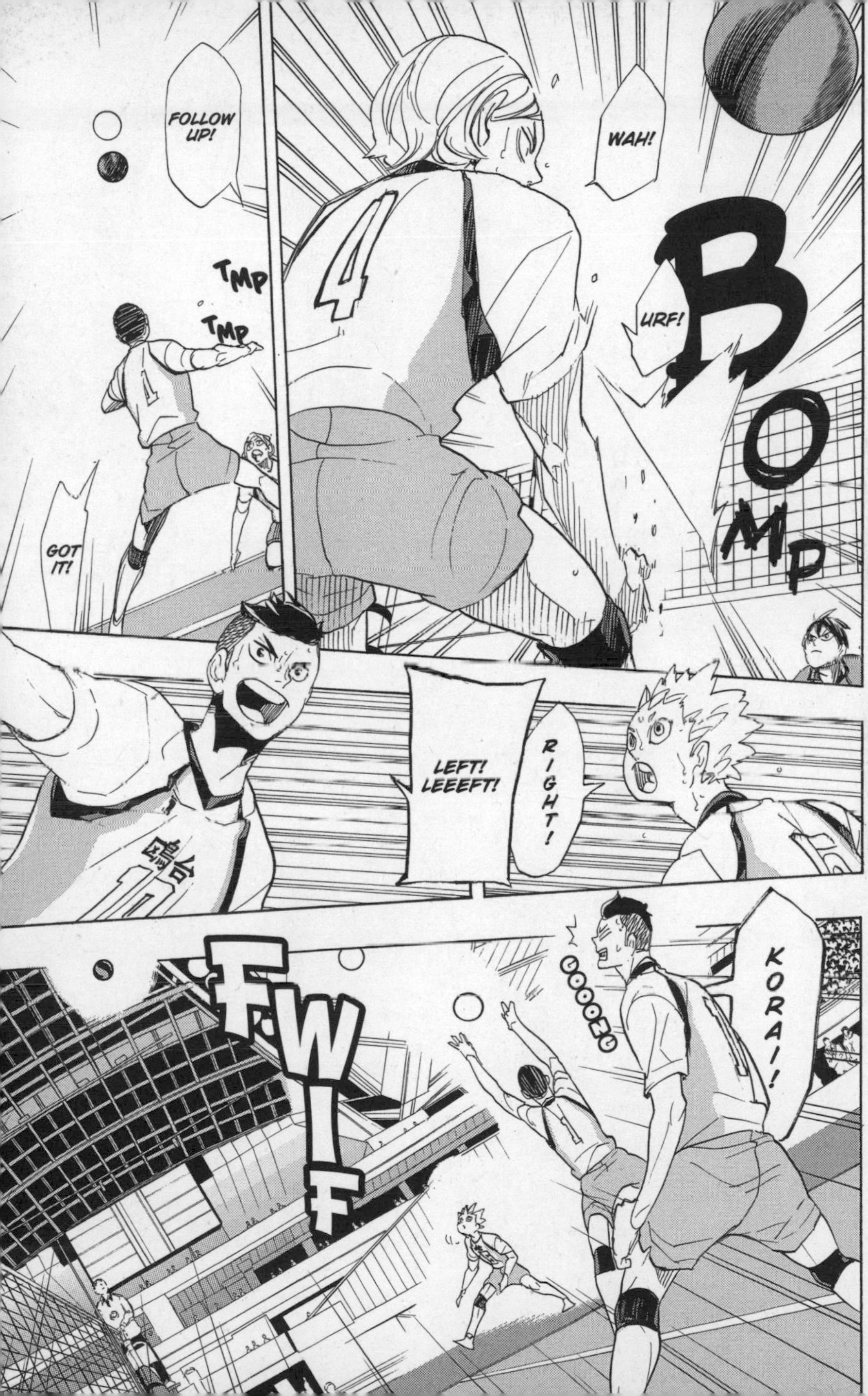
WAH!
BOMP
URF!
FOLLOW UP!
TMP
TMP
GOT IT!
RIGHT!
LEFT! LEEEFT!
KORA!!
GOOONG
FWIF

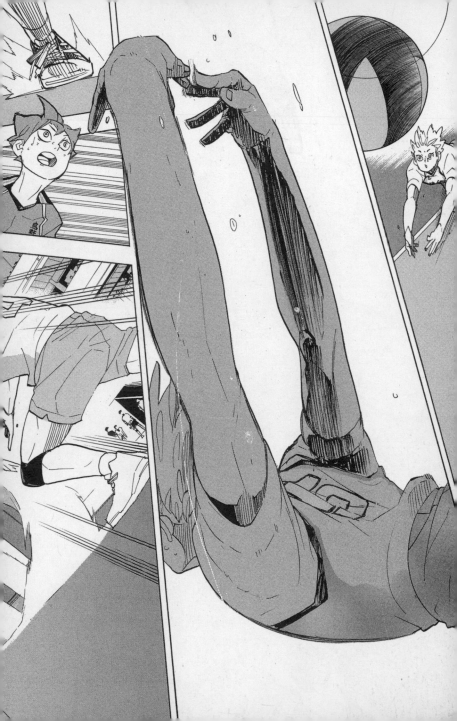

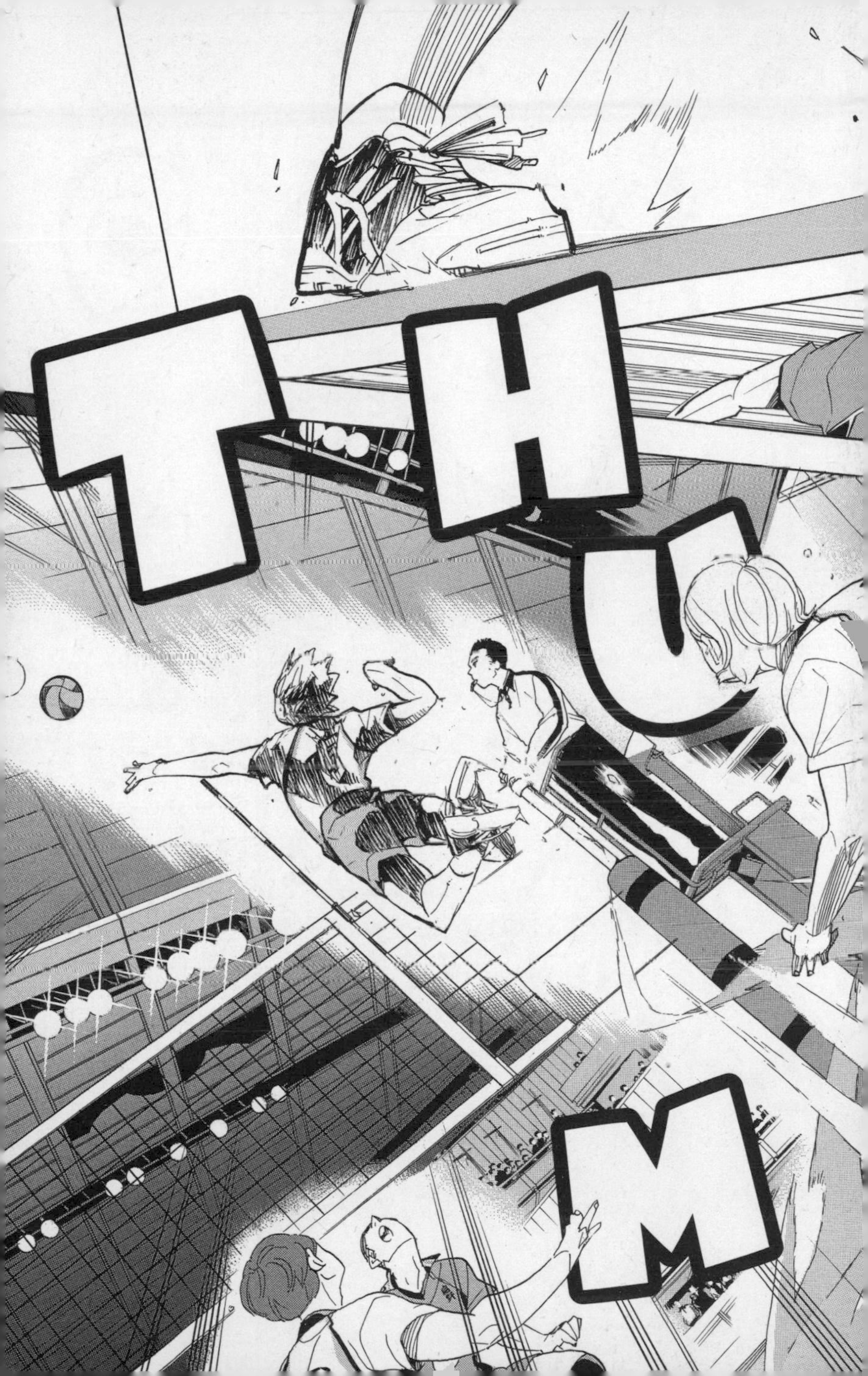
THUM

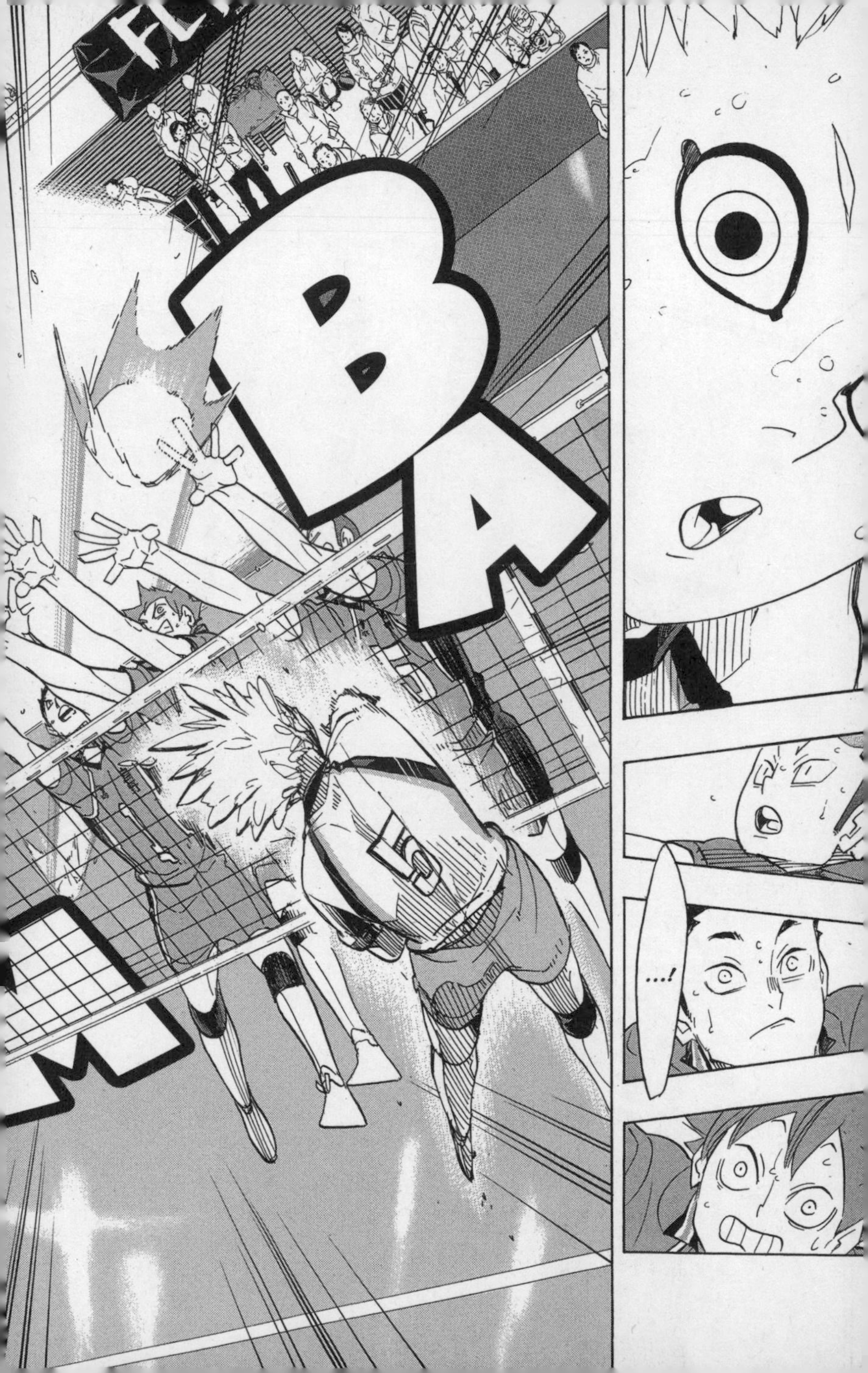
...!
BAM

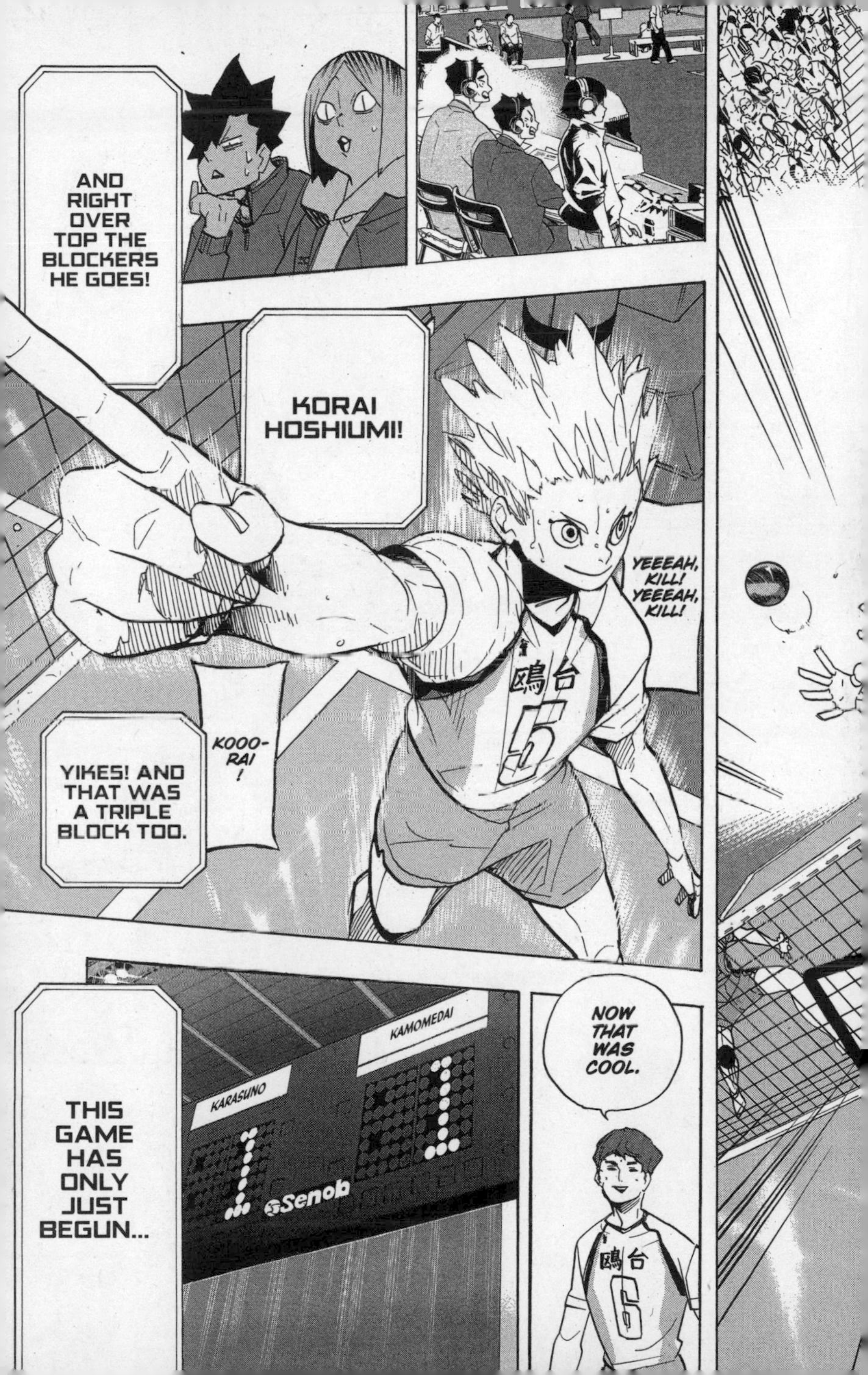
AND RIGHT OVER TOP THE BLOCKERS HE GOES!
KORAI HOSHIUMI!
YEEEAH, KILL! YEEEAH, KILL!
KOOO-RAI!
YIKES! AND THAT WAS A TRIPLE BLOCK TOO.
NOW THAT WAS COOL.
KAMOMEDAI
KARASUNO
Senob
THIS GAME HAS ONLY JUST BEGUN...

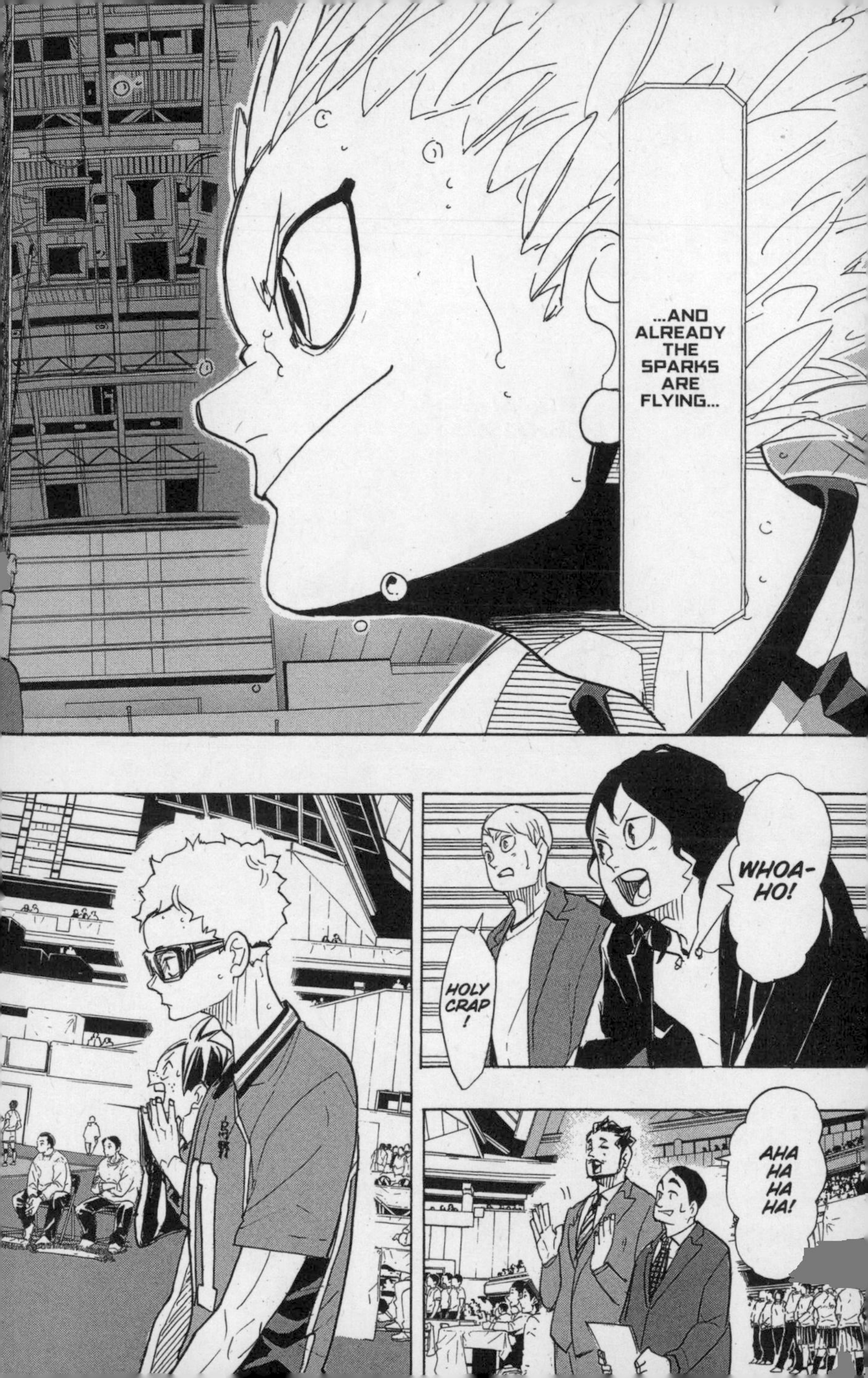
...AND ALREADY THE SPARKS ARE FLYING...
WHOA-HO!
HOLY CRAP!
AHA HA HA HA!

...BETWEEN THE TWO SMALLEST SPIKERS!

FWEEE EEE

HOSHIUMI SERVE

*CURRENT ROTATION

SERVE

| HOSHIUMI | SUWA | BESSHO (KANBAYASHI) |
| HIRUGAMI | HAKUBA | NOZAWA |

NET

| SAWAMURA | HINATA | TANAKA |
| AZUMANE | TSUKISHIMA | KAGEYAMA |

TIMING, GUYS. TIMING.

THAT WAS ONE HECK OF A SERVE HE HIT RIGHT OUT OF THE GATES.

DAMMIT, KAGEYAMA.

YES-SIR!

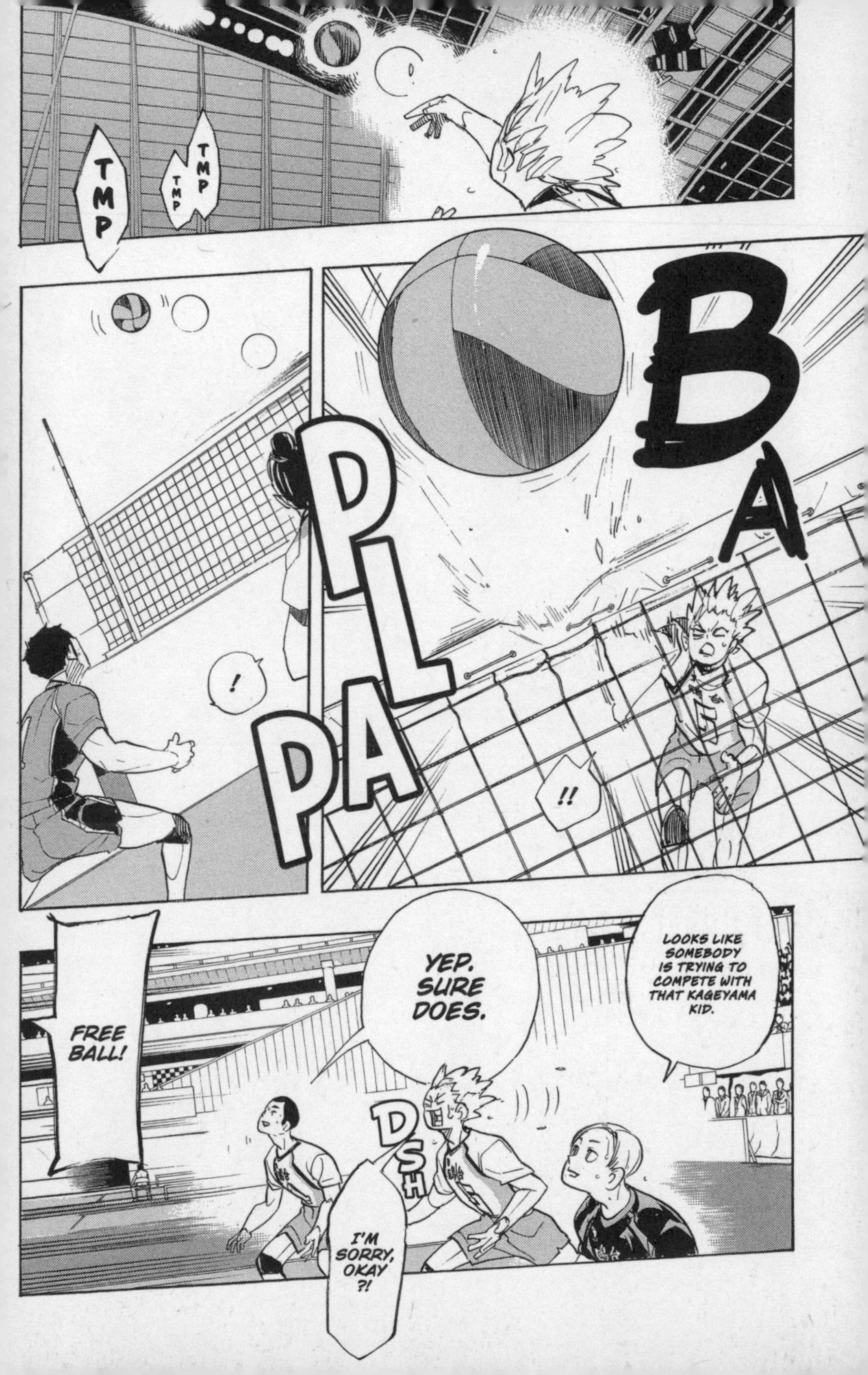
TMP
TMP
TMP
TMP
BA
!!
PA
PIL
!
LOOKS LIKE SOMEBODY IS TRYING TO COMPETE WITH THAT KAGEYAMA KID.
YEP. SURE DOES.
DSH
I'M SORRY, OKAY ?!
FREE BALL!

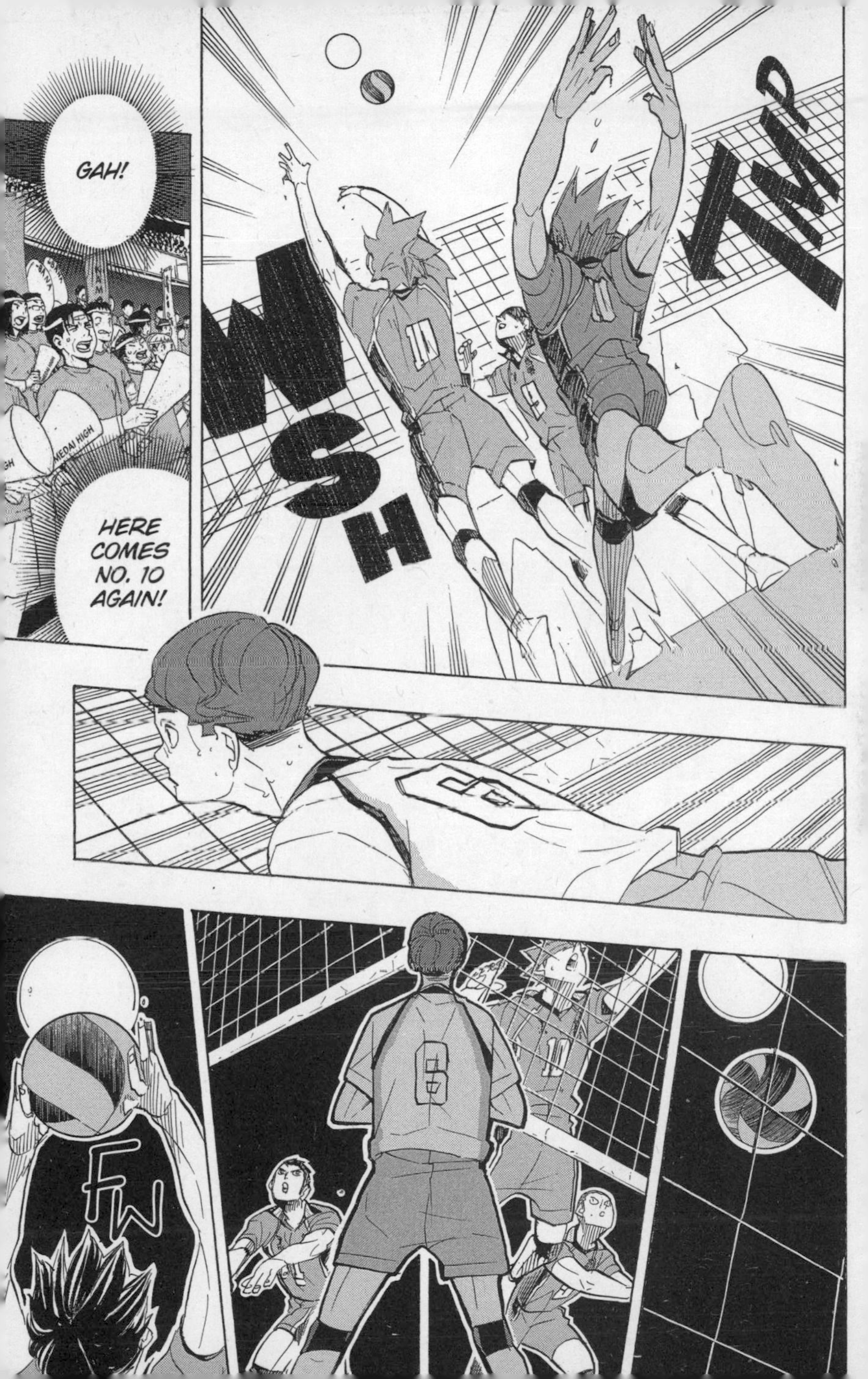
TMP
WHSH
GAH!
HERE COMES NO. 10 AGAIN!
MEDAI HIGH

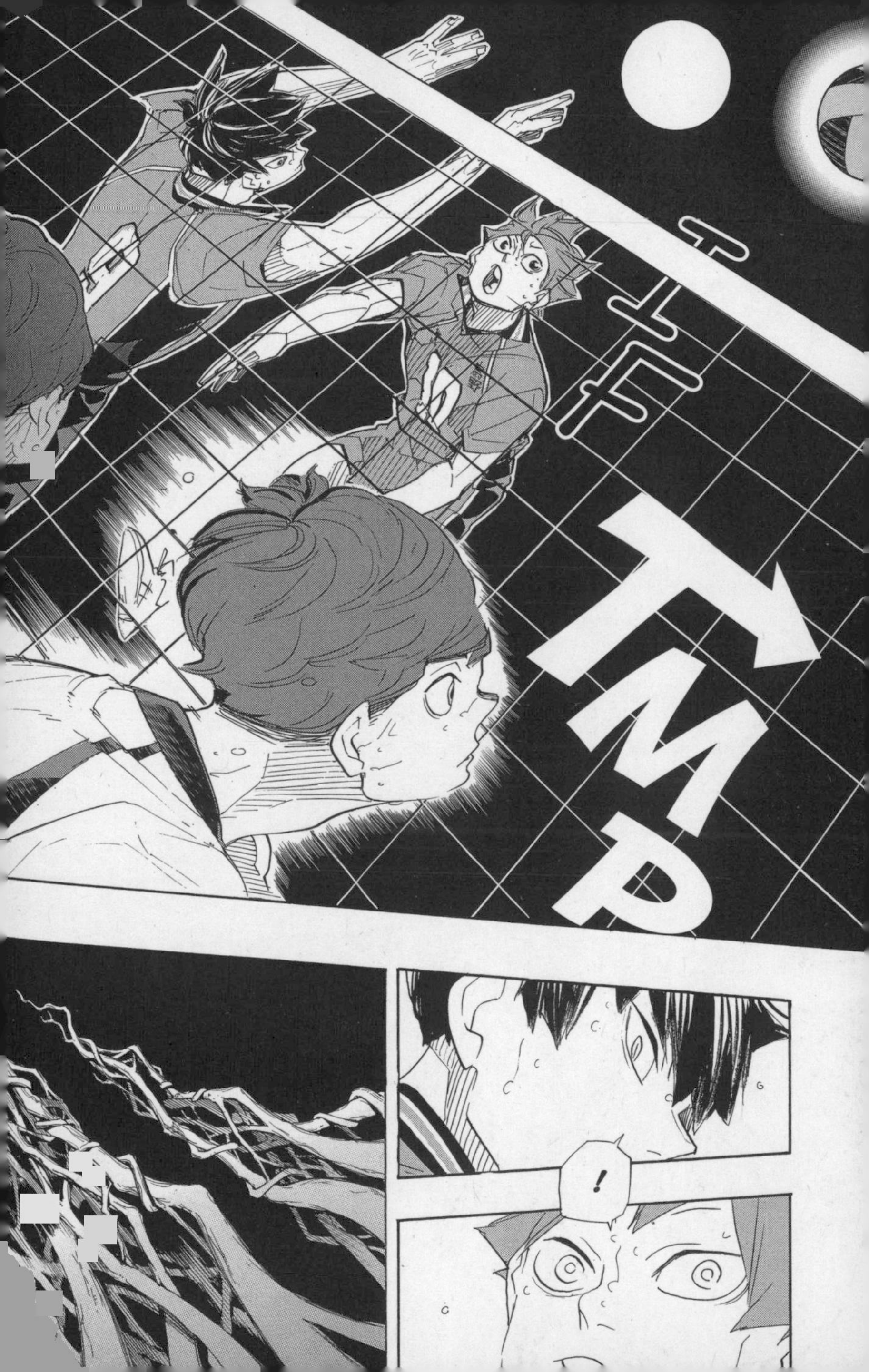
TMP
!

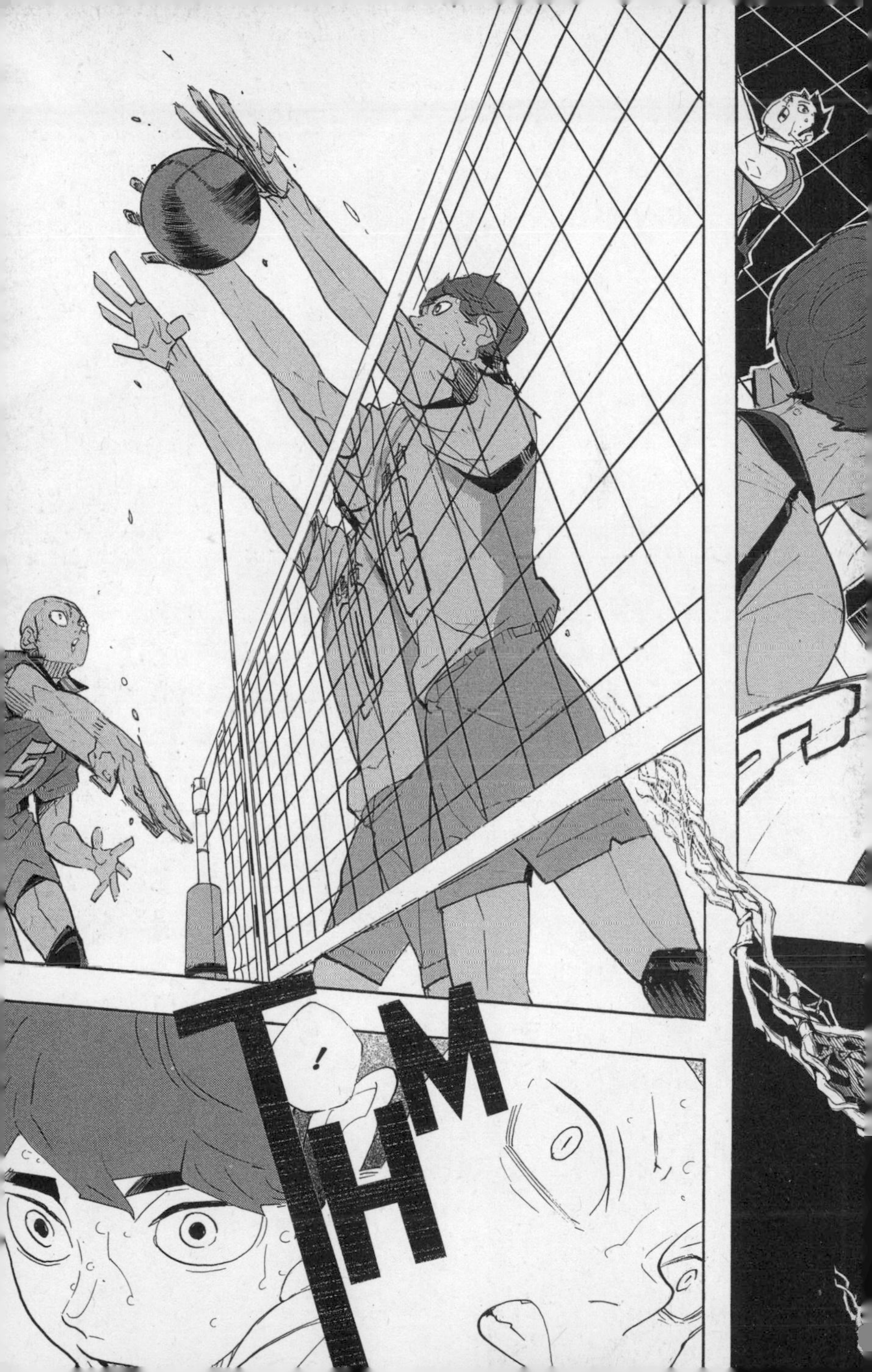
THM
!

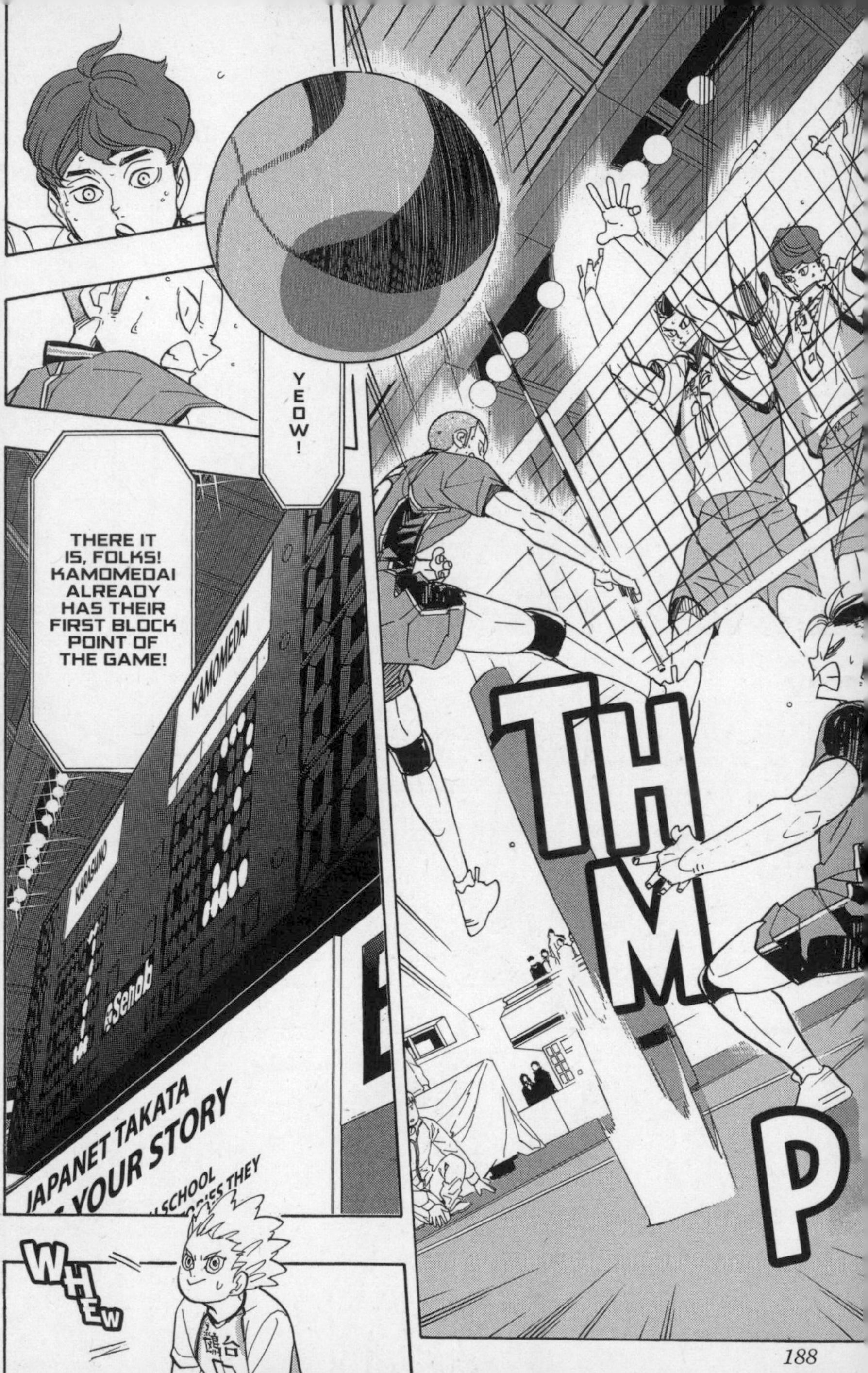
YEOW!
THMP
THERE IT IS, FOLKS! KAMOMEDAI ALREADY HAS THEIR FIRST BLOCK POINT OF THE GAME!
KAMOMEDAI
KARASUNO
JAPANET TAKATA
YOUR STORY
WHEW

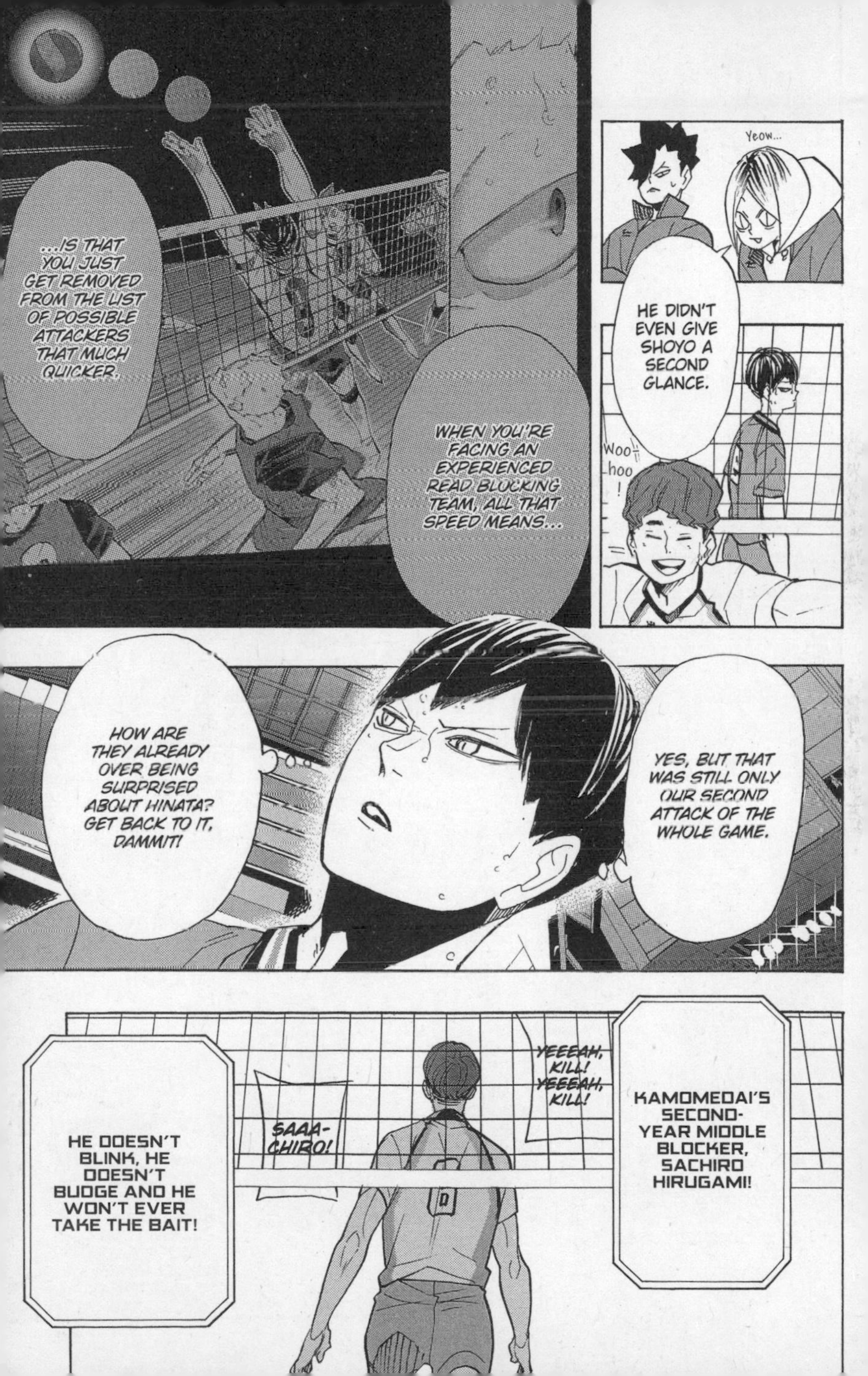
Yeow...
HE DIDN'T EVEN GIVE SHOYO A SECOND GLANCE.
Woo hoo!
WHEN YOU'RE FACING AN EXPERIENCED READ BLOCKING TEAM, ALL THAT SPEED MEANS...
...IS THAT YOU JUST GET REMOVED FROM THE LIST OF POSSIBLE ATTACKERS THAT MUCH QUICKER.
YES, BUT THAT WAS STILL ONLY OUR SECOND ATTACK OF THE WHOLE GAME.
HOW ARE THEY ALREADY OVER BEING SURPRISED ABOUT HINATA? GET BACK TO IT, DAMMIT!
KAMOMEDAI'S SECOND-YEAR MIDDLE BLOCKER, SACHIRO HIRUGAMI!
YEEEAH, KILL! YEEEAH, KILL!
SAAA-CHIRO!
HE DOESN'T BLINK, HE DOESN'T BUDGE AND HE WON'T EVER TAKE THE BAIT!

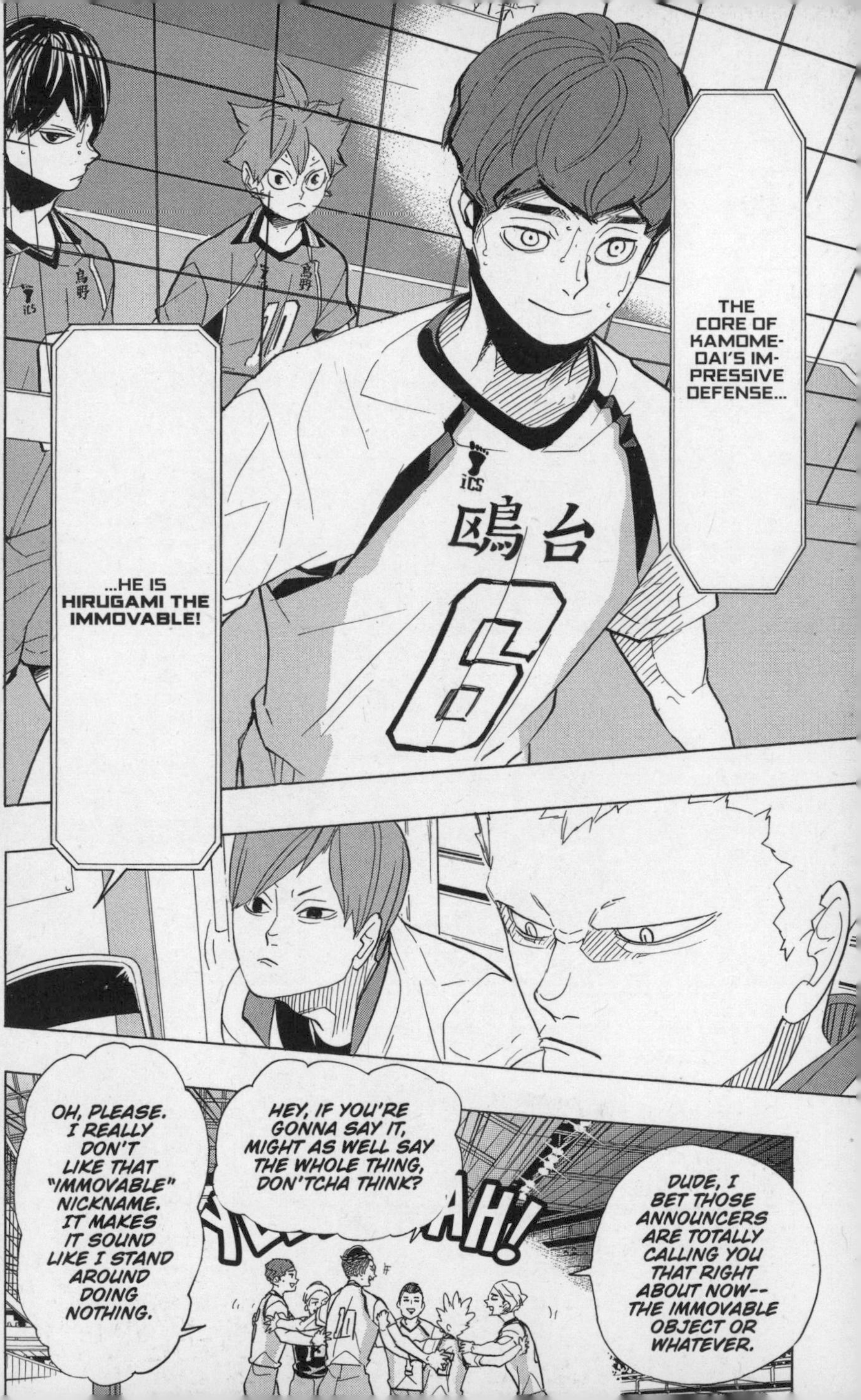
THE CORE OF KAMOME-DAI'S IMPRESSIVE DEFENSE...
...HE IS HIRUGAMI THE IMMOVABLE!
DUDE, I BET THOSE ANNOUNCERS ARE TOTALLY CALLING YOU THAT RIGHT ABOUT NOW-- THE IMMOVABLE OBJECT OR WHATEVER.
HEY, IF YOU'RE GONNA SAY IT, MIGHT AS WELL SAY THE WHOLE THING, DON'TCHA THINK?
OH, PLEASE. I REALLY DON'T LIKE THAT "IMMOVABLE" NICKNAME. IT MAKES IT SOUND LIKE I STAND AROUND DOING NOTHING.

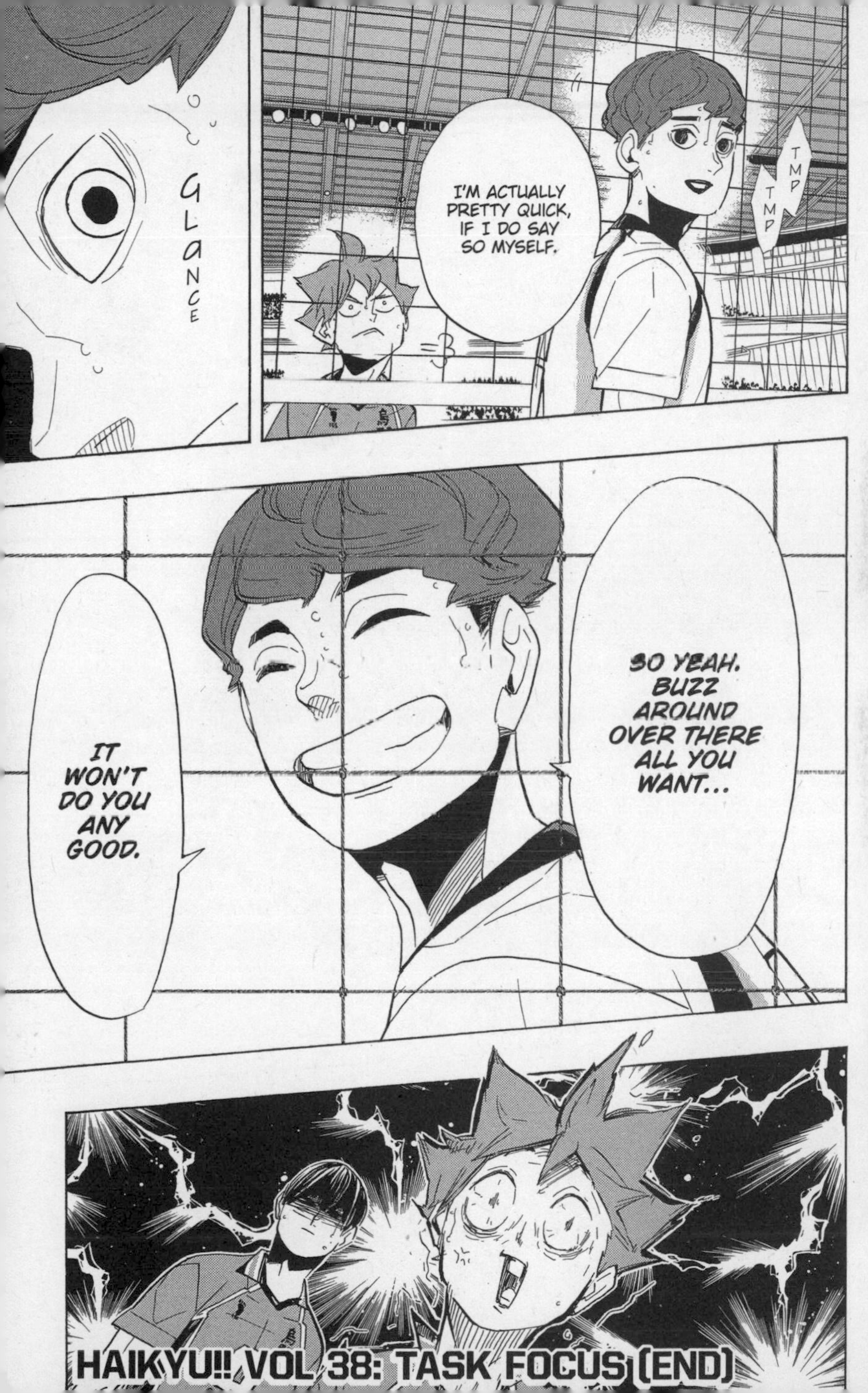
I'M ACTUALLY PRETTY QUICK, IF I DO SAY SO MYSELF.
TMP TMP
GLANCE
SO YEAH. BUZZ AROUND OVER THERE ALL YOU WANT...
IT WON'T DO YOU ANY GOOD.
HAIKYU!! VOL 38: TASK FOCUS (END)

EDITOR'S NOTES

The English edition of *Haikyu!!* maintains the honorifics used in the original Japanese version. For those of you who are new to these terms, here's a brief explanation to help with your reading experience!

When saying someone's name in Japanese, a suffix is often attached to indicate how familiar the speaker is with the person. Some are more polite and respectful, while others are endearing.

1 *-kun* is often used for young men or boys, usually someone you are familiar with.

2 *-chan* is used for young children and can be used as a term of endearment.

3 *-san* is used for someone you respect or are not close to, or to be polite.

4 *Senpai* is used for someone who is older than you or in a higher position or grade in school.

5 *Kohai* is used for someone who is younger than you or in a lower position or grade in school.

6 *Sensei* means teacher.

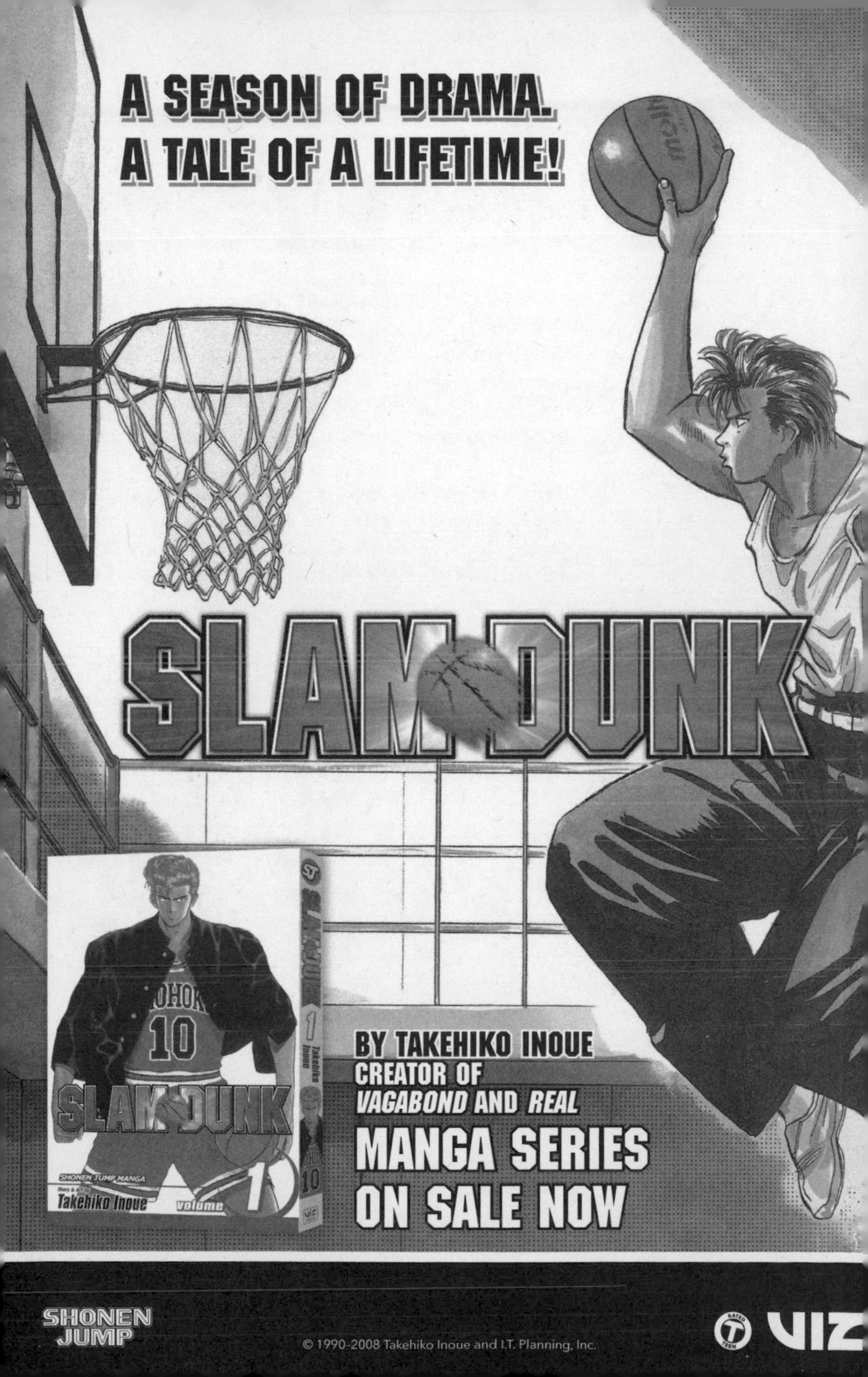

A SEASON OF DRAMA.
A TALE OF A LIFETIME!
SLAM DUNK
SLAM DUNK
SHONEN JUMP MANGA
Takehiko Inoue
volume 1
BY TAKEHIKO INOUE
CREATOR OF
VAGABOND AND *REAL*
MANGA SERIES
ON SALE NOW
SHONEN JUMP
© 1990-2008 Takehiko Inoue and I.T. Planning, Inc.
VIZ

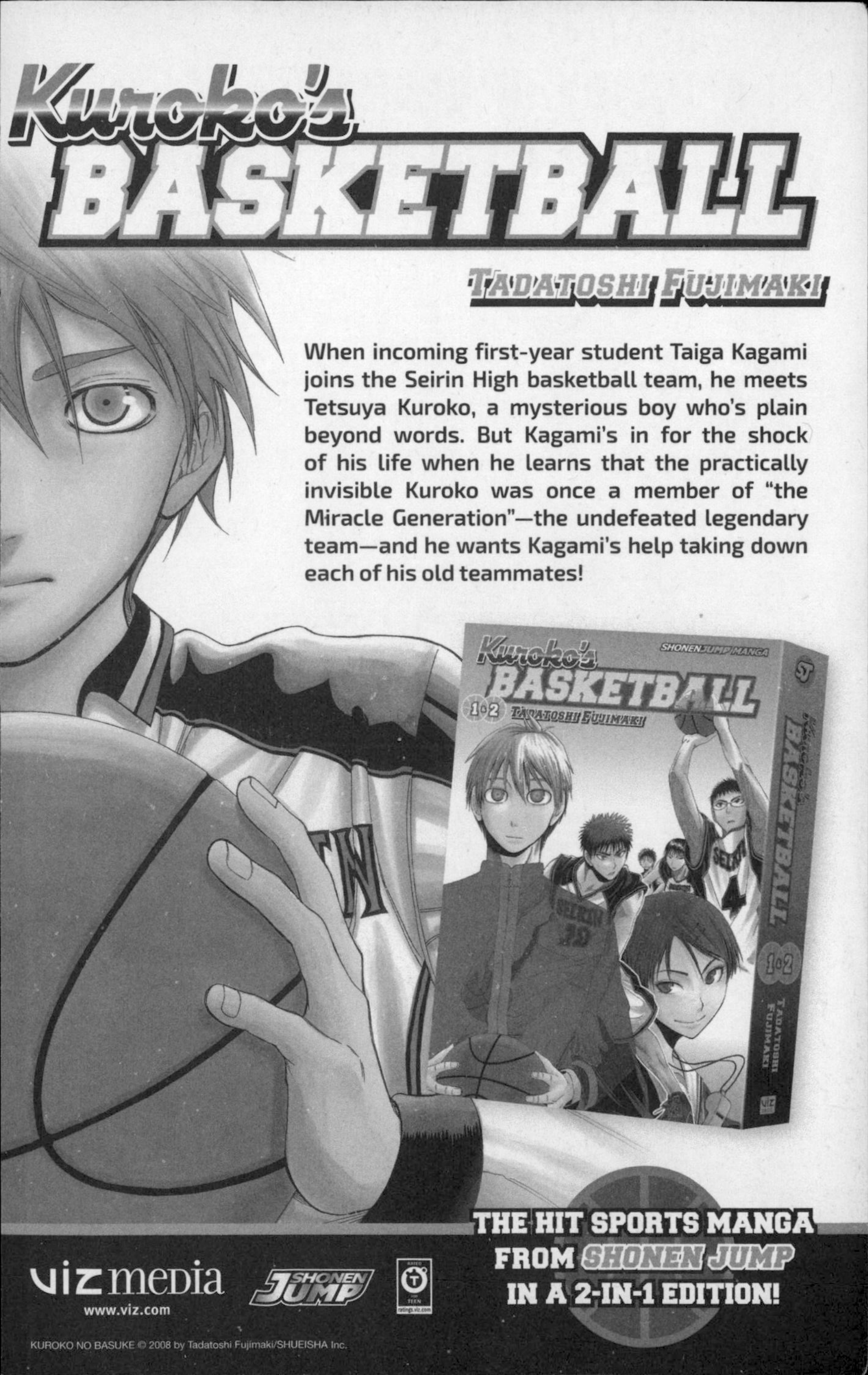
Kuroko's
BASKETBALL
TADATOSHI FUJIMAKI
When incoming first-year student Taiga Kagami joins the Seirin High basketball team, he meets Tetsuya Kuroko, a mysterious boy who's plain beyond words. But Kagami's in for the shock of his life when he learns that the practically invisible Kuroko was once a member of "the Miracle Generation"—the undefeated legendary team—and he wants Kagami's help taking down each of his old teammates!
Kuroko's BASKETBALL
SHONEN JUMP MANGA
1•2
TADATOSHI FUJIMAKI
THE HIT SPORTS MANGA
FROM SHONEN JUMP
IN A 2-IN-1 EDITION!
viz media
www.viz.com
SHONEN JUMP
RATED T TEEN
ratings.viz.com
KUROKO NO BASUKE © 2008 by Tadatoshi Fujimaki/SHUEISHA Inc.

テニスの王子様

THE PRINCE Of TENNIS

ON SALE NOW

Action Duels have become a global sensation, but what is the dark secret behind them that threatens to destroy the world?

Yuzu Hiiragi and her father run a Dueling school that's seen better days. If only they had a star teacher to bring in new students! When a rogue Duelist known as Phantom appears in the city, Yuzu may have found a savior, but Phantom will have to deal with the Leo Corporation's special forces before he can get into any community service!

ORIGINAL CONCEPT BY **Kazuki Takahashi**
PRODUCTION SUPPORT: **STUDIO DICE**
STORY BY **Shin Yoshida**
ART BY **Naohito Miyoshi**
DUEL COORDINATOR **Masahiro Hikokubo**

SHONEN JUMP
www.shonenjump.com

viz media
viz.com

YU-GI-OH! ARC-V © 2014 by Kazuki Takahashi, Shin Yoshida,
Naohito Miyoshi, Masahiro Hikokubo/SHUEISHA Inc.

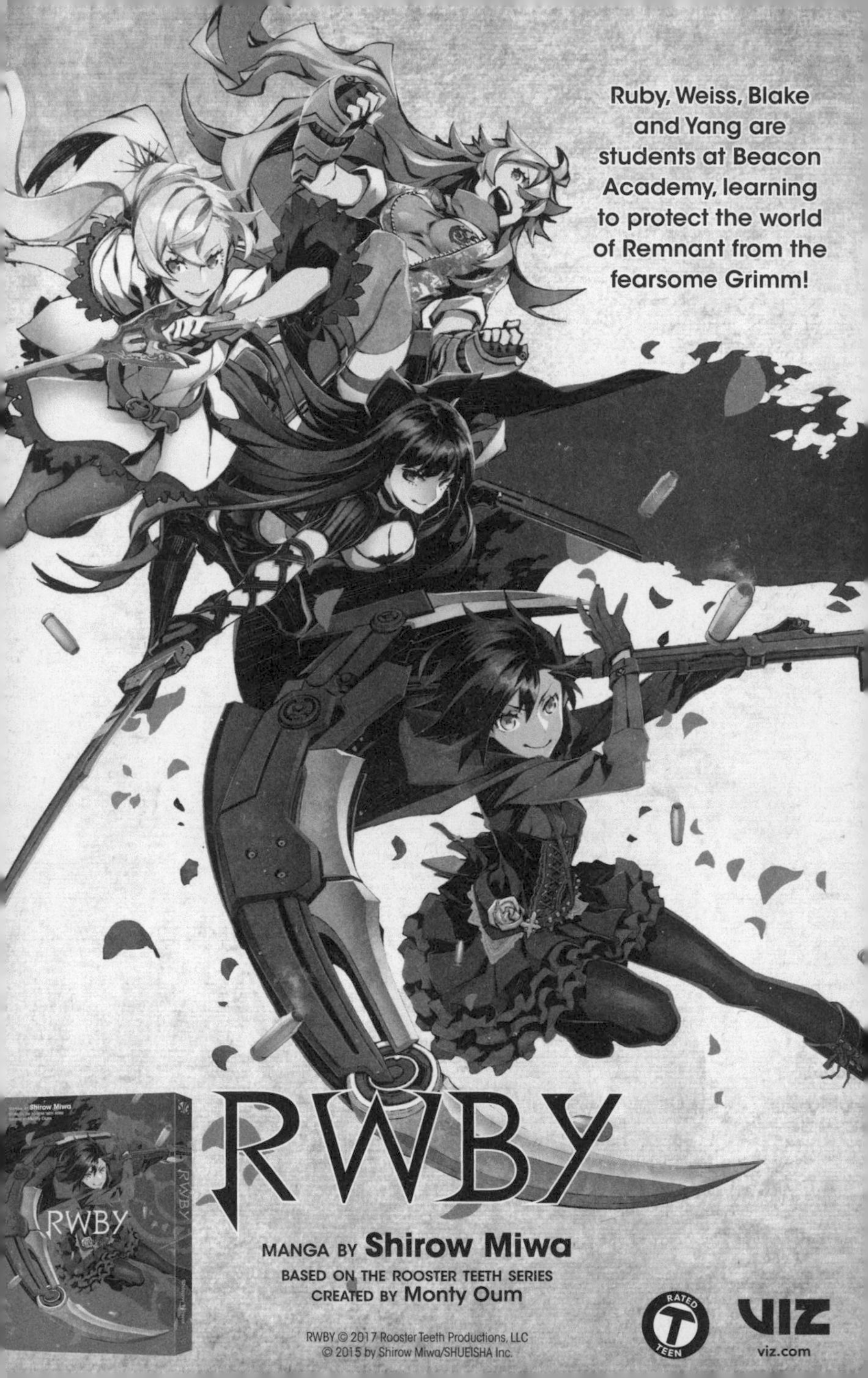
Ruby, Weiss, Blake and Yang are students at Beacon Academy, learning to protect the world of Remnant from the fearsome Grimm!
RWBY
Shirow Miwa
RWBY
MANGA BY Shirow Miwa
BASED ON THE ROOSTER TEETH SERIES
CREATED BY Monty Oum
RATED T TEEN
VIZ
viz.com
RWBY © 2017 Rooster Teeth Productions, LLC
© 2015 by Shirow Miwa/SHUEISHA Inc.

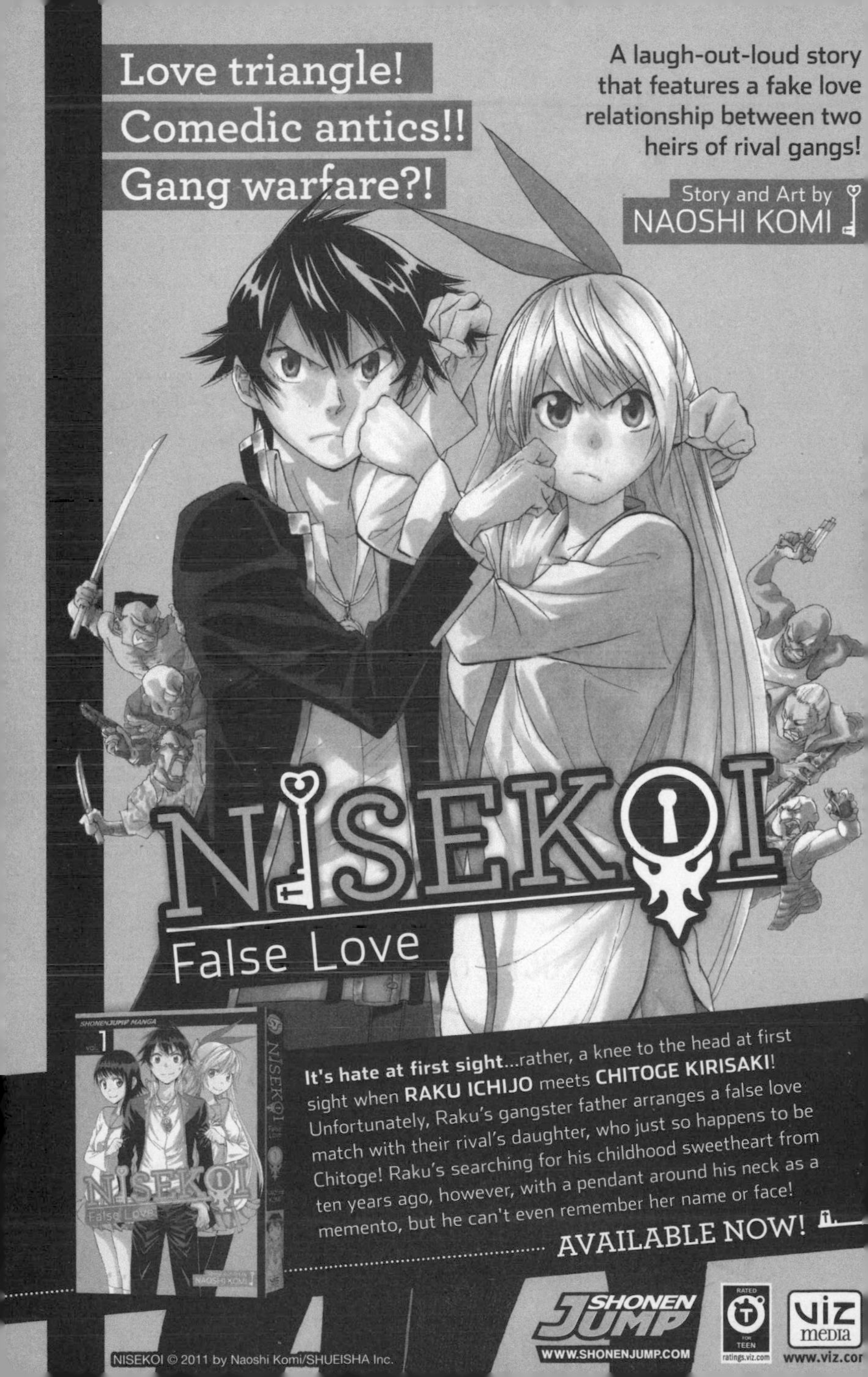
Love triangle!
Comedic antics!!
Gang warfare?!
A laugh-out-loud story that features a fake love relationship between two heirs of rival gangs!
Story and Art by NAOSHI KOMI
NISEKOI
False Love
SHONENJUMP MANGA
vol. 1
NISEKOI False Love
NAOSHI KOMI
It's hate at first sight...rather, a knee to the head at first sight when **RAKU ICHIJO** meets **CHITOGE KIRISAKI**! Unfortunately, Raku's gangster father arranges a false love match with their rival's daughter, who just so happens to be Chitoge! Raku's searching for his childhood sweetheart from ten years ago, however, with a pendant around his neck as a memento, but he can't even remember her name or face!
AVAILABLE NOW!
SHONEN JUMP
WWW.SHONENJUMP.COM
RATED T FOR TEEN
ratings.viz.com
viz media
www.viz.cor
NISEKOI © 2011 by Naoshi Komi/SHUEISHA Inc.

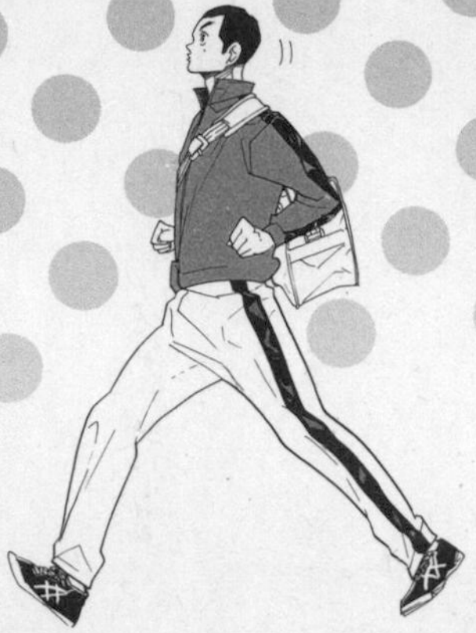

You're Reading the WRONG WAY!

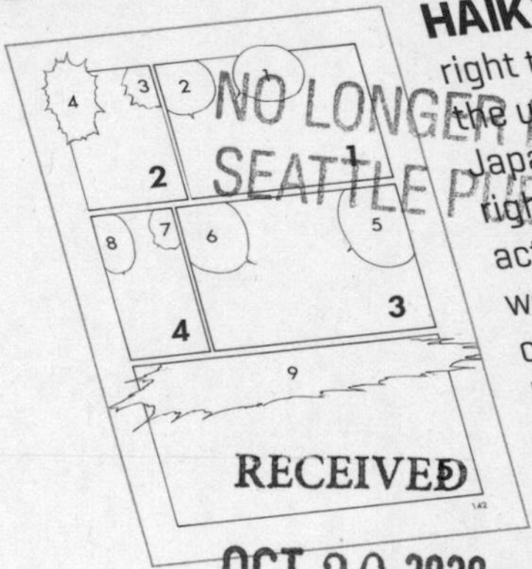

HAIKYU!! reads from right to left, starting in the upper-right corner. Japanese is read from right to left, meaning that action, sound effects and word-balloon order are completely reversed from English order.

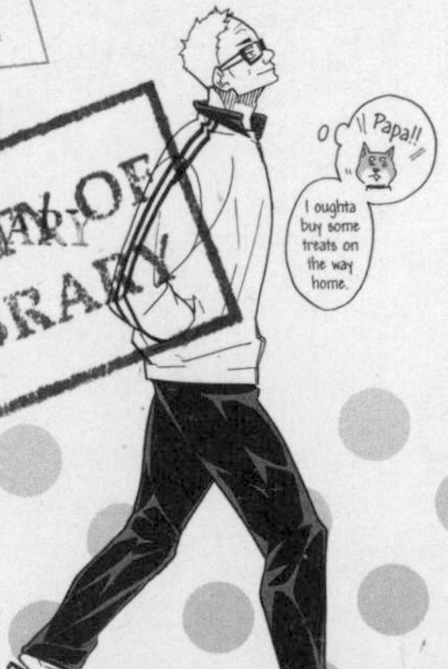
Papa!!
I oughta buy some treats on the way home.

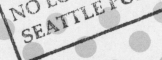